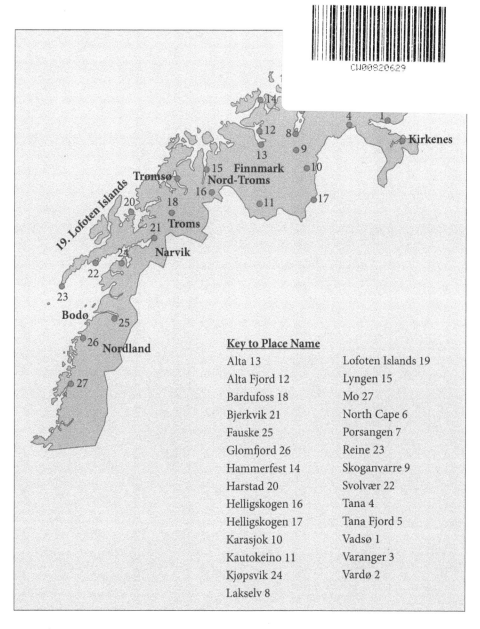

Key to Place Name

Alta 13	Lofoten Islands 19
Alta Fjord 12	Lyngen 15
Bardufoss 18	Mo 27
Bjerkvik 21	North Cape 6
Fauske 25	Porsangen 7
Glomfjord 26	Reine 23
Hammerfest 14	Skoganvarre 9
Harstad 20	Svolvær 22
Helligskogen 16	Tana 4
Helligskogen 17	Tana Fjord 5
Karasjok 10	Vadsø 1
Kautokeino 11	Varanger 3
Kjøpsvik 24	Vardø 2
Lakselv 8	

North Norway

NORWAY IN THE SECOND WORLD WAR

NORWAY IN THE SECOND WORLD WAR

POLITICS, SOCIETY, AND CONFLICT

Ole Kristian Grimnes

Translated by Frank Stewart

BLOOMSBURY ACADEMIC

LONDON • NEW YORK • OXFORD • NEW DELHI • SYDNEY

BLOOMSBURY ACADEMIC
Bloomsbury Publishing Plc
50 Bedford Square, London, WC1B 3DP, UK
1385 Broadway, New York, NY 10018, USA
29 Earlsfort Terrace, Dublin 2, Ireland

BLOOMSBURY, BLOOMSBURY ACADEMIC, and the Diana logo are trademarks
of Bloomsbury Publishing Plc

First published in Great Britain 2022

Translated by Frank Stewart. This translation had been published with the financial
support of NORLA.

Cover design by Tjaša Krivec
Wehrmacht Mountain Troops German gebirgsjager on cross country skis in the
Norwegian mountains in WWII (© Lordprice Collection / Alamy Stock Photo)

A catalog record for this book is available from the British Library.

A catalog record for this book is available from the Library of Congress.

ISBN: PB: 978-1-3502-1460-6
HB: 978-1-3502-1459-0
ePDF: 978-1-3502-1461-3
eBook: 978-1-3502-1462-0

Typeset by Deanta Global Publishing Services, Chennai, India
Printed and bound in Great Britain

To find out more about our authors and books visit www.bloomsbury.com and
sign up for our newsletters.

CONTENTS

Contents

Contents

ILLUSTRATIONS AND MAPS

Illustrations

Maps

PREFACE

My new history of Norway during the Second World War provides readers with a comprehensive coverage of the many unique experiences of this Scandinavian country and its people forced into a deadly military, ideological and genocidal conflict. It is now more than thirty years since a similar book was published. Since then, previously unknown sources and unheard narratives have been discovered. Further challenging questions have been asked about the attitudes and activities of the occupiers and the occupied, and today's readers have different expectations of what should be covered in a history of a war that changed Norway forever. A new book is now needed to bring together all of this history including the political, ideological, military, economic, and social aspects.

For most Norwegians, there is a patriotic historical master narrative about Norway during the war. Essentially, the war was about Norway fighting the good fight against evil forces. The good fight was to defend the values on which Norwegian social order is based. The evil forces were the Nazis. The great majority of Norwegians were on the good side. Opposing them were Germans and Norwegian Nazis on the side of evil. The narrative has been important in confirming national self-awareness and identity in Norway. It underpins much of the popular literary, film and television portrayals of the war such as *The King's Choice* (2016). The strength of this narrative is shown by the many groups which insisted on being given credit for their participation in this dominating patriotic story.

However, the narrative has also been challenged as too over-powering and one-sided, leaving little room for a broader understanding of the many different aspects of the occupation. The war, it is said, has been portrayed too much in black and white, without the necessary shades of grey. That said, historical writing about the years of occupation has become more discriminating and nuanced. It is more than twenty years since Odd-Bjørn Fure wrote his article 'Norway during the Occupation. Consensus, Taboos and Fear of the Untouchable'.[1] In it, he suggested there were aspects of the history of Norway during and after the war that were so difficult and traumatic that neither the Norwegian public nor Norwegian historians were able to handle them satisfactorily. Fure pointed out that the Jews, the *Waffen-SS* volunteers, assassinations, and the fate of enslaved foreign prisoners of war in Norway had all been neglected. This unacceptable situation

---

[1]Odd-Bjørn Fure, 'Norsk okkupasjonshistorie. Konsensus, berøringsangst og tabuisering', in Stein Ugelvik Larsen (ed.), *I krigens kjølvann. Nye sider ved norsk krigshistorie og etterkrigstid* (Oslo: Universitetsforlaget, 1999).

has been overtaken. There is now good, well-documented coverage of all these themes. Indeed, today it is difficult to point to any aspects of the history of the war that are considered taboo or untouchable.

My book aims neither at confirming nor at demolishing the patriotic narrative. The narrative is too important for understanding the role that the war years have played in the shaping of Norwegian historical consciousness. This importance justifies the space that is accorded to war and resistance in the book. But the patriotic narrative cannot determine the general structure and scope of a history of the war years. Instead, my aim has been to introduce as broad a spectrum of the war years as possible.

Over the years, many books about the war have been published. A good deal of them are focussed on particular personalities, dramatic events, and exciting incidents. Although this book also portrays people and events, it presents them in a broader context and a less dramatic style, seeking to trace key developments and present clear explanations of complex phenomena. My hope is that it will help understanding not only what happened during the war but also the reasons why it happened and what motivated those who were involved, for better or for worse.

The book then aims to meet the need for a multifaceted exposé of the years of war and occupation. The institutions set up by the Germans to consolidate their hold on Norway are discussed fully because they laid the foundations for the historical developments that followed. The Norwegian Fascist Party, *Nasjonal Samling* (NS), needs to be examined closely. With its grip on state power, the party became the most important German tool for promoting a Nazi revolution in Norway. The struggle between an NS-controlled state wanting to Nazify the country and a Norwegian people opposed to this is the story of extraordinary resistance unique in Europe.

The prelude to the German invasion, the military campaign that followed, and the political considerations and events of the summer of 1940 are well-trodden paths in the historiography of the period, requiring a synthesis of a wide range of literature. I do, however, challenge some previous points of view. The prelude to the invasion was a political interplay of great powers, and the military campaign in 1940 was a continuation of this, to be considered more as a European phenomenon than as a purely Norwegian one. The part played by the king needs to be seen in a wider perspective and not merely as part of regal mythology. The political negotiations in Norway during the summer of 1940 have always been portrayed in a negative light, and the politicians handling the negotiations on the Norwegian side have been regarded as compromised by their attempts to reach a settlement with the Germans. In fact, the political arrangements they accepted had much in common with those agreed to by other occupied countries in Western Europe.

The Norwegian civil and military resistance movement on one hand and the home front in Norway on the other are considered and re-evaluated separately. The civil resistance movement in fact was the most important. The time is overdue to give Norwegian communists their rightful place in the total picture of the resistance. There is now good and well-documented literature about their role. The tragedy of the Jews and the Holocaust is also covered with a degree of attention that was not given in the early post-war years. That history has been extensively researched, though aspects of the topic are still widely debated. The Norwegian economy during the occupation was strongly impacted by German economic policy and was decisively affected by the war. Norwegian historians have long neglected this topic, but I have been able to draw on the results of important research in this area in recent years.

Norwegian history usually concentrates on Norwegian people on Norwegian territory. But prisoners of war and forced labour meant that tens of thousands of foreigners were sent to Norway and so a book about Norway during the Second World War cannot be so restrictive. Although these two groups were not part of Norwegian society, they do form part of the history of Norwegian territory. Conversely, part of the Norwegian state moved abroad and created an extraterritorial 'Norway outside Norway'. In this way too, the history of the occupation must be more than just the story of Norwegian society on Norwegian territory.

The book starts at the beginning of the Second World War and ends when the war ends. The legal proceedings and other settlements in the first years after the war and the continuing discussion about the war years are deliberately not included as specific topics. The reason is that the moment the war was over, its effects, memories, and debates were strongly influenced by the conditions and requirements of peacetime. This interweaving of war and peace requires its own, distinctive presentation. I have, however, included some aspects of the post-war settlements in order to put the war years into perspective.

The book is compiled from my own research but is also based on what others have written. I have not read all the literature about the war; to do that would be beyond anybody. But I have been working on Norway's wartime history for half a century and have tried to follow what appeared to me to be the most important accounts and the main trends in the literature. Several research projects in recent years have provided new knowledge and understanding and I have integrated those into this broader history.

This book is a shortened and revised version of my Norwegian book that was published in 2018. After each chapter in the Norwegian book, there is a comprehensive bibliography of the literature I have either read fully or consulted, which provides the basis of my historical presentation. In this translated text, I have restricted the bibliography to a selection of relevant literature published in English.

This book could not have come into being without the initiative taken by John Gilmour, Honorary Fellow at the Department of Scandinavian Studies, University of Edinburgh. He arranged to have the Norwegian text translated into English and has in numerous ways helped to secure its publication, including partially abridging the Norwegian text for translation, arranging funding and production of the maps, and preparing the Index. I owe him a great debt of thanks. Likewise, I wish to thank Frank Stewart for his translation, cartographer Barbara Taylor for her maps, and both for their fruitful collaboration in this process.

ACKNOWLEDGMENTS

There have been many less obvious contributors to this book translation in addition to Rhodri Mogford and Sarah Skinner at Bloomsbury Publishing, both of whom have been patiently involved in its development and production.

Particular thanks must go to Jill Stephenson together with Alan Fraser, Brian Houston, and Tom Watson. Their suggestions for topics and issues were invaluable in helping to develop a new Introduction chapter to better inform readers of the English edition about pre-war Norway and its people.

For the cost of translation, NORLA (Norwegian Literature Abroad) has provided a substantial award of grant towards the translation cost. NORLA's Dina Roll-Hansen and Torill Johanson have been supportive with advice and help.

In addition to translation funding from NORLA, a Crowdfunding appeal also raised a substantial sum towards the cost from a diverse group of generous individuals and organizations in Scotland, Norway, and Sweden. Both Sally Garden and members of the Norwegian Scottish Association and Ken Kristoffersen and members of Scottish Norwegian Society (Glasgow) donated and spread the word. Donors are (in alphabetical order):

Laila Marie Bakke, Jens Buus, Tom Ellett, Ida Sølvi Fleming, Alan Fraser, Joan Fraser, Sally Garden, Ian Giles, John Gilmour, Peter Graves, Lars Gyllenhaal, Alex Houston, Brian Houston, Anders Johansson, Freddy Kristoffersen, Kenneth Kristoffersen, Alan Macniven, Edith MacQuarrie, David McDuff, Asle Moldestad, Catherine Muir, Robert Pearson, Robert B Robertson, Manja Ronne, Jill Stephenson, Dot Stewart, Eleanor Stewart, Janet Stewart, David and Britta Sugden, Bjarne Thorup Thomsen, Thomas Thompson and Tom Watson.

Their support is very much appreciated.

ABBREVIATIONS

ANCC	Anglo-Norwegian Collaboration Committee
AT	Arbeidstjenesten: The Compulsory Labour Service
DCO	Directorate of Combined Operations
FO	Forsvarets Overkommando: The Norwegian supreme military command
GSSN	Germanske SS Norge: Germanic SS Norway
HL	Hjemmefrontens Ledelse: The Home Front Leadership
KK	Koordinasjonskomiteen: The Co-ordination Committee
Komorg	Kommunistorganisasjonen: The communist resistance organization
Kripo	Kriminalpolizei: The German criminal police
Milorg	Militærorganisasjonen: The Military Resistance Organisation
NKP	Norges kommunistiske parti: The Norwegian Communist Party
NKVD	Soviet Security Service
Nordag	Nordische Aluminiumgesellschaft: The Nordic Aluminium Company
NRK	Norsk Rikskringkasting: Norwegian Broadcasting Corporation
NS	Nasjonal Samling: The Norwegian Fascist Party
NSB	Norges Statsbaner: Norwegian State Railways
NSPOT	Nasjonal Samling Personalkontor Offentlig Tjeneste: Nasjonal Samling's Personnel Office for Public Servants
NSUF	Nasjonal Samlings Ungdomsfylking: The NS Youth Division
OKW	Oberkommando der Wehrmacht: Wehrmacht High Command
OSS	Office of Strategic Services (American)
OT	Organisation Todt: German military engineering and construction organization
RSHA	Reichssicherheitshauptamt: Head Office of German Security
SA	Sturmabteilung: The original paramilitary wing of the German Nazi Party
SD	Sicherheitsdienst: The German Security Service
SHAEF	Supreme Headquarters Allied Expeditionary Force
Sipo	German Security Police
SIS	Secret Intelligence Service (MI6) (British)
Sivorg	Sivilorganisasjonen: Civil Resistance Organisation
SOE	Special Operations Executive
SS	Schutzstaffel: Protection Squad. Originally a small paramilitary wing of the German Nazi Party, that grew to become one of the most important power blocs in the Third Reich
Stapo	Statspolitiet: The Norwegian Nazified State Police
XU	Norwegian secret intelligence organization. The origin of the abbreviation is not known.

INTRODUCTION
WHO WERE THE NORWEGIANS? NORWAY BEFORE THE SECOND WORLD WAR

When the Second World War broke out in September 1939, most Norwegians thought that it would be like the First. Norway would again manage to assert its neutrality and stay out of the war. Things didn't work out like that, however. Germany invaded Norway on 9 April 1940 and conquered the whole country after a couple of months. That was the start of an occupation lasting five years which led to a resistance movement at home and participation in the war overseas, with far-reaching consequences for Norwegian society and the economy.

But what kind of country was Norway as these dramatic events began to unfold? How had 'the long march of history' shaped the nation, and how had the short stretch of history between the First and Second World Wars affected Norwegian society?

Long-term history was strongly influenced by geography. Norway consists largely of mountains. About half of Norwegian territory is above the tree line, with high moorland and wild mountain ranges. In Western Norway, the sea cuts into the land in the form of fjords between the mountain tops. Rivers have carved deep valleys through the mountain ranges. Flat land is found mainly in Østlandet and in Trøndelag, where the rivers descending from the hills broaden out into wide straths. It is not easy to conquer a country with such a topography.

In such a mountainous country, the population was small: three million. The people lived on the plains, mostly in Østlandet, and in the valleys and along the coast where most of the towns were. Fishing and farming were important in the coastal districts, farming and forestry inland. Good soil was scarce. Only 3 per cent of the land area was under cultivation, whereas 23 per cent was productive forest and a whole 70 per cent of the land was unproductive. Nevertheless, agriculture was an important industry which alongside forestry and fishing provided employment for one-third of the working population. The nation was not self-sufficient in food production and was able to produce only 30–40 per cent of the cereal it needed. The need to import the rest made the Norwegian economy vulnerable.

Norway was also an industrial nation. Industry had been the biggest driver of economic development since the end of the nineteenth century, with crafts and manufacturing employing almost as many people as agriculture, forestry, and fishing. Much of the industry was based on resources available within Norway, such as timber, fish, and ores. There were also significant resources of hydropower, based on which major electrochemical and metal industries had grown up since the beginning of the twentieth century, many of them started by foreign capital.

Norway is an extraordinarily long country, stretching 1,750 kilometres from top to toe. It is broadest in the south and becomes progressively narrower towards the north until it broadens out again in Finnmark in the very north. It looks to the sea in the south, west and north. The coastline is particularly long. Maritime industries such as fishing, whaling, and shipping were therefore important to the Norwegian economy. The merchant fleet was the fourth biggest in the world and was also very modern. At the end of the interwar years, it accounted for as much as 40 per cent of the nation's export earnings.

The sea and the coast drew Norwegians westward towards the Atlantic. Before the First World War, a greater proportion of the population had emigrated to the United States from Norway than from any other country except Ireland. The sea linked Norway to Great Britain. Norway had a very outward-looking economy. Exports of goods and services accounted for an unusually large part of the gross national product. No other country imported so much per inhabitant as Norway, and only Sweden exported more.

The boundaries of Norway had been stable since the seventeenth century. No foreign state laid claim to Norwegian territory, and Norway made no claims to the territory of any other state. Ethnically, the population was almost homogeneous apart from minorities such as Sami and Finns in the north and about 2,000 Jews who had mostly migrated to Norway during the decades before the First World War. The question of minority groups played little role in foreign policy. There was no internal minority seeking protection by a foreign power, and no foreign states attempted to involve themselves in the politics of any minority group within Norway.

Together, Norway and Sweden make up the Scandinavian Peninsula. The geography indicates that they should be one nation, but that has never been the case. The boundary between the two countries runs mostly through forests or across mountains that have kept the populations of the Scandinavian Peninsula apart. As the long frontier between Norway and Sweden largely runs through uninhabited territory, it has been difficult to control.

Norway and Sweden were two among four small states in Northern Europe. The other two were Denmark and Finland. Three of them – Norway, Sweden, and Denmark – constituted Scandinavia. Together with the fourth – Finland – they made up 'The Nordic Countries'. There was a certain uniformity between them. They were small states in a world dominated by great powers. The three Scandinavian countries were constitutional monarchies with royal families as symbols of national unity, whereas Finland was a republic. All four were parliamentary democracies. Their relationships with each other were amicable, and they resolved their differences peacefully. The last war between Nordic States had been in summer 1814 when Sweden and Norway had waged a brief war without great losses.

The Scandinavian States also have much in common in the matter of language. Norwegian, Swedish, and Danish are really three different dialects of the same language. Norwegians, Swedes, and Danes can understand each other, albeit with a little difficulty. Finnish belongs to a completely different language group, though Finland had been united with Sweden for many centuries until 1809 and this left its mark. Swedish had been an important language in Finland. It remained an obligatory subject in school, and there is still a Swedish-speaking minority in Finland. There were also cultural and religious similarities between the Nordic Countries, including Lutheran Christianity which had been introduced as part of the Reformation in the sixteenth century.

The history of the four countries was also interwoven. The three Scandinavian kingdoms of Norway, Denmark and Sweden came into being around the year 1000 – possibly a little later in Sweden. In the High Middle Ages, the kingdom of Norway was a great power in Northern Europe, though this era did not last long. In 1380 Norway entered a union with Denmark, in which Denmark became increasingly dominant. This would last right up to 1814. During that time, Denmark and Sweden continued as two Northern European powers that were often at war with each other.

The union with Denmark lasted for 400 years and left deep traces on Norway. The country lost more and more of its independence and became a dependency. In 1537 it lost its governing body, the Council of the Realm. From 1660 onwards it was integrated in a Danish-dominated autocracy. The country was governed from the Danish capital, Copenhagen. The government officials were either Danish or were Norwegians who had been educated at the university in Copenhagen. The army officers were German. The business classes in the towns were of either Danish or German origin. The written language was Danish, and the government officials and urban middle classes spoke Danish, which was different from the many Norwegian dialects of the general population. The Danish influence on the Norwegian language and culture was strong.

The Napoleonic Wars decisively influenced developments in Norway and in all the Nordic Countries, setting off a century-long process that ended with four small states. An early stage in this process occurred in 1814 when Norway was detached from Denmark and forced into a union with Sweden. This arrangement was much less restrictive than the union with Denmark had been. In 1814 Norway ceased being part of autocracy and became a recognized state with its own constitution and its own government, parliament, army, national bank, and currency. Only the king and foreign policy were shared with Sweden. The union with Sweden did not leave such deep traces as the union with Denmark had done, and the Swedish cultural and linguistic influences were minimal. In effect, this rather loose union provided a favourable framework for the development of the Norwegian nation and the Norwegian constitutional monarchy during the nineteenth century.

The Norwegians opposed Swedish attempts to extend the union but were otherwise mostly satisfied with the status quo. That changed at the end of the 1880s. Radical nationalists – the people who would characterize development after 1890 – were no longer satisfied with the union as it was and wanted to achieve greater independence. Their basic demand was for Norway to have its own foreign minister. At the same time, the country began to arm itself. For fifteen years the question of the union dominated the relationship between Norway and Sweden and internal political debate in Norway. Finally, the political parties and the nation agreed to request that the union be dissolved. After difficult negotiations, the Swedes agreed to this, and the union was dissolved in 1905. For the first time since the Middle Ages, Norway was a fully sovereign state.

For half of the thousand years of its existence, Norway had been united with another country. The memories of dependency and subsequent liberation have played an important role in the nation's history and influenced Norwegians' sense of national identity. The experiences of a union can be seen as one of the reasons why Norway today remains outside the European Union, in contrast to Sweden, Denmark and Finland. For historic reasons, 'Union' does not resonate in many Norwegian ears. In two referenda, the Norwegian public has by a narrow majority said 'No' to the EU. During the campaigning ahead of the referenda, opponents of the EU used Norway's experience of unions as an argument against membership.

Norway had been a separate kingdom throughout this time, even though foreign kings had sat on the Norwegian throne for centuries and the kingdom had long been essentially a formality. With the dissolution of the union with Sweden in 1905, Norway again got its own royal family. The Danish prince Carl was elected king. He took the Norwegian name of Haakon and became Haakon VII. One must go far back in history to find the previous Haakon, who died in 1380 as the last king of an independent Norway.

The Norwegians were not just cultivating their relationship with Denmark by choosing a Danish prince as their king. An equally important reason was that the future Haakon VII was married to a British princess, Maud. This secured the relationship with Britain. Also, the couple had a son, to secure the succession. Maud was something of an outsider in Norway, but Haakon soon found his role in Norwegian affairs and gradually became a respected and generally popular monarch. During the union with Sweden, the Swedish king had held significant political power as late as 1905. Haakon rejected royal power and served first and foremost as a symbol of national unity, above party politics.

From 1814, nation building and cultural liberation became important themes in Norwegian history. The task was to create a distinctive national culture, built on perceptions of Norwegian history, folklife and natural landscape. There was a national reaction directed against 'the Danish time' in Norwegian history and the strong Danish influence to which Norwegian society had been exposed. The language question was central to this but was also the most disputed issue. From the 1880s there were two official Norwegian languages. One was a Norwegianized version of Danish, known as *Bokmål*. The other was a new language, *Nynorsk*, that was built on Norwegian dialects. Most people used *Bokmål*. *Nynorsk* was promoted vigorously, but *Bokmål* won in the end and today only a minority use *Nynorsk*. *Bokmål* is a striking example of how strongly Norway has been influenced by its Danish past.

In the late nineteenth century, Norway developed into a parliamentary democracy. In 1884 the parliamentary principle won through, and the country got its first parliamentary government. There were three political parties. The Liberals and the Conservatives alternated in government, and the Labour Party grew steadily before and during the First World War. With the foundation of the Farmers' Party in 1920, the country acquired a multiparty system in which no single party dominated. Universal suffrage was introduced step by step until women got the vote in 1913. Democracy was enhanced by a diverse press that largely acted as spokespersons for the political parties. This in turn depended on the literacy of the population, nurtured by obligatory schooling.

From the end of the nineteenth century up to the First World War, the development of Norway as a nation and the development of democracy ran parallel, in a fortunate marriage of ideas. There was, however, a darker side. Norwegian nationalism included a racist tendency that was directed against the Sami and Finnish minority in a heavy-handed policy of Norwegianization. They were to be converted into permanently settled, assimilated, Norwegian-speaking citizens. The Jews were aware that there was also antisemitism within Norwegian society, expressed not as an articulated ideology but rather as a vague dislike.

Norway was a newcomer to the field of foreign policy. After 1905 it had to carve out its own foreign policy for the first time since the Middle Ages. It built this policy on the premise that as the country was situated on the fringe of Europe, it would be possible to remain detached from the political interplay of the great powers and avoid major international conflicts. Among the major powers, Great Britain was the one to which Norway was most attracted. Britain's liberal values and institutions and its parliamentary system served as a model. Anglophile Norway did not trouble itself about the less attractive aspects of Great Britain, such as its imperialism and colonial domination. Like Norway, Britain was a sea power. The British Navy ruled the waves between Norway and the British Isles. Britain was seen as a friendly state which didn't threaten Norway, so long as the Norwegians did not ally themselves with an enemy of the British.

However, during the First World War Norway was hard-pressed both by Britain and by Germany. Each of the powers attempted to acquire Norway's resources and hinder the other from getting hold of them. Norway did not wish to take either side and insisted on maintaining its neutrality. Although Norwegian neutrality survived formally right to the end of the war, it operated steadily more in favour of the Western Allies. This was an important experience. The nation's success in staying out of the Great War vindicated and reinforced its policy of neutrality. Only the merchant fleet had suffered major harm. Half of the tonnage was lost and over 2,000 sailors died.

The development of the Nordic Countries into a group of small states was largely completed during the First World War, when Finland also joined the group. Finland had been an integral part of Sweden until 1809, when it was invaded by Russia and incorporated into the Russian Empire as a separate dukedom. During the Russian Revolution, Finland broke free and declared itself a fully sovereign state in December 1917. Only Iceland, which we shall not discuss here, had to wait until 1944 to free itself from Denmark and become the fifth member in the ranks of the Nordic Countries.

The Scandinavian States' shared interest in preserving their neutrality brought them closer together during the First World War. Their kings met to demonstrate the new Scandinavian solidarity, and the premiers and foreign ministers in their respective capitals negotiated how they could co-ordinate their foreign policies. The Nordic Association was founded in 1919 and has worked since then to promote Nordic fellowship. The Nordic Countries worked together within the newly formed League of Nations. Groups and institutions in the various countries co-operated in practical ways, held joint conferences, and experienced the benefits of coming together. The feeling of unity among the Nordic nations grew during the interwar years.

The sense of Nordic identity was not strong, however. If the Nordic Countries in some sense comprised an entity, it was largely a divided entity. National interests trumped Nordic. People considered themselves as Norwegian, Swedish, Danish, or Finnish, not as 'Nordic'. Nationalism influenced attitudes in all four of the countries. Their past histories had been woven together, but up until 1800 these had been histories of internecine war and strong disagreements rather than peace and understanding. They were also pulled in different directions in their relationships with the great powers. For Finland, the Soviet Union was the most important power and a permanent threat. In the case of Denmark, Germany occupied a corresponding position. Sweden shared no direct boundaries with any great power and did not feel threatened, but as a Baltic Sea power, it had to cohabit with other Baltic powers such as Germany and the Soviet Union. Norway was the most westward-facing of the Nordic Countries, looking primarily towards Great Britain.

The First World War changed the international situation. In its aftermath, Germany's power had been reduced, and Germany was no longer considered to be a threat to Norway. The sea separated the two countries. On the other hand, trade and cultural relationships with Germany were important. Norwegian cultural life before the war had been orientated towards Germany, with poets, painters and composers living there for long periods. These relationships continued after the war. German was the main foreign language in school, and there was noticeable German influence both in the University of Oslo and in the technical college in Trondheim. Many of the students who went abroad were educated at German universities, especially in engineering and science subjects.

Russia, now in the form of the Soviet Union, was also a diminished power and was largely preoccupied with its own internal problems. It too was not seen as a threat. Few people considered the possibility of a Soviet attack on Norway. It did, however, represent an ideological challenge. The Norwegian labour movement was strongly influenced by the Russian Revolution, and in the 1920s the Labour Party became a revolutionary party that regarded the new Soviet Union as a model. The middle classes, on the other hand, saw the Soviet Union's communism as an ideological threat, and this served to deepen Norway's internal political divisions.

The period between the First and Second World Wars can be divided in two. The first part, extending to just before the middle of the 1930s, was a problematic time of economic crisis, industrial conflict, and debt. It was further characterized by weak government and left- and right-wing radicalization, as well as a reliance on international law and disarmament.

Like other countries, Norway was hit by the economic crisis of the interwar period, initiated in autumn 1920 by a violent fall in prices. With only one exception, prices continued to fall every year for the next twelve years. During this long period, wholesale prices fell by as much as 67 per cent. Business income weakened and companies either had to reduce in size or close completely. Bankruptcies increased. The crisis went through three waves in the years between 1920 and 1934, with production falling each time and picking up again at a higher level than before. Seen as a whole, the interwar years were therefore a period of significant economic growth. The gross national product increased by 70 per cent between 1920 and 1939.

Part of the crisis was the problem of debt. Many people and organizations had taken out loans during or shortly after the war and were now having difficulty repaying them. The central government and local authorities trying to pay down their debt had less money for social support and measures to combat the crisis. In some local authorities, the financial situation became so serious that they lost the right to manage their own affairs and were put under government administration. When interest and instalments were not paid, the banks came under pressure and many of them failed. In 1920 there were 192 commercial banks; by 1935 only just over half of them had survived.

The worst aspect of the recession, however, was unemployment, which was both an economic and a social problem creating misery and despair. Unemployment struck early in the crisis and maintained its grip. At the start of the 1920s, it stood at 17 per cent among workers in organized trades. It then fell but rose again, and from 1930 onwards it was never below 17 per cent, reaching a peak of 33 per cent of people out of work in 1933. The need for social support grew, and in 1935, 15 per cent of Norwegians were dependent on poor relief to survive.

Not everybody was hit by the economic recession and accompanying social problems. Those who still had work coped and, despite everything, were still the majority. Among workers in full-time jobs, real income and living standards increased. When prices fell, wage earners were able to buy more for their money and even a nominal wage reduction could be associated with increased real income because prices fell more than wages.

The crisis led to unusually bitter industrial strife with strikes and lockouts. Both caused the loss of many working days. The workers went on strike to prevent their wages from being reduced, and the employers locked them out to force them to accept the reduction. The industrial battles came to a climax in 1931, when the employers imposed a widespread lockout that lasted from February to August, affected 60,000 workers and caused the loss of 7.5 million working days. On one occasion, demonstrating workers and police clashed in a pitched battle and several policemen were injured. The authorities dispatched two naval vessels to the location and soldiers were called in. Nobody died in the conflict. Indeed, despite the scale of the crisis there was no loss of life associated directly with the industrial disputes of the interwar years.

The depression struck farming, forestry, and fishing just as hard as it afflicted industry. A severe fall in the price of agricultural produce reduced the farmers' income. They too struggled with debt, as they had taken out loans which they now had difficulty paying back. Industrial owners could compensate for falling income by cutting back production and dismissing workers to reduce expenses. This remedy was not available to the farmers, who responded instead by increasing production in order to sell more. This in turn led to overproduction and a further fall in prices. In earlier times, emigration to the United States had eased the pressure on the rural population, but the Americans had now closed their borders and rural overpopulation increased.

The number of forced sales of farms rose dramatically and reached a peak in 1932 with 6,600 instances. However, most of the owners managed to avoid having to leave their farms. The eviction order often served as a sort of readjustment of the debt. The farmers were able to buy their farms back at a reduced price, and the smaller debt was easier to service. However, at the start of the process nobody could be sure of getting their farm back. About 20 per cent lost their farms permanently by eviction.

Parliamentary democracy had difficulty coping with the depression. Governments were weak, short-lived and had no coherent policy for dealing with the crisis. Most politicians thought that the problem would resolve itself and that no special measures were necessary. The nation was caught up in the age of prohibition. The sale of spirits was forbidden between 1916 and 1927, and much of the political debate was about whether this ban should be lifted. Such a question had little to do with the economic crisis and was not likely to arouse interest in how it should be resolved.

The depression created a seedbed for the growth of the radical wings of the political parties. In the 1920s, democracy faced challenges from two directions. On the left, the Labour Party became revolutionary and wanted to reorganize society on socialist principles, bypassing the democratic institutions. The party had joined the new Communist International, Comintern, in 1919. They did withdraw from it as soon as 1923 when only a minority remained members of Comintern and proceeded to found the Norwegian Communist Party. Even outside Comintern, however, the Labour Party continued to see itself as a revolutionary party.

The Russian Revolution and the revolutionary tendencies within the labour movement stimulated the germination of groups on the extreme right. These had little respect for parliamentary democracy, which they thought was too feeble in tackling the revolutionary trends. These trends had to be suppressed, using harsh measures. The biggest of these right-wing groups was *Fedrelandslaget* (the Fatherland Organisation), which around 1930 reportedly had as many as a hundred thousand members. They wanted to ban the Labour Party and the communists and strengthen the power of the government in relation to parliament. A strong, authoritarian, and unifying figure should stand at the head of the government. The radical right brought an authoritarian tendency into Norwegian nationalism for the first time.

After 1930, developments on the right diverged. In 1933 the fascist *Nasjonal Samling* (NS) party was founded, with Vidkun Quisling as its leader. This would seem to indicate that the radical sections of the political right were becoming more extreme. On the other hand, they were now losing their mass appeal and capacity for mobilization. One might have expected that when the economic crisis was at its worst at the start of the 1930s, there would have been increasing support for the most radical option on the political right, but that did not happen. NS never achieved mass appeal.

The new League of Nations organization founded after the First World War was the first worldwide coming together of states to protect peace and security and develop international co-operation. It gave the small nations a defined place in the system of international relationships. By working together, they were able to influence the work of the League in the 1920s. This was where Norway found the forum to advance its ideals of peace and disarmament. Up to the beginning of the 1930s, the League of Nations provided an increasingly more important framework for Norwegian foreign policy. Together with the other Nordic States, Norway worked to increase the scope of the

International Court at The Hague and to extend international law to require obligatory mediation and arbitration to resolve conflict.

However, the League's principle of collective security presented small states such as Norway with a problem. The member countries were obliged to come to each other's aid if one of them was attacked. This was contrary to Norway's policy of neutrality and could lead the country into war. So long as there was no risk of another war between the great powers, Norway continued to balance the two principles.

Norway had armed itself ahead of the dissolution of the union with Sweden in 1905, maintained military readiness in the following years and strengthened its defences during the First World War. After that, it started on a process of disarmament. The bloodbath of the war had created an aversion to war and military forces. Many people thought that militarization was a cause of war and should therefore be avoided. The economic crisis made it difficult to spend money on the military when the state faced debt problems, falling tax revenue, and rising social costs. The disagreements among the great powers were not so great that a major war seemed likely. Norwegians did not feel that their country was particularly threatened. There were no apparent enemies, and it was difficult to oppose the policy of disarmament.

A defence commission worked for several years on proposals for a reorganization of the armed forces. Its recommendations were approved by parliament in 1927 but were never implemented because they were too expensive. A new and cheaper reorganization was approved in 1933. The length of national service would be a total of 84 days, but this would be introduced gradually. The number of permanently commissioned officers was reduced to 470. The plan was to be able to set up a force of six small brigades as the first line of defence to protect neutrality. Since no practice exercises were arranged beyond initial training, these units would never have operated together, and the military commanders would never have had the experience of leading them. To set up bigger forces than those called up in the first round of mobilization would require preparations and extra budget allocations, which would take several years to achieve.

Military equipment gradually became worn out and was seldom replaced, and new types of weapons were hardly ever introduced. An air force was set up, but it had obsolete planes and no bombers and was considered just as a support for the army and the navy, rather than as an independent arm of the forces. There was little civil or military defence against air attacks. The navy had to depend on old ships, had few modern vessels and was not a force to be feared. The army lacked tanks and anti-tank defences, and the artillery had little firepower. The period of basic training was the shortest in Europe. The result was that 'in 1936 the army stood out as one of the least modern, most scantily equipped and worst trained in Europe', according to *Norwegian Defence History*. The Conservative Party was the most supportive of the defence forces, followed by the Farmers' Party, with the Liberal Party between these two on one side and the anti-military Labour Party on the other.

From 1934–5 there were new and more positive developments. The economic situation and prospects improved. Sections of industry expanded, and employment rose. This was not enough to cure the economic ills, however, as a rise in the number of school leavers increased the demand for jobs. Unemployment continued to swing between 18 and 22 per cent. There were fewer evictions from farms. Problems in servicing debt did not loom so large as before but neither did they disappear, either in rural areas or in the economy as a whole. On the other hand, the bitter industrial disputes died down. Many fewer working hours were lost by strikes or lockouts, and working life became more peaceful.

Nor were political divisions so acute. Governments ceased to come and go, and the process of government became more stable. In 1935 Johan Nygaardsvold formed a Labour government that lasted until the end of the decade. He was able to do this because the Labour Party had changed course radically. In 1930 it still presented revolutionary aspirations, but in the following years, it modified its policy. It would no longer wait for a revolution that never came, but now advocated combatting the economic and social crisis with practical measures and reforms, using parliamentary democracy to drive these through.

The electorate demonstrated its approval of the new policy by giving the party successively more of the votes in the parliamentary elections – 31 per cent in 1930, 40 per cent in 1933 and 43 per cent in 1936. The party did not achieve an overall majority but had to seek support first from the Farmers' Party and later from the Liberal Party. These two now recognized the Labour Party as part of the parliamentary system and found positive aspects in Labour's policy of reform, even though its revolutionary past was not forgotten.

The extreme political wings that had threatened democracy in the 1920s nearly disappeared in the following decade. The Labour Party became reformist, while the radical authoritarian right and the new Fascist Party lost their appeal.

After the First World War, several new states grew up that had all started as democracies but where democracy eventually collapsed, except in Czechoslovakia. Developments took the opposite direction in Norway and the other Nordic Countries, where democracy was stronger at the end of the interwar years than it had been at the start. Parliamentary democracy's strongest hold in Europe was now in Great Britain and the Nordic Countries.

The socialist parties in all the Nordic Countries played an important role in this development. After the Norwegian Labour Party had changed course, it sought like the others to combat the crisis using economic and social reforms, with varying support from the non-socialist parties. In the second half of the 1930s, the socialists were in government in Norway, Sweden and Denmark and were participating in the government in Finland. This was the prelude to what has been called the high point of social democracy and it points forward to the development of the Nordic welfare states after the Second World War. Despite these good signs and brighter times, the decade nevertheless remained securely implanted in collective memory as 'the hard thirties'.

The big changes in the international picture in the second half of the 1930s had consequences for internal, foreign and defence policies. There were now three major political identities in the international arena, each with its own ideology. The first was the fascist phalanx which consisted of Germany and Italy and behaved more and more aggressively. The second was the Western democratic states which tried to pursue a policy of appeasement against Hitler's expansionism. The third was the communist Soviet Union which wanted to stem the advance of fascism.

The new constellations influenced political and ideological relationships in Norway. Foreign and internal policies became more closely connected. Within Norway, the Fascist and Communist Parties played a minimal role. The Conservative Party, the Liberals and, to a large extent, the Farmers' Party subscribed to the Western pattern of democracy, and the Labour Party now also joined that camp. However, some of the earlier sympathies for the revolutionary Soviet state persisted within the Labour Party, even though Stalinism seemed steadily more repulsive. Despite the Stalinist excesses, the Soviets in the 1930s did stand for an anti-fascist ideology and a foreign policy that appealed to socialists. In conservative circles, people maintained their old scepticism about socialism, whether of the communist or the social-democratic type.

In the Spanish Civil War of 1936–9, the European fascists supported the authoritarian General Franco, who eventually won. The Soviet Union and the communists sided with the republicans, and the Western powers followed a non-interventionist policy, supporting neither side. The Norwegian Labour government followed the Western powers in refusing to offer any form of military support. Recruitment of volunteers and voluntary military participation was forbidden. Around 300 Norwegians nevertheless ignored the ban and took part in the war. Most of these were communists, but there were also some adherents of the Labour Party. The Conservatives sympathized to some extent with Franco. The labour movement identified with the republican side, set up a number of Spanish committees throughout Norway, expressed its sympathy for the republicans and offered humanitarian help.

Events in the 1930s undermined the League of Nations, which proved to be incapable of preventing aggression and war. This also revealed the gap between the Norwegian wish for neutrality and the ability of collective security to ensure it. In 1935, Italy invaded Ethiopia. The League instructed the member states to implement economic sanctions against the aggressor. Norway took part in these, but many people now became concerned about what could happen if Norway were to become involved in further sanctions. The country might risk being drawn into conflicts with an aggressive great power. Norway and six other previously neutral states considered it best to withdraw from the provisions about collective security.

The Labour Party foreign minister, Halvdan Koht, still wanted to work through the League of Nations, but specifically to pursue an active peace policy. He thought that the small states could play a role as intermediaries between the great powers and act as driving forces for a policy of disarmament. For some people, such a peace policy gave the small states an aura of moral authority. In retrospect, it is easy to see that the policy was unrealistic, not to say naïve and that it totally underestimated the expansionist urge of Hitler's Germany. Even among the other small states, Koht had difficulty raising support for his policy. Only after Germany had conquered the Czech parts of Czechoslovakia and made Slovakia into a subordinate state in March 1939 did Koht abandon his peace policy in the international arena. He considered that a European war would probably break out soon, in which case it was important to follow as balanced a neutrality policy as possible. Only thus could the country hope that the warring powers would leave it in peace. This was the policy that Norway was following when the Second World War broke out.

Defence policy became more and more important, but it was mainly seen in the light of Norway's experiences during the First World War. If war broke out in Europe, it would probably affect Norway as a war at sea, with random incursions of Norwegian territorial waters and sinking of Norwegian merchant ships. Some people went so far as to think that the warring powers might land troops on the southwest coast to set up a base there. War in the air was a new factor. During both the Ethiopian War and the Spanish Civil War, people had experienced the effects of bombing. The reality that Norway could now be struck by bombers was difficult to take in and respond to.

As the governing party, Labour was responsible for defence policy. Since 1906 its manifesto had included unilateral disarmament, but the party gradually abandoned this policy during the 1930s. Defence policy now developed alongside the new policies of economic and social reform. The party took the first step in 1933 when it proposed setting up a *vaktvern* ('national guard') with purely police duties. When the party came into government, it initially continued the non-socialists' defence arrangements and budget. In the autumn of the following year, it proposed an extra allocation to the defence budget. In the same year, the party's national conference deleted 'disarmament' and 'police duties' from the defence programme but retained the expression *vaktvern*. However, this alteration in defence policy made slow progress and led to long-lasting splits within the party. There was never as much consensus about defence policy as there was about economic and social policy.

It was obvious that the question of defence was now a matter of concern not just for the political parties but for the public. The government could risk losing political control and possibly facing an opposition majority in parliament if they did not pursue a more active defence policy. So, in 1937 Nygaardsvold sought a compromise with the non-socialists about defence. They agreed to allocate an extra twenty million kroner to defence over three years, and further allocations were made over the next couple of years. The money was to be used primarily to strengthen sea and air defence.

However, there was still disagreement within the Labour Party about defence. Most members of the government and the parliamentary group were reluctant to spend too much on defence. Nygaardsvold and others still harboured antipathy to the military. Koht was preoccupied with his peace policy and had little interest in or understanding of military matters. Although there were now more people in the party executive who dissociated themselves from the labour movement's previous negativity about defence and were willing to spend more, many were sensitive about anything that sounded like rearmament. In two successive years, the government demanded a vote of confidence about the length of military service. They would not approve more than 72 days, and they refused to increase it to the 84 days that had been scheduled in 1933. The extension to 84 days was not approved until 1938. The Conservative Party proposed motions of no confidence against the government because of defence policy in both 1938 and 1939, but both motions were rejected.

One basic question was never resolved in the interwar years. Should Norwegian defence be designed for combatting minor territorial infringements without going to war, or should it be capable of taking up the fight against an intruder and continuing until the conflict was resolved? The most important reason for this uncertainty was not, and could not be, expressed openly. If Great Britain, seen as Norway's protective guardian, threatened Norwegian territorial rights only a formal defence would be instigated to signal the infringement. If another of the powers attacked, Norway would be more likely to take up the fight seriously, though it was difficult to see which power that might be.

Whereas the Nygaardsvold government's economic and social reforms have subsequently been recognized and have been little criticized, its foreign and defence policies have been sharply, indeed violently, criticized. The underlying premise of the criticism has generally

Figure 1 A snapshot from the conquest of a nation. The Germans have advanced to Lundamo in Sør-Trøndelag, where they have been in battle against Norwegian forces. A Norwegian volunteer has been captured. His right shoulder is dislocated, and he is unable to hold his right arm up against the wall. © BUNDESARCHIV, Bild 1011-759-0125-37A/.

been that a more competent foreign policy and a more active defence policy could have prevented the German attack on Norway in 1940. However, the Labour Party did not have sole responsibility for defence policy, as there was a non-socialist majority in parliament that could have forced through a different policy. At the same time, the Labour Party as the party of government had a decisive influence on defence policy and acted as a brake on the aspirations of the non-socialist parties. This was partly because of the party's long-standing anti-militarist and pacifist traditions, and partly because of the exigencies of the economic crisis. The party concentrated, above all, on dealing with economic and social policy, not the defence. Asked to select between 'butter' and 'guns', most Labourites chose 'butter'.

At 11.00 pm on 8 April 1940 the first shots were heard in the outer reaches of Oslo Fjord and the first Norwegian fell as a casualty of war. German warships were on their way in towards the capital. The world of Norwegian assumptions and perceptions crumbled to dust. Confidence that peripheral status was protective vanished. Expectations that neutrality was a guarantee against being drawn into the war proved to be mistaken. The conviction that Norway was under the protective wings of a great power was shattered. The view of the North Sea as a barrier between peaceful Norway and the warmongers of Europe evaporated. The idea – if anybody had believed it – that small states were more moral than great powers and therefore deserved to avoid the conflict was without foundation.

PART I
A COUNTRY IS CONQUERED

German forces invaded Denmark and Norway at the same time on 9 April 1940. Denmark surrendered after only a few hours. It took the Germans five days to occupy the Netherlands and six weeks to gain control of France. Hitler had reckoned on capturing Norway as quickly as he had taken Denmark, but he miscalculated. It took two months to defeat Norwegian, British, French, and Polish troops on Norwegian soil, and even longer – almost six months – to impose a new system of government on the occupied territory. The German army, a German civil administration, and a German police force were imposed on the land. What the conquerors could not agree about was the role that Quisling's *Nasjonal Samling* (NS) Party should play in the new regime.

CHAPTER 1
INTO WAR

The Second World War broke out when Germany invaded Poland and the Western powers responded by declaring war on Germany on 3 September 1939. The German divisions conquered Poland in just a few weeks, and at the end of September Hitler told his generals that he wanted to start an offensive in the West as soon as possible. Right up to the end of January 1940 he reckoned that this could be set in motion very soon. Even after he had deferred it until the spring, this was his major obsession. Meanwhile, the German divisions had been stood down from action after the campaign in Poland. On the western side, Britain and France were not strong enough to initiate an attack. Instead, they relied on the traditional British strategy of the blockade, attempting to prevent Germany from getting necessary supplies from other countries.

Winter 1939–40 was the period of 'The Twilight War' or 'The Phoney War'. There was hardly any fighting on land. The airborne activity was limited. The war was mostly being fought at sea, but this too was limited except for U-boat activity. As had happened in the First World War, most of the German surface vessels were tied up in their German ports. The defeat of Poland had left a pause in the action, and the question was how the flames of war would be reignited.

At the outbreak of the war, Norway and the other Nordic States declared themselves neutral. They did not wish to ally themselves to either side, and they wanted to stay out of the war, just as they had done at the start of the First World War.

Much was reminiscent of 1914–18. As before, the struggle over Norwegian trade and shipping was very important. Both the warring sides wanted to acquire Norwegian products and merchant shipping services and hinder the enemy from doing the same. There were long, intricate negotiations between Norway and Britain and between Norway and Germany. These ended with agreements that gave the two sides some of what they wanted (mostly to the British), guaranteed Norwegian import and export trade, and regulated the use of Norwegian shipping.

Those whose lives were most affected by the war at this stage were the seafarers. Reports of losses soon started coming in. Some ships were torpedoed, and several ran into mines and were blown sky-high. The newspapers carried reports of daring rescues of sailors. By 1 April 1940, 380 seafarers had perished, and 55 Norwegian ships had been lost.

As before, neutrality needed military protection. The entire navy was mobilized to prevent any of the warring nations from infringing Norwegian territorial waters. A new feature, however, was the risk of foreign aircraft entering Norwegian airspace, and such planes as were available were also mobilized. On the other hand, the coastal defences

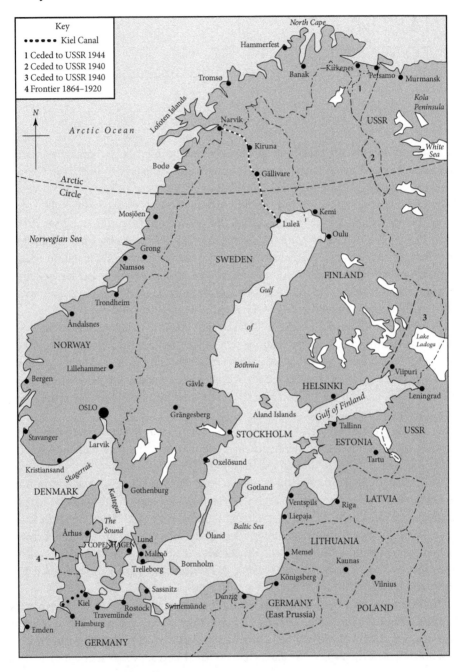

Key
●●●●●● Kiel Canal
1 Ceded to USSR 1944
2 Ceded to USSR 1940
3 Ceded to USSR 1940
4 Frontier 1864–1920

N

Arctic Ocean

North Cape

Hammerfest

Kirkenes
Banak
Petsamo
Murmansk

Tromsø

Kola Peninsula

USSR

Lofoten Islands

Narvik

Kiruna

White Sea

Bodø

Gällivare

2

Arctic Circle

Norwegian Sea

Mosjöen

Kemi
Luleå

Oulu

Grong

SWEDEN

FINLAND

Namsos

Gulf

3

Trondheim

of

Lake Ladoga

Åndalsnes

NORWAY

Bothnia

Lillehammer

Gävle

HELSINKI

Viipuri

Bergen

Grängesberg

Leningrad

OSLO

Åland Islands

Gulf of Finland

Stavanger

STOCKHOLM

Tallinn

USSR

Larvik

ESTONIA

Kristiansand

Skagerrak

Oxelösund

Tartu

DENMARK

Kattegat

Gothenburg

Gotland

LATVIA

The Sound

Ventspils
Riga

Århus

Lund

Liepaja

Baltic Sea

Öland

COPENHAGEN

Malmö

LITHUANIA

Trelleborg

Bornholm

Memel

Kaunas

4

Sassnitz

Danzig

Königsberg

Vilnius

Kiel
Rostock
Swinemünde

GERMANY
(East Prussia)

POLAND

Travemünde

Hamburg

Emden

GERMANY

Map 1 Scandinavia and the Baltic 1939.

were only partly mobilized, and a mere scattering of army units was called up. Few people expected a real war, and the perceived need was to ward off random infringements of sea and air boundaries.

This attempt to defend neutrality would turn out to be more difficult to implement than it had been in the First World War. The British did not conceal their dissatisfaction with Norwegian neutrality, as they thought it gave the Germans too many advantages. German ships, including warships, could sail safely through Norwegian waters and thereby pass back and forth between Germany and the Atlantic Ocean. The German war economy was dependent on Swedish iron ore. Much of this came from the Swedish mines at Kiruna and was sent by rail to Narvik to be shipped southwards along the Norwegian coast. The Germans were benefitting from Norwegian territory as a safe zone, and so long as they respected the regulations governing Norwegian neutrality, the British could do nothing to prevent it.

Both warring parties had fewer inhibitions than before about entering Norwegian waters. In December 1939 a German U-boat torpedoed three ships in British service. The Western Allies claimed that this had happened in Norwegian waters, a claim that was later shown to be correct. The Allies quoted this as evidence of Norway's incapacity to defend its territory. A note from the British on 6 January 1940 referred to the torpedoing and threatened that it would now be legitimate for the British Navy to operate in Norwegian territorial waters. Norway now faced more than just random infringements of her boundaries while the British felt justified in transgressing them as part of their naval operations.

In February the British moved on from diplomatic warning into naval action within Norwegian waters. On 14 February the German ship *Altmark*, that had been serving as supply ship to a German battleship in the South Atlantic, entered Norwegian waters north of Trondheim Fjord with 300 British prisoners on board and set course southward along the coast towards Germany. Two days later, *Altmark* sought shelter in Jøssingfjord, between Egersund and Flekkefjord, where she was followed in by the British destroyer *Cossack*. British sailors boarded *Altmark*, and after a fight that cost seven German lives the British prisoners were freed, and *Cossack* put out to sea again. Two Norwegian torpedo boats that were standing by protested, but they had orders not to use force. This incident was widely reported in the world press. The British had deliberately operated in Norwegian territorial waters, ignoring Norwegian neutrality. Now it was the Germans' turn to protest about Norway's incapacity to defend its neutrality.

It was proving more difficult than before to keep the great powers out of Norwegian waters. On the other hand, there was little reason to anticipate operations on Norwegian soil, with troop landings and occupation. An extension of the war at sea to include engagements between British and German warships along the Norwegian coast seemed more likely.

In late autumn 1939 circumstances in the Nordic region took a harsh and fateful turn. A completely new factor came into being: the 'Winter War' between the Soviet Union and Finland. This broke out on 30 November, when the Soviets invaded Finland because the Finns would not agree to Soviet demands to cede parts of Finnish territory. The Winter

War would last for three and a half months. In Norway, it aroused widespread sympathy for the Finns. Money and equipment were collected, and committees were established to promote voluntary war service. The first group of Norwegians left for Finland just after New Year. A total of 725 men travelled to Finland, though they did not arrive in time to take a significant part in the war.

This widespread goodwill towards the Finns did not, however, change Norway's policy of neutrality. The Norwegian government remained neutral even in respect of the Winter War. However, it did secretly allow the Finns to be given twelve field guns with ammunition and it did not oppose the transit of weapons and ammunition to Finland, which was allowed by international law. It would give no form of military help other than this. Norwegian officers were not allowed to volunteer. Sweden was more supportive. The Swedes declared themselves not as neutral but as non-belligerent. They gave significant arms supplies and other support to the Finns, and they allowed both officers and others to volunteer.

The intrusive Allies

There was no direct connection between the Winter War and the main war in Europe. The Winter War was not part of the Second World War, and neither the Russians nor the Finns were at that time engaged in the fighting between Germany and France/Britain. But the Winter War turned relationships in Scandinavia upside down. The major European powers – Great Britain, France, Germany, and the Soviet Union – suddenly all became interested in Scandinavia, considered engaging there or, in the case of the Soviet Union, were already engaged. It appeared that the spark that would reignite The Phoney War might come from the North.

When the Western powers declared that they wanted to help Finland, this was mainly a cover for other motives. The principal motive was to acquire control of Swedish iron ore. Plans were made to despatch the aid to Finland via Norway and Sweden. The Allies would land troops in Narvik to proceed from there to northern Sweden, where they would take control of the ore fields and continue to the Gulf of Bothnia to gain mastery of the shipping ports. Only then would a part of the force move on to Finland.

Swedish iron ore was so important to the German munitions industry that the Allies reckoned that the Germans would send troops to Scandinavia to block the Allied advance. The Allies would hinder this by landing troops in Stavanger, Bergen and Trondheim and sending forces via Trondheim to southern Sweden to cut off a possible German advance there. The project for Allied landings was not only on a large scale; it also made it very likely that a new front would flare up in the stalled land war. That was just what the Allies, and especially the French, wanted. They wanted at all costs to avoid a war on French soil that could be just as bloody as a quarter of a century earlier. The French wanted to offload hostilities onto Norwegian soil.

It would have been difficult to carry out these plans without consent from Norway and Sweden. The Scandinavians could easily hinder the Allies from crossing their territory by cutting off the power supply to the railway or blowing up any of the many bridges. On 2 March the Allies contacted Norway and Sweden, appealing to their sympathies for Finland and asking permission for Allied troops to be allowed safe passage. Both countries responded with a flat refusal. They were not willing to turn their countries into battlefields on that account.

By the second week in March the Allies' preparations had reached the stage where they could set their operations in motion at short notice. Troops were standing by, and ships lying at anchor at ports of embarkation were waiting for the final order. The troops had orders to defy symbolic or minor Norwegian opposition, but not to combat a resolute Norwegian defence. The Allies were not expecting the Norwegians to react strongly.

The secret invasion plan

The Winter War was viewed in the same way in Germany as in the West. Hitler began taking an interest in Scandinavia at about the same time as the Allies. His interest was encouraged by a particular individual, namely Major Vidkun Quisling, the leader of the tiny Norwegian Nazi Party, the *Nasjonal Samling* (NS). When Quisling visited Berlin in December 1939, he was welcomed in influential circles: Erich Raeder, the head of the German Navy; Alfred Rosenberg, the head of the Nazi Party's Foreign Affairs Department; Hans-Wilhelm Scheidt, who led the department's Scandinavian section; and finally Albert Viljam Hagelin, a Norwegian businessman who had lived in Germany for a long time and who cultivated important connections in the German capital. Hitler was told of the visit, and he suddenly became interested. The two men met on 14 and on 18 December 1939.

Quisling set out his view of the situation in Norway. He claimed that Norway had a secret agreement with Britain about free access if Norway were to come into the war with one of the great powers. In Norway, the president of the parliament, C. J. Hambro – 'Hambro the Jew', said Quisling – controlled the government, the parliament, and foreign politics. As Norway was ruled by a Labour government, it was on the slippery slope towards Marxism. In Quisling's opinion, this government would no longer be legal after 10 January 1940. Parliament (*Stortinget*) had not only extended the period of the parliament from three to four years but had also extended this provision so that the current parliament that had been elected in 1936 would sit until 10 January 1941. This gave Quisling the pretext for a coup. He proposed that his party, the NS, should take over the government and encourage Germany to send troops.

Quisling must have made an impression on Hitler. The *Führer* later claimed that he owed Quisling a debt of gratitude for making him aware of the British threat in the North. This would come to be of great significance, as it was only by Hitler's support that Quisling and his party later gained a prominent position in occupied Norway. Without the meeting between Hitler and Quisling in December 1939, Quisling would not have become a major figure in the history of the years of occupation.

After his first meeting with Quisling, Hitler gave orders to the military to investigate how Germany could occupy Norway, and plans were then drawn up. When he was shown the first outline of the plan, known as 'The Northern Study', Hitler decided on 27 January that the planning should be continued by a special task force in the High Command, *Oberkommando der Wehrmacht* (*OKW*), under his 'personal and immediate influence' and be code-named *Weserübung*. This became the title from then onwards of the German plans for the occupation of Norway and Denmark.

Hitler must have had several motives for his invasion project. Lessons from the First World War were important. At that time the surface vessels of the German Navy were locked in their home ports, unable to break out into the Atlantic. Now, it was important to avoid a repetition of this and to strengthen Germany's position in the sea war against Britain. Control of Norwegian territory would give the navy easier access to the open sea. With harbours, U-boat bases, and airfields in Norway, Germany would be in a much stronger position to attack the supply lines to the British Isles. Alongside this major strategic maritime consideration, the transport of iron ore through Narvik was also very important. German occupation of Norway would make this route secure. A third consideration was to forestall an Allied landing in Norway. As Britain and France were thought to be making plans to establish themselves in Scandinavia, a German occupation should be set in hand as early as possible. With Allied troops in Norway, Germany would lose all its benefits from Norwegian neutrality.

After the Finnish Winter War

When the Winter War ended on 13 March 1940, Hitler and the Allies both lost the political pretext for intervening in Norway. On the German side, preparations continued at full pace, guided by two overriding considerations. Norway is a long, narrow country whose most important towns lie by the sea, often far inside fjords and therefore rather isolated from each other. To attack at one point and deploy from there would not be effective. An invader would gain the quickest and most effective grip on Norway if he captured all the most important towns at once and then occupied the land from these bridgeheads. So, bridgeheads would be established in Oslo, Kristiansand, Stavanger, Bergen, Trondheim and Narvik, while small units would take Arendal and Egersund. That was how the attack was launched on the morning of 9 April.

The second consideration was that the British fleet was dominant. If the Germans were to succeed in reaching Norway and establishing their positions there, they would need to act quickly and decisively. They would not be able to move all their troops in slow transport ships which would be vulnerable to attack. They decided instead to send the first contingent of the invasion forces in rapid warships that would have a better chance of avoiding discovery or of managing to make their way through if they were discovered. This greatly reduced the size of the first wave of the attack. The available warships could only take 8,850 men. Another quick way to transport troops would be by air, but planes could take even fewer, 3,000–3,500 men in the first round. Airborne troops would only take Stavanger and be a supplement to the forces travelling by sea to Oslo.

Weserübung was a risky operation. The British Navy could have stopped it if the British had not misjudged the situation. When at the last moment they got reports of the movement of the invasion fleet, they thought that it was a naval force on its way out into the Atlantic and they deployed their own ships accordingly. The Germans were taking a calculated risk, knowing that the day of the invasion and the first few days thereafter would be critical. Their situation would ease as reinforcements were brought in, provided the British did not manage to stop them. The reinforcements were sent by the shortest sea route to Norway from Northern Denmark across the Skagerrak, where the British would not dare to send in their warships to be exposed to German air attack.

The purely military invasion did entail political considerations. In Oslo and Copenhagen, the landing troops would secure the country's leadership, including the king, as soon as they arrived. The military occupation would be combined with diplomatic action. The minister heading the German Legation would visit the country's foreign minister and lay out requests for immediate surrender. In exchange for this, the country would be allowed to keep its political system and its internal freedom. The demands would be backed up by the landing forces simultaneously occupying the palace, the parliament building, government buildings and broadcasting headquarters. It was thought that flypasts over the capital city would also have this effect. In Copenhagen this scheme all went according to plan, but in Oslo, it failed because the troops did not reach the city in time.

The end of the Winter War had a greater effect on the Allies than on the Germans. The Allies abandoned their expeditionary project. It was not long, however, before the Allies agreed on a new initiative. They would lay mines in Norwegian shipping lanes to force German vessels out into the open sea where British warships could attack them. At 6.00 am on the morning of 8 April Norway received a message from the Western powers to inform them of the minelaying. At the same time, the Allies revived their plans for landing troops to ward off German counterattacks.

The Allies did finally carry out a naval operation in Norwegian waters, at the same time as they were ready to set bigger operations in motion on Norwegian soil. Behind this decision lay a long and complicated process. Many plans had been put forward in addition to those that were finally accepted. Plans and preparations had to be agreed on both politically and militarily, within and between both Britain and France. The co-operation between these countries was not without hitches. Important considerations held the Allies back. They retained some respect for Scandinavian neutrality and preferred not to defy Norway and Sweden against their will. When help for the Finns could no longer be used as a justification for the landing project, they abandoned it. Then they revived it again after only a few days. Allied policy was vacillating.

Ever since the dissolution of the union with Sweden in 1905, Norwegians had regarded Great Britain informally as a sort of protective power. It would be in Britain's interests to keep other countries out of Norway, and her powerful navy gave her the means to do that. The British would have no need to occupy Norway themselves so long as the Norwegians were friendly towards them and did not ally themselves with Britain's enemies. Norway's big problem in the winter and spring of 1940 was that their informal defender changed into a threat. The Allies deliberately flouted Norwegian neutrality when they sent their warships into Jøssingfjord, and they threatened to turn Scandinavia into a battlefield with their plans to march through to Finland.

This pressure roused more fundamental aspects of the Norwegian neutrality policy. The evident expression of this policy consisted of maintaining a balance between the combatants and keeping Norway out of the war. But what if it became no longer possible to stay out and they had to choose between sides? This choice was predetermined. Norway must not come into war against Great Britain, must not join 'the wrong side'. Norwegians based this on prior experiences. During the Napoleonic Wars it had been unfortunate for Norway that the united country of Denmark-Norway had been on the opposite side from Great Britain. At that time, the British had blockaded Norway's flourishing foreign trade and the import of grain on which Norway was so dependent.

This less obvious aspect of the neutrality policy now came into the open. Norway protested about the British naval operation in Jøssingfjord but wished to avoid becoming engaged in a military confrontation with Britain. Two old torpedo boats were sent to escort the British warships out of the fjord, with orders not to open fire. This part of the neutrality policy inclined towards symbolic, rather than real opposition to an Allied landing. That was the Allies' assessment of the situation when their troops stood ready to be transported to Norway on 8 April.

The prelude to 9 April 1940 has been much debated. Many historians have claimed that the German and the Allied action plans and preparations ran parallel and have considered the relationships between them. The German plans can't have had any influence on the British because the British did not know about them. Only at the very last moment did the German invasion project influence the British operations. When the British discovered the German ships that were on their way to Norway, they thought that they were trying to break out into the Atlantic and put all their efforts into stopping this. So, the British ships carrying troops intended for Norway were called back, the soldiers disembarked, and the ships redeployed into the hunt for the German warships.

Some authors have suggested that Britain and France were trying to draw Norway into the war to lock German troops up there and that the Allies were therefore partly responsible for the German invasion. There is some truth in this. The Allies, especially the French, saw some benefit in a new front being set up in Scandinavia. Their plans for landings were an important factor in Hitler's decision to occupy Norway. He wanted to get ahead of the Allies, because he feared that the Allies had immediate plans to take possession of Norway and he considered that they would do that anyway, sooner or later. But Hitler also had other reasons, as we have seen.

Others have concentrated on the different ways the Allies and the Germans planned and executed their projects. The Germans planned and executed their invasion project much more resolutely, professionally, systematically, and ruthlessly than the Allies. The Allies had difficulty coming to shared decisions and they made inadequate military preparations. Hitler's objective was to occupy the whole of Norway, whereas the Allies were just aiming for towns along the coast. Hitler had no scruples about infringing Norwegian neutrality.

Norwegian foreign policy in the prelude to 9 April was paradoxical. The biggest threat came from Germany, but this threat was unrecognized and played no part in Norwegian foreign policy. The other threat came from the Allies and was well enough known. The Western policy could lead to Norway being dragged into the war. This was the risk that Norwegian foreign policy sought to avoid. Norway protested when the British Navy violated Norwegian neutrality and refused the Allied request to be allowed to send troops across Norway on their way to Finland. This policy had some influence on the Allies, causing them to hold back. Norwegian foreign policy had no influence on Hitler and no effect on the German invasion, which went ahead as planned.

The government's refusal

Nygaardsvold's government could have responded to the German attack on 9 April by surrendering. There was much to be said for doing that when confronted by Europe's most powerful army and air force while one's own military forces were weak and unprepared. The Danes surrendered almost immediately when Denmark was attacked the same day. But the Norwegian authorities rejected the German demand. They refused to surrender, thereby bringing Norway into the Second World War as a combatant nation. Why? To answer that question, we need to look more closely at the two major decisions the government made about the war.

The first decision was made in the government building in Victoria Terrasse in Oslo on the morning of 9 April. The government had assembled there in the hours after midnight and received regular reports about the German attack that the country now faced. As soon as it became clear that the warships sailing into Norwegian waters were German, the government made a disputed decision to mobilize. Around 4.30 am Curt Bräuer, the German ambassador, arrived to meet the Norwegian foreign minister, Halvdan Koht. Bräuer gave the government an ultimatum to surrender immediately, warning that all resistance would be vigorously suppressed. In compensation for this, the Germans confirmed that their only reason for occupying Norway had to do with the conduct of the war. They did not intend to interfere in the country's government and administration. It was a question of strategic and military occupation without political or ideological control.

Koht put the German demands to the government, who had their reply ready quickly and almost without debate. They refused the German ultimatum and chose war. The reason for this was the unofficial part of their neutrality policy. Norway must not find itself on the 'wrong' side in the war, must not be at war against Britain. If Norway surrendered and was occupied by the Germans, they would end up on the 'wrong' side. There was not much time for discussion, and not much discussion was required.

The decision was also influenced by the immediate circumstances. The German attack on Oslo had been held back when the invasion group was stopped at Oscarsborg Fort.

Under the leadership of Colonel Birger Eriksen, the Norwegian forces there managed to sink the spearhead of the invasion force, the heavy cruiser *Blücher*, and delay the attack on Oslo. So, when the government made its decision there were no German troops in the capital as the Germans had planned. Because of fog, German planes had not arrived either. This gave the government the breathing space that it would otherwise have lacked. A further consideration was that the government could not avoid war on Norwegian soil even if they did surrender. The Allies would probably land in Norway to fight the Germans anyway.

It was the government alone that made the decision to bring Norway into the Second World War on the morning of 9 April 1940. Throughout the day, however, the political debate about war and peace widened. King, government, and parliament left Oslo with all haste in the early hours. They moved north to Elverum, where parliament assembled for an evening sitting, still under the authoritative leadership of Carl Joachim Hambro. Several important decisions were made in the day. The government led by the Labour Party would be joined by representatives from centre-right parties to become more of a government of national unity. The government was given full authority to operate on behalf of the parliament. This 'Elverum authorization' was later much debated.

Eventually, the parliament decided to negotiate with the Germans and appointed their own delegation for this purpose, readily accepting an invitation to negotiate sent by the German ambassador in Oslo. There was little talk of what benefits might be gained from these negotiations, and both then and since there have been conflicting views on what the parliament was thinking of agreeing to. Some commentators have maintained that the Norwegians did not want to be occupied on the Germans' conditions and that they wanted to hold fast to the government's refusal of the ultimatum. Others have said that they wanted to do as Denmark had, agreeing to the occupation in return for the country's democratic system being allowed to continue and the Germans not interfering in the government and administration of the country.

Germany attacked Norway and Denmark simultaneously and gave each of them the same ultimatum to surrender, and the same promises to respect their political systems. The Danes accepted the ultimatum and surrendered. When the Danish authorities had to decide whether to submit or not, German soldiers were already marching through the streets of Copenhagen and German planes were flying low over the rooftops.

That evening, while parliament was meeting in Elverum and deciding to appoint negotiators, the situation in Oslo was changing fast. Quisling launched a coup, appointing himself as prime minister of a new government. Two Norwegians and one German were behind this attempt to set up a counter-government opposed to the Nygaardsvold government. The Norwegians were Quisling, who became 'prime minister', and Hagelin, who was a key person at that time. The German was Hans-Wilhelm Scheidt, also a leading figure as Hitler's special envoy. The German naval attaché in Oslo gave the members of the coup direct access to communications with Berlin without censorship by other German authorities.

Quisling, Hagelin and Scheidt had all been involved in December 1939 in a plan for Quisling to form a government that would support a German invasion. It is uncertain to what extent the three were informed that their proposal was not included in the German invasion plan, or how long they continued working on it. But the instigators of the coup cannot have abandoned it, as otherwise, it would be difficult to understand how they could act so resolutely on 9 April.

The three conspirators had complementary roles. Quisling had a public role as leader of the government formed by the coup, but Scheidt and Hagelin were pulling the strings backstage. Together, the three formed a strange link between German and Norwegian national socialism. The Norwegian Nazi Party that Quisling led and that would be the basis for a new government was kept out of the preparations. Quisling did not inform any of his NS Party members about his meetings with Hitler in December, and he did not involve any of them in the planning of the coup.

Throughout the morning of 9 April Quisling began unsuccessfully to act as if he were the prime minister, but it was not until the evening that the coup was first exposed to public knowledge on the radio. Scheidt made the airwaves in the Norwegian Broadcasting Service (NRK) available to Quisling, and Quisling spoke to the Norwegian people twice during the evening to tell them that the Nygaardsvold government had been ousted and he had formed a new government. In his second broadcast, Quisling added that any resistance to the German forces was useless, and he demanded that officers and civilian officials obey only his government.

The coup came as a complete surprise to the German authorities in Oslo. Its architects had acted without involving the official diplomat in the German Legation or the German military authorities. Neither the German ambassador nor the High Command had heard anything about an NS government beforehand. Ambassador Bräuer had to telephone his superior, Foreign Minister Joachim von Ribbentrop, who in turn passed his enquiry on to Hitler late on the evening of 9 April. It then became apparent that the *Führer* supported Quisling's coup. The Nygaardsvold government had rejected his peace offer, and he would have nothing further to do with them. There would now have to be a firm demand to the king to appoint Quisling as prime minister. Other things were negotiable, but not Quisling's position.

Within twenty-four hours, the German invasion had changed character. What had started as a purely military action had now with Hitler's support for Quisling as prime minister also become an ideological and political mission. When Quisling presented a programme for his new government on 12 April, he did not conceal his intention of reforming the Norwegian political system. Party politics should be abandoned, and the parliament replaced by a national assembly built on business and cultural organizations.

Bräuer had the task of presenting the Norwegians with Hitler's demand that Quisling be appointed prime minister. On the night between 9 and 10 April, he requested an audience with the king. He travelled to Elverum, where he met King Haakon and Foreign Minister Koht on the afternoon of 10 April. Bräuer laid out Hitler's demand; the king must appoint Quisling as prime minister, but the appointment of other members of the government was open to negotiation. Bräuer was informed that this must be put to the government, which had moved during the night to Nybergsund.

When the government met in Nybergsund on the evening of 10 April, it decided unanimously that it could not agree to the German demand. The Norwegian authorities again rejected the German ultimatum to surrender. The government had again chosen war. It was now a war not only about defending Norwegian territory but also about defending Norwegian democracy.

Addressing the meeting at Nybergsund, the king affirmed that he could not appoint Quisling as prime minister. He said that the government must make the decision, but that if they decided to recognize Quisling he would have no option but to abdicate. His speech made a strong impression on the government. However, the threat of abdication played no part in their decision. The government was of the same view as the king. They were just as opposed to the demand as he was. But the decision lay with them, not with the king. Norway did not cease functioning as a constitutional monarchy on 9–10 April 1940.

This does not mean that the king was unimportant in these times. He was important to the Germans, who tried to split the king from the government and have the king on their side. He was important to opinion-leaders in the capital who were trying after 9 April to connect with those who had left the city. But first and foremost, the king was important because he showed such solidarity with his government. The meeting at Nybergsund established a pattern that remained valid for the rest of the war: the king and the government were as one.

These decisions on 9 and 10 April were all taking place within the context of continuing military operations. Three times the Germans tried to put the king and government out of action, and three times they failed. First, they did not manage to occupy the capital in time. The second occasion was on the evening of 9 April, when they sent a detachment of paratroopers to take the government and the king as prisoners. During the night, when the paratroopers had reached halfway between Hamar and Elverum, an improvised Norwegian unit managed to stop them at Midtskogen. On both these occasions, the Germans were trying to win control of the king and the government by taking them into custody. Their third attack was an attempt to eliminate them. The day after the decision at Nybergsund, German bombers attacked in a blatant attempt to kill the king and the government, but luck was not on the German side that day either. From then on, the king and the government were constantly on the move throughout southern Norway, until they came to Molde at the end of April.

There has been no lack of criticism of the Nygaardsvold government. The foreign and defence policies before the war have been strongly criticized, as has the failure in the early days of April to recognize the many indications of a pending German invasion. An especial criticism is that they didn't manage to come to a clear decision for general mobilization. The government should have consulted with the military chiefs on the morning of 9 April to discuss the situation with them. If they had done that, the mobilization would have been less confused and the military chiefs would have been clear about what the government wanted.

The government also failed to inform the population of their decision. They should have issued a proclamation so that the public had something to hold onto. They forgot to make use of the radio broadcasting system, which had not been destroyed. The Germans were soon able to put it to use and spread confusion over the airwaves. Not until 11 April did the king and the government begin to reach out to the population with the news that they had refused the German ultimatum and appointed a new and more belligerent commander-in-chief, Otto Ruge.

Criticism would continue to be directed towards the government throughout the war. It gradually subsided as more people came to support the government's policy of resistance, but there was always an underlying opinion that there would need to be a reckoning after the war was over. When the time came, this was carried out by an investigating commission that came to sharply critical conclusions.

In retrospect, the government has not been criticized for its chosen policy of resistance. In the course of the war the great majority of Norwegians came to see that policy as correct, and today the wartime resistance is an important part of the national identity. At the time, it was not so clear that the king and the government made the right decision when they took the country into war with a defence force that had been starved of resources during most of the interwar years. Many saw the king's and government's policy not as a line of resistance but as a line of escape; they fled to save themselves instead of 'sticking to their post'. However, this criticism played only a minor role in the evolution of events, for at the time most people were not asked what they thought about resistance or surrender. Even parliament gave no clear indication of whether to pursue war or surrender. The government alone, supported by the king, made the crucial decision that took Norway into the Second World War.

CHAPTER 2
THE NORWEGIAN CAMPAIGN 1940

The great powers' interest in Scandinavia during the winter of 1939–40 developed in April 1940 into military intervention in Norway. The campaign that followed was a multinational affair in which all the warring powers were engaged. For a short time in this early stage of the Second World War, Norway was an important focal point. Troops from Norway, Germany, Great Britain, France, and Poland all took part. The small nation of Norway played a significant, though not the biggest, part in this.

The campaign involved battles at sea, on land and in the air. The military operations on land were the most important because the ultimate aim of all the participants was either to capture or to recapture Norwegian territory. For Germany and for the Allies the war at sea was also important because both sides wanted to secure their seaborne lines of communication with Norway. Germany and Britain both committed considerable resources to this and suffered bigger losses of life at sea than on land. The British lost 2,500 men at sea as compared with 1,900 killed, wounded, or taken prisoner on land. The Germans lost 2,400 at sea, with 1,300 killed and 1,600 wounded in land battles.

The war in the air was also important, though. The Germans immediately took control of the biggest airfields in southern Norway, and they continued to benefit from their dominance in the air. The British didn't dare send their warships into the Skagerrak for fear of attack by German planes. British bombers on long sorties from home bases did carry out some raids, and fighters operating from aircraft carriers off the Norwegian coast were fully occupied providing cover for Allied troop landings. Neither side clearly dominated in the air around Narvik. Only the Germans used paratroopers. The plan was for them to take Fornebu Airport near Oslo, but airborne regular troops got there first. Paratroopers captured the airbase at Sola and were also dropped as reinforcements around Narvik and around Dombås.

Norway had little to contribute in the air. Fighter pilots based at Fornebu attacked German planes in a brief engagement on the morning of 9 April, but otherwise, the Norwegian air force was too small to play much part. The Norwegian navy was also able to make only a small contribution to the defence of the country. The fleet was taken by surprise at Narvik on the morning of 9 April, losing 2 old battleships and 276 men. Norway's naval defence was weakened on the very first day.

On the other hand, one of the coastal fortresses played a short, but significant, part. These fortresses were critical points in relation to the German attack because they could control the entrances to Oslo, Kristiansand, Bergen, and Trondheim. The German assault fleet relied on being able to pass them without being stopped. They succeeded in

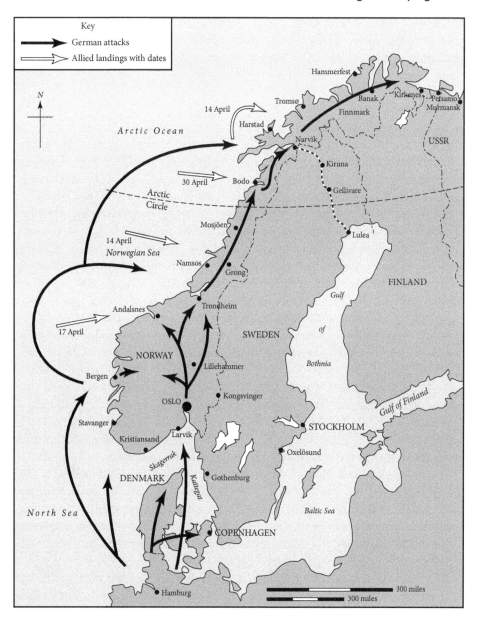

Map 2 The German invasion of Norway 1940.

this, except in the Oslo Fjord, where the artillery at Oscarsborg Fort delayed the invasion force by sinking the cruiser *Blücher*.

From the Norwegian point of view, this was mainly a war on land, where Norwegian ground troops played a significant role. Norwegian losses were smaller than those of the other participants. The 850 killed and a similar number of wounded were less than the German losses on land mentioned earlier, and less than the Allied losses of 1,900

British and 500 French and Polish soldiers. Nothing illustrates better that this was a war not primarily between Germany and Norway, but between Germany and a coalition of Great Britain, France, Poland, and Norway. Norway had to find its place in this coalition.

South Norway

The pattern of the fighting in Norway was largely set by the starting positions that the Germans had acquired in the opening phase. As they had planned, on 9 April they had attacked and occupied all the most important towns along the coast of south Norway: Oslo, Arendal, Kristiansand, Stavanger, Bergen and Trondheim. They had also established themselves in Narvik, the iron ore exporting port that had played such an important part in both the Germans' and the Allies' previous deliberations.

The German advance detachments around the captured towns were gradually consolidated into bridgeheads from which they could move on to take possession of bigger areas, while the Norwegians and eventually the Allies tried to stem the German advance and launch counterattacks. Several of the areas of operation were isolated, developing without any relationship to the main theatre of war in south Norway. The Germans' main objective was to establish a connection between the bridgeheads in Oslo and Trondheim. A steady flow of new troops was sent from Germany to the northern tip of Denmark, ferried over to Norway in a shuttle service of smaller boats and sent on to Oslo. The connection with Trondheim had to be made by forces from Oslo because the only way the Germans could bring reinforcements to their small force in Trondheim was by air. The Germans pushed northward from Oslo along several lines of advance, first across the flatter parts of Østlandet and then into the long valleys, mainly Gudbrandsdalen and Østerdalen which both lead towards Trondheim.

The Norwegians were the first to confront the German attack on land, as it took several days for the Allies to land their troops in Norwegian ports. The government had appointed General Ruge to conduct the war. Having opted for war, they left the military free from interference in carrying it out. The basic principle both for the government and for the military command was to hold out until the Allied help arrived. There was no way that Norwegian troops alone could repel the enemy.

Ruge's first task was to block the German forces that were heading north from Oslo. In an important directive on 15 April, he ordered that the units must prepare to carry out delaying tactics. Troops should hold their positions until the opposition became too strong, then pull back and mount another defence until they had to withdraw again. In the next phase, they would try to hold a line for longer while the main operation developed, the attack to recapture Trondheim.

Ruge faced an extremely difficult, if not to say impossible, task. He estimated the number of Norwegian troops in Østlandet at about 15,000–20,000 men, of whom not more than 10,000–12,000 were front-line soldiers. The Germans were relatively few, to begin with, but they steadily received reinforcements and they ended up with more than twice the number that Ruge had available. The German troops were well trained and well equipped, and they had quickly taken possession of most of the munitions stores and assembly points, which caused muddle and confusion for the Norwegians in organizing their units. There was also doubt in the early days about whether the government really would take up the struggle.

Ruge was not commanding troops who had been calmly organized into companies in a regular manner before being sent out to fight. The companies were organized 'on the hoof', while on their way into battle. Apart from a brigade that was sent over from Western Norway and distinguished itself in the fighting in Valdres, the units fighting in Østlandet were improvised. Personnel came and went. Very few of them had had more than six weeks' military service, and many of those who presented themselves for service had had no military training at all. The officers were not accustomed to leading large units. Equipment was in poor condition, and the lack of fighter planes, air defence, anti-tank defences and, to some extent, artillery was particularly felt.

It was clear from the start that the Allies would send troops to engage in Norway. They had been wanting to do that all winter, and now the Norwegians were inviting them to come. However, the Allies were afflicted by the same weaknesses as the Norwegians. The German attack on Norway had also taken them by surprise, and they too faced the reality that the Germans had already established themselves in so many positions on the very first day. There was much confusion during the Allied landings in Åndalsnes and Namsos affecting the unloading of weapons and equipment, while some of the Allied forces were poorly trained. German dominance in the air was just as discouraging to the Allies as it was to the Norwegians, and they had hardly any more anti-aircraft guns than the Norwegians themselves. The regular German air attacks not only caused material damage but also had a demoralizing effect on the troops being bombed and shot at from the air. Nor did the Allies have much to contribute against the German tanks and armoured vehicles.

The Allies had their own strategy that was drawn up in London. In south Norway their objective was to recapture Trondheim by a pincer movement. On 14 April the British, later joined by the French, started landing in Namsos. From there they advanced southward past Steinkjer until they met the Germans, who drove them back to the area around Steinkjer. There, they and later the French joined up with the Norwegians. Neither the Allies nor the Norwegians had been defeated at the end of April when the British and the French received orders to withdraw, and the Norwegian forces had to abandon the fight.

In the southern arm of the pincer movement, the first British soldiers arrived at Åndalsnes on 17 April. The plan was for them to move south-east to Dombås and then turn northwards towards Trondheim at the same time as the forces landed at Namsos were making their way south. Trondheim was to be taken in a combined attack from both north and south by Allied and Norwegian troops.

It soon became clear to Ruge that the Norwegian forces were not strong enough to hold back the Germans and cover the Allied attack on Trondheim. He recommended therefore that the British troops should defer the advance towards Trondheim and instead move south down Gudbrandsdalen to relieve the Norwegian troops in Østlandet.

Even though this meant postponing the recapture of Trondheim, the British accepted this plan and sent their troops south from Dombås. Under Ruge's command they fought alongside Norwegian forces on both sides of the northern end of Lake Mjøsa and later in Gudbrandsdalen.

The British help was insufficient, however. The British and Norwegian forces together were soon forced to retreat. The German advance continued relentlessly, and on 30 April they completed the link between Oslo and Trondheim. By then, the Allies had already decided to abandon the struggle in south Norway and had started moving their troops out. In the first few days of May, the Allies were out of south Norway, the last Norwegian units surrendered and all of south Norway was in German hands.

In Britain, there was sharp criticism of how badly the campaign in south Norway had gone, and the defeat led to political upheaval. After a key debate on Norway in the House of Commons on 7–8 May, Neville Chamberlain's Conservative Government was overthrown and Britain got a government of national unity led by a more warlike prime minister, Winston Churchill, who led Great Britain throughout the rest of the war.

The Allies did not intend to give up the struggle around Narvik. That would continue, and the British offered to transport the Norwegian king, government, and High Command to north Norway to continue the war there. The Allied retreat was a bitter disappointment for the Norwegians, but General Ruge encouraged them to go on fighting in the north, and despite everything, the government would not give up. The king, government and High Command sailed north from Molde on British ships to continue the war in north Norway.

Narvik

There were in a sense two very different military campaigns in Norway in 1940. One was in south Norway; the other centred around Narvik in north Norway. In the north, the fighting was characterized by Allied and Norwegian victories and German retreats. Towards the end, it appeared only a question of time before the Allies would win and the Germans would be driven out of the area around Narvik.

In the south, the war was largely between the Germans and the Norwegians. The British and French only managed to land about 10,000 men at Åndalsnes and Namsos. According to Ruge's estimate, 40,000–50,000 Norwegians took part for varying lengths of time in south Norway, though there were never so many in action at the same time. In north Norway there were more Allied than Norwegian troops. British, French, and Polish forces amounted to 24,500 men when they finally abandoned Narvik, whereas Norway in the course of a few weeks provided 8,000–10,000 men. The Germans were able to ship reinforcements to south Norway across the Skagerrak, but the British controlled the northern sea routes. The *Luftwaffe* never achieved air supremacy around Narvik as it did in the south.

At the start of the Battle of Narvik the German forces consisted of not more than 2,000 men, but this number was gradually reinforced by parachute drops and other means until it amounted to 5,000–6,000. By then they were facing a combined Allied and Norwegian force of over 30,000.

The British dealt with matters at sea. In two daring attacks in Ofotfjorden they wrecked all ten of the destroyers that the Germans had used in the attack on the town. That amounted to about half of the German destroyer fleet, a loss that they never entirely managed to replace during the war. The British provided all the vessels needed for the landing operations. British planes operated from aircraft carriers, and towards the end of the battle, British fighter squadrons made use of the airbase at Bardufoss. British ground troops fought alongside Norwegians to halt the German advance northwards from Trøndelag. The French sent troops to the most important landing operations, and in the last weeks of the campaign, they were also joined by Polish soldiers.

The German troops had captured Narvik on the first day of their attack and then consolidated their position in several directions. Their mission was to hold on and protect the bridgehead for as long as possible. The Allies' preparations went slowly, but they gradually assembled for what was to be the main attack. French Foreign Legionaries were landed at Bjerkvik and defeated the Germans there, giving the Allies an unopposed route to Narvik from the north. On 28 May landing craft brought two French and one Norwegian battalion over the Rombak fjord. From there they advanced to Narvik, which they captured over the day.

Norwegian troops took part in the recapture of Narvik, but the Norwegians' real specialty was mountain warfare. Led by General Carl Gustav Fleischer, they pushed the Germans back into the mountains. They continued their offensive for five weeks across a trackless terrain of valleys, hills, and plateaus. It was just as much a fight against nature as against the enemy – a struggle against snow, ice and cold.

After Narvik was recaptured on 28 May, the Norwegians continued their mountain warfare inland towards the Swedish border. Meanwhile, French, Polish, and Norwegian troops were also pushing eastward from Narvik and the surrounding district. It could not be many days before the Germans would have to surrender. However, on 10 May the Germans had started their major offensive on the continent. Now it was the turn of the Netherlands, Belgium, and France to be invaded. Narvik disappeared from the headlines in the world's press. The Allies needed their troops elsewhere, and at the end of the month, they decided to withdraw from the town of Narvik that they had recaptured. The German troops trapped near the Swedish border avoided having to surrender. By 10 June the Norwegian Campaign had come to an end.

The campaign and the occupied areas

The German invasion came as a shock to Norwegians. The general reaction of the civilian population in the occupied areas was to fall back on familiar routines and procedures. Holding onto normality gave a feeling of confidence. There was nothing to be gained from panic or resistance; it was better to keep the wheels of normal life in motion and integrate the Germans into daily life.

This suited the German policy in occupied regions. They quickly set about establishing good relationships with local authorities and populations, and mostly they succeeded. It was in the interests of both sides for Norwegian society to function as normally as possible. The Germans needed help with accommodation for their soldiers, hospital beds for injured personnel and many types of provisions, and such help was by and large offered. This peaceful cohabitation was helped by the fact that from the very start, the Germans paid for the goods and services that they used. The Germans placed their orders and the Norwegians supplied and were paid. Some Norwegians seemed eager to be of service, but the usual attitude was just to see the Germans as normal customers. Many didn't think too much about the purpose to which their goods and services might be put, even though they could be of direct use in the German war effort.

A common notion at the time was that war was conducted by regular troops facing each other across a front. It hadn't anything to do with the civilian populations behind the front. The Norwegian constitutional authorities had difficulty getting their messages through. In the occupied zones, the Germans controlled the Norwegian Broadcasting Corporation (NRK), newspapers were censored, and political activities were restricted. So, it was easy for the king, the government, and their war to be seen as something remote, arousing less awareness than the demands of each day, all the new requirements brought about by the occupation and the need for normality.

In a later chapter discussing the political struggle about government during the occupation in the summer of 1940, we shall consider attitudes similar to those that were prevalent during the campaign – an idea that war does not concern the part of a population that is already under occupation and whose members must first and foremost consider themselves. This reaction readily attracted surprise and retrospective criticism in later years. By 1945, many people had forgotten the first year of the occupation when there had been little or no resistance in the occupied regions. They looked back with amazement and displeasure, an attitude that passed on to the post-war generations. The wartime resistance has such a central place in the Norwegian sense of self-identity today that the state of mind in the occupied zones in 1940 can seem impossible to understand and difficult to accept.

Bitterness

The defeats in 1940 provoked much bitterness among Norwegians. Some of this was directed against the Allies, who were thought to have fought badly in the south and had twice abandoned the Norwegians by withdrawing, first from south Norway and then from north Norway, without warning or discussion. There was also criticism in Britain, as we have described, and the Norwegian Campaign does not have a good reputation in Britain. The French, on the other hand, have taken pride in their part in the Norwegian Campaign, seeing the victories in north Norway and the recapture of Narvik as a contrast to the humiliating defeats that Hitler's armies on the continent inflicted on

France in 1940. In France, there are still many streets and squares with 'Narvik' as part of their name.

The Norwegian officers were subjected to criticism. They faced bitterness and complaints both from the soldiers and from the public, who thought that many of the officers had been incompetent and should bear responsibility for the defeats. The officers' angry reaction to this was directed mostly against the Labour government, which they claimed had starved the armed forces and weakened their defence capability. The government had started a war without the means to fight it.

The strongest manifestation of the officers' anger was among several hundred who were captured by the Germans and found themselves in the prisoner of war camp at Grini, near Oslo, in early May after the end of the campaign in south Norway. They started a political rebellion wanting to appeal to the king to stop the war in north Norway and return to Oslo. There had been far-right and even fascist tendencies in part of the officer corps during the interwar years, and these now found full expression in demands for extensive political reform. Local democracy should be reduced, party politics eliminated from parliament and more power given to the government. Compulsory labour should be introduced and strikes and lockouts banned. However, the rebellion quickly died away when it became clear that the Germans would not allow any emissary to be sent to the king.

The bitterness and criticism could not be expressed in newspapers or other publications, as would have happened in an open, democratic society. Press and broadcasting were now censored. There couldn't be any public debate about who was responsible for the defeat. Therefore, the argument about the conduct of the campaign was deferred until after the war, when a military investigating commission was set up. Some of the officers did not emerge well from its report. Also, the criticism and depression following the defeat in the campaign became overshadowed by the wider development of the war. Oppression, victimization and a growing resistance movement at home, plus the varying fortunes of the war elsewhere, took attention away from the campaign. The defeat was turned into victory. When people in 1945 looked back at what had happened five years earlier, it seemed like a distant past, far remote from what they had experienced in the subsequent years.

However, there were important connections from the campaign in Norway in 1940 to the conduct of the war in the following years. After the campaign, what was left of the navy and the air force was taken to Great Britain, to become part of the Norwegian sea and air forces that were built up abroad. The leading resistance organization, Milorg, had some of its roots in the campaign. Officers and men seeking revenge created the first military resistance groups. Officers from the campaign were among the pioneers who built up the clandestine intelligence agency, XU.

There were also developments in the opposite direction. Experience in the campaign gave some people, not least among the officers, a distaste for the democracy that had mounted so weak a defence, coupled with an admiration for German military efficiency and for the Germans' or the Nazis' values and organization. Some of the officers and men who had taken part in the campaign later fought as volunteers on the German side. A fifth of the senior officers joined the NS Party after 9 April.

The government decides to continue the struggle

In north Norway, the king and government had taken up residence in and around Tromsø. From there they could see the war with some degree of optimism, as the Allies appeared to be winning around Narvik. However, on 1 June the course of events changed when the Allies told the Norwegians that they would have to abandon the campaign and withdraw from north Norway. They no longer had the resources to fight in Norway when they needed every available man on the continent.

The question was what to do now. When the Allies told the king and government that they were going to withdraw, they offered the Norwegian authorities the opportunity to go with them and continue the war from Great Britain. Such an offer was very difficult for the Norwegians to accept. It would mean abandoning the homeland and weakening the connection with their people. Many people would see it as fleeing and leaving the people at home in the mire. With the king and government based abroad, it would be easier for the Germans to set up a new government in Norway. In the war elsewhere, the Allies had gone from one defeat to another, and further defeats were expected to follow. When the king and government were starting to discuss what they should do, the Germans had just crushed the Allies in the Netherlands and Belgium, and France was next in turn. The British Expeditionary Force on the continent was in the process of withdrawing via Dunkirk. Linking one's fate to such a weak Britain was not an attractive prospect.

The king and government considered several possibilities. One option was to start peace talks and surrender. This possibility was available but was easily rejected. The Norwegian authorities were not willing to become prisoners or puppets. Another was to fight on alone after the Allies had left. This too was soon rejected as unrealistic. Norwegian forces on their own were no match for the Germans.

The government then tried to go for a ceasefire. Their proposal was that the Germans should halt their advance at the same time as both sides ceased their military operations. The king and government would continue to operate in north Norway, where there were neither Germans nor Allies. There would be a demarcation line north of Bodø, monitored on both sides by peace-keeping troops from Sweden, which supported the plan. The Germans had little reason to agree to such a plan, and they never replied to the Norwegian proposal. The king and government did not have much confidence in it either, but they clung to it for several days in a desperate attempt to be able to stay in Norway.

This idea should mainly be seen as an expression of how difficult it was for them to contemplate leaving Norway. Every time the possibility of leaving was discussed, proposals were put forward that at least some of them must remain to share the fate of their compatriots. The crown prince suggested that he should remain, which would help the nation to understand that the king and government were not fleeing from the enemy to abandon Norway. On 4 June the king wrote secretly to the British to say that he had decided to remain in Norway, but he changed his mind just as quickly. General Ruge insisted on staying, so that nobody could accuse the supreme commander of fleeing. He also hinted that it would be good if a couple of ministers of state resigned and stayed behind. They could tell people about the government's work and counteract the German propaganda that would try to blacken the regime as a 'fleeing minority government'.

The question of whether to go to Britain to continue the war from there was so difficult that the government would probably have split if it had had to decide immediately. Instead, the members gradually concluded that there was no alternative. On 7 June the government made a unanimous decision endorsed by the king: it would continue its policy of resistance from exile in Britain. That same day the king, the crown prince and the government boarded a British warship which succeeded in evading the German Navy and brought them safely to Britain.

The decision on 7 June was an expansion of the decisions taken on 9 and 10 April. Then, the government had decided to take part in the war without specifying for how long. Now, they had decided to continue to the end.

To implement this policy militarily, they ordered all naval vessels and all planes with sufficient flying range to make their way to Britain. They also encouraged all flying officers who could make the journey to do so. Many of them did, to become part of the Norwegian Airforce that was already being built up abroad. The first naval ships were in service off Britain by early July.

It would have been difficult to take any of the troops from the front, as they were needed to cover the Allied withdrawal which had to be kept secret for as long as possible. The government could have taken senior staff officers, but they were given free choice and were not urged to go into exile as the flying officers had been. Only one of them decided to leave. The biggest resource available to the Norwegian government in exile was the huge Norwegian merchant fleet, which it had already decided to bring under government control by setting up a national shipping company, Nortraship. The government's main priority at this time was to maintain itself as an independent Norwegian institution that would symbolize Norway as a sovereign state and could look after Norwegian interests when the war ended.

Even if we maintain that the king and government in exile were continuing to resist the Germans on behalf of a Norwegian state that they legally and legitimately represented, there remains a question of how 'Norway' was now to be understood. The king and government's decision to leave Norway and continue the war from abroad had split the nation in two. From now on there were in a sense two Norways: a Norway at home and a Norway abroad. There is no doubt that Norway abroad was at war, but what was the status of Norway at home in respect of wartime activity and in relation to Norway in exile? How and to what extent could the Norwegian authorities in exile place obligations on Norway at home? In the summer of 1940 leading circles in Norway at home started acting as if they were under no obligations to the Norwegian authorities fighting the war from abroad.

CHAPTER 3
HOW TO GOVERN AN OCCUPIED COUNTRY?

In autumn 1939, Poland became the first country to be occupied by Germany during the Second World War. Denmark and Norway followed next, in April 1940. There was a fundamental difference in German policy about Denmark and Norway, as compared with Poland. The Polish state was broken up and disappeared. The Polish elite was to be eradicated. Deportation, ethnic cleansing and forced relocation were integral parts of German policy in occupied Poland. The Poles were Slavs, Germany's old enemies from the East and not considered worthy of consideration by the *Herrenvolk,* the Germanic master race. The Norwegians and Danes, on the other hand, together with the Swedes, the Dutch and Flemings were considered members of precisely that race. They, therefore, had to be treated respectfully, with the prospect of becoming parts of a future racist Germanic Reich.

An occupied country needs to be governed, and the question immediately arises: To what extent should the occupying power hold the reins and to what extent should they be left in the hands of representatives of the local population? The plan was for Norway and Denmark to keep their existing organs of government, which would continue as normal so long as they complied with German military interests and on condition that the country did not resist the German invasion.

The Danes accepted this condition, capitulated almost immediately and were allowed to keep their democratic system. When the invasion of Norway failed to achieve its full objective on the first day, however, Hitler had no 'Plan B' for the government of the country. There was a political vacuum in the Norwegian capital that called for improvisation both by the Norwegians and by the Germans. Who should take responsibility for filling the vacuum, and how should it be filled? The struggles over this would go on for almost six months – until 25 September, when an arrangement was set up that would continue with some modifications for the rest of the war.

The first person to try to fill the political vacuum was Quisling, when he announced his coup over the radio on the evening of 9 April. The Germans allowed him to move into the parliament building, where he set himself up with his staff and three 'cabinet ministers'. He called a press conference, where he announced that party politics was to be abandoned permanently. Instead of political parties, Norway was to have organizations representative of business life and of cultural interests. A business assembly and a cultural assembly would be set up and would come together to form a combined parliament, called *Rikstinget,* that would take the place of the traditional parliament, *Stortinget.* The new prime minister wanted to start right away on creating a new political order.

Quisling's attempted coup provoked the Norwegians into a will to resist. The Germans were aware of this, and the commander of their forces in Norway, Nikolaus von Falkenhorst, would have liked to remove the 'prime minister' who was causing so many difficulties in their conduct of the war. There were still insufficient German troops on Norwegian soil, and their position was vulnerable. The formation of Quisling's government was, however, a political matter that would need to be handled by Curt Bräuer, who up to now had been the German ambassador but who now bore the title of 'Plenipotentiary Representative of the German State'. He still operated under the aegis of Foreign Minister Joachim von Ribbentrop and the Foreign Ministry in Berlin.

Hitler's demand that King Haakon should be persuaded to appoint Quisling as prime minister had presented Bräuer with a very difficult task, but after a few days, Hitler began to vacillate. Reports of the Norwegians' opposition to Quisling and the difficulties this was creating for the German campaign made an impression on him, and he became less firm in his demand. This gave Bräuer an opportunity to find a solution that did not include Quisling.

The Norwegian side with whom Bräuer negotiated consisted of an elite group that was trying to fill the political vacuum left by the departure of the king and the government. It included prominent members of the legal establishment led by Paal Berg the chief justice, and senior officials from the church, the civil service, government departments, voluntary organizations, business and political parties. They consulted each other and they consulted or were approached by German representatives, with Bräuer as the key person on the German side.

Among the numerous opinions on the Norwegian side, two main trends can be detected. Many people's priority was to put an end to the hostilities. The aim was to stop the bloodshed, save Norwegian lives and stay out of the war. The Norwegians would rather accept the occupation as a fact, try to make the best of the situation and restore business activity and employment to normal. They would encourage the king and the government to put a stop to the war as soon as possible. The other trend running through the discussions was the desire to get rid of Quisling and come to an accommodation with the Germans without him and his NS Party government. This view was promoted especially by members of the administration, who anticipated disturbances and poor organization if an illegitimate government such as Quisling's tried to rule.

Bräuer's objective in these negotiations was to set up a Norwegian governing body that would have both the approval of the Norwegians and the ability to work with the Germans. Such an institution should preferably have the approval of the king. However, it proved impossible to contact the king and Bräuer had to abandon this requirement. The assembly should be a type of counter-government that could compete with the Nygaardsvold government. In this, however, Bräuer met opposition from the Norwegians, who demanded an institution with a more limited remit. It should confine itself to administering the occupied territory and imposing order on areas of unrest and chaos. Even though there were many on the Norwegian side who disagreed with the king and government's policy of resistance and wanted to make peace with the Germans, they did not want to betray their king and government by openly opposing their decision. The

Norwegian negotiators insisted that the new central administrative organ should not have any opinion about the elected government's policy in relation to the war.

The various demands on the Norwegian side that something must be done and that an accommodation had to be reached with the Germans soon converged on one person, Paal Berg. He had served as a minister in two Liberal governments, but his background and political leanings were broad enough for him to be acceptable to many. As chairman of the Labour Court for many years, he won the respect of the labour movement. Most significantly, however, as chief justice he represented the third branch of government in the absence of the legislative and the executive branches. In these circumstances, the Supreme Court was the one constitutional organ that could give legitimacy to new arrangements in the occupied zones. That was why Berg was so important.

The Administrative Council

On 15 April the Supreme Court appointed a new assembly, the Administrative Council, to be responsible for administration in the occupied areas. To emphasize that this was not a political organization and even an alternative government, only civil servants and other professionals were appointed to it. I. E. Christensen, the regional commissioner of Oslo and Akershus District, was appointed as chairman. The Administrative Council immediately issued a manifesto encouraging everyone to 'show calm and self-control' and to 'contribute to the best of their ability to keep work and business going'. 'Everybody will on reflection understand that acts of sabotage and creating difficulties for civil life would just cause problems.'

To have the Administrative Council recognized in Berlin, Bräuer had to resort to creative use of language. He described it in German as a 'government committee'. Under the impression that this was a sort of alternative government that could compete with the Nygaardsvold government, Hitler approved the arrangement. The Norwegians, on the other hand, refused to call the assembly anything more than an 'Administrative Council'.

People in the occupied areas generally accepted and approved of the Administrative Council. The political parties and the main business and trade organizations supported it. A line had now been drawn, and a definition provided of what was acceptable behaviour under occupation. Norwegians should have nothing to do with Quisling and his NS Party. On the other hand, there had to be some degree of co-operation with the occupying power. This arrangement was better than leaving the Germans to rule on their own. Norwegians in the occupied areas should not publicly oppose the king, the government, the Western powers or the war policies that these were pursuing in the unoccupied zones. Nor could they support these policies publicly. Disturbance and sabotage in the occupied areas were banned, and economic life had to be kept going so far as possible and even actively promoted.

The Administrative Council managed a wide range of national governance and activity during the five months of its existence. Members of the council led the various departments of government with the same authority as ministers of state. The council took the place of parliament, and several of the most important issues it considered would normally have been decided by parliament. The Germans wanted to publicize that they were not interfering directly in Norwegian administration, which should be carried out as much as possible by Norwegian authorities. The Germans would issue regulations only when absolutely necessary, and there were only three such decrees prior to 25 September.

The Administrative Council made some important economic decisions. In response to German demands, strikes and lockouts were forbidden and wages and labour conditions would be set by the administration. The council gradually took over leadership of all economic policy, including control of production, wages, prices, and trade. All economic links with the West were blocked, and Norwegian trade was directed towards Germany, German-controlled or neutral countries. The council appointed a special committee for trade and industry which worked actively to facilitate adaptation and ensure effective economic co-operation with the Germans.

Important changes had to be made in monetary policy. The Germans brought in their own banknotes, which were to be recognized as legal tender alongside Norwegian kroner. The Finance Ministry and the Bank of Norway, concerned that this would cause monetary chaos, arranged instead for the Germans to receive Norwegian kroner directly from the bank, without any limit on how much they could withdraw.

The Administrative Council tried to follow a consistent policy that it was not a competitor to the government in exile and that it had no opinion about the war that the government in exile was conducting. On the other hand, they were unable to prevent the Germans from making use of Norwegian-produced goods and services in the conduct of the war and they had to tolerate the role of the Bank of Norway in financing the German war effort.

There were obvious differences between the policies of the government and the Administrative Council, and there were contrasting attitudes in the free and the occupied zones in Norway. The government and the council both did their best not to exacerbate the differences or the contrast, but there was inevitably a tension between them. The government was conducting war formally on behalf of the whole country, but it was cautious in saying anything about whatever practical obligations its policy might entail for people in the occupied zone. The Administrative Council pursued a policy of peaceful co-existence as more and more of the country was brought under German occupation.

Most of the Norwegians living within the zone administered by the council felt positive about it at the time, and the number living under its control grew steadily as the area of German occupation expanded. Five years of living under wartime occupation changed attitudes towards it, however. By the time the investigating commission had started its work in 1945, there were more critical voices to be raised. The population had lived through five years of occupation and had either experienced or heard about sabotage behind enemy lines. The idea that war took place not only between troops at a military front but also involved civilians behind the lines had become more widely accepted.

The investigating commission took up these questions and concluded by not criticizing the Administrative Council. It pointed out that the council was in a sense a resistance organization, in that it opposed Quisling and saved Norwegians under occupation from being ruled by a Quisling-led government. Mainly, however, it pointed out that nobody was calling for a policy of open sabotage at that time. The parliamentary protocol committee discussing the commission's report in 1948 was less sympathetic. It took the view that it would have been better if the country had not had a means of co-operation that weakened the policy of military resistance.

Opinions about the Administrative Council will probably continue to be divided. Seen through the eyes of those in the occupied territory at the time, it was right to establish an organization to keep Quisling and the NS Party out of power and keep the wheels of society turning. Seen later by those who wish to be identified with the policy of resistance, the Administrative Council should not have been set up and more should have been done to hinder the German war effort.

Reichskommissar Josef Terboven

In the days around 15 April Hitler was in a foul mood, worried about the situation at Narvik. He feared that the German troops there would be defeated. One moment, he thought that they should fight their way southwards out of the situation and the next, he wanted them to be airlifted out – which was impossible, as his generals said there were not enough long-distance planes. He swung from one state of mind to the other.

Worried by his sense of crisis, Hitler made new decisions about the governing of occupied Norway. He had agreed to the establishment of the Administrative Council because he thought that it was a sort of alternative government that would put a stop to Norwegian resistance. When it soon became clear that was not the case, he became furious with Bräuer and the foreign service. His deep-seated mistrust of traditional diplomacy welled up. Bräuer fell into disfavour and was transferred to military service in the *Wehrmacht*, and occupied Norway was removed from the foreign minister's remit.

By 18 April Hitler had decided on forty-one-year-old Josef Terboven as Bräuer's successor, and the following day he appointed Terboven as *Reichskommissar* for the occupied zones in Norway. Terboven was a regional leader (*Gauleiter*) in the German Nazi Party and at the same time provincial governor (*Oberpräsident*) of the Rhine Province. In a mood of crisis, Hitler instinctively turned to a party veteran. Terboven had shown his energy and loyalty when the Nazi Party was striving for power. Now he was to apply the same talents to sorting out Norway. He made a quick visit to Oslo on 21 April, and on 24 April he received his marching orders from the *Führer*. He flew to Oslo the next day to begin his new appointment. Hitler formalized this appointment on 24 April with a *Führer* decree that defined the *Reichskommissar*'s position.

Terboven appears to have been recommended for the position by Hermann Göring, who at that time was at the height of his power. Göring had become minister president in Prussia in 1933, and supreme commander of the *Luftwaffe* in 1935. In 1936 he was also appointed as leader of the four-year plan to rearm Germany and prepare the country for war. Göring had so much power in this role that he almost became an economic dictator. He had plans to draw Norway into the German war economy. On 5 June Hitler decreed that Göring could give Terboven directives in relation to the economy. Terboven was clearly Göring's man in Norway.

By then Terboven had already entered an alliance with an emerging power bloc in Hitler's Germany, namely the *SS* under the leadership of Heinrich Himmler. Before Terboven made his first visit to Oslo, Himmler had asked for a meeting with Hitler, where Göring, Terboven and Martin Bormann from the Nazi Party were present. Himmler wanted to establish the *SS* in Norway, and Terboven was of the same mind. That would give him access to the *SS* with its police and enforcement apparatus and enable him to assert his power and compete with the military power of *Wehrmacht*. Hitler was clearly in agreement with this arrangement, and the *SS* was established in Norway at the same time as and in close association with the *Reichskommissar*. As part of the deal, Terboven was given influence on appointments to key positions in the *SS* in Norway.

Terboven had much more wide-ranging powers than Bräuer had had. The decree of 24 April placed him immediately under Hitler, from whom he was to receive his guidelines and instructions. From the start, Terboven strove to ensure that the terms of his appointment were not just a formality, and he always ensured that nobody came between him and the *Führer*. He could always demonstrate that his power came directly from Hitler, and that was how it remained for the rest of the war, until May 1945.

The *Führer* decree was an attempt to balance between competing institutions, to fine-tune the potentially difficult relationship between the *Reichskommissar,* the *Wehrmacht* and the *SS*. This was delicate because none of them was subordinate to any of the others. The *Reichskommissar* would have no authority over military matters, which were under General Falkenhorst's control, but decrees from Falkenhorst relating to civilian life could be implemented only by the *Reichskommissar*. Terboven could use the services of the *SS* police force, but he was not in command of it. *SS* police services were also available to Falkenhorst if necessary, subject to the *Reichskommissar's* requirements having priority. This gave Terboven some sort of veto over the military in this respect.

Hitler's decree also set out the relationship between the *Reichskommissar* and the Norwegian authorities. Terboven could make use of the Administrative Council and other Norwegian authorities to carry out his instructions. The Norwegian legal system should continue to operate, provided its decisions were compatible with the occupation, but the *Reichskommissar* could make new laws by decree.

Hitler was probably trying to do more than just formalize Terboven's appointment. He must have discussed with Terboven how he wanted the situation to develop in Norway, where the building of the future National Socialist and Greater Germanic *Reich* could already begin. He left it to Terboven to specify what sort of political arrangement would be needed, once he was in post. This was in a way a continuation of the policy that Hitler had introduced so suddenly on the evening of 9 April when he recognized Quisling as prime minister. The democratic institutions in Norway could be set aside or manipulated to allow the development of national socialism, but as the Quisling experiment had failed, Hitler now had to start again in a different way, and he entrusted that task to Terboven.

Terboven spent the first few weeks orientating himself and building up his administrative staff in the *Reichskommissariat*. First and foremost, he strengthened the alliances he would need on the German side, rejected the institutions he wanted to have nothing to do with and made agreements with the key people and organizations whose support he thought he would need most. There was constant rivalry between the various power blocs around Hitler, and Terboven had to position himself so that he would not be overruled from Germany and lose control of Norway. Terboven mastered the art of finding his way through the political labyrinth that had Hitler at its centre. He immediately rejected two German institutions in Norway; he would have nothing to do with the diplomatic service or with Alfred Rosenberg's Foreign Affairs Department. Instead, he allied himself with the SS and the police.

A new government?

Terboven waited until the fighting in north Norway had ceased and the king and government had moved to London, and then he set about changing things. He wanted to create a new organization to replace the Administrative Council. Like the council, the new organization should be acceptable to the Norwegians and should promote calm and good order. Unlike the council, however, it should be a government that the Norwegian parliament (*Stortinget*) recognized as a legitimate replacement of the king and government in exile. Terboven also had a further requirement – it should serve as an instrument for the gradual Nazification of Norway.

On 13 June Terboven laid forth his demands: the king and government in London should be dismissed and Norway should get a new government that could work with the Germans. Following suggestions from Norwegians, it was to be called *Riksrådet* ('Council of the Realm'), which had been the title of a governing council of the Norwegian kingdom in the Middle Ages. To establish the council, parliament would need to be recalled and would need to give approval. The election of new members to parliament would be postponed, and in the meantime, the Council of the Realm would rule with the authority of a law passed by parliament giving it full powers. As the German side of the bargain, the *Reichskommissar* with his wide plenipotentiary powers would be replaced by an emissary who would be more like a German ambassador to Norway. Terboven's proposal was accompanied by a threat: if the Norwegians didn't accept it, Germans would be appointed as heads of all ministries and German control would be harsher than before.

Terboven's aim was to carry out a 'legal revolution' in Norway with the help of the Council of the Realm. This would inevitably be a slow process if he was to have any hope of getting support from Norwegians. So, the council would need from the start to have a majority of members who had public support and who were neither Nazis nor known to be pro-German. His strategy was to infiltrate the council gradually with more and more Nazi or pro-German members. Meantime, the Germans demanded that four new departments be set up: Interior; Culture and Popular Enlightenment; Labour Service and Sport; and the Police Department. These were obviously modelled on the political and administrative structure in Nazi Germany, indicating that the Germans planned from the start to use the Council of the Realm as a means towards a Nazi revolution in Norway.

The Norwegian side was horrified by Terboven's demands, and the question now arose of who should take on the task of negotiating to assert Norwegian interests. The Supreme Court immediately made it clear that it could not legitimize any initiative that was contrary to Norwegian law. It claimed that the king had not lost the right to exert regal authority and that parliament did not have the authority to depose him. The Supreme Court, therefore, refused to play the same role in establishing the Council of the Realm as it had in setting up the Administrative Council. Somebody else had to step in, and that role fell to the politicians in parliament, through *Stortinget*'s joint presidency which became Terboven's opposite number in the negotiations. The members of *Stortinget*'s presidency did this very much against their will, for they knew what a thankless task they were taking on.

To understand what happened next on the Norwegian side, we need to remind ourselves of the war situation at that time. Norway had lost the battle on home territory and was now occupied by German troops. On the continent of Europe, Paris fell on 14 June and France capitulated three days later. The outlook was depressing, and Germany looked unbeatable.

Within a few days *Stortinget*'s presidency had accepted all Terboven's demands except one. The Germans wanted to remove the royal family, even though they would allow Norway to continue as a kingdom. The presidency agreed that the king could not function, as he was living abroad, but they proposed that the future of the dynasty should be decided when the war ended. On 18 June they sent a letter to Hitler, asking that sometime in the future the throne could be offered to Prince Harald. Hitler refused the request.

As there was still disagreement on the question of deposing the king, the Germans stood ready to impose German heads of departments. I. E. Christensen, president of the Administrative Council, stepped in to try to resolve the deadlock. In a night-time meeting with the German negotiator, he offered to invite the king to abdicate, considering that it would be better for the king to abdicate voluntarily than to be deposed. Christensen obtained *Stortinget*'s presidency's approval for this, and on 27 June a letter was sent to the king, inviting him to abdicate. If the king refused to do this, the presidency would work for a parliamentary resolution that the king must step down. With this manoeuvre, the presidency was yielding to Terboven's demands on this point also; the dynasty would be removed with parliamentary approval. The king gave his reply on 3 July. He refused to abdicate.

The membership list of the sixteen ministers of state that the parties finally agreed on 29 June included six or seven men who were close to the Germans or to Quisling's NS Party or who were members of NS. Terboven had succeeded in building a solid base within the proposed Council of the Realm, a springboard for further pro-German influence and Nazification. His 'legal revolution' appeared to have a good chance of success.

Throughout the summer, influential circles in Oslo and in Stockholm tried to secure a place for at least some of the Royal Family within the new order. The starting point for this was that part of the family was living in Stockholm as guests of King Gustav, namely Crown Princess Märtha, Prince Harald and his two sisters, who had all taken refuge in Sweden when the Germans invaded. The idea was that Märtha and the young prince should stay in Sweden, ready to return to Oslo if an opportunity arose to secure a future for the Royal Family in Norway. Märtha put this suggestion to her husband in a telegram to London, but the king and the government in exile wanted to avoid splitting the monarchy in two, with one line in London and one in Stockholm. Märtha complied with this reply, and on 12 August she and the children left Stockholm to travel to the United States, where they stayed for the rest of the war.

The Council of the Realm is abandoned

The negotiations in Oslo about the Council of the Realm were completed by the end of June. The Norwegians had agreed to all the German proposals. Terboven travelled to Berlin to put the outcome of the negotiations to Hitler for approval. He must have been quite confident of approval, as he had instructed the propaganda department in the *Reichskommissariat* to prepare for a magnificent ceremony on 15 July to inaugurate the Council of the Realm.

However, Terboven had reckoned without Quisling's supporters in Berlin, who thought that Terboven had treated Quisling unfairly and who wanted to give him a more prominent place. Hitler listened to them, and around 20 July he decided that Quisling must be included more conspicuously in the council project, that the *Reichskommissar* should not withdraw and the *Reichskommissariat* should not be closed. Both elements of this decision entailed important changes to the plan for the Council of the Realm and made Terboven's task more difficult. He now had to find a place for Quisling, which he knew would provoke the Norwegians. At the same time, he would have less to offer at the bargaining table, since the *Reichskommissariat* was not now to be abolished. During August and September Terboven and Quisling negotiated between themselves and with Hitler. Quisling demanded that his NS Party should immediately have a greater share of government power, though he did not insist that he himself should be prime minister to begin with.

Having obtained Hitler's approval, Terboven resumed negotiations with *Stortinget*'s presidency on 7 September, by which time there had been a certain change of mood on the Norwegian side. The king's refusal had become known, and the first illegal publications had sprung up. When the presidency called the various groups in *Stortinget* together for wider consultation, a majority voted to suspend the king until the end of the war, but they were not willing to reject him entirely. There was, however, still a readiness on the Norwegian side to set the king aside, dismiss the government in exile and distance themselves from the king and government's policy of resistance, but when Terboven suddenly demanded a fifth place on the Council of the Realm for a nominee from Quisling's NS Party, that was too much for the presidency to accept. They finally understood that the proposed council could not serve as a protector of Norwegian interests, and the negotiations were abandoned.

During the negotiations about the proposed council, it became apparent that the king was regarded differently from the government in exile. The Norwegian negotiators' greatest difficulties were about abandoning the king. One might have expected the labour movement representatives who met in Oslo to have defended the government, as it had been formed by the Labour Party, but they did not. The labour movement that took part in the negotiations had been weakened. It had lost some of its most important members, who had joined the government in exile. There was also a Marxist-inspired faction with a good deal of influence, the 'Trade Opposition of 1940', that wanted a new political order based on a unification of the working class. This group obviously had no interest in defending either the king or the government in London.

Terboven's political revolution

After the negotiations about the council broke down, Terboven had to decide how occupied Norway was to be governed. The road was now open for Quisling and his NS Party. Terboven obtained Hitler's approval at a final meeting with him on 24 September. 'Terboven's political revolution' was announced on the following day, 25 September 1940, a fateful day in the history of the occupation. In broad outline, the system of government decided that day persisted for the rest of the occupation. Delivering a speech in his characteristically brutal style, Terboven poured scorn on the professional politicians, for whom he had no respect. His disdain for parliamentary politicians and parliamentary democracy dated from his participation in the Nazi struggle for power in Germany during the Weimar Republic and had now been amplified by his dealings with vacillating politicians who were willing to jettison their king, government, and constitution.

With the stroke of a pen, Terboven deleted Norwegian democracy. He dismissed the king, the Nygaardsvold government and the Administrative Council. All political parties, except the NS, were dissolved, and new political groupings were forbidden. Using the powers given to him by the *Führer* decree of 24 April, Terboven appointed thirteen ministers of state who all derived their authority from his position as *Reichskommissar*. Nine of these were already members of NS and a tenth was an NS supporter who soon joined the party. Terboven stressed that the Germans now recognized *Nasjonal Samling* as the only political party in the land, and he emphasized that it was the only means by which the Norwegian people could regain their freedom and independence.

Only three economic ministries – Finance, Trade and Supplies – were to be led by experts who were not members of the NS Party. Terboven was not taking chances with amateurs here. He also imposed a more compliant leadership on the Confederation of

Trade Unions. There was no mention of the parliament. Terboven probably wanted to keep that 'in reserve'.

While the Administrative Council had been governing the country, the Germans had mostly complied with international law. Nor was it in conflict with international law for the occupying power to nominate a government that consisted of Norwegians, even though it was subordinate to the occupying authority. But it was an obvious breach of international law to interfere so deeply in domestic politics and appoint legislators whose mission was to carry out a National Socialist Revolution in Norway.

The political revolution that Terboven carried out on 25 September was not something that he had originally wanted or worked towards. In a sense, he had suffered a defeat. He had not managed to bring the Council of the Realm into being as he had intended, and he had not managed to hold Quisling and his NS Party at bay. He probably would have wished to move on and take up a more fulfilling position elsewhere, but that was not within his power. He was tied to Norway.

On the other hand, his position as *Reichskommissar* had not been shaken, and he had at least as much power after 25 September as he had had before. He could now build up the organizational base he had acquired through the *Reichskommissariat* and his alliance with the SS and the police. He retained full control over developments in Norway, he was still the country's highest civil authority and he still held control of the police. He did have enemies, but there were none who could threaten his position as *Reichskommissar* so long as he had Hitler's support and there was nothing to suggest that Hitler was dissatisfied with him.

Göring must have been satisfied with Terboven's revolution; he still had Terboven as his man in Norway. Himmler and his SS could also have reason to be satisfied, as they had achieved a foothold in Norway through the *Reichskommissar* and among the NS members of the new government. Three of them were not only SS men but were in departments of particular interest to the SS. Jonas Lie had become head of the Police Department, of which Himmler must have had high expectations. Sverre Riisnæs led the Justice Department, and Axel Stang was in charge of the Department for Labour Service and Sport.

The alliance between Grand Admiral Erich Raeder and Party foreign policy chief Alfred Rosenberg could record a political victory. They had played a decisive role in the lead-up to 9 April and had been important in the summer of 1940 in advocating Quisling's case to Hitler. They continued to act as Quisling's supporters and Terboven's opponents in Germany. It may appear strange that Raeder, who was not himself a national socialist, could be such a strong supporter of a national socialist party in Norway. The explanation may be that he hoped thereby to acquire permanent naval bases in Norway. There may also have been some rivalry between Raeder as the navy's man and Terboven as Luftwaffe's.

The main winner in Terboven's revolution was Quisling, with his loyal party followers. From an insignificant position prior to 9 April, Quisling and his tiny political party had won through to a majority of Terboven's ministerial posts and achieved a solid grip on governmental power. From this power base, they could set about carrying out a political revolution in Norway. If the party succeeded in this, they would have prospects of being able to take over full powers of government, no longer subordinate to Terboven. They could also count among their assets the support that they had from Raeder and Rosenberg.

The big, overwhelming liability in their political balance sheet was that their position was founded on German bayonets. Their power was derived exclusively from the occupying forces, who were in direct control. No representative Norwegian organization had given the NS Party support, and there was widespread opposition among the population.

The NS Party's route to power was built on the remarkable relationship between Hitler and Quisling. Hitler had listened to Quisling before setting in motion the preparations for an attack on Norway. He had supported Quisling's coup on 9 April and had demanded that Quisling be held in reserve when the Administrative Council was being set up. Finally, he had insisted that Quisling and NS must have a leading position

Figure 2 Autumn Thanksgiving ceremony at Universitetsplassen, Oslo 1941, attended by leading powerful figures in occupied Norway. In the centre, Reichskommissar Josef Terboven, representing German civil and police power. Behind him SS and Police Chief Wilhelm Rediess. To his left is Vidkun Quisling, Fører of the NS state, inserted among the Germans. © KIHLE and JOHNSEN/NTB.

in the new political order in Norway. Hitler had persistently undermined the efforts of the Germans working locally who understood the political developments in Norway, first Bräuer and then Terboven, who both saw how unlikely Quisling was to succeed.

The clear loser on the Norwegian side was parliament. Despite making humbling concessions, *Stortinget*'s presidency had not achieved anything. They had been willing to sacrifice the king and dismiss the government. Parliament had considered suspending the king. It had not been a firm anchor in the hour of need. The emerging Home Front grew from support for the king's refusal from London and dissatisfaction with the negotiations about the Council of the Realm.

PART II
OCCUPIED NORWAY

The institutions of the German occupation sat heavily on Norwegian society. German civil administrators supervised and directed Norwegian central and local government. The German police became an instrument of terror and suppression. Several hundred thousand German soldiers and massive German building and construction works drained enormous resources from the Norwegian economy. Amid all this German activity was *Nasjonal Samling* (NS), the Norwegian National Socialist Party. With German encouragement, NS had taken upon itself a particular mandate: to convert the Norwegians to national socialism.

CHAPTER 4
THE *WEHRMACHT* IN NORWAY

The Germans imposed three separate institutions in Norway to assert their authority and maintain their presence as the occupying power: the armed forces or *Wehrmacht*; the civil authority or *Reichskommissariat*; and the security forces of SS and Police.

Each of these institutions had its own chief, with equal rank and authority in Norway. There was no local overall leader, no governor-general who could bring together the various strands of control. The overall leadership was in Germany. One reason for this was the situation in Norway at the time the regime was established. This is a feature found in many occupied countries, where the structure of the occupying regime was strongly influenced by the circumstances prevailing at the time it was set up. In Norway, much had already been put in place during April, prior to being formally completed on 25 September.

Another reason was the complicated interplay of power in Hitler's Germany. The *Führer* was surrounded by constant rivalry and shifting balances between different power blocs. Hitler allowed this to continue so long as it didn't threaten his own position. These rivalries gave his *Führerstaat* a dynamic energy, though they also imparted divisive tendencies. His tripartite regime in Norway mirrored the situation back in Germany.

A third characteristic distinguished the *Wehrmacht* from the other two. The *Reichskommissariat* had power and responsibilities only within Norway. Similarly, the police and SS units located in Norway only operated within the country. The *Wehrmacht* in Norway ranged more widely, however, as part of the German war effort at sea, in the air and on the northern part of the Eastern Front. Operations on this scale had to be seen from a strategic perspective and directed from Berlin.

The ultimate overlord of all this was Hitler himself. The extent to which he chose to fulfil this leadership role or could do so varied greatly from time to time. Norway was only a minor consideration on the pan-European level on which Hitler operated. There was a limit to how much attention he could give to decision-making on Norwegian issues. Nevertheless, Hitler had a remarkably strong influence on Norwegian history during the war.

He alone made the decision to invade Norway. He opened the door for Quisling and NS. Many of the German war leaders feared an Allied invasion of Norway, but none so deeply or persistently as Hitler. This had wide consequences for the German military presence in Norway and for the civilian population. Some of his utopian dreams for the future are related to Norway and they have left their mark on Norwegian history.

Leadership

The *Wehrmacht* in Norway was a divided entity. The army, the navy and the air force all went their separate ways. Each of the services had its own commander in Norway, who was subordinate to the High Command in Germany, *Oberkommando der Wehrmacht* (*OKW*), under Hitler as Supreme Commander. The major decisions about Norway, as elsewhere, were made in Germany. Meantime, the traditional rivalry between the armed forces continued. The navy complained that there were not enough reconnaissance planes to find targets for their warships. The army thought that the navy had too much responsibility for coastal defence.

There were, however, some elements of unitary command in the constitution of the *Wehrmacht* in Norway. Nikolaus von Falkenhorst was both commander of the army and senior commander of *Wehrmacht* in Norway as a whole, with the title of *Wehrmachtsbefehlshaber*. In this capacity he was responsible for co-ordinating the three armed services and representing them externally. The three services had common interests in matters such as supplies, transport and prisoners of war, and it was Falkenhorst's job to promote such shared interests. He did not have the authority of a supreme commander, however. He could give the heads of the navy and the air force directives, but he could not give them orders. If the heads of the forces disagreed about something and Falkenhorst could not bring them to a united view, the question would have to be put to the head of *OKW*, Wilhelm Keitel, or ultimately to Hitler. Falkenhorst was only the first among equals.

Falkenhorst was a typical Prussian army officer and a professional soldier, not a Nazi. However, he served a Nazi regime and loyally implemented the regime's war policy and racist objectives. The *Wehrmacht*, of which he was a part, was first and foremost a war machine that carried out the military duties that the regime required of it. But there was also an ideological aspect to the military power. Officers and men were indoctrinated in national socialism as part of their military training. This was a war between ideologies, and the soldiers were required to be ideologically aware. Even those who were not Nazis mostly considered that they were fighting a rightful war and continued to look up to Hitler, to whom they had pledged their personal loyalty.

National socialism's racist doctrines were applied to the *Wehrmacht's* use of Soviet prisoners of war as an important labour force in Norway. In other respects, the *Wehrmacht* adhered to the rules of war as set out in international law, with one exception. Hitler issued his Commando Order on 18 October 1942, decreeing that Allied commandos who were captured should be executed immediately, even though they were in uniform. British commandos, Norwegian soldiers from Company Linge and seamen from the Shetland Bus were all affected by this. After the war, a British military court sentenced Falkenhorst to death because the *Wehrmacht* had either shot British prisoners of war or handed them over to the SS who shot them. However, Falkenhorst's sentence was reduced to life imprisonment.

The army and the air force were not politically active, but the navy was. Admiral Erich Raeder, head of the German Navy, continued to support Quisling and the NS Party, as he had done prior to the invasion and during the negotiations about the Council of the Realm in the summer of 1940. He and his Fleet Commander in Norway, Hermann Boehm, did not agree with Terboven's heavy-handed political approach. They would have preferred Norway governed by Quisling, allied to Germany and able to make agreements about naval bases. In autumn 1942 Raeder tried to persuade Hitler to start peace talks with Norway, dismiss Terboven and appoint Admiral Boehm as the new *Wehrmachtsbefehlshaber*. However, Hitler was not persuaded. Raeder fell into disfavour and had to resign, followed soon after by Boehm. Hitler then appointed Admiral Dönitz, a U-boat specialist, as head of the navy and that put an end to the navy's political activism.

Defence against invasion

The *Wehrmacht* in Norway was responsible for four tasks. Their foremost responsibility was to defend Norwegian territory against possible Allied invasion. Throughout the whole war, Hitler worried that Allied troops might make a landing in Norway. This obsession caused him to commit large military forces to Norway.

His obsession arose largely from two raids that the British made on the Norwegian coast in 1941, in March at Svolvær in the Lofoten Islands and in December at Reine in Lofoten, and at Måløy and Vågsøy. He exaggerated the military significance of these. There might have been some grounds for his concern as the British did consider invasion plans in 1942. These plans were not so hard and fast as he suspected, but he clung to the idea that the British would try to invade Norway.

After the Lofoten raid in March 1941 Hitler gave orders to strengthen the Norwegian coastal defences, with 160 heavy artillery batteries to be mounted along the coast. The defence installations were to be concentrated in north Norway, as that was where he thought an Allied landing was most likely. There were several key points in his plan. To establish Trondheim as the main base for German submarines in the North, the U-boat bunker Dora 1 was started in May 1941 and completed two years later. In Bergen, the construction of U-boat bunker Bruno started in November 1941. The *Luftwaffe* was ordered to intensify its activity in the coastal areas, especially in the North. In December 1941 a new air force command post, *Fliegerführer Lofoten*, was set up to defend north Norway, secure the German supply lines to Kirkenes and attack Allied convoys. The biggest detachment of the air force was based near Kirkenes.

However, it was the British raids in December 1941 that really stimulated Hitler to react. He maintained that Norway was a critical zone where the outcome of the war might be decided. After the raids, he ordered most of the navy's surface vessels to be moved to Norway. By May 1942 the battleship *Tirpitz*, three heavy cruisers, eight destroyers, four torpedo boats and twenty submarines were stationed along the coast between Trondheim and Kirkenes. During just over six months north Norway had become the German Navy's most important base for surface vessels and Bergen an important support base for submarines. Trondheim also harboured submarines and the large surface ships that were later based in Alta Fjord.

The air force was extensively reinforced, until eventually there were more and bigger airfields than were required for the number of planes stationed in Norway at any one time. The intention was to have sufficient airfield capacity in case planes had to be relocated at short notice to repel an Allied invasion. Before the war Norway had had only three airfields with surfaced runways – Sola, Fornebu and Kjcvik – plus a few military airfields with grass or gravel landing strips. During the war the Germans either extended or built from scratch almost thirty airbases on land, twenty seaplane stations, several dummy airbases and numerous emergency landing strips. The *Luftwaffe* presence in Norway reached its peak in the summer of 1942 with a total of 264 aircraft, but this had to be reduced following the Allied landings in North Africa in November that year.

The scale of these preparations led to many Germans being stationed in Norway. By November 1940 the occupying force amounted to 231,000 people. These were mostly *Wehrmacht* soldiers, but the total also includes personnel (men and a few women) working in the *Reichskommissariat*, the police and other organizations. From December 1941 the forces were built up further until in July 1942 there were 300,000 Germans in Norway, and there were never fewer than that number from then until the war ended. A peak of 358,000 was reached in July 1943. This was surpassed only in November 1944, and in May 1945 there were 351,000 Germans in Norway. Right to the very end of the war, Hitler was obsessed about keeping enough troops in Norway to ward off an Allied invasion.

Norway is a long, narrow country with many potential landing places to be defended against invasion. At the cost of committing colossal resources, the Germans were turning it into a fortress, *Festung Norwegen*. They started by developing the lines of communication so that troops could be moved quickly to repel invaders. The Norwegian State Railways (NSB) completed the Southern Railway to give troops quick access to the South-West of the country, a likely area for landings. In the North, the Germans wanted to complete the Northern Railway with help from NSB and on their own extend it as the 'Polar Railway Line'. This was intended to transport troops northward by land, away from the risk of attack by Allied naval vessels, and to bring Swedish iron ore southwards from Narvik.

Troops and materials could also be transported along the roads, which needed to be improved. Particularly important was State Highway 50, nowadays European Route 6, which went all the way to Kirkenes but was not open all year. It was narrow and rough and included many ferry crossings. The Germans set about a major upgrading. With the installation of snow-plough stations, snow barriers and snow tunnels, by 1943 State Highway 50 could be kept open all year as far as Lakselv on the Porsanger Fjord. At times of heavy snowfall, the road onwards from there to Kirkenes still had to be closed and traffic had to detour across Karasjok and then onwards via Ivalo and Petsamo in Finland.

Fortifications were constructed all along the coast to block Allied landings and around 300 coastal batteries were built to house the guns that were the main component of the defence of Norway. This was the northern end of the defensive 'Atlantic Wall' that girded Europe from Biscay in the South to Kirkenes in the North.

Hitler also viewed Norway in a more romantic light. He dreamed of it as part of the new empire that would arise from German victory in the war and last for a thousand years. Norwegian granite would be used to build the huge victory monument that he was planning for his renewed capital city, to be called 'Germania'. Some of it still lies in quarries by the Oslo Fjord, a memorial to Hitler's dreams of victory. Trondheim was to have a special place in the new empire. A new town would be built on the peninsula west of Trondheim, with a big new naval base nearby at Øysand. Here there would be a German cultural and military centre, with German inhabitants governed directly from Germany and with Hitler as the town's patron. The first building works were started, but the Germans didn't get any further. After a couple of years, the grandiose project had to be abandoned.

Hitler's most fanciful project was the Polar Railway Line. The original plan was to extend the Northern Railway to Bodø, but in the winter of 1941–2 Hitler decided that a Polar Railway should be built right through to Kirkenes. There were some plausible military grounds to support this project, which would keep transport away from the sea routes that were vulnerable to Allied naval attack. Hitler's dreams, however, soared beyond purely military considerations. The Polar Railway would be part of a network linking the furthest fringes to the centre of the projected Greater Reich. It also gave the possibility of a further extension into the Soviet Union, establishing a link between Oslo and St. Petersburg. Hitler refused to drop his pet project, despite advice from his engineers and generals that it would be too heavy a drain on resources. To abandon his railway would be to abandon the thousand-year empire. Such a decision was unthinkable.

The geography of Norway, however, raised such formidable obstacles that Hitler had to agree reluctantly to reduce his ambitions and accept that the line should extend only as far as Narvik. The Germans and Norwegian State Railways worked together on the extension from Mo i Rana to Fauske, with the Germans working on their own from there northwards. As the work hit more and more difficulties demanding massive resources, Terboven and Falkenhorst wanted to put a halt to it, but their request was refused. Railway equipment continued to be despatched from badly bombed German railway stations to the promised line in the North. Hitler supported his project to the bitter end. In 1945 the Polar Line received the same priority as the German Navy in the allocation of coal and fuel oil.

By the end of the war, the line reached only a little beyond Mo i Rana. The rest had to wait until after liberation, and it has never been completed beyond Fauske. When the Germans withdrew from Finnmark and Nord-Troms in the autumn of 1944, they derived no benefit from their great railway project. The soldiers had to march on foot all the way to Mo i Rana before they could be put on trains and sent south. The Polar Line had run in Hitler's dreamworld but had been quite useless in Falkenhorst's military world.

In retrospect it is easy to see that Hitler squandered resources in Norway. He didn't need to station so many troops there or to build so many coastal forts against an Allied invasion that never came. He should not have invested so heavily in the Polar Railway Line.

Protection of coastal shipping

The second duty of the *Wehrmacht* in Norway was to defend Norwegian territory and sea areas against Allied operations. The Germans had to protect military targets from Allied reconnaissance and bombing flights. They had to prevent the Allies from landing men and materials to support The Resistance Movement. What was even more important, however, was the defence of coastal traffic. As road and rail connections in Norway were so poor, much of what the Germans needed to transport had to be taken by coastal shipping. German and Norwegian merchant ships and smaller vessels all took part in this.

German troops were transported both north and south. Freight shipped northwards included military and civil equipment for the *Wehrmacht*'s units, the coal and coke essential for shipping, trains and industry, and other civil goods such as building materials. Cargoes carried south included iron ore, pyrites, and other important metals such as molybdenum, copper and aluminium, plus vast quantities of fish, all destined for Germany. These were large-scale operations. In 1942, escorts were provided for 7,000 merchant ships that transported approximately 230,000 soldiers, 9,000 vehicles, 7,000 horses and 900,000 tonnes of goods.

This was the scale of the coastal traffic that the *Wehrmacht* had to defend against Allied raids from sea or air. The navy and the *Luftwaffe* escorted convoys of German and Norwegian merchant ships and hunted for Allied submarines and motor torpedo boats that attacked the ships. German planes scrambled to attack Allied planes that were shooting at the convoys, laying mines, firing torpedoes, or dropping bombs. Allied submarines, mini-submarines and motor torpedo boats were to be kept away by minefields, booms and closed harbour mouths, and German minesweepers were sent out to clear mines laid by the Allies.

The supply lines around the coast of Finnmark to Kirkenes required particular attention. After the German attack on the Soviet Union in June 1941 the defence of these routes became increasingly important. The German Lapland Army with its 230,000 men and 60,000 horses needed a steady flow of supplies which were brought all the way from Germany or from southern Norway, round the North Cape to depots in Kirkenes and Petsamo. The last part of the journey was the most exposed, over the Barents Sea past Vardø and across the mouth of the Varanger Fjord. Soviet planes and submarines attacked the German convoys, harbours, and storage depots. Along the stretch of coast between Tana and Kirkenes, by the spring of 1943 the Germans had a defence system consisting of no less than ten artillery batteries, several minefields extending towards the open sea, at least four radar stations and six airbases and seaplane stations. Each of the German convoys sailing to Kirkenes also had a strong naval escort.

Offensive forays

In addition to defence against possible invasion and the protection of coastal traffic, the *Wehrmacht* in Norway also had an attacking role. All three branches of the armed services were involved in defence, but the navy and the air force also carried out raids from Norwegian bases. In the early days of these operations German planes took off from Sola to attack Great Britain, but from autumn 1941 the *Luftwaffe* in Norway mainly concentrated on attacking the Allied convoys taking weapons and equipment from Britain to Murmansk and Archangel for the Soviet Army. The Russians badly needed these supplies, and the Germans put a lot of effort into stopping them.

Reconnaissance flights took off regularly to explore the sea area between Norway, Iceland, and Jan Mayen Island, locating Allied convoys. These could then be attacked by surface vessels, torpedoed by submarines, or assaulted from the air. Large battleships also took part in these operations. On one occasion, in September 1943, both *Tirpitz* and *Scharnhorst*, accompanied by nine destroyers, sailed north from the Alta Fjord to Svalbard to attack the Norwegian settlements there.

Defence against invasion, the need to control sea routes and the offensive forays against Allied convoys all tended to concentrate the activity of the *Wehrmacht* in Norway seawards towards the West. The eastern land border with Sweden was less significant. However, Hitler did sometimes fear that neutral Sweden might suddenly enter the war on the Allied side. German troops were stationed in eastern Norway as a warning to the Swedes and as a precaution against an invasion force from the West linking up with Swedish forces, but no defences were built, and larger units were never deployed along the Swedish border.

The attack on the Soviet Union

The *Wehrmacht* in Norway became heavily involved in its fourth task, which was to support the German attack on the Soviet Union. North Norway and Finland provided the launch points from which German and Finnish troops crossed the Russian border to create the northern end of the long Eastern Front. In the southern sector of Finland, the invading army was composed mostly of Finnish troops with some German units attached, all under the command of Finnish general Gustaf Mannerheim. In northern Finland it was the other way round, with mainly German troops and all under German command. There were close connections between the branches of the *Wehrmacht* in Norway, in Finland and in the invaded parts of the Soviet Union.

At the end of July 1940, Hitler ordered plans to be made for an attack on the Soviet Union. Finland's relationship with the Soviet Union was particularly tense at that time. Stalin's troops had occupied the Baltic nations of Estonia, Latvia and Lithuania in June, and Hitler feared that the same might happen to Finland. The combination of this fear, his anxiety about an Allied invasion and the prospect of a forthcoming attack on the Soviet Union led him to issue an order on 13 August that the defences in north Norway must be strengthened. The fjords were to be fortified better, particularly at ferry crossings.

In the autumn of 1940, German and Finnish interests coincided. The Finns received large quantities of weaponry and munitions from Germany, in exchange for the Germans being allowed to send troops and supplies over the Baltic and across Finnish territory to

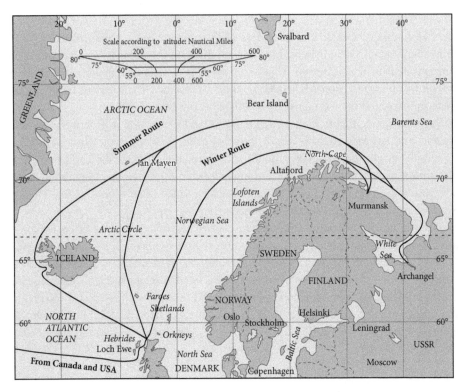

Map 3 Arctic Convoy routes. A total of seventy-eight convoys brought valuable cargo to the Soviet Union during the war. Because of ice, the convoys in winter had to sail further south than in summer.

north Norway. German troops were stationed along the transport routes in preparation for the attack on the Soviet Union to begin. This enabled the attack to be launched both from north Norway and from Finland.

In addition to being *Wehrmachtsbefehlshaber* and head of the army in Norway, General Falkenhorst was appointed commander of the German and Finnish troops in northern Finland. He moved to Rovaniemi in Finland and set up his headquarters there. The German air force in Norway, *Luftflotte* 5, also had its area of responsibility expanded to include Finland and the Murmansk Front. At the end of October 1941, a separate command unit was set up in Kemi to control *Luftwaffe* operations in north Norway and Finland, which included attacks on Allied convoys, Murmansk, the Murmansk railway, and Archangel.

Falkenhorst faced a difficult task. Hitler demanded that the defence of Norway must not be weakened because of the attack on the Soviet Union. In addition, in an order to Falkenhorst on 7 April 1941 he required that the defences along the most exposed stretch of coast between Narvik and Kirkenes were to be strengthened. This limited how many soldiers from Norway Falkenhorst could make available for operations towards the East. His predicament did not become any easier when it became apparent how dangerous it was to bring in reinforcements by sea. The campaign in the North was therefore not going well. The German troops soon became bogged down in their attempt to take Murmansk, and further south neither the Germans nor the Finns managed to cut the railway connection from Murmansk.

After the British raids in late December 1941, Falkenhorst was ordered to relocate immediately to Oslo, where as head of the army and *Wehrmachtsbefehlsheber* for Norway he would concentrate on the defence of Norwegian territory but no longer have responsibility for the battles on the Northern Front. Command over the troops there was given to General Eduard Dietl, hero of the defence of Narvik and a favourite of Hitler. On 15 January 1942, Dietl was appointed head of what for a while was known as the Lapland Army. There was now no longer any combined command for the German troops in Norway, northern Finland and northern Russia.

There were close links between them, however. The Lapland Army was given responsibility for coastal defence in the Varanger region as far west as the Tana Fjord. Troops and supplies were brought in by sea to be disembarked at Kirkenes, and some were also brought in along State Highway 50. Soldiers and supplies were sent forward to the front from Kirkenes, and soldiers were brought back to Norwegian territory by the same route. At Skoganvarre, 30 kilometres south of Lakselv, a large camp was set up where soldiers from the front could rest before being sent back. At the peak of activity there were 30,000 German soldiers and other personnel located around Porsanger, plus prisoners of war and workers, in a municipality with only 3,000 Norwegian inhabitants.

Although the navy and the air force were continuously engaged in operations at sea and in the air, the German military forces in Norway stood mostly as a reserve army that could be seen almost as a peace-keeping force. Most of the troops constituted an army of occupation and did not take part in active operations on Norwegian soil until autumn 1944. Many soldiers stationed in Norway had a peaceful time and could be content with preparing themselves for the invasion that never came. They could consider themselves lucky so long as they remained in Norway, but many were transferred elsewhere and sent to the front, bearing happy memories of their stay in Norway.

The *Wehrmacht* and Norwegian society

The *Wehrmacht*'s major concerns were events beyond Norwegian soil. At home in Norway, their activities in relation to the civilian population were minimal. There was no need to deploy German military units against angry mobs or rebellious crowds. Martial law was never imposed. The *Wehrmacht* did not arouse disquiet and popular resistance by brutal oppression. Strong discipline prevailed within the *Wehrmacht*, and instances of assault on civilians were few and were punished hard. Norway was a peaceful country. The military resistance movement did not shoot at German soldiers. There was no partisan war in Norway. Only towards the end of the war did the relationship between the *Wehrmacht* and part of the civilian population break down, when German armed forces were deployed against the people of north Norway, in Finnmark and Nord-Troms.

Even though the *Wehrmacht* didn't need to send troops in to suppress rebellious mobs or repel attacks by Milorg groups, the German war machine did keep track of its opponents. The military intelligence organization *Abwehr* tracked down resistance organizations. The counter-espionage section in *Abwehr* with its many Norwegian informers was a lead organization in exposing The Resistance Movement, though it did not undertake arrests or violent interrogations under torture. The *Sicherheitspolizei* (*Sipo*) attended to that part of the process, but thorough investigation by *Abwehr* was often the prelude to a successful action by the *Gestapo*.

Norwegian citizens could also be subject to the jurisdiction of either of two types of military court. The higher of these two courts, the *Reichskriegsgericht*, was headquartered in Germany but travelled around the occupied territories to hear serious cases. It ceased holding hearings in Norway in December 1941. The other type of court was the field court, which was based on the various branches of the forces. In the years 1941–3, the *Wehrmacht* courts condemned seventy-eight Norwegians to death and passed many lesser sentences. After 1943 the SS and Police Court handled most of the cases.

To accommodate the increasing number of people stationed in Norway, the military commandeered numerous buildings. Private houses, communal buildings and state-owned buildings were requisitioned according to the *Wehrmacht*'s needs, preferably in co-operation with the Norwegian authorities who tried to distribute the burden as best they could. The requirements were mainly met, however, by new building. Norwegians had to make vacant sites available for the building of barracks, stores, workshops, ammunition depots and stables. Camps with barracks shot up throughout the country.

The presence of the *Wehrmacht* in Norway and the building of *Festung Norwegen* transformed the landscape. Barrack buildings, military camps, coastal forts, gun emplacements and airfields formed new features. They lay in forbidden zones no longer accessible to the Norwegian public, surrounded by barbed wire, minefields, warning signs and guard patrols. This created a physical boundary between the occupying army and the civilian population. A force of several hundred thousand men lived isolated in their camps. The army was kept busy with military exercises and guard duties, while the naval and air force personnel also took part in active military operations. Outside the confines of the camps and the closed military sphere there were German institutions that attracted officers, other ranks, and officials from the *Reichskommissariat* and *Sipo*, keeping them apart from Norwegian society: a German theatre, bookshops, social clubs, casinos, sports huts, restaurants and even a German newspaper, *Deutsche Zeitung in Norwegen*.

The Germans needed many goods and services from Norwegian civil society, which led to co-operation between German and Norwegian officials and business people. Norwegians working on German building sites necessarily encountered German personnel. German military and civilian personnel could also meet Norwegians in their free time. Norwegian women and German men established relationships, formed close bonds, and even married. Between 10,000 and 12,000 children were born to Norwegian mothers and German fathers. The biggest opportunity for close or intimate relationships occurred when German soldiers were quartered in private homes, which was particularly the case in north Norway.

The *Wehrmacht*'s strategic deployment of its armed forces had major effects on Norwegian civil society. Parts of the army of occupation were relocated from the central region to the coastal defences, from east Norway to west or north Norway, or from towns to surrounding areas. The location of the German military and other establishments determined where it was most dangerous for Norwegians to live. Allied bombs struck not only the Germans but also Norwegians who lived in the vicinity of naval depots, airfields, or industrial sites. The coastline became a front line alongside a mainly peaceful inland territory and the only battlefield in Norway other than east Finnmark in autumn 1944. Along the coast, losses were suffered not only by the German forces but also by the civilian population. Coastal travel was dangerous; 1,000 Norwegian sailors and passengers perished, and 170 ships were lost.

CHAPTER 5
THE *REICHSKOMMISSARIAT*

The *Reichskommissariat* for the occupied Norwegian region had been established in haste, in a crisis situation in April 1940, and was obviously considered a temporary solution. The Germans set up similar organizations elsewhere, for example, in Eastern Europe and in the Netherlands. In each location, the *Reichskommissariat* was created as a temporary response to distinct local circumstances. This distinguished it from the *Wehrmacht* and the *SS*, which were both permanent institutions in Nazi Germany.

The *Reichskommissariat* set up to govern occupied Norway was a civilian, political institution with wide-ranging powers and a significant degree of independence. Its authority did not, however, extend to the *Wehrmacht* and military matters. This was a major limitation, relative to the power and significance of the military. Right from the start of the occupation there was a civil-military dualism that became an important feature in the governance of occupied Norway. A civil power and a military power, each with its own mandate, legitimacy and power base, stood as equal partners beside and against each other, required to co-operate and fated to clash.

The *Reichskommissariat*'s guiding principle was indirect rule. It should not govern directly, but through a Norwegian authority. During the negotiations about setting up the Council of the Realm, the Germans had threatened to appoint their own people and govern directly if the negotiations failed. The solution to the impasse had been to appoint NS members to most of the positions in the government. Norwegians would run Norway under the supervision of the *Reichskommissariat* and according to their directions, depending on how interested the Germans were in a particular topic and how deeply they wished to engage in it.

From the German point of view, the advantage of indirect government was that it required fewer of their own people to be involved and that they could leave the Norwegian apparatus of state to bear the burden of reaction against unpopular decisions. The guiding principle was not applied fully, however; German censorship was imposed directly on the newspapers without any Norwegian intermediary, and the Germans did sometimes take matters into their own hands and rule directly without going through the Norwegian administration.

The *Reichskommissariat* had three main tasks that were difficult to combine. First, it was to contribute to the German war effort and strive towards a German victory by creating favourable circumstances for the *Wehrmacht* in Norway. Second, it had responsibilities for the Norwegian population. The Norwegians were a Germanic race who could not be treated in the same brutal manner as Slavs and Jews. Orderly calm, however, must prevail in the occupied zones. Any threat to the German utilization of

Norwegian resources must be firmly suppressed. Third, it should promote the spread of the Nazi Movement, which it did mainly through the agency of Quisling's NS (*Nasjonal Samling*) Party.

Terboven

The *Reichskommissariat* was an institution, the supreme leader of the institution was the *Reichskommissar,* and the *Reichskommissar* was Josef Terboven. So far as can be known, the *Führer*'s trust in Terboven weakened only once. That happened after the mass arrest of students in autumn 1943. The publicity and opposition that this event aroused in Sweden enraged Hitler, and he directed his anger against the *Reichskommissar.* He may even have considered removing Terboven from power, but the crisis blew over and Terboven remained as secure – or insecure – as before.

The *Reichskommissariat* was primarily a tool to be used by the *Reichskommissar.* Terboven came first, the institution second. He created it from the start and set his mark upon it, influenced by his experiences in Germany during the First World War and in the interwar period. These were mirrored in the way he established the institution, in the way he used it as a tool and in the basic political style that he promoted.

Terboven had joined Hitler's German National Socialist Party, the *Nationalsozialistische Deutsche Arbeiterpartei* (*NSDAP*), in 1923. He took part in Hitler's unsuccessful attempt at a political coup in a beer cellar in Munich that same year. His serious contribution to the Nazi Party started in 1925, when he founded a branch of the party in his home town of Essen in the Ruhr district, right in the industrial heart of Germany. In 1928 the branch in Essen was recognized as a distinct county organization within the party, a *Gau*, with Terboven as *Gauleiter.*

Loyalty to the *Führer* became the basic foundation of his life. He remained ardently devoted to the Nazi movement that his leader had created. So long as Hitler was committed to the struggle, so was Terboven. When Hitler gave up the struggle and committed suicide in 1945, so did Terboven. There was never any question of opposing a clear directive from the *Führer*; the problem was that Hitler often did not issue clear orders, and then Terboven and others had to act on their own initiative. So Terboven developed his role as an independent, committed and autonomous local *Führer* with significant freedom of action. Hitler liked to see his *Gauleiters* perform in this way, and they became like minor kings owing homage only to the *Führer*.

Terboven became a man of power. He had an appreciation of power and knew how to acquire and handle it. Politics was a contest to win positions and defeat opponents. He calculated soberly, did not allow his feelings to influence his decisions, was hard-hitting and if necessary ruthless, and recognized violence as a political instrument. In Norway he suppressed opposition severely, with death sentences and shooting of hostages, but his use of violence was purposeful and rational rather than random and chaotic. His style was direct. He said what he thought, without circumlocution or evasion. He was often caustic, ironic and abrasive in what he said, and he did not hold back from appearing superior or arrogant. He was not a great orator. As a committed Nazi he supported Hitler's ideology, but his motivation came primarily from his loyalty to the movement rather than from ideological considerations. His roots were in the Nazi movement, through which he had developed his capabilities as a practical man of action.

From 1930 onwards the National Socialist Party in Germany was sailing before a following wind. Terboven was elected to the *Reichstag* as a party representative, a position he held for the rest of his life. His personal income, which had been meagre, was now enhanced by his salary as a member of parliament. However, his status in the new Germany under Hitler's leadership derived mainly from his position as a *Gauleiter*. The *Gauleiter* were the hard core of the movement that was now taking over power. They had driven the movement forward from its foundation, under Hitler's overall direction and control. Hitler honoured and identified with his *Gauleiters*, and they with him. After the takeover of power in 1933, they were the people who were given much of the responsibility for indoctrinating the German public. So when Terboven came to Norway in 1940 he already had experience of how to reorganize and indoctrinate schools, organizations, cultural life and local government.

In 1935 Terboven was appointed *Oberpräsident* in the Rhine Province, meaning that he now had parallel positions in party and state (*Gauleiter* and *Oberpräsident*). *Oberpräsident* was one of the highest government appointments in Prussia. It strengthened Terboven's regional position and opened up new areas of experience that further developed his political skills. He now had to deal with matters of public administration. The Rhine Province had to be governed according to the dictates of party policy, which was the purpose of merging party and state.

Through this appointment, Terboven became engaged in new areas of political struggle. He was drawn into conflicts between the party and public administration but also conflicts which crossed the borders between them, a typical feature of Hitler's Germany. He developed his understanding of the relationship between politics and administration. He formed good working relationships with business interests in the Rhine Province and the Ruhr, and he began to take an interest in economics and economic development. He made use of this experience when he was building up his German administration in Norway and had to adapt the *Reichskommissariat* to German politics and to various administrative organizations in Germany, while at the same time being involved in Norwegian politics and public administration and taking an interest in economic development.

Terboven initially took a short-term view of his appointment as *Reichskommissar* in Norway. He would sort out the confused entanglements left by his predecessor, set occupied Norway on the right course and then leave it to others to steer the ship of state forwards. But that was not how it worked out. The *Reichskommissariat* was not dissolved, and he himself had to continue as *Reichskommissar*. He still did not see his position as permanent, and later tried in vain to get out of it. He would have preferred to take a responsible post in the Ruhr or Rhineland or as *Reichskommissar* in Belgium. That would have brought him closer to the areas in which he still held appointments as *Gauleiter* and *Oberpräsident*, where he appointed deputies to attend to the day-to-day work but still held overall control. He didn't want to lose his established foothold in Germany.

Some Germans could for racial reasons take an interest in Norway as a Nordic-Germanic country and value the Old Norse tradition and Norwegian culture, but most had a rather restricted knowledge of Norway and Norwegians. Terboven travelled widely throughout Norway to assess how the natural and commercial resources could be put to use for the benefit of the *Wehrmacht* and the German war effort, but he took little interest in the Norwegian people, their culture or their history. He did not learn the Norwegian language; he discouraged its use in the work of the commissariat and he ordered that his title of *Reichskommissar* should not be translated into Norwegian. He kept himself alien from Norwegian lifestyle and democratic culture and operated as the representative of a *Herrenvolk*.

The *Einsatzstab* – a political taskforce

As soon as Terboven arrived in Norway he started building up his staff and situating them in the parliament building. He took up residence in the crown prince's estate at Skaugum outside Oslo. However, while the political situation remained uncertain and the outcome of the negotiations about the Council of the Realm was unknown, it was difficult for him to make progress in setting up the *Reichskommissariat*. After 25 September 1940 the situation changed and he was able to enter fully into his duties as *Reichskommissar*. By late autumn the commissariat had an organizational structure which in the main persisted throughout the war.

The heads of departments in the *Reichskommissariat* were given considerable freedom of action. Terboven sketched out what was to be done and left his colleagues to carry it out. This way of working made it possible for him to be away travelling for considerable periods of time, giving him time and opportunity to protect his own interests and those of the *Reichskommissariat* abroad and to nurture all the connections and alliances that it was important to maintain in the complexities of Nazi Germany. There were no competitors for his position as *Reichskommissar*, and he faced no serious opposition from within his own ranks other than at the very end of the war. He chose not to appoint any permanent second in-command who might have built up a power base from which to challenge him.

One of the special departments within the *Reichskommissariat* was a political taskforce known as the *Einsatzstab*, whose role was to develop relations with Quisling's *Nasjonal Samling* Party and provide it with support. This group was initially known as *Einsatzstab Wegener*, after the name of its first chief, or sometimes as *Einsatzstab NSDAP*, signifying its status as an offshoot of the *Nationalsozialistische Deutsche Arbeiterpartei* and a channel by which the German Nazi Party could provide personnel and the benefits of its organizational experience to its Norwegian sister party.

The *Einsatzstab* was a means to implement Hitler's instruction to Terboven in the summer of 1940 that NS was to be given a place in the new arrangements. It was decided that the small and immature Norwegian Nazi Party would need a helping hand from German experts in party organization. The *Einsatzstab* was set up after discussions with the leadership of the German party, namely Rudolf Hess whom Hitler had appointed as 'Deputy *Führer*' and Martin Bormann who was Hess's powerful secretary and chief of staff. Terboven proposed that Paul Wegener, a former member of Hess's staff, should be appointed leader of the *Einsatzstab*, and Hitler approved the appointment.

Between 6 and 9 September 1940, twenty-four *NSDAP* officials arrived from Germany. They were given a briefing about the situation in the NS Party and then allocated as advisers to the local organizers. By autumn 1941 there were seventy people working in the *Einsatzstab*, which was now a large department within the *Reichskommissariat*. The NS was glad of this help, at least to begin with. Many party members looked at the German party with awe and accepted that they needed professional help to build a similar party in Norway. On the other hand, conflict was inevitable. The cultural differences were great. The Germans had little understanding of the NS members' nationalism, and they tended to act as if they knew better.

Economic departments

The biggest and most important section in the *Reichskommissariat* was the Economic Department (*Hauptabteilung Volkswirtschaft*), which by the beginning of February 1942 had grown to include 258 personnel. Terboven's interest in trade and industry was one reason for this, but a more important reason was that German economic activity in Norway was so extensive. The Economic Department spearheaded this from the start.

The department's function was to advance German economic interests in Norway. Leading and co-ordinating these was not so easy, as they were many and diverse. Not least, there was a balance to be maintained between German requirements and the needs of the Norwegian economy. The task was to incorporate Norwegian businesses and Norwegian trade and industry into the German war economy without damaging or destroying them to the extent that they could no longer serve German interests.

The department had widespread contacts with Norwegian trade and industry and with those parts of the Norwegian administration that dealt with business and economic matters. The Germans as the occupying power were in a strong position to put pressure on the Norwegians, though Terboven and the Economic Department preferred to derive as much benefit as possible from voluntary German–Norwegian co-operation.

As head of *Hauptabteilung Volkswirtschaft* throughout the war, Carlo Otte had a major influence on the Norwegian economy. Otte was a convinced Nazi, but he combined his ideological zeal with a sense of economic reality, a willingness to listen to experts and a talent for protecting the economy against ideological pressures. Otte's wish to shield the economy from ideological considerations and his trust in experts set limits on the influence of the *Nasjonal Samling*. He feared that NS would allow ideological considerations too much weight and that they would recruit economic dilettantes.

A second economic department was set up in the *Reichskommissariat*, though without 'economic' as part of its title. In spring 1942 the big, half-military construction organization *Organisation Todt (OT)* set up a branch in Norway, *OT Einsatzgruppe Wiking*. This gradually took over more of the German building and construction activity in Norway. *Einsatzgruppe Wiking* was administered by the central *OT* organization in Germany but included as a technical department in the *Reichskommissariat* in Norway, *Hauptabteilung Technik*.

Propaganda

The Department of Popular Enlightenment and Propaganda (*Hauptabteilung Volksaufklärung und Propaganda*) was led by Georg Wilhelm Müller. He was a close colleague of Goebbels, and his department operated like a branch of Goebbels's Ministry of Propaganda in Berlin. Müller therefore served two masters – Terboven and Goebbels – without this causing any great difficulty. Terboven relied on his close relationship with Goebbels and wanted to develop this further by allowing Goebbels's ministry and his trusted collaborator to have a powerful position in the *Reichskommissariat*. Beyond that, Terboven was not particularly interested in the propaganda activity.

The role of Müller's department was to propagandize national socialism and the whole range of German culture and history that national socialism identified with and wished to promote. Within the department there were sections for propaganda, press, broadcasting, schools and culture. Müller also controlled the censorship that instructed press and broadcasting in what they should tell the public and how they should present it. The department worked to import German information material, literature and films. It arranged several book fairs with material promoting Hitler and the Third Reich. It supported a Norwegian-German Association that had already been in existence before the war. It sponsored newly established German cultural institutions such as a German Institute and a German Theatre, and it invited German artists to Norway.

The *Reichskommissariat* set up local offices throughout Norway. During most of the occupation these operated in Kirkenes, Tromsø, Narvik, Trondheim, Bergen, Stavanger, Kristiansand and Lillehammer, relating both to the *Wehrmacht* and to the local Norwegian population and authorities. They ensured that *Reichskommissariat* directives were followed, and they dealt mostly with economic matters. Otte's department was therefore represented in all of the local offices.

The *Reichskommissariat* and Germany

Terboven visited Germany frequently. These trips must have been important, but we know little about them because Terboven wrote little and many documents were destroyed as Germany faced defeat towards the end of the war. There is, however, one source that indicates how effortlessly Terboven moved in the highest circles of Nazi society. Goebbels recorded in his diary that in late November 1944 he had a long conversation with Terboven, who had been to visit Göring. Terboven's former mentor had by then lost much of his status. Terboven and Goebbels were both concerned about Göring's isolation, his poor reputation and the decline in the *Luftwaffe*. Hitler was also concerned about Göring at that time.

Goebbels wanted to strengthen Göring's position, and Terboven needed a strong Göring to be able to face up to Martin Bormann, one of the most powerful men in the narrow circle around the *Führer*. The two of them agreed that Terboven should visit Göring to try to promote a closer working relationship between Goebbels and Göring. Terboven's discussion with Göring must have been successful, because Goebbels was later able to record how his own relationship with Göring had subsequently improved.

The *Reichskommissariat* had to relate to several different organizations in Germany. This required not just correspondence but also visits and discussions. It must always have been important for Terboven to have a sense of how power and relationships were shifting at home in Germany. He needed to know which power blocs were flowing or ebbing, and which influential people had the *Führer*'s favour at any particular time. Terboven's visits to Hitler were, of course, particularly important and he must have tried to keep in with the people who had access to Hitler and could submit or argue a case to him.

Terboven wanted to have as much control as possible of the connections with Germany. It was not possible for him to have full control, as the *Wehrmacht* had its own lines of communication. This was also true to some extent of the SS and Police, but Terboven had a better grip of these, as we shall see later. He took care to ensure that nobody came between him and Hitler. He chose not to set up any branch of the *Reichskommissariat* in Germany, other than a small travel office that dealt with postal and air connections to the *Reichskommissariat*.

Terboven faced an enormous task in responding to the numerous initiatives emanating from various institutions in Germany. He always had to try to filter and co-ordinate them so that they fitted in with his policies for administering the occupation and did not threaten his position as the highest civil authority in Norway. As Göring's man, he allowed the economic departments in the commissariat to promote Göring's special interest in the building up of the aluminium industry. He was close to Goebbels and allowed Goebbels's ministry to have a branch in the commissariat. Himmler's SS and Police were a power bloc that could have caused Terboven difficulties. He largely avoided such problems by means of a personal agreement with Himmler and by forming personal political relationships with the SS and the police. The Ministry of Munitions under Albert Speer was another power bloc, with its associated *Operation Todt*. He dealt with this, as we have seen, by giving OT's branches in Norway considerable freedom but at the same time incorporating them within the administration of the *Reichskommissariat*. The Nazi Party (*NSDAP*) was grafted on to the commissariat from the start through the *Einsatzstab*.

Not all German ministries and organizations were incorporated into the *Reichskommissariat* in this way. The German Finance Ministry, Trade Ministry and

Food Ministry were not included, though officials from these were recruited into the commissariat. Such ministries could, however, exert influence when Terboven and Otte's department really needed their expertise, or through the informal links that the ministries sometimes maintained with their former officials.

Terboven had enemies both in Norway and in Germany. The navy was the most significant of these, until he managed to get rid of its politicizing elements. In the conglomerate of the *SS* and Police there could always be some who were doubtful about Terboven. This led to friction between Terboven and the departments in the *SS* responsible for recruitment of volunteers to the *Waffen-SS*, namely *SS Hauptamt* in Germany and *Germanische Leitstelle* in Norway. They thought that Terboven's policy was unnecessarily harsh and that this created difficulties for them in recruitment. Likewise, the security service in Norway and its masters at the German headquarters of the Reich's security services were dissatisfied with Terboven because they thought that his policy was turning Norwegians into enemies of the German occupation. However, doubts and dissatisfactions such as these were not a serious problem for him.

Altogether, Terboven succeeded in fashioning the *Reichskommissariat* into an organization where the interests of the *Reich* and of the occupation authorities came together and were harmonized. He managed to keep control over forces that were already diverging in Germany and could have done so even more in Norway. That was no small achievement. It would have been impossible without his harsh experiences in the political struggles of the interwar years and the constant conflict between the party and the public authorities in Germany in the 1930s.

Relationships with the *Wehrmacht* and the NS Party

The *Reichskommissariat* and the *Wehrmacht* each had their own area of authority, independent but interlinked. They were not fundamentally opposed, but their relationship was marked by disagreements and power struggles. The decisive factor was that they shared a common objective, to support the German war effort. As the organization responsible for waging the war, the *Wehrmacht* had the lead role in this and the commissariat's main function was to support it.

Such a support function might suggest that the commissariat should be subordinate to the *Wehrmacht*. That was exactly what happened in countries such as France and Belgium, where the military had overall control in the occupied areas. Falkenhorst had originally expected such an arrangement in Norway. He was apparently surprised to find a high-ranking party man as *Reichskommissar* beside him. 'What are you doing here?' he reportedly asked Terboven when they first met. The *Wehrmacht* had to adapt to having a civil administration by its side, right until the end of the war.

Though the *Reichskommissariat* had a supporting function in relation to the *Wehrmacht*, Terboven did not interpret this as meaning that he must be subordinate to the military. On the contrary, he maintained his own independence and defended the power of the *Reichskommissariat* in relation to the *Wehrmacht*. He could always point out that he stood directly under the *Führer*. If there were conflicts between Falkenhorst and Terboven that could not be resolved locally but had to be decided at a higher level, Terboven held the trump card. He could take the matter directly to Hitler, whereas Falkenhorst always had to go via the *Oberkommando der Wehrmacht* (*OKW*) to reach the highest authority. On the other hand, Falkenhorst's route to Hitler did have an advantage: *OKW* could influence Hitler in its daily contact with him, whereas Terboven either had to undertake the long journey to see him or send him telegrams and written reports.

Terboven always regarded his relationship with the *Nasjonal Samling* Party as of secondary importance. What mattered to him were his relationships with the great German power blocs such as the *Wehrmacht*, the *SS* and Police and Speer's Ministry of Munitions. However, the *Führer* had decreed that NS should have a place in government and be given the opportunity to initiate a National Socialist Revolution in Norway. Terboven was therefore obliged to support this project, and he had the *Einsatzstab* available as the administrative organization he needed to help in this. He had little faith in Quisling as party leader, which made it difficult for him to support Quisling and NS wholeheartedly.

The NS Party's political campaign did, however, create significant problems for him, forcing him to intervene forcefully when NS activities aroused opposition that threatened German interests. It was more important to Terboven to suppress such resistance than to promote the interests of NS. He was hardly concerned that the brutal way he did this could also harm the NS Party. As it steadily became more apparent that the attempt by NS to promote a Nazi revolution was a fiasco, there was correspondingly less reason for Terboven to pay any heed to the party. Nevertheless, as a party of government it remained a force he had to reckon with right to the end. NS people continued to sit as heads of department in a public administration that the Germans could not manage without. NS ministers of state could be pressurized, circumvented or ignored, but they continued to exist as a barrier between German officials in the *Reichskommissariat* and Norwegian officials and workers in the government departments.

CHAPTER 6
THE *SS* AND POLICE

Terboven needed to be able to suppress those who threatened German interests and to have a means of punishing those who opposed his orders. For this, he required organizations that had physical means of exerting authority. There were no such organizations in the *Reichskommissariat*. Physical power was, of course, available in full measure in the *Wehrmacht*, but that was defined as military and was beyond Terboven's field of action. However, the physical resources for exerting his authority were available in the third institution on which the occupation regime was based, namely the *SS* and Police. That was where Terboven found the security organization and the means of suppression that he required. The relationship with the *SS* and Police was vitally important to him.

Hitler's hardmen

The *SS* was a unique institution, inseparably connected with Hitler's Germany. The *SS* could exist only in a Nazi environment. In Nazi Germany, it was integral from the start and steadily became more powerful. When Germany started to expand, the *SS* expanded with it and established itself in the countries that the *Wehrmacht* conquered.

The *SS* was set up in the 1920s as a small guard for Hitler and the *NSDAP*, but under the leadership of Heinrich Himmler, it became a progressively bigger and more influential force in Nazi Germany. Ideologically, the *SS* represented prevalent dogmas of national socialism such as anti-communism, anti-liberalism, contempt for democracy, racism and a *Führer*'s leadership cult. What singled the *SS* out was that from an early stage it aimed to become an elite racist organization promoting the Germanic race, that it expanded violently and that it ended up becoming a pervasive, sprawling conglomerate within Hitler's Germany.

Basic to the *SS* was its racial doctrine which divided mankind into a hierarchy of races. At the bottom of the hierarchy were the Jews and above them but still well down the ranks were the Slav peoples. Supreme above all was the Germanic race, standing out as best of all. The cultivation of all things Germanic and the idea of a fellowship of Germanic peoples were integral, shared concepts in German national socialism. These concepts were, however, in competition with an alternative idea – that the people of Germany, rather than the Germanic peoples as a whole, stood atop the racial hierarchy. The *Führer* himself was pan-Germanist, but not exclusively and entirely so. His national socialism had in its time had a German nationalist origin.

A distinctive feature of the *SS* was the emphasis it put on physical power and on the struggle in its most physical form, armed conflict. In the *SS*, the glorification of conflict came to overshadow everything to the extent that the most important branches of the institution came to be concerned with the development of physical power. The *SS* took on more and more tasks that led to it growing as an apparatus of physical power.

At the end of the 1930s in Germany, the *SS*, the Security Service and the Police were combined. The police were thereby torn loose from the civil administration to become part of an ideological movement. The police officers were indoctrinated in national socialism, were expected to act in accordance with national socialist principles and were deployed to persecute the enemies of national socialism. Judicial and legal considerations were to be set aside. The combination included the Criminal Police, the Order Police and the political police, the *Gestapo*. For Norway, the most important feature of the *SS* was this combination of the *SS*, the Security Service and the Police. The security and repression apparatus that had been created could be transplanted to Norway and continue its work there for the duration of the occupation.

The first concentration camp, Dachau, was established in Germany in 1933. This was the start of an enormous empire of camps run by the *SS*, consisting of work camps, concentration camps and extermination camps. The *SS* did not set up concentration and extermination camps in Norway, with one exception: the *SS* work camps for 3,700 Yugoslav prisoners in 1942–3. These 'Serb camps' functioned as extermination camps, with a death rate of 65 per cent. The German police set up internment camps in Norway for political prisoners, where the conditions were less inhumane than in the work camps elsewhere in occupied Europe.

The *SS* not only had a strongly antisemitic ideology but was also responsible for the practical implementation of the Holocaust. The Jews were sent to *SS* camps, and there they were killed. The *SS* had started murdering Jews in large numbers behind the front lines after Germany invaded the Soviet Union in June 1941 and then gone on to a universal programme to eliminate them. All Jews were to be killed. Norway was included in this extermination programme in autumn 1942.

The *SS* set up its own army, the *Waffen-SS*, alongside and in competition with the *Wehrmacht*. The *Waffen-SS* grew significantly and took an active part in the hostilities on the Eastern Front. Members of the *Waffen-SS* underwent normal military training and fought as regular front-line soldiers, but they were also given ideological instruction, educated in racial theory and indoctrinated that they belonged to a racially elite organization. The *SS* considered its men to be both military and political soldiers. When they took part in the war on the Eastern Front, they were fighting not just in any conventional war; they were taking part in a war against inferior races who must be culled and subdued, such as Slavs, or exterminated, such as Jews. The *Waffen-SS* eventually included several nationalities, including Norwegian volunteers whom the *SS* welcomed as they were considered to be of the pure Germanic race.

As the police and the *Waffen-SS* became more dominant, they threatened to overshadow the *SS* as a political and ideological movement. To correct the balance, the *Allgemeine SS* (the Civilian SS) was set up.

Altogether, the SS was a very special and more than slightly chaotic mixture of an ideologically aware and idealistically motivated institution; a subjugation and elimination apparatus; and an army that was both a regular fighting force and a political/ideological instrument. People in Norway came to know all these aspects of the SS, but mostly the SS as a police force and an instrument of suppression. Their experience matched the official description, which was not just 'SS' but SS und Polizei.

The SS in Norway

Himmler tried from the very beginning to establish the SS and Police in Norway. By June 1940 there were already 5,000 Waffen-SS soldiers in Norway, and the number continued to increase. They did not take part in the military campaign in 1940 but were soon transferred north to be engaged in the attack on the Soviet Union. A nucleus of police and security services was already present in April 1940 and was soon installed in Victoria Terrasse in Oslo which became the German Security Police Headquarters for the rest of the war; an ominous address that became synonymous in the public consciousness with German police oppression and torture. The Security Police initially held back while it was unclear what form the regime would take, taking up their duties in earnest only after the upheaval of 25 September 1940.

From autumn 1940 the SS and Police in Norway operated under an organization structure that they retained. At the top was an SS and Police Chief (Höhere SS und Polizeiführer Nord), Wilhelm Rediess. Under him were three main branches, each with its own head: the Waffen-SS, the Order Police and the Security Police/Security Service. The police service as a whole, therefore, consisted of two parts. One was the Order Police (Ordnungspolizei), which was a militarized police force indoctrinated in SS ideology and national socialism. Six battalions of the Order Police amounting to 3,400 men arrived in 1940, a number that had risen to seven battalions and 4,600 men by the end of 1941. The second component of the police was the Security Police, which was linked with the Security Service. In German these were known as the Sicherheitspolizei, abbreviated to Sipo, and the Sicherheitsdienst, abbreviated to SD.

The Security Police (Sipo) included the Criminal Police who dealt with purely German cases, but the main component was the Gestapo. Strictly speaking, the Gestapo was just one part of Sipo, though by far the most important part. The Gestapo investigated and made arrests in all cases that were to do with resistance against the regime. They were the regime's main instrument of suppression.

The Security Service operated alongside Sipo under one leader, Heinrich Fehlis. SD was a political surveillance organization that tracked the development of opinion among the Norwegian public and provided reports on its findings, the Meldungen aus Norwegen. In the course of its surveillance activity SD came across and passed on information that would be of interest to Sipo and generally supported Sipo's activity. The titles SD and Sipo are sometimes used synonymously in Norwegian and German sources, but it is important to distinguish them from each other. The Security Service did not have a duty to hunt down Norwegian resistance; that was the work of Sipo (the Gestapo).

Sipo and *SD* came under the administration of a central head office in Germany, the *Reichssicherheitshauptamt* (*RSHA*), which co-ordinated the work of the police and the security services throughout all German-controlled zones. The first head of *RSHA* was Reinhard Heydrich.

By the end of the war *Sipo* and *SD* in Norway had grown to almost a thousand personnel, with regional offices in Stavanger, Bergen, Trondheim and Tromsø, and in Oslo where the regional and central offices were combined. Under the regional offices, there were numerous local offices (*Aussendienststellen*) in smaller towns and villages. *Sipo* made use of Norwegian prisons and also set up its own internment camps: Grini near Oslo; a camp near Ulven, then Espeland in Bergen; Falstad outside Trondheim; and Sydspissen and later Krøkebærsletta near Tromsø.

There was a parallel resource available to the German security apparatus, in the form of the Norwegian police, mainly the new NS police, known as Stapo, but also the police in general. The SS acted quickly to gain control of the police by setting up a separate Ministry of Police under Jonas Lie. Whereas other departments of state had matching counterparts in the *Reichskommissariat*, matters referred from the Police Ministry to the *Reichskommissar* passed via the SS and Police Chief Rediess.

The *Gestapo* used torture and maltreated prisoners severely. It was no coincidence that all of the fourteen Germans who were condemned to death and executed in Norway after the war were *Gestapo* personnel condemned for gross torture or murder. Unlike the concentration camps on the continent, however, few people were killed in the internment camps in Norway and the maltreatment of prisoners that occurred in Grini and the other camps was not widespread.

In *Sipo* 1,145 Norwegians served. Some of these were drivers, interpreters or ordinary investigators. Others were informants or provocateurs who infiltrated The Resistance Movement. Without the co-operation of all these Norwegians it would have been much more difficult for *Sipo* to track and neutralize the resistance networks. The Germans had the basic handicap of not knowing the Norwegian language and culture and therefore being dependent on help from Norwegians. In Trondheim, the Norwegians who assisted *Sipo* formed their own group, later known as 'The Rinnan Gang'. They infiltrated and broke up resistance groups over a wide area, and they maltreated and tortured prisoners just like their German masters. As many as nine of the group's members were condemned and executed after the war.

Reichskommissar Terboven and the SS

Terboven had had formative experiences in the *Sturmabteilung* (*SA*), an organization that was eventually overshadowed by the SS. He was not a typical SS man; rather an SA man. He was rather indifferent to the SS's pan-Germanism, even though he was signed up to it as part of national socialism. This was of little importance, however, as Terboven's relationship to the SS was primarily a matter of power politics. He needed to ally himself with an institution that had access to physical means of enforcement.

As the highest-ranking *SS* and police chief in Norway, Rediess answered directly to Himmler in Germany. It would appear, therefore, that the *SS* and Police were positioned parallel to the *Wehrmacht* and the *Reichskommissariat*. All three were independent authorities within Norway, each with an overlord in Germany. The reality was not so simple, however. Through his agreements with Himmler and his own political manoeuvrings, Terboven had formed close connections with the *SS* and Police, including a dominant relationship with Rediess, who was not a strong personality. It was not by chance that the two of them lived under the same roof, at Skaugum. He also had a close relationship with Fehlis, which gave him a good sense of the work of *Sipo* and *SD* and enabled him to evaluate the political and security situation as a whole.

Despite Terboven's close link with the *SS* and Police, the *SS* and Police force was never formally subordinated to the *Reichskommissar*. Rediess and Fehlis remained under Himmler and the central *SS* authorities in Germany. Terboven couldn't ignore the status of the *SS* and Police as a separate institution or the fact that Rediess and Fehlis were Himmler's men. Despite this, however, he managed to gain extensive control of the German security apparatus in Norway. Head office security officials at *RSHA* were concerned about this and criticized Fehlis for his apparent subordination to Terboven, but their criticism was ineffective.

German courts functioned alongside the *SS* security system. In the early years, cases that Terboven and *Sipo* wanted to refer for trial had to be sent to military courts. Terboven would not have been satisfied to be dependent on the military in this way. The *SS* and Police already had its own court for internal disciplinary matters. On 10 September 1941 Terboven asked Himmler if he could make use of this court, for which Himmler readily granted permission.

A new court quickly came into being, known as *SS und Polizeigericht Nord*. It passed its first death sentences on 28 February 1942 and dealt with most of the bigger and more important cases from April of that year onwards. The military courts still heard cases concerned with resistance activity directed against the *Wehrmacht*, German military personnel or military buildings or equipment, and they pronounced death sentences in both 1942 and 1943. Most cases, however, were about minor offences with lesser penalties. From then on, it was mainly the *SS* and Police Court that combatted The Resistance Movement with harsh sentences, including death.

The *SS* and Police Court was not a mere subsidiary to *Sipo* and Terboven. The judges had a certain amount of independence, though Terboven and Fehlis largely got their own way. It was they who decided which cases should be sent to the court for trial. They could confidently refer cases that they thought were self-evident and where they could be reasonably sure of the outcome. Cases were judged according to German laws and regulations, and human rights guarantees were few.

The activity of *Sipo* and the German courts led to over 40,000 Norwegians serving time in prisons or internment camps, with or without trial and for shorter or longer periods. Most of these were political prisoners, arrested because they had shown dislike, opposition or resistance to the occupation regime. Most were held in prisons or camps in Norway, but several thousand were sent to Germany. In the course of the war, 20,000

Norwegians spent shorter or longer periods in Grini, which was the biggest of the prison camps.

The prisoners in Grini could be subjected to solitary confinement and a diet of bread and water, and some were beaten. Those in a special punishment unit underwent harsh punishment exercises, including hard labour, forced marches, crawling on all fours and creeping face-down through the mud. However, these punishments were relatively mild in comparison with conditions suffered by the prisoners, especially the Slavs, in German concentration camps. The prisoners at Grini were not hanged, shot dead or beaten with sticks. The food was scant and poor and the prisoners' physical condition deteriorated, but there was little serious illness in comparison with the concentration camps. Access to treatment was not too bad, and the pace of work was not really hard. The main punishment of imprisonment in Grini was the loss of freedom.

Of the 40,000 Norwegians who were imprisoned, between 8,000 and 9,000 were sent to Germany, where they were scattered among several prisons and concentration camps. Around 1,500 found themselves in regular prisons or in prisons that went by the rather old-fashioned name of *Zuchthaus* ('houses of correction'), where the conditions were harder, the work heavier and the prisoners' rights fewer than in the normal prisons. By far the most, however, were sent to one of the many German concentration camps. There were Norwegian prisoners in Buchenwald, Mauthausen, Dachau, Bergen Belsen and the women's camp at Ravensbrück. Most of the Norwegians, around 2,500, were gathered together in Sachsenhausen, a camp a few miles north of Berlin.

All things considered, it was worse to be a prisoner in a German prison, *Zuchthaus* or concentration camp on the continent than in a German prison camp in Norway. There were, though, big differences between the prisons or camps and between the categories of prisoners. The officers, police personnel and students who were deported to Germany in autumn 1943 got off relatively lightly. The people who suffered the worst fate were the Jews. Next to them were the *Nacht und Nebel* (*NN*) prisoners, who were mostly sent to Natzweiler Camp in Alsace. They were kept isolated, and they were either condemned to death or set to hard labour intended to kill them. Ordinary prisoners could write a short letter home once a month and receive letters from home, but this was never permitted to *NN* prisoners. Their relatives never got to know anything about their fate. About a thousand Norwegians were sent to the continent as *Nacht und Nebel* prisoners, and several hundred of them were killed directly or indirectly.

Sachsenhausen was a particular case. Initially, the conditions there were about as hard as in other concentration camps. Most deaths of Norwegians in Sachsenhausen occurred in this early period. From spring 1943 conditions improved, however. The Norwegians were gathered into their own barracks, where it was easier for them to look after each other. They were allowed to receive parcels from home, not least Red Cross parcels. These eventually became very abundant, to the extent that the prisoners started putting on weight and ended up eating better than many people back home! A little of the content of the parcels could also be used to help other prisoners or to bribe the guards. The favour given to the Norwegians was probably because of their status as a Germanic race, though it may also have been thought that better nutrition would improve their work efficiency.

The Germans swung between starving their prisoners to death and feeding them better to get more work out of them.

Terror politics

Seen as a whole, the German policy on policing, law courts and sentencing was a policy of terror. The objective was to create a climate of fear that would inhibit Norwegians from opposing the German occupation regime or the Norwegian NS government. A powerful security police force used brutality to create terror. The courts paid scant heed to human rights, and the German law code was alien and harsh. Collective punishments were common, with no distinction between the guilty and the innocent. Hostage-taking and the shooting of hostages were part of the machinery of terror. Exemplary deterrent sentences were sometimes deliberately combined with other fearsome actions. How or whether death sentences should be carried out was decided by what would have the greatest effect on public opinion. Choices between execution and reprieve oscillated according to Terboven's current political aim.

From a Norwegian sense of justice, the policy of terror appears illegal. On a strict understanding of international law, the matter is not so simple. The policy of terror was not entirely without a legal foundation. International law as laid down in the Fourth Hague Convention in 1907 gave an occupying power certain rights in relation to the occupied population. Summary courts, death sentences with subsequent execution and the use of courts-martial in a state of emergency were all within the bounds of international law.

One feature of the policy of terror was that people who had not taken part in any form of resistance were liable to be arrested and punished. The idea behind this was that resistance fighters would think twice when they saw that they were exposing not only themselves but also others to danger. On similar considerations, the general population would react against the resistance and distance themselves from it. Collective punishment was a characteristic manifestation of this aspect of terror politics.

A milder form of collective punishment was to impose extra taxes on a community when the population had shown undesirable behaviour. In April 1941, the town of Arendal was fined 20,000 kroner because somebody had cut the rope on the German swastika flag at the harbour. Stavanger had to pay out three times, the last of these payments being of two million kroner on account of 'offences against German service establishments and members of the German defence forces', plus damage done to German telegraph and telephone cables.

Communal fines such as this were just on the fringe of the policy of terror. Terboven could turn the screw further. In the first two years of occupation, the Germans imposed drastic collective punishments on local communities that had supported operations initiated from Britain. In 1941 the British carried out three major raids on the Norwegian coast. These were followed by German reprisals against local populations who had supported the British. After the raid on Svolvær in March 1941, sixty-four Norwegians were arrested and sent to prisons and prison camps in Oslo. Two months later, six men were sentenced to *Zuchthaus* for their collaboration and were sent to Germany. Twelve houses were burnt to the ground. After a landing at Måløy around Christmas that same year, fifteen men were sent to Grini and two were taken as hostages. At Reine in Lofoten, which was raided at the same time, the Germans burnt down parts of the village and took three men as hostages.

However, this was mild in comparison with the reprisals inflicted on the village of Telavåg, near Bergen, where two men from Company Linge were in hiding. At the end of April 1942, they were in a skirmish with the *Gestapo*, in which two Germans and one of the Company Linge men were shot dead. The Germans responded by burning all the houses in the village and sinking all the boats. Nearly all of the men were sent to Sachsenhausen, and of the seventy-two who were deported, thirty-one died in captivity. The remainder of the population was interned for two years. Eighteen Norwegians who had no connection with Telavåg but who had tried to flee to Britain were executed. 'Telavåg' became a symbol of German terror politics.

One form of collective punishment was the arrest and possible deportation of selected groups. In the spring of 1942, a thousand teachers were picked out and arrested, and half of them were sent to forced labour, as a punishment for refusing to join a Nazified professional organization. In the autumn of the same year, groups of officers, police personnel and students were arrested, and many of these were also deported to Germany. This was a pre-emptive operation to weaken possible resistance in future, but it was also intended to dampen down continuing resistance activity. The Jews were also arrested that autumn and sent to Germany, where they were killed. This too was a form of collective punishment, but it was unique in that the Jews were punished just for being who they were; they were to be condemned without exception if the police got hold of them.

Hostage-taking was another aspect of the policy of terror. When somebody fled to Britain or to Sweden, the Germans would hold a relative hostage in a prison or in an internment camp, hoping that this would discourage others from fleeing abroad. There was also a far more drastic form of hostage-taking. Terboven used the execution of hostages to demonstrate that anybody at all could be condemned because of a serious act of resistance, and to encourage the population to desist from such actions and to oppose them. Ten men were executed as scapegoats during a state of emergency in Trøndelag in October 1942. Five citizens of the Drammen district were executed in autumn 1943 after a sabotage action at Mjøndalen. The victims may have shown an anti-Nazi attitude, but they had not done anything so serious as to deserve a death sentence.

Sometimes hostages who had participated actively in The Resistance Movement and might or might not have been executed anyway were hastily executed in response to resistance activity in which they had no part. The Germans thus killed two birds with one stone: they punished individual members of the resistance and at the same time using them as parts of a deterrent collective punishment. In 1942, as mentioned earlier, eighteen men were imprisoned and then executed because they had tried to escape over the North Sea. They could have been condemned for trying to abscond, but instead, they were condemned collectively as scapegoats for the action at Telavåg. In February 1945 several Norwegians were condemned and executed, ostensibly for their resistance activity. This may have been the reason in some of the cases, but not in all. Their executions were first and foremost a collective reprisal for an act of murder in which none of them had been involved.

In the first couple of years, Terboven made use of a particular method of deterrence, the declaration of a state of emergency. Such a measure was traditionally within the remit of the *Wehrmacht*, which could impose a state of emergency if there was such strong unrest among the population that it threatened military interests. However, *Wehrmacht* in Norway never declared a state of emergency. When Terboven issued a regulation on 31 July 1941 giving himself the right to declare a state of emergency and to set up a summary court that could sentence people to death or to ten years or more in *Zuchthaus*, it was something new. At the same time, the chief of the *SS* and Police was given wide powers to uphold law and order. During a long tug of war between Terboven and Falkenhorst, the relationship between civil and military authority with regard to emergency powers became more closely defined.

Declaration of a state of emergency was a momentous occasion. A curfew affected people's lives directly. Bus and tram journeys were suspended, restaurants closed and cinema and theatre performances cancelled. The biggest impression on the populace, however, was created by the mass mobilization of police and the associated multiple arrests, plus ominous reports in the newspapers about death sentences, executions or long-term sentences to *Zuchthaus* in Germany. Imposition of a state of emergency on an area caused feelings of fear and dread locally, with ripples throughout the rest of the country.

The first such declaration was in Greater Oslo on 10 September 1941, in response to a strike. During the state of emergency, Goebbels spoke with Terboven by telephone. He advised Terboven not to lift the state of emergency too soon, but rather to show clemency to see how that would affect the Norwegian public. Terboven followed this line. On 11 September Rediess announced that the summary court had passed two death sentences, that these had been carried out and that four men had been sentenced to *Zuchthaus* in Germany. One man was sentenced to death the following day, but this time Terboven commuted the sentence to lifelong *Zuchthaus* and justified his decision by claiming that industrial calm had been restored. Three more men were sentenced to *Zuchthaus*. On the third day, there were no death sentences, but five men were given *Zuchthaus* sentences and one was acquitted. Nothing happened on the fourth day, because it was a Sunday. On the last day, Monday, 15 September, twelve new sentences were announced. Two of these were death sentences, but these were also commuted by Terboven to *Zuchthaus* for the same reason as before: the restoration of industrial peace. The ten others were also sent to *Zuchthaus*.

The second time a state of emergency was declared was from 6 to 12 October 1942, in Trøndelag. This time it was directed against Norwegians who had helped Norwegian soldiers from Company Linge who had come from Great Britain. The Germans had lost two men in an exchange of fire at Majavatn on the boundary between Nord-Trøndelag and Nordland. Following this, most of the local Norwegians were arrested. Soon after the events at Majavatn an act of sabotage against the power station in Glomfjord and another against the mines in Fosdalen on 5 October provoked Terboven to a serious response.

He travelled to Trondheim on a special train, accompanied by Rediess and Fehlis, forty *Gestapo* officers, a German police company and an execution squad. About 2,000 men from German and Norwegian Order Police, *Sipo*, *Abwehr* and Stapo took part in the operation. On 7 October the newspapers reported that ten people had been shot as scapegoats for various sabotage attempts. The next day it was reported that a further fifteen had been condemned to death and executed, accused of illegal transport of weapons. On the third day came the report that the last nine had been executed because they had transported explosives for use in sabotage.

Contrary to what one might expect, the hardest collective punishments occurred early in the war, in the form of the reprisals in Telavåg and Trøndelag. The number of death sentences carried out was also greatest in 1942, when the German fear of invasion was at its peak. The reprisals connected with Telavåg and in Trøndelag were directed against a resistance movement that the Germans readily interpreted as preparation for an impending invasion.

The German terror policy swung between two courses. For a long time, it was aimed at frightening the populace into submission by announcing punitive measures. On the other hand, such announcements could be counterproductive; they could create martyrs who inspired increased resistance. So the terror policy could also be applied in a different way, by keeping punishments secret. The secrecy would create uncertainty and unease that would deter people from resisting. This was the purpose behind the *Nacht und Nebel* order. *NN* prisoners would just disappear in 'Night and Fog'.

The use of the courts swung between these two ways of implementing the policy. Up to summer 1944, most of the people who were executed had been sentenced by a court and the sentence had been announced publicly. Then Hitler intervened. At the end of June and beginning of July a big general strike occurred in Copenhagen. The German authorities struggled to keep the situation under control, they opened fire on the crowd and ninety-seven Danes and several German soldiers were killed. These events echoed throughout the whole allied world.

Hitler was furious. He thought that the strike had occurred because the German court had condemned eight saboteurs to death and announced the executions. Such publicity just created martyrs. The *Führer* recalled heroes from German history who were famous because they had suffered judgement from the court of a foreign power. In July/August 1944 he forbade the use of courts in the struggle against resistance movements in occupied countries. This obviously implied that executions should not be announced publicly. From now on, *Sipo* would investigate, condemn and execute without public knowledge.

Terboven was opposed to this policy. He thought that the execution of hostages would be a more effective deterrent if given the necessary publicity. During a visit to Hitler in January 1945, he persuaded the *Führer* to modify his point of view. Following this visit,

Terboven would be able to publicize several sentences passed by summary courts in February and March.

Altogether, the Germans executed almost 400 Norwegians during the war: 151 sentenced in the *SS* and Police Court; 92 without sentence; 80 sentenced in a military court; 42 by a summary court and 29 in Germany. Other Norwegians died in the course of *Sipo*'s police work: 108 were shot in a skirmish or while attempting to flee or were systematically murdered; 35 died as a result of torture; and 22 committed suicide in prison to avoid being tortured and forced to betray their colleagues.

In Norway, the policy of terror succeeded in achieving much of the deterrent effect that was intended. The fear that it generated in the long term did sharpen the will to resist, but at the same time, it shaped the resistance into a pattern that suited German interests. The declaration of a state of emergency in September 1941 in response to a strike deterred Norwegians from using industrial strikes as a means of resistance. Drastic reprisals against military-style acts of resistance made the growing Milorg network restrict itself for a long time to building up preparations for future actions. The result was a public that worked in industry without laying down tools, a non-communist resistance movement that refrained for a long time from acts of sabotage and a population with whom the *Wehrmacht* had few problems.

The 'racially pure' Norwegians

In Norway, the *SS* and Police was first and foremost a brutal and oppressive security agency. But the *SS* was also something more – an institution that wanted to advance its Germanic ideals. The *SS* regarded the Norwegians as a particularly pure example of the Germanic race. Himmler, therefore, took a particular interest in Norway. When he visited Norway for almost three weeks in January/February 1941, he had great expectations. He wanted not only to meet his contemporary pure-race Germanic Norwegians but also to experience the many historic links that Norway had with Germanic culture. He found such connections in museums, in old buildings such as Nidaros Cathedral in Trondheim or in old farm buildings. The day he arrived in Norway, he went to see the rock carvings near the nautical college at Ekeberg. Later in his stay, he visited Maihaugen Folk Museum at Lillehammer and old farmsteads in Gudbrandsdalen. A visit to the Viking Ship Museum and the Folk Museum in Oslo was a highlight of his trip. In the restaurant at the Folk Museum, there was a presentation of folk dances, ballads and readings from the sagas.

The *SS* promoted its Germanization of Norway in four different areas of activity. Himmler wanted to recruit Norwegians as volunteers in the *Waffen-SS*, to fight alongside the Germans on the Eastern Front and return to continue working for the Germanic cause in their homeland. He also wanted to establish a general *SS* movement that would be directed towards Germanization and the spread of *SS* ideals in Norway. He wanted to reform the Norwegian police so that it would become more effective and could serve in the building up of the future *SS* state. Finally, he wanted to protect newly born Germanic children in Norway.

Volunteers for the *Waffen-SS*

Unlike in other occupied countries, the SS in Norway had to relate to an indigenous national socialist party that had governmental authority, to the extent that the *Reichskommissar* allowed the party to use it. Quisling's NS Party was both a partner and a competitor with the SS, mostly a partner to begin with but soon becoming more and more a competitor. There was a fundamental contradiction between the nationalism of the NS Party and the supranational pan-Germanism of the SS. There were also, however, pan-Germanic trends in the NS Party, and a willingness in the SS to go some way towards tolerating NS's national line. Disagreement and friction did still occur on many issues. The relationship between the SS and NS was particularly problematic in the question of recruiting volunteers for the *Waffen-SS* on the Eastern Front. The SS wanted primarily to bring recruits into German units under SS control to serve the institution's main Germanic purpose – to convert the soldiers into pioneers of a future supranational SS state. NS wanted to create units that had a Norwegian character, could serve NS objectives and would be under NS control.

The SS had the advantages of physical power, access to resources and influence over where the volunteers should be posted on the Eastern Front. The NS Party really held only one card: It could influence recruitment. The party could promote and facilitate recruitment or could oppose it. The SS soon realized that the best source of recruits was to be found among the members of NS and its subsidiary organizations, particularly its militarized branch known as the *Hird*. So, the SS couldn't just dissociate itself from NS in its recruitment efforts; it was better to have NS positively supporting them.

During spring and early summer 1940 the Germans had invaded regions that included four Germanic nationalities: Dutch, Flemish, Danish and Norwegian. The SS wanted to set up *Waffen-SS* volunteer divisions from these nationalities. On his birthday, 20 April in 1940, Hitler gave orders that *Regiment Nordland* should be created, consisting of Norwegians, Danes and Germans to give it a shared Germanic ethos. *Regiment Nordland* would become part of the newly established *SS Division Wiking*, which also was made up of *Regiment Westland*, originally for recruits from the Netherlands and Flanders, and *Regiment Germania* for Germans. The majority of *Division Wiking* was German, and the officers were German. The language of command was German, the only language that the German officers and the multinational troops could use in common.

The SS gained the support of NS to launch the new volunteer project. On 12 January 1941, Quisling issued a general invitation to join *Regiment Nordland*, which was published in all the major newspapers the next day. On 30 January the recruits were assembled in the Hippodrome at Vinderen in Oslo under Himmler's command. Himmler, Falkenhorst, Quisling and Terboven gave speeches and the recruits swore loyalty to Hitler, Himmler and the SS. The ceremony was broadcast and was reported on the front pages of most of the Norwegian newspapers.

Division Wiking was intended to support the German war effort and strengthen the SS as a military power, but it was also considered a means of promoting the SS's Germanic ideals and values. Most of the Norwegian recruits were disappointed when they discovered that they were not to be organized into Norwegian units but were to be put together with other nationalities. That was, however, an important part of the Germanic integration policy of the *SS*. Himmler's plan was for the soldiers to return from the battlefield as hardened *SS* men, ready to continue working for the Germanic vision. What was important was not the number, but the creation of a nucleus that could be built up further. Soldiers returned from the field would be expected to get leading positions in the administration and the police and would form the core of a 'National Defence Corps' that would defend the future *SS* state against enemies within. They could also be considered as possible *Wehrbauern* ('Defence farmers') in Eastern Europe, taking part in the big colonization project that the Germans planned.

Prior to the start of the attack on the Soviet Union on 22 June 1941, between 650 and 800 Norwegians were recruited to the *Waffen-SS*, but less than 300 of them took part in the invasion. Between 800 and 1,000 served in *Division Wiking* in the course of the war. The division took part in the battles on the Southern Front, came as far east as the Caucasus and then was involved in the Germans' long retreat.

There has been much controversy about whether the Norwegians in *Division Wiking* took part in the war crimes that the division committed when it went into Ukraine in summer 1941. There is no doubt that the Norwegians witnessed such crimes, but it has been difficult to establish whether or to what extent they themselves took part in the massacres. The Norwegians were scattered among different units, and it has been difficult to link individual Norwegians with specific war crimes. Researchers have had to depend on circumstantial evidence that suggests participation.

Germany's attack on the Soviet Union on 22 June 1941 led to the recruitment of volunteers to the *Waffen-SS* taking a different turn. NS saw this as an opportunity to raise a Norwegian volunteer regiment, the Norwegian Legion, that would fight alongside the Germans as part of the *Waffen-SS*. Similar initiatives arose in other countries. This was contrary to SS policy, which aimed for combined Germanic units. Individual legions were seen as undesirable expressions of nationalism. However, Himmler considered it wise to go with the flow and he approved the establishment of national legions that would operate as independent units within the *Waffen-SS*.

It was easier to propagandize for the Norwegian Legion than for *Regiment Nordland*. NS could now appeal to patriotic sentiments. A specifically Norwegian military entity was being created for the first time under the new government. The enemy was more challenging. The thought of fighting the British was much less motivating than the idea of fighting the archenemy, communist Russia. Moreover, there was a promise that the Legion would be sent into Finland. The NS propaganda was, therefore, able to play upon the strong sympathy for Finland following the Winter War.

The Norwegian Legion was officially established on 29 June in an announcement by the *Reichskommissar* that was published in the papers the following day. Terboven said that the *Führer* had approved the Norwegian request and authorized the setting up of a Norwegian Legion. Enrolment continued throughout July. The volunteers were brought together and quartered in Bjølsen School in Oslo, before being transferred later in the month to Gulskogen camp near Drammen. At the end of July, 700 legionnaires were shipped to

Germany. They amounted to a battalion and were thought of as the first of seven battalions. However, it remained the only such battalion as there were not enough recruits for more.

Arriving in Germany at the beginning of August, the battalion was quartered in Fallingbostel for military training under the direction of the SS. Then, to the great disappointment of the legionnaires and of NS, the battalion was sent in February 1942, not to Finland, but to the Leningrad front. They remained there until February/March 1943, when the Legion was disbanded. A total of 2,300 men had joined the Legion, but its maximum size at any one time was a force of 1,200 men.

Quisling had extensive plans and big ambitions when the recruitment to the Legion started. He considered the Legion as a good starting point for a new Norwegian army that would be trained by Norwegian officers following Norwegian guidelines. A Legion staff was set up in Oslo to form the embryo of a future Norwegian General Staff. The methods of registration and recruitment made use of the organization for compulsory labour service (*Arbeidstjenesten* or *AT*) that functioned as a continuation of the pre-war military conscription system.

The SS soon put a stop to this development towards a Norwegian army. Himmler had authorized national legions to make use of their appeal to recruits, but he wanted to be in full control of them. The SS, therefore, forced through a requirement that the troops would not be trained in Norway and along with Norwegian guidelines as the Norwegians had wanted, but would be sent to Germany for instruction by German officers. They would have to wear SS uniforms with German badges. They swore loyalty to Hitler, not to Quisling. The Legion staff had to be disbanded.

From summer 1941, therefore, there were two competing directions of recruitment for Norwegian volunteers wanting to fight on the German side. One led to a multinational *Waffen-SS* division, *Division Wiking*, that had SS pan-Germanism as its overarching ideology. The other led to an NS-inspired Norwegian unit, the Norwegian Legion, made up of Norwegians and with a clear Norwegian identity. There was also a third type of force, the 'police companies', sponsored by the SS and Jonas Lie. These would give Norwegian police personnel experience at the front and make them capable of supporting a future SS state. In July 1942 Lie encouraged all the nation's policemen to join a Norwegian police company that served at Leningrad alongside the Legion from October 1942. Two new police companies were formed later.

In 1943 each of these two directions was developed further by the creation of new units. The SS took *Regiment Nordland* out of *Division Wiking* and upgraded it to a division, known as *Division Nordland*. The Norwegians in the new division were allocated to Regiment Norge, or Pansergrenaderregiment Norge to give it its full name. Here they were mixed with other nationalities, under German command and with German as the language of command. There were probably about a thousand Norwegians in the regiment or in other parts of the armoured corps of which the regiment was part. They were sent to take part in the siege of Leningrad and ended their days in the battles around Berlin at the end of the war.

In the other direction, the Norwegian Legion was withdrawn from the Leningrad front in spring 1943 and disbanded. NS then worked to create another purely Norwegian unit. Since autumn 1942 there had been a ski-mounted company that had been trained in Germany and sent to the SS division at the Finnish Front in Russian Karelia. NS now built this up further to create SS-skiløperbataljon Norge, which was trained in Norway and Finland. This battalion was also sent to Karelia, where its main work was in patrol and security duties, and it suffered severe losses during a Soviet attack in June 1944. Between 500 and 700 men served in the battalion before it withdrew to Norway in autumn 1944. This was the most Norwegian of all the volunteer units. Its identity was linked to skiing, the officers and the language of command were Norwegian, and it was allowed to serve in Finland, which was what NS had always wanted for the volunteers.

Thus, there was no single volunteer unit to which all recruits were allocated. In the course of the war, the volunteers were scattered among five different units – two German and three Norwegian – if we consider the police companies as one. This dispersal mainly reflected the rivalry between the SS and the NS recruitment policies, but to some extent, it also indicated differences on the Norwegian side, as when the police wanted to have their own units. Altogether 4,500–5,000 men served in these various units, though there were never so many fighting at any one time. Between 800 and 1,000 lost their lives.

Despite the deployment in different units, there is a common term used to refer to all the volunteers: 'front-fighters'. Much of the literature presents the front-fighters as pure fighting men, like the soldiers in the *Wehrmacht*. This view of them downplays the role of the racist and national socialist ideology. The front-fighters have wanted to see themselves as soldiers, and they have largely obtained approval for their view. This self-image has been reinforced by the fact that the front-fighters' experience on the Eastern Front was first and foremost an experience of military combat.

However, recent research shows that the front-fighters cannot be considered just as purely military soldiers but must also be seen from an ideological point of view. Ideological indoctrination was part of their military training. There was much in the ideology that must have appealed to the volunteers. Many of them had a radical right background that was a good seedbed for the SS ideas. At the same time, these ideas were combined with a strong nationalism. The research also shows that the front-fighters were never convinced pan-Germanists. They felt primarily that they were fighting for Norway, an NS Norway, not for a Greater Germany.

The Civilian SS

The SS wanted to set up a branch of the Civilian SS in Norway, *Allgemeine SS*. Again, they had to work through Quisling's NS Party. On 28 March 1941 Terboven, Lie and Riisnæs met with Himmler at his headquarters in Berlin to discuss plans to establish an SS formation in Norway. Himmler thought that the nucleus should be recruited from Quisling's inner circle, the *Hird*, and that Lie and Riisnæs should lead the organization. The plans were put to Quisling the following day and he approved them. 'The Norwegian SS' was established on 21 May in the Masonic Lodge in Oslo, in the presence of numerous important people: Himmler; Terboven; Falkenhorst;

representatives of the *Reichskommissariat* and the *Wehrmacht*; Quisling; and the NS ministers of state. Himmler appointed Lie as leader of the new organization and promoted him to the SS rank of *Standartenführer*, equivalent to a colonel. Riisnæs was appointed deputy leader.

Staff for the new organization were recruited by ordering in members of the *Hird*. They were medically examined, and about 150 men who were approved donned German SS uniforms on which the German eagle was replaced by the *Hird*'s armband. They marched in close order to the Masonic Lodge, where they swore loyalty first to Hitler and then to Quisling. The new organization was to be both a part of the SS and a special unit of the NS Party. The recruits were sent to a newly built camp near Elverum, where they were met by German SS and Norwegian officers. Here, they were given both ideological and military training.

This attempt to create an SS movement in Norway shows several noteworthy features. The SS and NS worked together on it, but it was the Germans who were dominant. The lavishness of the opening ceremony suggests that it was thought of as the beginning of a more widespread SS movement. The Norwegian SS was different from what one usually associates with a political movement in Norway, and it obviously took the SS in Germany as its model. It was strongly militarized from the start. Not only was it uniformed, but the recruits were immediately sent on courses that included political and ideological indoctrination in addition to military training, delivered by professional officers. Service at the front would be a natural posting for the new SS men.

The Norwegian SS did take part in the war on the Eastern Front, but not as a separate unit. Most of the members joined the NS's newly established Norwegian Legion, which almost led to the dissolution of the Norwegian SS. The SS therefore took an initiative to reorganize the SS movement, and again there was a compromise between the SS Germanic and the NS national points of view. In Quisling's call for volunteers on 21 July 1942 when the establishment of 'Germanic SS Norway' was announced, it was said that the new organization should be both a part of the Greater Germanic SS organization and an independent branch of the NS Party. In practice, it became mainly an SS unit which eventually came to be strongly opposed to NS and the *Hird*. The uniform was to be a black SS uniform with Norwegian SS badges. The organization never grew very big. In November 1944 it had 1,300 active members, nearly all of whom were front veterans, policemen or members of the *Hird*.

The Norwegian police

Himmler saw the Norwegian police not just as part of a security organization but as a way to spread the SS ethos in Norway. He planned to reform it on a German model and gradually unite it with the SS. Such a police force would both disseminate SS ideology and combat enemies of the regime. It would be a main pillar of the anticipated National Defence Corps. At the start of September 1940, fifty police officers travelled to Germany on a six-week study tour with the SS and the German Order Police, to become better acquainted with German methods. The plan for a reorganization of the police accelerated early in 1941. Many in the police welcomed such a move, but it was mainly the *SS* who pressed for it. There was to be a new, centralized police force, the National Police Corps. Following a German pattern, 'police presidia' were established in the four biggest cities, each headed by a president of police.

As in Germany, the force was divided into Security Police and Order Police. The Security Police included the former Criminal Police and the newly established State Police (Stapo), which corresponded to the *Gestapo* on the German side and had the task of hunting down enemies of the NS regime. In practice, Stapo came to stand under the direct control of the minister of police and the *Gestapo*. Standby units were to be set up within the Order Police. New police personnel would be taught at Kongsvinger Fortress, where the *SS* set up a training centre with German and Norwegian instructors.

The *SS* made considerable progress with its plans for the police and its reorganization of the police force. For purely professional reasons, many police personnel were in favour of centralization and strengthening of the force. Prominent police officers such as Jonas Lie wanted both reorganization and membership in NS. Many officers serving in the local police forces joined NS in the autumn and winter of 1940–1, with the result that the police became the most Nazified of all the departments of the state. Lie also set up police companies that were sent to the Eastern Front. He thought that service at the front should be a natural part of a policeman's training and make him better equipped to combat enemies of the regime.

Lebensborn – The *SS* breeding programme

The Germans saw Norway as the country that contained the very best Germanic bloodlines. New genetic stock was created when Norwegian women had children by German soldiers or *SS* men who were stationed in Norway. Such precious human stock had to be protected and preserved. During his stay in Norway, Himmler raised this question with Terboven at a meeting where several German representatives were present. Terboven suggested that the *Reichskommissariat* should attend to the matter, but Himmler wanted it to be handled by the *SS*. The solution was to establish the German institution of *Lebensborn* ('Fount of Life') in Norway. The *SS* had founded *Lebensborn* in Germany in 1935 to help families with many children and support unmarried mothers. To give birth outside of marriage would no longer be shameful, provided the child was racially valuable.

Lebensborn would now serve the same purpose in Norway. When German men fathered children with Norwegian mothers, the mothers and children must get the help they needed. Experts were summoned from the *Lebensborn* programme in Germany, and in summer 1941 the first mother and baby home was established at Hurdal Manor. Twelve such homes were set up throughout Norway over the following years, all staffed by German midwives and doctors. The mothers received help around the time of giving birth and economic help thereafter. The children were considered German. Around 1,200 children were born in the organization's maternity homes, but many more mothers and children received help in other ways. The *Lebensborn* records account for about 8,000 children from an estimated total of 10,000–12,000 wartime babies with German fathers and Norwegian mothers.

CHAPTER 7
NASJONAL SAMLING (NS) – NORWAY'S FASCIST PARTY

Nasjonal Samling was a political party. It was founded in the early 1930s and survived alongside the other parties throughout the decade. It was a small party from the start, it soon became politically insignificant and it was always far from power. However, it took shape in the 1930s and later retained several of the characteristics it had developed at that time, which came to be significant in defining its role during the occupation. Although it was not an institution of the occupying power, it became incorporated into the workings of the regime.

The 1930s: An insignificant party

NS regarded Norway's national day, 17 May, as the date of its foundation in 1933. This was an appropriate choice of date for a party that aimed to appeal so strongly to nationalist feelings. NS arose as a continuation of reactionary right trends in the 1920s, but with a further radicalization of these ideas. In the early 1930s, it rode the crest of a wave of fear of communism, of revolution and of the Labour Party (*Arbeiderpartiet*), which had been revolutionary in the 1920s and still had remnants of its revolutionary profile at the start of the 1930s. Fear of 'the Red Terror', 'the Bolsheviks' and a threatened revolution was strong in parts of middle-class society and found expression in voices and requests that pointed beyond the established political system towards dictatorship, 'the strong man' and harsh measures. At the same time, the economic crisis and labour disputes of the interwar years were reaching their climax in the early 1930s.

The fear of revolution and the demand for a strong man focussed on one person, Major Vidkun Quisling, and attached itself to him. He had entered the political scene in 1930 when he pointed out the danger that was threatening from communist Russia. He quickly and unexpectedly became defence minister in the 'Farmers' Party' (*Bondepartiet*) government that was formed in March 1931. From this position, he launched a violent attack the following year on the Labour Party and the communists, claiming that they received money from Moscow and fomented discord and revolution in Norway. The Labour Party struck back with equal force. In this way, Quisling kindled and nurtured the section of public opinion that yearned for 'the strong man'. He had suddenly become a man for his time.

Although Quisling used his position in the government as defence minister to advance his own interests, *Bondepartiet* itself was weak, with a slender parliamentary base, and was plagued with strong internal disagreements to which Quisling himself contributed. It fell from power in March 1933, and NS was established two months later with Quisling as its head. The new party's first objective was to win votes in the parliamentary election in autumn 1933. This was a disappointment. It appeared that the wave of anxiety that Quisling had ridden and that had brought the party into being had not spread wider throughout the electorate. NS got 2.2 per cent of the total votes, or to express it a little more favourably: 3.5 per cent of the votes in the constituencies where they had a candidate; yet no parliamentary seats.

Things didn't go much better in the local elections the following year, although the party did achieve a number of local representatives, a total of 69. The parliamentary election in 1936 clearly indicated a decline, with only 1.8 per cent of the votes, even though the party had campaigned actively and had entered the list in every constituency. From a height of 10,000 in 1935, the party membership fell steadily throughout the following years. After the unsuccessful election, the party fell apart. In the last couple of years before the Second World War broke out, it consisted only of Quisling as party leader and a few hundred active followers.

After 1937 the feeling of being part of a global fascist movement that was obviously on the advance was important for Quisling and his small band of followers. The party seemed to be just a minority sect, and we may wonder why it didn't just disappear. However, it did not disappear and the explanation can be found in the feeling among the party members that history was on their side. As Quisling saw the situation, the fascist movements and countries with whom NS identified were progressing towards new solutions to the problems of the time and were succeeding. They would finally defeat democracy, capitalism, liberalism, Marxism and Judaism, which were all enemies that would succumb. A new order would grow up shaped, as Quisling would say, in a new nationalist era.

A new Norway would also arise when the time was ripe. The process had not stopped. The fascist movement throughout the world was growing steadily and still had a future ahead of it. The party would play a part in the birth of the new order that would inevitably come in Norway. This was the conviction that sustained the little band of followers and gave Quisling the strength that was needed.

After the election defeat in 1936, NS abandoned plans of becoming a mass party and started instead to prepare itself to take over the leadership of the country in a crisis situation where the fascists, led by Germany, would clash with the Jewish-Bolshevist Soviets and the bourgeois democracies in a gigantic struggle. Then Germany would win and the war conclude with a new order in Europe, under German leadership. Quisling gradually became a supporter of Germany, even though he thought first and foremost that Norway ought to be neutral.

Such were the thoughts in Quisling's head when he met Hitler in 1939, showed himself willing to assist the Germans in their attack on Norway, and fought to advance his position throughout the summer of 1940 until they installed him in power on 25 September: He was not a man betraying his country; he was an agent of a world movement that by means of the German invasion brought its blessings to an afflicted nation.

Despite the steady decay of NS as a more and more marginalized party and the obvious failure of Quisling as a politician in the 1930s, there were several features of the party that were historically significant. The first was that there was in fact a fascist party in Norway that Germany had to relate to when it invaded the country, a party which Germany chose to back through Hitler's intervention, despite the party's initial insignificance. The second was that the powerless party did have an unchallenged leader. After 1937 there was nobody who could threaten Quisling's position as party leader. The third was that this leader, who competed with his party in insignificance, nevertheless managed to make an impression on Hitler when the two of them met in December 1939. Against all the odds, Hitler decided to back Quisling and his party in Norway.

Ideology

In January 1938 Quisling considered what name would best suit the political doctrine and the political system that NS was fighting for. He listed several descriptions that had been current but rejected them all: 'socialism', 'national socialism', 'fascism'. No, what best characterized NS was 'nationalism', and this was the expression that Quisling advised his followers to use when they described in one word what NS stood for. When the Germans arrived, however, it was not long before Quisling accepted 'national socialism'. The *Nasjonal Samling* was a national socialist party. On the other hand, NS people did not refer to themselves as 'Nazis', and they felt slandered when described as such. Their opponents used the word against them as a term of abuse.

Nationalism was and continued to be, an essential ingredient of NS ideology. NS cultivated the nation, national fellowship, national history, and national culture. The party's name, '*Nasjonal Samling*', indicated how important this was. The nation was divided. The party's first objective was to bring it together and encourage national unity. NS therefore considered itself not as a normal political party. It stood above the parties that were dividing the nation and from its high position it would bring about unity.

Like all Norwegian nation-builders in the nineteenth and twentieth centuries, NS looked back nostalgically to the great days of the Viking Age and the High Middle Ages. Quisling pointed out how the Viking voyages had contributed to the creation of both the Russian and the British Empires. In its rituals and its terminology, NS was inspired by Old Norse history. It reintroduced the old *heil og sæl* greeting. It made use of the word *Hird*, which had been the term for the king's retinue and bodyguard in the Middle Ages. And it held its assemblies at places such as Hafrsfjord, where Norway was said to have been brought together as a nation, and Stiklestad, where the saintly King Olav died in battle.

NS members admired the same aspects of national culture as other Norwegians. They used national symbols such as the Norwegian flag together with the party flag. Rural nationalism was a branch of general nationalism that was particularly strong in NS. The farmers were the heart of the nation. Tilling the soil was an activity beyond the purely material.

For Quisling and NS, a strong nation could not be built through party democracy and class warfare. The nation could only stand together as united and strong when it was moulded by one movement, one party, one leader. NS stood for dictatorial nationalism, with a dream of one leader who personified the nation. The *führer* principle was a way towards unity and strength that NS followed in its own party and would promote in state and society. Just one person, the leader, should be responsible for a decision. In this way, the fragmentation of responsibility that NS considered so typical of democracy could be avoided.

Quisling's ideal was corporatism. The political system should not be built on political parties. That just caused divisions. The system should be based on the corporations, the organizations of commercial and industrial life. Within these organizations the employers and the employees should sit together and work forward to an agreement. Class conflict and wasteful industrial disputes would disappear through this collaboration. The organizations would select their representatives to a new type of national assembly, to be known as *Rikstinget*.

In this corporate national assembly, not only would class conflict disappear and the parties be superfluous, but one would also be assured of competent, professional government. The party politicians were unskilled, according to NS. Representatives coming directly from industrial and commercial life would have a better grasp of things and look for more appropriate and realistic solutions to the problems of the time than politicians. *Rikstinget* was expected to have an important function during the occupation. It would give NS a platform and the legitimacy it badly needed.

NS was racist. The party thought that humanity was divided into races and that some races had more valuable qualities than others and were, therefore, more important. NS succeeded a prior organization, *Nordisk Folkereisning*, that Quisling had founded in 1931. This organization had claimed that Norwegians and the other Scandinavian peoples were 'the nucleus of the great family of peoples that represent the most valuable racial element of mankind *the great Nordic race*'. World civilization had been largely shaped and advanced by this race and by input of Nordic bloodlines into other racial groups.

After the Germans had occupied Norway, Quisling set about linking this Nordic racial idea with Germanic racism. It was time to fashion a shared racial philosophy. The Germanic race was the world's most worthy race which had had the strongest influence on world history and had carried culture to quite different heights than other races. Within this, the North Germanics had a degree of precedence because they had undergone the least racial intermixing. Thus, there were no sharp distinctions between Germanic, North Germanic, Nordic and Norwegian, which mutually overlapped. These Germanic or pan-Germanic ideas featured most strongly within NS during the first years of the war. They followed the course of the German victories, so to say, and reached a high point at the party's national conference in September 1942. Thereafter they declined.

NS became an antisemitic party in 1935. This happened under obvious influence from developments in Germany. The Jews were seen as the prime enemy race who had penetrated everywhere and allied themselves with national socialism's other enemies. They infiltrated communism and the government of the Soviet Union, and they lurked behind the Western democracies and the capitalists. They could therefore have a big influence in Norway, even though they were few. They worked by influencing the political and economic system. Quisling's wartime speeches are full of attacks against the conspiratorial Jews who were creating an international plot, fighting for world domination.

Communism was another archenemy of all fascist parties. Socialism was also an enemy, and NS was not particular about distinguishing between communism, Marxism and socialism. Quisling and his party followers saw them rather as a three-headed troll where each was part of the others. The troll was a threat because it split the nation. Class was set against class, instead of co-operating and coming together to strengthen national unity. The communists were not nationalists, but internationalists led by Comintern in Moscow.

There was, however, another type of socialism that Quisling recognized, and that enabled him, like Hitler, to call his party 'national *socialist*'. The socialist element within fascism rejected all class conflict and wanted to strengthen national unity, while at the same time improving the workers' conditions and introducing social benefits. Among the various ideological trends in NS, there is a 'socialism' that got a foothold at the top of the Nazified trade union movement.

Liberalism was NS's other great enemy. NS was an anti-liberal party, which attacked liberalism on two fronts. On the one front, liberalism represented political democracy as it had developed in Europe. As an anti-democratic party, NS claimed that democracy weakened the nation because it was based on having several parties, which constantly threatened national unity. For the national socialists, the will of the people must be channelled through one party, one movement. This applied in the 1930s when NS policy was to bring the other parties together, and during the occupation when it was the only party allowed.

On the other front, NS attacked liberalism as an economic doctrine that preached the value of the free market and free play of market forces in the economy. This freedom led only to damaging competition, bankruptcies, unemployment and class divisions. NS wanted instead to introduce a planned economy with a stronger national direction of commercial and industrial life. NS saw itself as an anti-capitalist party, and it had its own derogatory jargon for capitalists. They were 'plutocrats', and Britain and the United States were typical 'plutocracies'. However, NS did not carry its anti-capitalism very far. It wanted to maintain the right of private ownership, market interaction and the exercise of private initiative as factors in the economy. Moreover, there was a pro-business trend within NS itself.

History and the mission of NS

History played a decisive role in NS's and Quisling's ideology and self-image. Quisling often quoted examples from history, and he had an outline of how Norwegian history had developed, through alternating phases of national progress and setback. The first phase was the time of greatness in the Middle Ages. Then followed a setback in the 'Danish times' when Norway was united with Denmark for over 400 years. This was followed in turn by a national revival in the nineteenth century. To this point, Quisling was describing history just as the Norwegian nation-building historians had done traditionally. Thereafter, in his opinion, a new decline set in, starting with the breakthrough of the political parties and parliamentarism in the 1880s. This weakened executive power and divided the nation, and the decline just deepened further when the Labour Party brought class conflict and revolution into the mix. Then on 9 April 1940 began a new phase, a new era of national revival and progress in which NS had a fundamental role.

For Quisling, the German invasion showed what kind of abyss the Labour Party government had dropped the country into, and how the old order was now receiving its death blow. Instead of following a strict policy of neutrality, the government had favoured Britain in such a way that Germany was fully within its rights when it invaded the country as part of its war strategy. The government had neglected defence and nevertheless sent the country's depleted army into the field against the strongest land-based military power in Europe. Worst of all: Instead of staying at their post the king and government had fled, leaving their people in the lurch. The country was ungoverned. NS's time had come. He knew and had long known where the future lay: with the fascist movements. The party had a duty to fill the vacuum after the king and government had fled, a duty to save the nation.

So, from Quisling's point of view, it was not difficult to justify what he did when the Germans invaded Norway. He had clearly understood what was required when the system broke down. In this crisis situation, there had to be someone who went in and took initial responsibility. Then NS must set to work on the Sisyphean task of saving the nation in the only way possible – through a totally new order, a revolution. This would have to happen on an ideological basis of national socialism and with Germany as the model, but it had to be a Norwegian revolution. NS considered itself a party of national salvation.

NS held a twofold view of the German occupying force. From one point of view, NS considered that the German presence in Norway was justified by the needs of the war and that Germany naturally must dominate as the occupying power so long as the war lasted. Taking another point of view, the German occupation offered a historic opportunity for a National Socialist Revolution. Implementing this was a task not for the Germans, but for NS. German support was needed in the first phase, but it was NS as a Norwegian movement that must bring about the new, national socialist order that would enable Norway to enter New Europe as an independent nation equal to Germany. Norway could not be a great power like Germany, but it could take its place as a natural friend and ally of Germany since both countries stood for the same political system, the same ideology and the same world view.

The supreme leader

The *Nasjonal Samling* Party was led by a *Fører*. It did not have a 'chairman' or 'leader'. At one time there had been talk of using the word *Høvding* ('chieftain') as a reminder of the greatness of the times of the sagas, but the party finally decided on *Fører*, as a reflection of the German *Führer*, Adolf Hitler.

Nobody personified the party as Quisling did. It was he who had founded the party, and it was his prestige as defence minister that the party had built upon at the start. He had led the party through thick and thin. He had committed his whole career to it. His faith in his own and the party's mission appears never to have weakened. Nobody else devoted his life so completely to NS as Quisling did.

Quisling's strength was his ability to give his status as a supreme leader an aura of superior insight, of thoughtfulness and reflection. He gained recognition as the party's ideological visionary. The set of ideas that nourished the party's ideology was largely formulated and propagated by the supreme leader. He functioned as the common denominator for the various ideological currents in the party. He had a talent for putting the political issues of the day into a greater historical context. There was something magnificent about the supreme leader's historic vistas and the long connecting lines that he drew. He explained NS's historic mission and how it was spliced together with the great movements of history. He gave the party members and those who felt drawn towards the party a feeling that they were taking part in something great. In this area, Quisling was unchallenged within the party.

He was also the one who made the decisions in another area. He was the key person in assessing what status Norway and NS should have in relation to the Germans. He was the leading spokesman when such questions were discussed with Hitler. Quisling's relationship with the German *Führer* had been the prerequisite for NS gaining its position as a governing party and being able to start a National Socialist Revolution in Norway. It was he who then decided and formulated how NS's political aims were transferred into demands on the Germans. It was mainly he who strove for them, against Terboven in Norway and Hitler in Germany as his opponents.

Quisling's weaknesses were a lack of a sense of reality and a lack of skill in political manoeuvring. He had little understanding of the craft of politics, was almost helpless in negotiations and often reacted only with silence when he stood face to face with an opponent. He seemed at a loss when confronted with specific decisions in practical life and practical politics. His enemies and his followers both agreed that the *Fører* was ill-suited to day-to-day politics. He had no understanding of how one progresses from ideology to strategy and onwards to tactics and political horse-trading.

Because of Quisling's difficulty in relation to daily political leadership with all its requirements for tactical assessments and the balance of conflicting considerations, he does not stand out as a strong and unifying leader for the implementation of The National Socialist Revolution in Norway. A campaign of Nazification was set in motion over a broad field, but it leaves no impression of having had an overall leader who was working from a plan and exercised his authority to harmonize the different strains in the campaign. Instead, it was directed by the initiatives of the various NS ministers and their German advisers. The supreme leader was indeed involved and important decisions could be made by him or in his name, but he had no firm grip on the campaign as a whole.

A party led by a supreme leader naturally respected his supremacy. Party members could make suggestions and could try to influence him, and they could criticize him privately. But they could not openly disagree with or oppose a decision he had taken. The leader could and did listen to advice from his colleagues, but he was not obliged to do so and in some instances, Quisling made momentous decisions without informing anyone in his circle. He said nothing to the others about his meetings with Hitler in December 1939, and his attempted coup on 9 April 1940 came as a surprise to the NS members and aroused much discussion in the party. Quisling also aroused criticism in 1943 when without having discussed the matter with any of the ministers in his government he endorsed 'Lex Eilifsen', which provided a legal basis for the NS government to condemn to death and execute Norwegian citizens.

The principle of the supreme leader propagated itself from party to state. From 1 February 1942, Quisling as prime minister was also formally the state's *Fører*. This again implied an ambition to be the nation's *Fører*. In the eyes of NS, Quisling then embodied and symbolized the party, the state, and the nation as a unity. The great fascist leaders in other countries largely succeeded in fulfilling this ambition. For Quisling, the reality was quite different. He survived as supreme leader in a weakened NS state, but he never had a chance of becoming the nation's *Fører*, as the nation united in steadily stronger opposition to him and to NS.

Quisling wanted to use the authority of the supreme leader to carry out The National Socialist Revolution. The leader would decide, and the people would obey. Quisling had a particularly strong belief that the revolution in Norway could be set in motion from above, by means of regulations and laws. The Norwegians would accept these because they were law-abiding people, accustomed to obeying what emanated from governments, departments, county governors and district chairmen. It naturally followed that those who broke the rules and regulations must be punished. An established government and an orderly society could not tolerate anybody opposing lawful authority.

Like other fascist parties, NS sought to gather and inspire its members through frequent meetings and great gatherings. These occasions gave Quisling his most important channel of communication out to the party members and further out to the population. NS did not hold party conferences such as those found in liberal democracies. There were no debates. Instead, the meetings were an important platform for the leader to tell his followers how the current situation should be understood, how it should be interpreted in the light of great historical movements, what tasks lay ahead and what the future looked like. The meetings were not intended to be a channel in the opposite direction, from the membership to the leader.

Membership and organization

NS needed a large membership to be able to influence opinion, but above all, to influence the Germans. With enough members behind him, Quisling could demand a bigger share of power and a more independent status for his party. It was always assumed that NS would attain such a position when the party had enough followers. Prospects for recruitment looked good in autumn 1940. The Germans' backing of the party, their promises that the only way to Norwegian freedom and independence was via the party, the German victories and NS's new prominence in the media and in the public eye led to a stream of new members that increased the party membership to 14,000 in October 1940 and 25,000 at the turn of the year. This was a marked increase from the few hundred the party had had on 9 April and the membership of 4,000 at the end of August.

Recruitment was slower after that, but there was still a steady flow and by August 1941 membership had reached 30,000. A recruitment campaign was then launched with an optimistic target of 100,000 members, but this was unsuccessful. At New Year 1941–2 the tally was 34,000 members, rather comparable to the conservative parties in the 1930s but less able to be compared with the 100,000 in the Labour Party because the Labour Party was built upon collective membership from the trade unions. Staff in the *Einsatzstab* thought that NS had made sufficient progress to be able to have a greater share of power. Membership continued to rise slowly until it reached a peak of 43,400 members in November 1943. In addition, there were 5,000–6,000 members in the party's youth section. In all, between 50,000 and 60,000 people will have been members of NS for shorter or longer periods. Eight thousand three hundred people left the party in the course of the war.

Most of the members of NS came from urban areas and from eastern Norway, where most of the population was to be found. Oslo and the areas around Oslo Fjord were the party's best recruiting grounds. Western Norway was the part of the country where the fewest people joined. When the party was founded, it had had a strong intake of high-status workers such as military officers, independent businessmen, senior employees, engineers and technicians. The middle class dominated. This evened itself out during the war, although the proportion of officials was still high.

What is most surprising is that the party appealed so strongly to the workers, even as it was violently opposed to the Labour Party. The percentage of workers in NS was only slightly below the percentage of workers in the population. Part of the explanation may be that most of the workers in NS were unskilled, a group on whom the labour movement had a weaker grip. Another explanation may be that the party succeeded to a certain extent in presenting itself as anti-capitalist and intent on social reform.

NS tried to connect with nationalist trends in the rural population (*bondenasjonalisme*) and the glorification of working the soil. It found good support among the farmers in some parts of inland eastern Norway and Setesdal, but on the whole, the proportion of farmers in the party was less than in the general population. Young people were well represented, with 30 per cent of the members under the age of thirty-five. After 1941 more women than men joined the party, eventually making up a third of the membership. One explanation that has been given for this is that men in NS brought their families into the party with them as they became progressively more isolated and ostracized.

NS was constituted with a national leadership and the local district organization, both directly under the *Fører*. It also included several special organizations such as the

Hird, the Youth Division, the Women's Organisation, the Student Division, the Trades Group Organisation for workers and Farmers' Groups. The *Hird* was *Nasjonal Samling's* political activist organization in which 8,000–9,000 members served as 'political soldiers'. Members of the *Hird* were trained and indoctrinated in the movement's ideology. At meetings, training courses, leadership courses and summer gatherings they were told repeatedly about 'the national revolution', the national values that NS stood for, the national socialists' modes of thought and action, the supreme leader principle and Quisling's unique position as the movement's leader.

The *Hird* was a prominent part of the party's public image. The members of the *Hird* marched through the streets in close order on their way to meetings and rallies, with brass bands playing and flags flying, their own sun-and-cross flag and the Norwegian flag side by side. They served as stewards and guards at NS's many meetings and events. From time to time, detachments took part in bigger actions alongside *Sipo*, Stapo or the *Wehrmacht*. The *Hird* took part in the arrest of the Jews in autumn 1942 and the hunt for the heavy water saboteurs at Hardangervidda in spring 1943. The *Hird* was also important because it provided so many recruits to the German and Norwegian units fighting at the front. There were high expectations that members of the *Hird* would enlist. With its emphasis on military order and military virtues, the *Hird* was the natural starting point on a route to military training and service at the front.

The special organization for young people was *Nasjonal Samlings Ungdomsfylking, NSUF* (*Nasjonal Samlings Youth Division*). NS saw itself as a youthful organization and gave weight to its work in the Youth Division as an important source of recruitment to the mother organization. Members of the Youth Division automatically became members of NS when they reached the age of eighteen. The division's German advisers were from the Hitler-Youth organization. The division was also inspired by the Boy Scout movement and acquired part of the Scouts' assets and property when the Norwegian Boy Scout Association was dissolved in September 1941.

In some ways, the Youth Division was reminiscent of the *Hird*. It was defined as a fighting organization, for fighting both home and abroad. It inculcated readiness for defence and readiness for self-sacrifice and prepared young people in various ways for later military service. It had a militarily patterned, hierarchical structure, emphasized the importance of discipline and had its own uniform. It also took part in many of the same ritual events as other parts of NS. The young people went on parades and march-pasts. They went on torch-lit processions, provided standard-bearers, held bonfire parties, celebrated St. Olav's Day and held gatherings at important historical sites from the Viking Age.

Opposition

NS was intended to be a united party, a movement without fissures, projecting a unity that would spread out to government and nation. Schisms within the party were forbidden. Outwardly, the party was largely able to fulfil this need for unified action.

Nothing about conflicts in the party was allowed to get out. However, the illegal press and London Radio were able to gather bits and pieces about the internal conflicts in the NS regime and build them up. Such conflicts naturally existed, even though they could not be expressed openly.

When one party has a monopoly on power and freedom of expression is suppressed, different currents of opinion have to flow together within the one party. NS included both nationalists and supranational pan-Germanists, both worker-friendly socialists and supporters of free-market capitalism. When the conflicting opinions could not be expressed freely but had to be constantly held in check so as not to be too apparent and violate the image of the united body, the *Fører*-led, authoritarian party easily became a pressure-cooker. Rumours, suspicions of subversive activity and ideas of conspiracy took root and were further nourished by the obscure connections that existed between individual party members and Germans in the *Reichskommissariat* or the *SS*. It was not easy to face up to an opponent in the party if the person concerned could refer to support from a German authority.

Quisling was faced with two types of opposition within the party. One type arose among the members of the government. In 1943–4 there was opposition among some of the government ministers led by Hagelin, Quisling's old henchman from Germany and the one who had the most influence on Quisling in the first years of the war. Hagelin stood for resolute national independence and had been critical of the Germans early on. In August 1943 he wrote a paper in which he directed a violent attack against the *Reichskommissar* and his staff, who he thought was behaving too ruthlessly and irresponsibly without considering Norwegian interests. Several of the members of the government endorsed the paper, in which they threatened to leave the government.

There was also opposition between two pro-business groups within the government. One group, with Minister of Trade and Industry Eivind Blehr as its leading representative, proposed a policy of national self-sufficiency with limited foreign trade. Blehr was dismayed by the Germans' exploitation of Norway, and his self-sufficiency policy had an obviously anti-German sting. The other, more pro-German, group was represented mainly by Alf Whist, a rising star in the party. This group advocated an export-driven economy with Norway adapting to a large German economic bloc (*Grossraumwirtschaft*).

Quisling allowed these arguments to run on for a while, but he eventually took a stand. The opposition's people gradually disappeared from the government and were replaced by new members. In the conflict between Blehr and Whist, it was Whist who drew the longest straw. The relationship with the Germans was an important consideration for Quisling during these changes. He probably chose Whist because he was more amenable than Blehr to frictionless co-operation with the Germans. Hagelin also irritated the Germans so much that this must have been an important reason for his departure. Quisling was in an exposed position in this respect. He tried repeatedly to win concessions from the Germans, always without success. He was not willing to press harder – whether from weakness, a lack of skill in political manoeuvring or an understanding of what was really achievable.

The second type of opposition facing the supreme leader came from around the edges of the party. The most determined opposition came from the SS. Germanic SS Norway (GSSN) and the newspaper *Germaneren* had been set up as a shared project between the SS and NS, but the relationship between these participants was strained and went from bad to worse. GSSN and *Germaneren* promoted an unadulterated pan-Germanic policy and considered Quisling and NS far too nationalistic. The paper launched unusually bitter attacks against NS.

Another opponent was Klaus Hansen. His platform was the Norwegian-German Association, of which he was chairman. The association with its branches throughout the country had 8,000 members in 1944. Hansen was a member of NS, a pro-German pan-Germanist who could call upon support through his good connections with the propaganda department in the *Reichskommissariat*. He was dismissed from the party and also from his leadership position in the Norwegian-German Association.

Quisling experienced the particular problems associated with combatting opposition in an indoctrinated party in a one-party state. In order not to infringe the principle of the unified party, deviant opinions or outright criticisms were usually expressed in bland phrases with their sting hidden. Critics could argue indirectly. Within NS, violent and continuing accusations were raised against the freemasons. In fact, all national socialists came to consider the freemasons as their enemies. The Germans had already dissolved the Norwegian Order of Freemasons on 19 September 1940. Freemasons who were members of NS had to renounce all loyalty to the order. A vicious attack on freemasons in NS, without naming names, could nevertheless be interpreted as an attack on certain NS leaders who had in their time been freemasons.

The restricted flow of information in this top-down system led to the context being less transparent, knowledge of developments in society more restricted and the party leadership more uncertain about what was actually going on. The Germans had solved this problem by establishing their wide-ranging Security Service (*SD*), which gathered information for the highest leadership in Nazi Germany and leading German authorities in Norway about what was afoot. Quisling copied this when the party set up its own intelligence service to report on public opinion but more especially on internal relationships within NS. Like other institutions that NS established, this surveillance organization was rather slender, but it illustrates the problem that Quisling faced as supreme leader. He didn't know enough about what was going on in the party or in the indoctrinated public, and he had to fumble in the dark when he had to make decisions.

It was typical of the indoctrinated party that the *Fører* needed a special court to judge in disputes between members or pass judgement on members who had committed an offence against the party or not behaved as they should. They could be reprimanded for minor infringements or excluded for more serious offences. An internal court such as this is not usually a feature of democratic parties, where a question of exclusion would be handled through the party's usual channels. NS needed a party court that the leader could use to avoid having to decide delicate disciplinary matters himself.

Programme

NS adopted a programme in 1934 that continued subsequently and was applied in principle even during the occupation. It could not provide answers to the many new questions that the occupation presented for Quisling and the party, but no formal new manifesto was prepared. Some of the objectives towards which Quisling was working could, however, be linked to an informal programme that applied alongside the older one.

A key point in this informal programme was to set up a sovereign Norwegian state again. The NS government that was created on 25 September 1940 did not provide that, nor did the government that followed from the ceremonies at Akershus in February 1942. Quisling called for an end to German supremacy. The *Reichskommissar* with his full authority from Hitler's decree of 24 April 1940 and the associated *Reichskommissariat* would need to be withdrawn. Instead, the two nations should relate to each other through special envoys or exchange ambassadors and negotiate through diplomatic channels, as is normal between sovereign states.

Quisling proposed that the NS government should formally make peace with Germany. It should be clearly established in a peace treaty that the state of war between the two countries had ended. Then there would need to be negotiations about what rights Germany as the occupying power should have in Norway and what contribution Norway should make to the German war effort. An independent NS government would be prepared for a close and agreed relationship with national socialist Germany.

Quisling was eager to set up a Norwegian army. A defining characteristic of a sovereign state was to have its own military forces. A peace treaty would eliminate the formal objections to a Norwegian army. NS and the government would appear stronger in the eyes of the public if they managed to establish a national military force. As part of the agreement, Quisling would deploy some of the Norwegian armed forces on the German side. NS Norway identified itself with the German war effort and wanted to take part. The size of such a contingent and its contribution would, however, have to be the subject of negotiations and agreements between the NS government and the Third Reich.

As soon as Quisling was appointed prime minister in February 1942 and had achieved a formal position as head of government, he launched his first proposal for a Norwegian army. This would comprise an army corps of three divisions. In June that year, he proposed that Norway's independent defence force should be formally reinstated on 25 September, the second anniversary of NS's accession to power. The following year he busied himself with plans for a reintroduction of conscription to the army. In the autumn he proposed that 50,000 men should be mobilized for service on the Eastern Front and he considered using the system of call-up for compulsory labour service (*Arbeidstjenesten (AT)*) to recruit troops. When Quisling visited Himmler in January 1944, he spoke enthusiastically about setting up a Norwegian conscripted army that would be trained by officers educated at Norwegian officer training colleges. He probably also took the matter up with Hitler, whom he visited the same month.

It was natural for Quisling to put such emphasis on the military. Officers had played an important role in the preparations for the founding of NS and subsequently. Parts of the officer corps were well disposed towards NS, and after the German invasion, as many as 25 per cent of the officers had joined the party. There was a sympathetically inclined reserve of officers who were ready to join the new army. Also, NS's nationalist policy gave it extra impetus. A nation could not be strong unless it was able to demonstrate its power by means of an army.

All proposals of Quisling for an independent army fell on stony ground. The Germans were not interested. They were sceptical about an army that would just make Quisling and NS more independent. They were not as optimistic as Quisling was about enlisting enough recruits, and they pointed out that any mass mobilization of conscripts would create unrest and a mass exodus to Sweden. They had no confidence in Quisling's assertions that Norwegians would simply obey orders from above. On the contrary, an attempt at mass mobilization would undermine the NS government's authority. In addition, the Germans always had an alternative to a Norwegian army in the recruitment of volunteers to the *Waffen-SS*. That was the way NS should go, suggested the SS, if the party wanted to give its support to the German war effort.

Quisling didn't attain his objectives. An independent NS government was not established, and nothing came of peace talks or a Norwegian army. NS's attempt to carry out a National Socialist Revolution in Norway was better received by the Germans, but even this failed in the end. It was, however, driven forward with such strength and aroused so much opposition that it runs like a leitmotif through the history of the first years of the occupation. This aspect – 'The struggle over The National Socialist Revolution' – will be the main theme of a later chapter.

NS and the Germans

The Germans held the power in occupied Norway. NS had power only in so far as the Germans allowed them to exercise it. Nearly all military and police power were held by the Germans, and the resources available to them were formidable. The power of the civilian government was always in the last resort in the hands of the Germans. It was thanks to the Germans that NS had come to power, and the Germans always set the boundaries of NS's development. The party had no mandate from Norwegian constitutional organs or Norwegian voters to bring into play as a counterweight to the German dominance. They never had a representative platform on which to build their authority.

On the other hand, NS and the Germans largely embraced the same fascist ideology, and the Germans had declared that they would back NS. Both wanted NS to carry out a National Socialist Revolution in Norway, and the Germans were ready to support the party in realizing this project. The party, therefore, acquired most of the ministerial posts on 25 September 1940, and from 1 February 1942, Quisling stood as prime minister at the head of a purely NS government. In giving NS access to the resources of the Norwegian state, the Germans were giving them the basis for The National Socialist Revolution.

The problem was that the Germans had other interests that held higher priority than this revolution. Their military and economic needs set tight boundaries on how far they could give the Norwegian NS government a chance. Norwegian resources must first and foremost be used to sustain the numerous German troops, build up *Festung Norwegen* and achieve ambitious industrial projects. Security was a prime consideration. Orderly calm would need to prevail in occupied Norway if the Germans were to fulfil their military and economic aims. The National Socialist Revolution presupposed daring initiatives that aroused opposition and threatened public order. So, a sort of pattern developed: NS took a Nazifying initiative; the initiative aroused opposition; the opposition in some instances spread and became a threat to public order; and the Germans had to intervene, suppress the opposition and restrain NS.

NS was weakened by being blamed for the many controls, restrictions, reprisals and punitive actions that the occupation imposed, but for which the party was not directly responsible. Living standards sank, nearly all goods were either rationed or unobtainable, many Norwegians were arrested, thousands were deported and several hundred were executed. The occupying Germans who were mainly responsible for this received their due share of the blame, but the criticism, ill-will, dissatisfaction and hate were also directed at the party that shared leadership with the occupiers, had received its authority from the Germans and headed a government that issued laws and regulations that signified political repression and economic scarcity.

A particular problem for NS was that the Germans were not united among themselves. They didn't always speak with one voice. German pronouncements could appear confusing when they came from different organizations that were not necessarily on the same page. On the other hand, this gave NS an opportunity to exploit the situation by playing the Germans off against each other. There were always two 'Germanies' to be reckoned with – a Germany in Norway and German rule elsewhere in Europe. The final decisive authority in both places was always Hitler, and Falkenhorst, Terboven and Quisling all sought interviews with the *Führer*. Quisling's meetings with Hitler became a series of disappointments. He didn't get approval for his most important ambitions. Hitler did not completely wash his hands of him, but he gave him little or nothing.

However, under Hitler there were possibilities of forming alliances with various German institutions. The alliance between NS and the German Navy in Norway and Germany up to New Year 1942–3 was a partnership against Terboven and the *Reichskommissariat*. NS's relationship with the SS was problematic because the SS was so powerful both in Germany and in Norway and stretched its tentacles out into so many fields. NS vacillated between allying itself with the SS and trying to oppose SS power. It helped the SS to recruit volunteers for service at the front in the *Waffen-SS,* while also setting up its own units to send to the front.

One way to work against the SS was to seek help from other German institutions. NS could make alliances with some of the many German advisers, who had their own connections in Germany. The compulsory labour service (*Arbeidstjenesten (AT)*) provides a good example of this. With support from Herbert Bormann, who represented the German labour service in Norway, and his boss in Germany, NS managed to block the *SS* from recruiting front-fighters from *AT*. Another example is the Youth Division (*Nasjonal Samlings Ungdomsfylking (NSUF)*). NSUF sent some of its members to courses and camps in Germany and had its own representative in Berlin. Through him, NS managed to gather sensitive information about the *SS* that NS could use at home in Norway.

NS itself was not entirely united, though. This gave the Germans opportunities to back different trends within the party. The *SS* faction in NS and government is the most prominent example of this. The faction gave the Germans a foot inside NS. Another example is found in the connections between departments in the *Reichskommissariat* and certain elements in the periphery of NS that were critical of Quisling and the party leadership.

NS never broke off its relationship with the Germans. It remained in government until the very end. Over time, however, it changed from being pro-German to becoming partly anti-German. The strength the anti-German tendencies could finally attain is reflected in a letter from Rediess to Himmler on 2 December 1944. Quisling was due to meet Hitler, and with Terboven's approval, Rediess used the opportunity to raise strong complaints against the party secretary, Fuglesang. The Germans considered Fuglesang to be so opposed to them that they asked for him to be dismissed from his position.

This development of anti-German feeling within the party largely followed the trends of German fortune in the world war. NS positively wanted to team up with the Germans so long as they were winning but gradually distanced itself from them when they suffered defeat. NS always saw the Germans as both an ally and an occupier. The party initially emphasized the former, but later their status as an occupier became more important, especially as one whose main aim was to utilize and exploit Norway. Then NS had to take on the duty of protecting the country from the exploitation, within the limitations of not breaking off from their German Allies and not even seriously threatening to do so. Such limitations did not leave much leverage in an increasingly restricted negotiating position.

NS policy aroused strong public opposition. Not all parts of the policy were controversial, however. NS also passed resolutions or worked to promote causes that even their opponents could consider positively. Some of the members of the NS government fought a stubborn campaign to maintain the Norwegian laws on waterfalls and prevent the Germans from gaining control of Norwegian hydroelectric power. The minister of shipping worked to keep the home fleet in Norwegian hands and campaigned for support for seafarers' families when the breadwinner was away at sea, even if he was on an allied ship. NS also continued its social policy from before the war. Unemployment benefit and sickness benefit were expanded, and child benefit was introduced in Norway for the first time.

The history of this social policy provides examples of an almost normal bureaucratic tug of war between German and Norwegian interests. Child benefit, for example, was approved in December 1944 after a trial of strength between the *Reichskommissariat* and the Ministry of Social Affairs. The *Reichskommissariat* approved the principle of child benefit, but German and Norwegian bureaucrats pulled in different directions when it came to the details, and this resulted in a compromise. Another example relates to the introduction of a special war pension for both military and civilian personnel who had been injured in the military campaign in 1940. It was proposed that soldiers who had fought against the Germans should also be eligible for the pension. The *Reichskommissariat* agreed in principle but had many objections to the proposals and called, among other things, for strong evidence of need in each case. The Ministry of Social Affairs rejected such demands and pressed to have their proposals approved and implemented, which they achieved.

CHAPTER 8
IN THE GRIP OF WAR ECONOMY

Before the occupation, Norway was part of an international economy that was still quite open, with access to markets in many countries. Then it was suddenly dragged into a German-controlled economic zone where the Germans always had the final say. Norway was an outward-looking nation, whose trade with other countries was an important part of the economy. No other country imported as much per head of population, and only Sweden exported more per head. The German occupation suddenly put a stop to this. Overnight, trade was restricted to German-controlled regions and Scandinavia. Norway was cut off from all trade with Western countries. A major trading partner, Great Britain, disappeared. Germany had been Norway's second biggest customer before the war. Now the Germans were in full control.

Trade on a free international market with free currency exchange disappeared. Instead, there was a direct exchange of goods between countries, with payment through a special clearing system. Germany had full control of both the exchange of goods and the system of payment. Every consignment needed a currency licence or approval for payment. Such licences or approvals were given only for goods that were deemed vital. Goods important for the German war economy were given priority. Imports of items that the authorities considered unnecessary were refused licences, and export of items needed to meet needs in Norway was forbidden.

Norway was totally dependent on imports for some goods. This gave the Germans a trump card in negotiations with Norwegian authorities. They could threaten to reduce or stop the import of goods that Norway could not do without. Grain was one such commodity. The country could not grow enough grain for its needs and was always dependent on imports. The other key commodity was coal. Norway needed coal to keep the railways, industry and coastal shipping fleet running. Fuel oil for the fishing fleet was also necessary if both the Germans and the Norwegians were to get all the fish they required. The Norwegians did get grain and coal – less than they wanted, but enough to hold famine at bay and enable transport and industry to continue. Other necessary imported goods did become unavailable, however. In agriculture, the application of phosphate fertilizer and the use of feed concentrates stopped. It became difficult to sustain agricultural production without such important materials.

Before the war, income from the carriage of freight by the big merchant fleet had been important for the Norwegian foreign trade balance. This income compensated for the big deficit in the balance. Norway could depend on importing more than it exported. This source of income disappeared immediately when the Germans arrived. Norway at home now had to reduce its imports to a level that the exports could pay for. Instead, it was Norway in exile that benefitted from the merchant fleet's big earnings. The reduction in imports also led to reduced production, because part of the import consisted of important raw and manufactured products that were needed by industry.

Norway's total foreign trade fell drastically during the occupation. According to one calculation, imports in 1944 had fallen to a fifth and exports to less than a third of the 1939 levels. Norway had difficulties adapting to a situation with a single, all-dominant trading partner. There was less available to export because so much of the labour force and production in Norway was being used to meet German requirements. Germany itself had less to spare for export, which would have reduced the level of Norwegian imports anyway. On top of all this, there was a lack of shipping tonnage to carry the goods, causing a constant bottleneck in both military and civil supplies.

Although foreign trade as a whole fell, Norway's trade with Germany rose strongly. One might have expected the Germans to force the Norwegians to send more goods to Germany than they received back. That would have been one way to exploit Norway, and that was what generally happened in other occupied countries. In Norway it was the other way round; the Germans brought greater value to the occupied area than they took out. The Norwegians were not exploited through foreign trade. Instead, the exploitation was linked to the large requirements that the Germans had in Norway. These requirements were so massive that they had to be met both using Norwegian resources and by bringing in additional resources from Germany.

A new economic zone

The new political order that Hitler wanted to establish on the European continent had its economic counterpart. The Germans planned to set up a German-dominated economic zone, a *Grossraumwirtschaft*, that would be self-sufficient rather than dependent on other countries' raw materials and markets. It would consist of a centre, more or less like Germany, and a periphery of German-controlled zones. The centre would form a modern industrial economy, while the periphery provided food and raw materials to the centre, made use of its local advantages within the new zone and otherwise invested in primary industry.

There were many different ideas about the further design of the new economic zone, and no final plan was ever agreed. However, it did play a certain role in the first years of the war. In Norway's case, the idea was that the country should make use of its asset of cheap hydroelectric power to produce raw materials and semi-manufactured goods for German industry. Another of Norway's advantages was its access to fishing, which could provide the basis for a modern fishing industry. However, Norway should not become an industrial society. Primary industry would provide the foundation and Norway would remain a peripheral nation.

The basis for this was as much ideological as economic. The farmers and fishermen harboured particularly pure and valuable Germanic bloodlines. They should therefore become the mainstay of a society built on traditional values and counteract the changes that resulted from industrialization. The fascists dreamt of the old peasant society with strong links of kinship to the soil, at the same time as they were promoting modernization and industrialization. This created a contradiction that they did not want but were unable to avoid.

The plans for a new economic zone came into being in the early years of the war, when it looked as if Germany would win and preparations should be made for the post-war period. They gradually disappeared when Germany had to concentrate all its attention and all its resources on fighting the war. Ideas about a new economic order in Europe were no longer relevant to the current situation.

Important war goods

Norway produced several goods that were of particular interest to the Germans. The output from Norwegian mines, smelting plants and the metal industry was especially important for the German arms industry. An inventory of raw materials exported to Germany between June 1940 and April 1941 includes various ores, metals, ferrous alloys, and minerals. The most important ores were iron and pyrite. Sulphur from pyrite was used to make sulphuric acid, needed for the manufacture of explosives. Aluminium and copper were the most important of the metals. Aluminium was particularly important for the aircraft industry because it is so light.

A list from 1942–3 of seventeen different priority goods is topped by molybdenum, ferrosilicon, silicomanganese, copper, and aluminium. Molybdenum was a particularly sought-after metal, used to reinforce the steel in German armour plating. The deposits of molybdenum in the mines at Knaben in Kvinesdal were among the most important in the German-controlled zone. The manufacture of many products was largely based on supplies of ores coming from abroad for processing. This applied to aluminium, zinc, nickel, and several ferrous alloys such as ferrochromium, ferromanganese and silicomanganese. The cheap Norwegian hydropower was what made it worthwhile to transport the ores to Norway for processing.

The Germans always tried to keep the manufactured output of all these products as high as possible. The manufacturers stood near the head of the queue for their share of coal and the necessary raw materials. Nevertheless, the Germans did experience big problems in keeping production up, and in most areas, it sank. Particularly striking was the fall in the production of molybdenum, despite its importance for the war. The output of some products did increase, however.

Heavy water was a potentially important product for the German war effort. This was produced at Norsk Hydro's works at Vemork, near Rjukan. The quantity was small in comparison with other things that Norsk Hydro produced and relative to the production of other important war goods. But heavy water was significant because it could be used as a moderator in nuclear experiments that might lead to the development of an atomic weapon.

The Allies considered the war goods industry in Norway so important that they attacked it, either by bombing or by sabotage. The British Special Operations Executive (SOE) and the Norwegian High Command in exile executed as many as seven sabotage actions to stop the transport of sulphur and pyrite from Løkken mine to the export harbour in Thamshavn. The Fosdalen iron ore mines in Nord-Trøndelag and the power station in Glomfjord that provided electricity to the aluminium factory there were subjected to sabotage in autumn 1942. In January 1943 the Stordø Kisgruber company's mine that produced pyrite was attacked. In November of the same year, the same thing happened at Arendal Smelting Plant in Eydehavn, which produced siliconcarbide. The Knaben mines were bombed in spring and autumn 1943. Factories on Herøya important for the production of light metal were bombed, and the heavy water plant at Rjukan was both sabotaged and bombed in 1943.

Mining, smelting plants and the metal industry formed one part of the economy that was of special interest to the Germans. The other was fish. In 1943–4 around half of Germany's fish supplies came from Norway. This was an important source of protein as meat and other protein-rich products became scarce. Germany also received almost a hundred per cent of Norway's canned fish, which was very important as field rations. The Germans had little interest in the traditional salted and dried fish that Norway had always exported. They wanted to invest in more advanced technology and fishfreezing. There had not been much frozen fish in Norway before, but now it was being introduced on a large scale by the Germans.

Wehrmacht's building and construction programme

International law allows an occupying authority to require the local population to provide for the needs of the army of occupation. There were already 220,000 German troops in Norway by autumn 1940. This number fell, then rose again, but the average count was about 300,000 men, equivalent to 10 per cent of the Norwegian population. They needed food and clothes, which had to come from Norwegian producers, among others. The hundreds of thousands of soldiers had to be paid. Norway paid up. It was not, however, the provisioning of the army of occupation that came to absorb the most resources, but the Germans' military and militarily associated building and construction programme. This more than anything else stands out as the heaviest burden on the Norwegian economy during the war.

For a start, accommodation had to be found for all the 220,000 soldiers. Most of them would need to be housed in barracks, and the barracks had to be built. The building programme was under German management, but the work was done mostly by Norwegian companies and Norwegian workers. For Norwegian companies in the building sector, this was a boom time. Timber merchants, planing mills and sawmills had full order books. Forestry was the only large branch of Norwegian industry that produced much more during the occupation than in the pre-war years. Stove manufacturers made thousands of stoves for the new camps. Furniture factories flourished, equipping the barracks with tables and chairs. Electricians ran cables into the new buildings and plumbing firms were kept busy fitting pipes and water supplies. Workers streamed to the building sites in their tens of thousands.

The building of roads and railways in both north and south Norway needed big resources. The same applied to the building of *Festung Norwegen*, which required not only barracks but mainly huge amounts of building materials for the army's and the navy's gun emplacements, bunkers, trenches, and barbed wire fences. New airbases for the *Luftwaffe* also claimed their share of the resources, as did the building of U-boat bases, harbour facilities and shipyards that the Germans used for shipbuilding and repair. The forestry industry delivered boards and planks for shuttering and scaffolding. The metal industries provided iron for reinforcing concrete, plus spikes and nails. Vast quantities of cement were required, and the three cement factories at Slemmestad, Brevik and Kjøpstad worked to full capacity.

The German building and construction programme needed finance, building materials and labour. In the first year of the occupation, the Germans acquired these resources mainly from the Norwegian economy, which came under severe pressure. The pressure became even stronger after the British raids around Christmas 1941 and Hitler's decision to speed up the building of *Festung Norwegen*. It then became clear that organization needed to be improved and more resources brought from Germany.

Responsibility for this was given to *Organisation Todt (OT)*, a semi-military building and construction organization named after its first head, Fritz Todt. *OT* was gradually awarded contracts for big construction projects in the German-occupied regions. It was given the task of building the Atlantic Wall and eventually controlled over 1.4 million prisoners of war and forced labourers. When Todt was appointed minister of armaments and war production, his power increased further. After his sudden death in February 1942, Albert Speer took over his role. Under Speer, the Ministry of Armaments and *OT* grew to become one of the big power blocs in Hitler's Germany, in third place after the *Wehrmacht* and the *SS*.

Speer immediately set up several command groups under *OT* in the occupied regions. *Einsatzgruppe Wiking* would cover Norway and Denmark, from headquarters established in Oslo in April 1942. Willi Henne was head of *Einsatzgruppe Wiking* and also held an appointment in the *Reichskommissariat*, where he was head of the technical department. Until then *OT*'s only project in Norway had been to build a U-boat bunker in Trondheim. *Wiking* was now given responsibility for nearly all military construction work, following a special instruction that Speer received from Hitler on 13 May 1942. The instruction illustrates the policy that funding, building materials and manpower in the form of prisoners of war should now be provided from Germany. Funding would therefore come from the German war budget. Building materials would be given priority for shipment from Germany. The *Wehrmacht* was given the added duty of providing guards to supervise the prisoners. The establishment of *Wiking* created an institutional framework for German building work in Norway. The organization took control of more and more of this activity, until from autumn 1944 onwards *OT* almost had a monopoly of building.

OT worked with a combination of German administration and private capital. German companies were contracted to provide their own machines, tools and a nucleus of German workers. *OT* saw to it that the companies got enough building materials and the necessary workforce, which largely consisted of prisoners of war and civilian forced labourers. By July 1942 over 200 German companies had signed contracts with *OT*. Numerous Norwegian building firms took part in *Einsatzgruppe Wiking*'s programme as subcontractors, making their own staff available to the German firms and to *OT*. Few of the Norwegian firms used prisoners of war, though some did make use of civilian compulsory labour.

The failure of a giant project

Hermann Göring had had an ulterior motive in recommending Terboven as *Reichskommissar* in Norway. Göring wanted to make use of Norwegian hydroelectric power to build up a light metal industry to supply the *Luftwaffe*, and he wanted Terboven to take part in this. Soon after Terboven's appointment, Göring sent his man Heinrich Koppenberg to Norway to start setting up the industry. This would mainly consist of aluminium works, but as another light metal, magnesium, was also included in the plans, the project had a composite name, 'light metal industry'. These plans fitted well with the ideas of the new economic zone, in making use of a distinctively Norwegian asset.

From the start, the light metal project was characteristic of Göring's way of working: big plans, big enterprises, big words, and great impatience; but poor execution, poor understanding of local circumstances and poor administration. The project was to be brought into being by the combined work of German public administration, in the form of the *Luftwaffe* and the Four-Year Plan, and big German companies. The overall leadership of the project lay or was meant to lie, with the administration, while the companies were responsible for developing it. The commercial firms made alliances with competing branches of the administration while also competing between themselves.

On 3 December 1940 a German company was set up with capital from the Air Ministry. This was known as *Nordische Aluminiumgesellschaft*, abbreviated to 'Nordag'. In order to have more control over the development, Terboven insisted that a daughter company be set up in Norway. So, A/S *Nordag* was founded on 3 May 1941 as a Norwegian company but with German capital. This was the organization that would now see to the building up of the new industry.

The German company IG Farben and Norsk Hydro started their own light metal project. Norsk Hydro was interested in entering the aluminium market and was confident that the raw material for aluminium production, aluminium oxide, could be produced from Norwegian labradorite, with which they had experimented. The two parties agreed to create a Norwegian company, *Nordisk Lettmetall A/S*, which was registered the day before the Norwegian *Nordag* company. The share capital came one-third each from *Nordag*, IG Farben and Norsk Hydro. To be able to take part in the new company Norsk Hydro increased its share capital, with the Germans having a controlling share. A group of Norwegian capitalists, known as the Oslo consortium, also took part in the share issue. IG Farben would construct a factory for magnesium and aluminium at Herøya, while Norsk Hydro would build a factory to produce aluminium oxide. Norsk Hydro would also develop the power station at the Mår watercourse in Telemark.

The plans for the light metal project were ambitious and included several construction sites throughout the country. By summer 1941 work was proceeding at full pace on the factory at Herøya and the power station at Glomfjord, but construction of the aluminium factory there had hardly begun. Work was about to begin in other places such as Saudasjøen, Tyin, Årdal, Osa, Ulvik and Eitrheim.

Nordisk Lettmetall A/S was a well-managed business. The magnesium factory at Herøya was almost complete and would probably have been a success if the Allies had not considered it such an important military target that it was bombed by American planes in summer 1943. The factory was destroyed, and the Germans did not want it rebuilt. Progress was more difficult for *Nordag*, which hit one problem after another. The plans were too ambitious, the construction sites were too numerous and more and more bottlenecks delayed the building programme. After New Year 1941–2, the plans were gradually reduced. As minister of armaments, Speer decided to concentrate activity on the projects that could be completed before the war ended.

The mismanagement in *Nordag* eventually came under severe criticism, and in spring 1943, at Terboven's instigation, the firm was investigated for squandering public resources and it was arranged that a commission from *RSHA* and *Kripo* would come to Oslo in May to investigate the case in more detail. The only one of *Nordag's* projects that came to completion was the factory at Sauda which started production in January 1944, but even here there were great difficulties because the power station was not ready and there were shortages of coal and bauxite. The factory, therefore, had to close at the end of the year. At the same time, the existing aluminium industry was producing progressively less than it had produced before the war. Alongside the Polar Railway, *Nordag* was the leading example in Norway of the haphazard, chaotic and unplanned way the war economy could evolve under the German *Führer* government.

Run on the National Bank

Nothing illustrates the German pressure on Norway's economy better than the figures for the financing of the German projects in Norway. When the German troops came to Norway in April 1940 they brought their own money, which had the rather long name of *Reichskreditkassenscheine*. This would be legal tender that the Germans could use to pay for Norwegian goods or services. Norges Bank was reluctant to have this money in circulation alongside Norwegian kroner. The National Bank was concerned that it would lose control of the money supply and that monetary policy would be endangered. The bank, therefore, thought that it would be better if the Germans received Norwegian money directly from the bank. The Germans could simply go to Norges Bank and withdraw the money they needed. The sum would be entered on a special Occupation Account, and there was no ceiling on how much the Germans could receive. The *Wehrmacht*, the *Reichskommissariat*, the *SS* and *OT* all made use of this arrangement.

The *Wehrmacht* immediately started using large amounts. Money was needed not only for the soldiers' pay and subsistence but also for the German building programme. As recently as 1939–40 the state's annual budget had been 714 million kroner. By October 1940 the Germans had already used well over that amount. Money was pouring out of Norges Bank, the directors were frightened about this and even the economic experts in the *Reichskommissariat* became worried. They feared galloping inflation. Terboven took the matter in hand. In autumn 1940 there were several high-level meetings both in Norway and in Germany including representatives from the *Wehrmacht,* the German Finance Ministry, the Economic Ministry and the German *Reichsbank*. The experts tried to calculate how much of the occupation costs the Norwegian economy could bear, and a sum of 500 million kroner per year was proposed.

Nothing came of this at first. All proposals came up against the stone wall of the *Wehrmacht*'s opposition to reducing the drawings from Norges Bank. Falkenhorst referred to the commission he had from Hitler to secure the occupied territory as quickly as possible, which would inevitably cost a lot of money. He paid little heed to the advice of the economic experts, and the *Wehrmacht* continued to make large monthly withdrawals from the bank. These reached a peak in 1941, before flattening out as the Germans themselves took over more of the financing.

By the time the war ended, the occupying power had used 11,000 million kroner from Norges Bank, equivalent to 7.8 thousand million kroner in 1939 values. In other words, the Germans had used 130 million kroner per month, which was more than a Norwegian pre-war budget for 5 months. This was a lot, not only when measured in money but also when assessed in relation to the gross national product. The withdrawals from the Occupation Account were equivalent to about a third of the gross national product during every year of the occupation. The enormous withdrawals led to Norway paying out more per inhabitant than other countries. Norway's outgoings were double the average for occupied countries in Western Europe.

The demand for labour

The massive funding required for the Germans' building projects is not the only evidence of the enormous resources the Germans applied to their war effort in Norway. The demand for labour provides further proof. By October 1940 there were already 58,000 Norwegians working for the Germans – 15,000 for the army, 6,000 for the navy and 20,000 for the air force, plus 17,000 working on construction sites for the *Reichskommissariat*, building roads and military installations. The workers streamed in because there were jobs to be had and they were attracted by high wages. During the winter of 1940–1, a thousand Norwegians moved to Germany to work there, but that came to an end as they were all needed in their homeland where the occupying power even had to draw in extra workers. What applied to the financing of German projects and to the supply of building materials also applied to the labour force: The Germans had to supply this occupied region with extra resources from elsewhere.

The *Wehrmacht* wanted more and more workers for its construction sites, at the same time as *Nordag* and *Nordisk Lettmetall A/S* also needed labour. Terboven had reason to be concerned. He wanted to facilitate the conditions for military projects in the occupied zone, but he also had a responsibility to protect the economy to avoid public unrest and labour disputes. Uncontrolled movement of Norwegian workers could cause serious damage to the Norwegian economy. Terboven wanted the labour force to be controlled in a way that would have regard to both German and Norwegian needs.

The result was a series of decrees that did just that – regulated the labour market and directed the labour force towards priority areas. The most important and most comprehensive decree was issued on 9 July 1941. This instituted compulsory labour and established that the Labour Directorate could direct people's employment. Tens of thousands of Norwegians were conscripted in this way up until the end of the war, allocated to either German or Norwegian workplaces. Of 56,000 labour conscripts in 1942, 36,000 were sent to work in farming and forestry, and 17,000 to German construction sites as an addition to the voluntary building workers. On 22 February 1943, the law on national labour service was passed to improve the effectiveness of the labour force, by conscripting workers who were not being fully utilized. As a result, in 1943 as many as 85,000 workers were conscripted in accordance with various laws and regulations. The police were used to enforce conscription. Stapo and *Gestapo* both arrested people who failed to turn up at their appointed workplace or who abandoned their job.

The regulation of the Norwegian labour market did not release for the Germans all the labour force they needed, and they had to resort to bringing in workers from abroad. In July 1941 the *Wehrmacht* in Norway asked for the first time to be provided with prisoners of war for the labour force. The first batch of 3,300 arrived in autumn 1941. This was far fewer than the *Wehrmacht* had hoped for, and the military continued to press for more. The work speeded up when Speer took over, and the transfer of workers to Norway increased sharply. Between them, Speer's command centre and the *Wehrmacht* High Command arranged for 100,000 Soviet prisoners of war to be sent to Norway in the course of the war.

Responsibility for the prisoners of war and their camps lay with the *Wehrmacht*. OT supplied them with food, clothing, and most of the tools. German soldiers kept watch and escorted the prisoners to and from work, but OT personnel also served as guards. On the workplaces, the work was led by engineers from OT, personnel from German or Norwegian companies, or professionals from institutions such as the Norwegian State Railways or the National Roads Authority which were responsible for some of the construction works.

The prisoners lived in their camps, isolated from the Norwegian public, and they were forbidden to have any contact with Norwegians. The work camps were so widely distributed around the country that many Norwegians caught a glimpse of the prisoners on their march to or from the workplace or at work. Despite the ban, there was a certain amount of contact between Norwegians and prisoners. The Norwegians tried to help the prisoners in various ways and received small homemade presents from them in return. The guards partly turned a blind eye to this.

The way the prisoners were treated varied greatly according to what sort of German boss they were working under, but in general, they were treated badly. They were not to be eliminated, as they formed a workforce, but their accommodation was poor, their clothes scanty, their food wretched and their workload hard. The guards' handling of the prisoners could be brutal, exacerbated by the Germanic disdain of the Slavs. Fourteen thousand Soviet prisoners of war perished on Norwegian soil or in Norwegian waters during the war.

The Germans didn't set up extermination camps in Norway – with one exception. One of the first heads of the German Order Police in Norway was appointed head of the SS and Police in Serbia in January 1942. After a couple of months in the post there he made an offer to Rediess and Terboven to send Yugoslav prisoners to Norway. A total of 4,040 Yugoslav prisoners, mostly Serbs, arrived between June 1942 and March 1943. These prisoners were distributed in work camps in north Norway and near Trondheim. They were not categorized as regular soldiers, but as partisans and 'bandits', and they were destined not only to work hard but to be worked to death. The Yugoslavs were guarded by German Order Police and Norwegians from SS-Vaktbataljon Norge. The Germans kept watch inside the camps and the Norwegians outside and at the workplaces.

Both treated the prisoners brutally. Sick prisoners were executed en masse, and others were flogged to death. Many died from exhaustion, and others froze to death. Of the 2,600 prisoners who arrived in the first 9 months, 72 per cent died. In March 1943 the Wehrmacht took over responsibility for the prisoners, who were now for the first time treated as prisoners of war, in fact better than the Soviet prisoners of war. The death rate among the prisoners fell dramatically. They were no longer destined for extermination.

A particular group of German prisoners was also treated harshly. Most of the 2,600 who were sent to Norway were soldiers whom German military courts had sentenced to Zuchthaus. These prisoners were put to work in a number of different camps in north Norway. Only the Yugoslavs were treated worse than the German prisoners. The numbers are too uncertain to calculate a death rate, but the German Zuchthaus prisoners were evidently treated worse than the Soviet prisoners of war.

The imported workforce did not consist only of prisoners. Around 20,000–30,000 were civilian forced labourers from several nationalities. Most of these were from the Soviet Union, including several hundred women, plus many Eastern Europeans and some from Western European countries. The degree of compulsion varied. The civilian workers did not live under guard behind barbed wire fences. They could move around freely, they received wages and they were allowed to travel back to their homelands on leave. They had nevertheless been recruited against their will, and they could not simply resign from their employment. Eleven thousand Danes who were also employed in Norway were treated almost as normal employees.

The hierarchy in workplaces reflected racist Nazi ideology. At the bottom were the Yugoslav and Soviet prisoners of war. The Polish prisoners of war were on the next level above. On top were the German employees or the voluntary or conscripted Western European workers.

The regulated economy

The Norwegian wartime economy was a shortage economy. Most goods and many services were in short supply. The only thing there was enough of was money. Such a situation easily gives rise to imbalances. Demand for scarce goods creates an inflationary pressure that can quickly run out of control. The law of supply and demand does not function well in a shortage economy. German and Norwegian authorities, therefore, took control at an early stage, and the controls steadily became more and more extensive. Commercial relationships were restricted by rules and regulations, decrees, and prohibitions. The authorities' aim in imposing these regulations was to control how the economy developed as a whole. The shortage economy became more and more a regulated economy.

Several sections in the *Reichskommissariat* and several departments and directorates within the Norwegian administration negotiated and worked together on the arrangements for regulating the primary industries. The Ministry of Supply with its Directorate of Provisioning and Rationing led by Nikolai Schei was particularly important. The ministry and the directorate had been created after the outbreak of war in September 1939, because of experiences in the First World War when the authorities had been slow to start dealing with the question of supplies. The Norwegians did not want to make the same mistake again, and large stores were bought in. The Directorate of Provisioning and Rationing set up local supplies committees throughout the country, to provide a mechanism for rationing and distribution. These committees came to play a key role in carrying out the regulation of supplies agreed centrally by the Germans and the Norwegians.

Fish was of interest to both the German and the Norwegian authorities. The Germans wanted it for export to Germany, where protein-rich food was much needed. They made an early start on their fish-processing factories and direct purchasing from the fishermen. At the same time, the *Wehrmacht* in Norway wanted fish for its troops. The Norwegian Ministry of Supply was equally interested because it was thought that fish would come to be an important component of the Norwegian diet. The ministry negotiated with the *Reichskommissariat* about arrangements that would cover exports to Germany, deliveries to the *Wehrmacht* in Norway and supplies to Norwegian consumers. The Germans always held the trump card in these negotiations: control over the import of foodstuffs that Norway had too little of and had to import, mainly grain but also sugar and fat. They also controlled the import of fuel oil that the fishermen needed for their boats. The Germans, therefore, had ample means to put pressure on the Norwegians.

Norwegian authorities tried to facilitate better conditions for the fishing industry. This required negotiation and co-operation with German institutions. The fishermen would need to get the necessary supplies of fuel oil, net, tar, glass floats and other equipment. The *Wehrmacht* would need to be persuaded to modify the many military activities that impeded fishing. The fishermen needed to be allocated fishing grounds outside the minefields and safe routes into quays in harbours that were under guard.

Agriculture provided the authorities with better opportunities to issue regulations and decrees that would increase production. The first order was to extend the acreage in use, and the second specified that the arable acreage was to be increased first and foremost. Then came regulations about how much of the yield the farmers must hand over to the authorities for a fixed price. The farming family could have the remainder for their own use. Inspectors travelled through the farms to supervise what was being produced and what was being delivered. They didn't note everything, because it is not so easy to check what is happening on a farm, and they also turned a blind eye to some things. The farmers held back more or less of their production with a view to having more for their own use, sale under the counter or gifts to friends and family.

Increased production and compulsory sale were one thing, but allocation and distribution of the products were another. All the agricultural products were to be consumed in Norway. The question was just how to divide it between the Germans and the Norwegians. The situation was further complicated by the great variety of the products. Hay and straw are not easily damaged and can be stored in large quantities for a long time, but eggs soon spoil, and milk quickly turns sour.

In the discussion about the allocation of agricultural products, the *Reichskommissariat* and the Norwegian authorities were to a certain degree united in opposition to the *Wehrmacht*. The way things developed was the same as we have seen in connection with the run on Norges Bank. Initially, the German military purchased from Norwegian producers without any form of regulation. They paid with the money they received from the Norges Bank, and they paid well. This was something that both the *Reichskommissariat* and the Norwegian authorities wanted to avoid. Both wanted production and marketing to be controlled in order to achieve a system of allocation that had regard to both German and Norwegian interests. This was the basic question. How much should the Germans have and how much should the Norwegians? The negotiations ended with agreements that gave most to the Germans but also recognized Norwegian requirements.

The policy that the Directorate of Provisioning and Rationing followed along with the *Reichskommissariat* meant that the directorate disapproved of Norwegians trying to earn money by selling products directly to the Germans. Direct marketing such as this undermined the control of production and distribution. The directorate also disapproved of attempts to conceal products. The patriotic justification for sabotage like this was that the more products people hid away, the less there was for the Germans. Nikolai Schei's policy was the opposite. Norwegian interests were best served by a unified Norwegian organization having control of all production and distribution. This gave the best possibilities for manoeuvre and the best conditions for asserting oneself in the competition for resources. It also gave the directorate an opportunity to go behind the Germans' backs and allow goods to pass along unauthorized channels.

The authorities also wanted to increase forestry production and they, therefore, decided how much timber should be cut each year. This production target was divided among the districts and the individual woodland owners, who were then required to produce what they had been allocated. In contrast with the pre-war years, there was little thought of exporting timber products as these were in high demand within Norway, both by the Germans and by the Norwegians. More wood went for burning than before since coal and coke were no longer available for domestic use and the *Wehrmacht* needed wood for the stoves in its barracks. As a substitute for petrol, which was also no longer available, wood was used in generators mounted on lorries and buses to produce wood gas. The timber-processing industry still needed timber to make paper and cellulose. However, what interested the Germans most of all and from the very start was building materials from Norwegian sawmills and planing mills, which worked flat out to satisfy the requirements of the German building and construction works. The Germans made early demands for this market to be regulated.

The system that was built up on the Norwegian side to administer the regulated economy had a public and a private or semi-private component. The public component consisted of the various departments, directorates, and government offices – the whole apparatus of public administration. The other component was various combinations of business interests who co-operated with the officials.

The economy beyond the primary industries was also regulated. Tight price control was introduced early on, which was decisive in combatting the strong inflationary pressure created by the overwhelming German use of money. The Price Directorate was set up in autumn 1940, along with a special pricing police and a pricing court that would ensure adherence to the prices set by the authorities. They held the black market in check but could not eliminate it. Wage control and later wage freezes were introduced to keep wages down. The directorate also tried gradually to have wage regulation introduced on the German building and construction sites, where wage levels had originally risen out of control. Strikes were forbidden.

Controls were imposed on foreign exchange, imports and exports. This gave the *Reichskommissariat* the mechanism it needed to regulate the import of goods. Among these goods, coal was particularly important both for the *Wehrmacht* and for the Norwegians. The import quota was decided in Berlin. What had to be decided in Norway was how the imported coal was to be allocated. In this question, Norwegian civilian and German military interests largely coincided. NSB got coal because the national railways were also important for transporting German troops. The coastal steamers got coal because they carried goods for the Germans. The section of industry that produced important war goods also had priority in the demand for coal.

The regulations in the shortage economy were far-reaching, but they could not prevent the rise of two informal markets that were not subjected to regulation. In a society with goods in short supply and less to be had for money, a barter economy readily developed. People traded goods for goods. One person had something the other wanted, and the other could offer the first something he needed. A barter market system developed, a system of trade without money. The newspapers were full of advertisements of items for exchange: 'Portable gramophone wanted, have gentleman's bicycle.' People who had tobacco or spirits did well in barter trading. Non-smokers acquired tobacco ration cards just to be able to use them as a means of exchange. People in towns bartered with each other and with people in the country.

The other informal market was the black market. This was a much more serious enterprise than the barter system because the black market was illegal and punishable. It was mainly the farmers who participated in the black market. It was against the law to sell agricultural products that were subject to compulsory delivery. The price police carried out checks, and if someone was caught, they would end up with confiscation of goods, fines or, in the worst case, imprisonment. The black market was frowned upon by most people, but in the shortage economy, it was inevitable. For townspeople who could afford it, there was an irresistible temptation to obtain some extra food from the country – eggs for example, or meat, which were almost unobtainable through the rationing system. Payment on the black market was generally by cash, which showed that money did have some value after all. For the farmer, the point was not necessarily to spend the cash buying goods. He might instead be concerned to pay down debt.

A successful adjustment

It is remarkable that the Norwegian economy was so easily grafted onto the German war economy and that it could be regulated so tightly without serious conflicts arising. The Germans succeeded in getting the Norwegian economy to meet a significant part of the enormous German demands. This led to a fall in the Norwegian standard of living and to depreciation in the value of buildings and equipment because of poor maintenance, but it was achieved without the situation becoming critical for the occupied population or hunger or poverty becoming widespread.

In autumn 1940, Terboven said that the limit on how much Norwegian resources the *Wehrmacht* could exploit had already been reached, and he pointed out the risk of economic collapse. Norway could not contribute more. Then it became apparent that the country was capable of providing many times what Terboven and his economic experts had predicted, without the economy collapsing.

One reason why the integration of the Norwegian economy into the German war economy went so well was that both Germany and Norway had learned from their experiences in the First World War. At that time, people had initially not had the necessary knowledge to understand the massive resource needs of modern major war and the economic change and regulation that this requires. The pressure was naturally greatest on the war economies of the combatant countries, such as Germany, but neutral countries such as Norway had also felt the painful transition from a functioning market economy to a shortage economy that required intervention and regulation.

When the Second World War broke out, the approach was different. In the first phase, the government had set up the Ministry of Supply and started extensive purchasing. In the second phase, when the occupation took place, it was already understood that a war situation required extraordinary measures. Therefore, Norwegian and German officials were able to meet each other and work together on regulating the economy. Both sides saw the need for this. So, the rise in prices during the Second World War was able to be brought under control quite differently from the First War. On the previous occasion, it had taken three years before a price directorate was set up, whereas during the occupation it was in place within six months. The cost of living rose about 150 per cent during the First World War, but little over 50 per cent in the Second World War.

Another reason was that the Germans were determined to maintain a minimum of supplies to the Norwegian population. They did not wish to pursue a policy of starvation in occupied Norway. Their relationship with NS may have played a role. Hitler had wanted to give NS an opportunity to win the population over to national socialism. So, there were limits to how far Norway could be exploited if NS were to have any chance of success. Anyway, Norway was a Germanic country, and the Norwegians could not be treated in the same way as the peoples in Russia and Eastern Europe.

It was important to have within the *Reichskommissariat* a professional economic administration that shared understanding with its Norwegian colleagues in departments, directorates, and Norges Bank. The inclusion of professionally qualified ministers in the three economic departments – Finance, Trade and Supply up until 1 February 1942 – strengthened this professionalism. In the first period, it was possible to draw from the reserve stores. For the first time in twenty years, production capacity and the workforce could be fully utilized. In other words, the Germans could start the occupation by taking Norwegian means of production into use without entailing painful adjustments.

Brutal German suppression was also an important part of the complex set of reasons. Unrest in the labour movement and a strike in Oslo in September 1941 led to a state of emergency, executions, deportations, and NS taking over The Norwegian Federation of Trade Unions. The workers didn't strike again after that. The Germans' method of payment was another key reason for their success. They did not attract the ill-will that would have arisen if they had forcibly requisitioned Norwegian goods and services on a large scale. Nor were they dependent on receiving grants from Norwegian authorities, as they could just take money out of Norges Bank. They nearly always paid the Norwegians for their goods and services, and they often paid well.

An important prerequisite for the largely frictionless alignment of the Norwegian economy was ultimately the characteristic willingness to co-operate that was present in Norwegian business and working life. This was particularly marked in the early years, which counted most when it came to joining the Norwegian economy to the German.

Norwegian collaboration

Right from the start of the occupation, the Norwegians were keen to co-operate with the Germans in economic matters. Again, part of the reason for this was Norway's experience in the First World War. The business world had realized that there was money to be made from war and that the country's official policy of neutrality did not necessarily close the door to profitable trading deals with the warring nations. On the contrary, the neutrality policy provided a necessary framework for such connections. Business people initially saw the Second World War in the same way.

Then came the occupation. This did not significantly change their attitude. Whatever the prevailing political situation, the role of business was to manufacture and trade with a view to making a profit. The economic problems of overproduction, poor sales, and fluctuating exchange rates that trade and industry had faced during the interwar years also played a part in this. The occupation provided an opportunity to be rid of the remnants of the interwar economic crisis.

However, the most important reason for the willingness to co-operate lay in the current situation. Businesses were obliged to make new trading relationships with the Germans, get orders from them and deliver goods and services. To this extent, it was a compulsory adjustment, but the Norwegians went further. During the first two years of the occupation, many people thought that Germany would emerge from the war as a victor and that Norway would in the foreseeable future be locked into a German-dominated economic bloc. So the best thing to do was to secure one's place in that system.

During the negotiations to set up the Council of the Realm the readiness for economic collaboration had a parallel in the willingness for political co-operation to establish a collaborative Norwegian government in place of the king and government in exile. This parallelism disappeared in Terboven's political revolution of 25 September 1940. A legitimate government with public support from Norwegians was no longer a political reality in the occupied region. The willingness for economic co-operation did not disappear, however. The events of 25 September did not create a fault line in the economic field or in the attitudes of business leaders as it did in the political field.

One piece of evidence for the widespread willingness for economic co-operation in the early years is to be found in the foundation of the German Chamber of Commerce in Norway (*Deutsche Handelskammer in Norwegen*) on 19 November 1940. The chamber was closely connected to the *Reichskommissariat* and planning for it had started in August on Terboven's initiative. The Federation of Norwegian Industries was particularly keen for it to be set up, and prominent Norwegian and German business leaders took part in the preliminary working party. At the time of its foundation, the chamber already had 850 members, 500 of whom were Norwegian companies or individuals. By 1 March 1941 the numbers had increased to 833 Norwegian and 512 German members.

The attendance at the foundation ceremony in the Rococo Room in the Grand Hotel and the reception in the evening is at least as telling. From the German side, there were Terboven, Falkenhorst and Rediess, plus many other representatives of the state, party, and business both in Germany and in Norway. From the Norwegian side, there were not only many of the government ministers appointed by Terboven (both members and non-members of NS) but also: Nicolai Rygg, governor of Norges Bank; Rolf Stranger, mayor of Oslo; the president of the Federation of Norwegian Industries; the president of the Federation of Trade Guilds; the managing director of Norwegian Railways; the managing director of Norsk Hydro and many others from the public administration and from business. The only major business organizations that chose not to attend were the Federation of Norwegian Commercial Associations and the Norwegian Insurance Federation.

The Chamber of Commerce is of interest mainly as a sign of the times rather than as a significant player, as it came to have only a limited role in commercial life. It was created when people were anticipating a new economic zone (*Grossraumwirtschaft*) and the founders were aiming to promote trade and co-operation between German and Norwegian companies within this zone. As economic activity became more and more tightly regulated, voluntary co-operation between German and Norwegian firms came to play a steadily lesser role. The regulations determined which directions trade would take and how it would develop.

In late autumn 1942, Terboven was still able to pull the same strings among the same groups as at the foundation of the Chamber of Commerce two years earlier. With help from the chamber, he invited a number of business leaders to a social gathering in his residence at Skaugum on 8 December. Terboven, Rediess and Fehlis were present, along with several NS people, but none of the government ministers. The business representatives were mainly from industry, including such leading figures as the managing director of Hydro, the managing director of Borregaard, the director of Askim Rubber Factory, a couple of bank directors and the director of Siemens – a total of sixteen people who were not members of NS. This shows that there was still a desire to co-operate commercially. People in the business world were willing to accept a dinner invitation to what had been the pre-war residence of the crown prince, where both NS and the German civil and military establishment were represented.

The fortunes of world war changed that winter, and one can also sense a change in attitudes within business and commerce. There were reactions to the meeting at Skaugum. A directive was issued against such gatherings. This appears to have had some effect. When invitations were received to a further meeting at Skaugum on 18 February, the guests conferred beforehand and sought advice from civil resistance groups. However, they accepted the invitation and the dinner with nineteen non-Nazi business leaders did take place. One reason for the businessmen turning up at Skaugum may have been a slight hope of persuading Terboven to soften his policy. If so, Terboven did respond to their hopes. Six days after the gathering, the newspapers were able to report that he had reprieved ten men from Kristiansand.

Initially, the willingness to co-operate was just as great among the Norwegian employees as it was among the employers. Again, the experiences from the interwar years were important. There was still a lot of unemployment at the end of the 1930s. The Germans offered well-paid work on their sites, and the workers readily accepted the offer and streamed to the German building and construction sites in their tens of thousands. Even after the many laws and regulations controlling access to labour came into force, many Norwegians were employed at German workplaces without compulsion.

Economic resistance

The attitude to economic interaction with the Germans and working on German building and construction sites changed during the second half of the war. It was no longer so obvious that it was acceptable to work with the Germans. Economic resistance became part of The Home Front. This type of resistance could not demonstrate spectacular deeds or come to play the same role in the national consciousness as the victories in the civil and military resistance.

There were two forms of economic resistance. One was about resistance to the German use of the Norwegian labour force. Workers stopped turning up at German workplaces or abandoned work. Admittedly, thoughts of the national interest were often not the main motive. People left because working conditions on the German sites were often wretched, with long working hours, rough and leaky sheds, poor food and difficult employers. But resistance could also be initiated by the organized Resistance Movement, as when the communists started boycotting compulsory labour conscription for the first time in the summer of 1942. The resistance to compulsory labour became stronger after the leadership of the civil resistance movement launched its campaign against the law on the national labour service in spring 1943.

The other form of resistance on the economic front was silent sabotage. This consisted of working less, using poor workmanship and avoiding making deliveries to the Germans. When the communists set about creating national committees within the firms, their intention was for the employers and the employees to agree together about how they could organize silent sabotage. In 1942–3 illegal organizations were set up with silent sabotage as one of their aims. In autumn 1943 the illegal labour movement issued a directive to delay German orders with companies, and the following spring the illegal industrial leadership encouraged employers to sabotage deliveries to the Germans. In autumn 1944, the twenty commands from The Home Front Leadership included this instruction: 'He who other than being compelled by the circumstances makes means of production, goods or labour available to the enemy is fighting on the enemy's side along with NS. Let him know what you think of him.'

It is inherent in silent sabotage that it is difficult to measure its extent. There can, however, be no doubt that quite a lot of silent sabotage was carried out in the second half of the war. It was accepted nationally as respectable to maintain a slow work pace and do poor quality work if one was working for the Germans. One sign that silent sabotage was widespread was the concern aroused by poor morale among workers and problems in many workplaces after the war when the country needed to be built up again.

The economic resistance did not aim to halt all supplies to the Germans or stop all work for them. Production of goods and services had to continue, to meet the basic needs of the occupied population. But the supply of goods and labour to the Germans was not considered so legitimate and routine as it had been in the early years, and it was more liable to be criticized. The directives urging economic resistance gradually took effect. There was increasing ill-will against those who enriched themselves by their economic co-operation with the Germans. Terms of abuse such as 'Barracks Barons' were applied to such collaborators.

Resistance and collaboration lived side by side, in both economic and administrative spheres. Silent sabotage was the hidden, illegal side of the normal work for the Germans.

The Directorate of Provisioning and Rationing within the Ministry of Supply negotiated with the Germans while at the same time manipulating the statistics to gain advantages. Supplies were siphoned off to The Resistance Movement, and the department issued thousands of fake ration cards to hand over to Milorg. Railway personnel secretly conveyed illegal material through the lines of communication that they operated every day for the benefit of both the occupiers and the occupied population. Intelligence organizations such as XU depended on having employees within the administration as sources of information that was significant both for The Resistance Movement at home and for the authorities abroad. Blowing up a factory important for war production required detailed knowledge which had to be acquired through someone who worked there and who therefore could be said to be functioning as an economic collaborator.

Problematic accounting

Soon after the liberation, the social economists Odd Aukrust and Petter Jakob Bjerve published their book *What the War Cost Norway*. When they wrote it, they had a perception that was common at that time – that the war had cost a lot, and that this must be shown in the accounts. They were thinking about possible reparations from Germany. From that point of view, it could be advantageous to use rather big numbers. They probably also had it in mind to motivate people to make an extra contribution towards post-war reconstruction.

The authors took as one of their starting points the high total of the Occupation Account. They adjusted this a little by adding in several requisitions the Germans had imposed and making a deduction for the import excess in the Norwegian balance of foreign trade. They came thus to the conclusion that the Germans had used Norwegian goods and services to the value of 7.8 thousand million pre-war kroner. They increased this sum by adding in a further five billion kroner for war damage, lack of maintenance and deterioration of buildings and machinery – fixed capital depreciation. Finally, they reckoned that if Norway had avoided occupation the national income would have risen by 2 per cent per year, and they assessed this loss as 4.7 billion. They did make a cautionary reservation that they had not included the value of what the Germans had built in Norway.

Post-war history books for a long time referred to *What the War Cost Norway*, without making any attempt to evaluate the figures more closely. In more recent years, economic historians have questioned the calculations. One puzzling question has been why the economy recovered so quickly after the war. Measured in fixed value prices, the gross national product in 1946 was already on a level with 1939. Even the capital depreciation had been recovered by 1948. Historians have pointed to the durable goods that the Germans created and that Aukrust and Bjerve ignored. Well over twenty permanent airstrips were built or extended. Before the war Norwegian civil aviation was largely by seaplanes that flew only in summer. In 1945 almost the whole of the Norwegian airport network stood ready, and land-based aircraft that flew all year round could take over the routes. The Southern Railway was complete, and the work that had been done on the Northern Railway provided the basis for the extension of the line to Bodø after the war. Narrow-gauge lines were converted to broad gauge and a stretch of 210 kilometres was electrified. The Germans had extended the telephone and telegraph systems, and the number of telephones increased by 65 per cent to over 200,000.

Many roads were widened particularly National Highway 50 to Kirkenes. Twenty new power stations were put into use, and if we include eight large installations that were nearly complete when the war ended, the total generating capacity had been increased by 30 per cent. The electrical distribution network was extended, and big dams increased the capacity of the reservoirs. Several of the works in the light metal programme, particularly the one in Årdal, had progressed so far that after the war they could soon be completed and become important companies in the Norwegian aluminium industry. The Germans had also contributed something new and useful to the fishing industry with their freezing plants.

It has also been pointed out that the Germans changed the Norwegian energy policy with lasting effect. The Germans wanted a rapid increase in Norwegian hydroelectric power and they prioritized energy-intensive industry, export and big establishments. Energy-intensive industry and public supply would be co-ordinated, and construction would be financed by a combination of private and state investment. After the war, the Labour Party continued this type of policy to develop the power industry. More recent presentations of the histories of the railways, telecommunications, the fisheries, and Hydro demonstrate how the Germans realized existing Norwegian plans and increased the pace of development.

One difficulty with calculations such as those Aukrust and Bjerve tried to work out is that we don't know how things would have developed in different circumstances. What would have happened if the Germans had not occupied the country? The alternative development could have gone many different ways. One or two per cent, more or less – it's a matter of guesswork which number to choose.

Nobody has drawn the conclusion that Norway's domestic economy was a success during the war. The economy was operating full tilt, but large resources were used for unproductive purposes such as the maintenance of the occupying army, building barracks and the enormous development of fortifications. There was little left over for Norwegian purposes and Norwegian use. But the picture that is drawn today of the economy during the war is more nuanced than before, and it shows more clearly than before the positive aspects of the Germans' activity in Norway.

CHAPTER 9
LIFE IN AN OCCUPIED SOCIETY

After the end of the military campaign in 1940, the Norwegian population's experience of military actions was limited. In the first years of the war, the British carried out several raids on places along the Norwegian coast. Apart from these, there were no land-based military operations on Norwegian soil for a good four years. War was being waged continuously in Norwegian territorial waters, however. Land-based military operations resumed in autumn 1944 when the Soviets invaded east Finnmark and the Germans withdrew from Finnmark and Nord-Troms.

Allied bombings of military targets and militarily important industrial installations were acts of war, and they could cost lives. Soviet air attacks were frequent in north Norway. One hundred ninety-three people died in an air raid on Laksevåg in Bergen on 4 October 1944, and a further forty perished in a second raid on Bergen the same month. A raid on Oslo on New Year's Eve 1944 took seventy-seven lives, and fifty-two people were killed in the air raid on Vallø near Tønsberg on 26 April 1945. A total of 752 Norwegians died because of Allied bombing. Two large accidental explosions in German ammunition stores also accounted for fatalities. An accident in Oslo killed thirty-eight people on 19 December 1943, and ninety-four were killed by a similar explosion in Bergen on 20 April 1944.

For most Norwegians, the physical signs of the war consisted mainly of the numerous German soldiers, the military camps, the barbed wire fences with warning notices and the tank barriers in the streets of the coastal towns. *Wehrmacht* personnel were conspicuous in Norwegian towns, and in those parts of the countryside where there were camps and other military structures, especially along the coast. These were the physical manifestations of the war, constantly present as a reminder of military operations that *could* also happen in Norway.

This threatening reminder created fear, which was part of communal life under occupation. It was not the fear that civilians feel in a war zone where there are active hostilities. It was a fear of possible future hostilities, a fear that increased strongly towards the end of the war; but also, a fear of what could happen when the air-raid siren sounded and people sought protection in the air-raid shelters; or a fear of being caught up in acts of sabotage. It was a fear of being arrested, felt not only by people taking part in The Resistance Movement but also by the public because of random arrests and hostage-taking by the *Gestapo*. It was a fear that blended with two other emotions characteristic of life under occupation – a feeling of national unity and a worry about one's daily bread.

Some regulations, such as the blackout, could have a profound effect on people's daily lives throughout the whole country. Blackout curtains were compulsory on all windows.

The whole of Norway was to be covered in darkness so that Allied planes couldn't navigate by lights on the ground. The blackout also required almost complete darkening of all streets in the towns. Only a few streetlamps were left on to give out a streak of light. The imposed darkness made people fearful of going out in the evenings in the winter half of the year. People were at risk of bumping into unseen walls, tree trunks, or fenceposts. It was almost pitch black in the streets until the moon eventually shone through and the town appeared in a new and distinctive light. Life under occupation was dark in a completely literal sense.

The darkness outside had its antidote in a new intensity of life together at home within four walls. People stayed in and read more than before. The libraries lent out more books. People sang as never before. More people came together to sing – national songs, the national anthem, old working songs, or well-known songs without any special national or social content. They gathered in each other's houses to play and listen to music and to read out poems – forbidden poems by Nordahl Grieg and Arnulf Øverland and innocent poems about love and the beauties of nature.

The war also intruded as a topic of intense concern and interest. The eternal questions were: 'When will the war end?' and 'How will it end?' Many people learned a lot about European geography as they followed the progress of the war on the map. The fact that the sources of information about this were so diverse gave rise to a discussion about how to interpret them. People had to read between the lines in the censored newspapers. The alternative source, the illegal newspapers, gave the Allies' version of events and were less readily available, but they were generally considered more reliable than the censored newspapers.

All this attention to what was happening at the fronts, out there in the world, lifted people out of the enclosed space in which many felt restricted. Nobody could leave the country without special permission, which was seldom given. Inland travel was also restricted. A travel permit was needed for long journeys or for travel to the border zones. For the border zones, this was a security measure, but the Germans wanted to restrict civilian travel generally, in order to save coal. The media's limited and biased information services omitted much of the news of events that people had previously been able to read about in the papers or hear about on the radio. So, people let their thoughts and their conversations revolve around what was happening out there where war was raging.

The war also affected social relationships through the divisions that arose as part of The Resistance Movement. A basic feature of daily life was the tripartite division within which most people categorized their neighbours: jøssinger ('Patriots'), nazister ('Nazis' or 'quislings') and stripete ('Scabs' or 'Blacklegs' who supported both sides). This division was created by the majority, the 'Patriots', who were largely synonymous with 'good Norwegians' or 'The Home Front'. The 'Patriots' and the 'Nazis' diverged increasingly. The social distance that the 'Patriots' applied – mostly against the 'Nazis', less sharply and clearly against the 'Blacklegs' – penetrated more and more aspects of urban social life. In the rural areas, the relationships varied, according to how many NS members there were in the locality, how much sympathy the farmers had had for NS before the war, and how committed the leader of the local commune was to NS policies.

The 'Nazis' enjoyed certain advantages over the 'Patriots'. NS members were invited to hold office in national and local administration and other areas of public life where the party wanted to appoint its own people. They got to keep their radios while everybody else had to surrender them, and they were allowed to go hunting, which was forbidden to others. Most of them, however, experienced the same social dislocations and the same scarcities as everybody else. The ration cards were the same for everybody.

Town and country

In Norway, the Germans used about a third of the gross national product for their own purposes. There was correspondingly less available for the Norwegians to use and invest. The population was worse off. They had less to spend, and the standard of living fell. The question is whether there was any social displacement within this framework of overall regression and whether there were any exceptions, with some people better off than before.

The occupation brought two undoubted benefits. The first was an end to unemployment. For those who had been unemployed in the 1930s, the occupation brought about a socio-economic improvement. A particular rural group, forestry, and agricultural workers, who had been particularly hard hit by unemployment before, now had their conditions improved. Their wages almost doubled, and they were often paid even more when they worked on German sites. The improvement of this group's conditions and the employment of people who had previously been unemployed are what led the Norwegian historian Edvard Bull to point out 'the paradoxical result that mass poverty in Norway disappeared precisely in the years that the country became impoverished'. The number of people receiving poor relief fell every year during the occupation and continued to fall in the post-war years.

The other benefit brought about by the occupation was the abundance of money. This generated a demand that the supply of goods in the shops was not able to meet, but it also made it easier to pay down debt. Problems with debt had afflicted society in the interwar years like a nightmare. Local authorities had been placed under administration because they could not pay their debts, and farmers had had to leave their ancestral land. Now the debts were reduced or paid off, and memories of the many compulsory sales by auction before the war lost their intensity.

Better pay for forestry and agricultural workers and more money among the farmers led to an economic leveling between town and country, which was the most widespread social change that happened during the occupation. People in the country were now better off than they had been before, in comparison with townspeople. People in the towns became aware of this mainly when they saw that country people ate better than they did because they could set aside produce for their own use or lived near farmers or fishermen who could acquire produce for them. The ration cards were less significant in these circumstances. In the towns, the occupation weighed heaviest on people earning fixed incomes. Standard wages fell between April and June 1940 and remained fixed thereafter for the rest of the war, while the cost of living rose. Wages were increased in mining and shipping, and workers who turned to building and construction could reckon on increased earnings. Also, the increasing introduction of piecework contributed to an actual increase of about 10 per cent in average earnings. We know less about the earnings of white-collar workers, but they probably also rose a bit. Gift parcels and other humanitarian aid from Sweden and Denmark may have helped to some extent. So, it is not easy to be precise about the fall in the standard of living. It may have been about 30 per cent.

Did the material difference between 'middle class' and 'working class' in the towns increase or was it reduced? One question is whether there really was a social dislocation. Another is, if so, whether this affected mental attitudes and changed class consciousness. The available sources do not show that. The feelings of community, of unity, of being together in the same boat, and of facing the same enemy counteracted the feeling of social differences. The most important political fault lines came to follow not social, but rather national, boundaries. The difference between 'Nazi' and 'Patriot' was decisive. There was obviously a social protest in hostility towards the black-market sharks, war profiteers, and 'barracks barons'. But the sharp edge of the protest came from its national overtones.

Shortages and women's experience

The aspect of the regulated economy that ordinary Norwegians were most aware of, especially in the towns, was the rationing of all sorts of everyday goods. The first decisions about rationing were made when the war broke out. Then they continued one by one over five years. One type of goods after another was rationed. The authorities developed an ingenious system of rationing that customers faced day by day. They were provided at regular intervals with a ration card, which they needed to be able to buy the rationed goods. It was an offense to give or sell the card, and it was difficult to falsify. If you went to a restaurant or were admitted to the hospital, you had to take your card with you for the necessary coupons to be clipped off. In the shops, the coupons were sorted and counted, and accounts were kept for each category of goods.

Rationing requires a bureaucracy. The more extensive the rationing, the more extensive the bureaucracy. For people's day-to-day needs, institutions such as the local supply committees were at the bottom of the bureaucracy and the Ministry of Supply, later the Ministry of Trade and Industry, was at the top. The supply committees had to ensure that the inhabitants received the most essential wares. They oversaw the sales, supervised the stores and reserve stores, and, not least, were responsible for distributing the ration cards.

The basic rations, which were gradually reduced, gave a poor basis for supporting life. The calorie content fell below the needs of an average consumer. However, the nutritional value of the rations was not all that was available to sustain life. There were sources that could supplement the ration to make it a little more generous and nutritious. A certain amount extra came in help from Sweden and Denmark during the second half of the occupation. Quite a few town dwellers got further supplies from their friends and relatives in the country.

What counted for more, though, was the home growing of food. People cultivated crops in their gardens, dug up the lawn, and planted potatoes or sowed vegetables. The local councils made some of their parks available to be shared out as allotments that people could apply for. This noticeably changed the townscapes, with green belts of crops around and within the towns. Some people also kept livestock in the garden, bred rabbits, started keeping hens, or reared a pig.

Scarcity led to substitution. As there was hardly any butter and there was only a little margarine on the ration cards, cod liver oil was used instead, even though it too was rationed. Cod liver oil (known as *tran*) was drunk, added to bread dough, and used for frying. The smell of cod liver oil permeated Norwegian homes. Great ingenuity developed, with floods of recipes about everything that could be done with potatoes, turnips, and herring in straitened times. The bread available in the shops was not good, and advice was given on how to eke out flour with potatoes, fishmeal, or even seaweed if one wanted to bake at home.

The wartime scarcity created new areas for social intercourse. People queued up in front of the shops to get hold of things before they were sold out. A queue was a channel for the exchange of information and opinions. The men in the towns met in discussions about their allotments, newly dug gardens, and domestic pigs. As novices in the mysteries of agriculture, they needed to exchange their experiences. Housewives making jams and preserves needed to confer together in small groups. The conversations were dominated not by total destitution, even though there were individual instances of that, but by shortages. There was less of most things, and people came together to discuss what they could do to overcome the shortages.

The housewife's duties were heavier than before. She had most of the additional work of buying and preparing food. Much of her time was spent standing in queues to acquire what was needed from the shops. A typical queue consisted of women except for the queues at the tobacco shops, which were male territory. The housewife was also mainly responsible for the family's clothes. As time went on, there was little or no good clothing available to buy. Utility clothes made with paper yarn were hardly worth having. Instead, worn clothing had to be patched and mended to be kept in use. Old clothes were fetched from the closet and loft to be resewn. The interwar generation had been economical, and there was much that they had not thrown away. That was now all to the good. Housewives could get busy with needles and thread.

In a sense this was the real 'Home Front', and the women were honored for their part in it. London Radio praised them in a broadcast in January 1945: 'And many, many mention the women, the mothers. Nobody can forget what hardships and burdens they bear without complaint.' They were praised for their commitment to making the most of what little was available to them, and they were also praised for making it possible for other members of the family to take part in the resistance activity.

Even though the number of women employed in remunerative work increased more than the number of men in employment, both relatively and absolutely, the war did not greatly change the gender balance in society. The Germans eventually tried to increase the number of women in employment, but they didn't get very far. Few women were conscripted into obligatory work. The war reinforced the trend in the decades before and after the war that married women were housewives and their workplace was in the home.

The women's movement and feminism in the 1970s protested against the promotion of the housewife and the woman's place in the home and therefore found it difficult to take part in the tributes to women's contribution 'on The Home Front' during the war. Instead, there has in recent years been interest in women's participation in The Resistance Movement. They are to be remembered not as wives and mothers but as combatants. Several books have directed attention towards women who took part in the organized resistance. We find them, often young and unmarried, serving with the illegal press, in the underground intelligence service, or in the organizations helping people to escape. They worked as couriers or helped people in hiding, and in the illegal press, they edited, printed, or distributed the newspapers. A woman was the deputy leader of the intelligence organization XU. In Milorg it was the men who filled the ranks and who in the final year of the war carried out the acts of sabotage and assassinations, but women took part in the supporting organization around Milorg's central leadership. It was women who started the big reaction by parents against NS's youth section in spring 1942.

However, the real war was, and continued to be, the men's war. The central statistical office figures for war deaths tell their story. War deaths were fatalities because of war operations in Norway or abroad, the fight on The Home Front, or attacks on the civilian population. The statistical report gives the total war deaths as 10,262, of whom 883 were women and 9,379 were men.

Health and birth rate

One would think that war and occupation would lead to deterioration in the health of the population. The effect is not so simple, however, as illustrated by the difference of opinion between two professors of medicine who disagree on whether health was better or worse during the occupation.

Axel Strøm thinks that it improved. He writes that, with certain reservations, the death rate can be used as a measure of the health of a population. Among adults in all age groups over the age of fifteen, the death rate from illness was lower during the occupation than before. 'If we [. . .] take the death rate as an expression of the health status of the population, this would indicate that the health of adults was *better* during the war than before', he concludes. He also has an explanation of why that was so. It was due to the fall in heart and vascular diseases, especially myocardial infarction. The diet was healthier during the war than it had been before. Scarcity and rationing meant that people ate less fat, since there was hardly any butter, and margarine was tightly rationed. Therefore there were fewer cases of heart and vascular diseases.

The other professor, Anders Gogstad, maintains that it cannot be correct that health status improved. The overall death rate had been falling steadily in the years before the war, but this trend was broken between 1940 and 1945. The death rate for men was about 10 per cent higher between 1940 and 1944 than it had been in the years just before the war. For women, it stayed about the same in the first few years of the war and then varied. The higher death rate indicates that health deteriorated.

The major health problem was infectious diseases, caused by bacteria or viruses. Children were particularly vulnerable, and it was obvious that child health deteriorated. Strøm and Gogstad both agree about this. The incidence of nearly all the common infectious diseases increased sharply, with a corresponding increase in deaths. The five-to nine-year-old age group was particularly hard hit, with a death rate as much as 57 per cent higher than before the war.

Pneumonia became particularly widespread. In 1944 nearly 167,000 cases were reported. Many places experienced local epidemics. However, the disease that stands out was diphtheria. Norway has never experienced such a diphtheria epidemic as occurred during the occupation. In the late 1930s, there were 1,660 cases of diphtheria, with 55 deaths. From 1940 to 1944 the numbers rose to 48,000 cases with 1,720 deaths. In the last of the pre-war years, there had been several diphtheria epidemics in Central Europe, caused by a type of diphtheria bacillus little known in Norway. This was now brought to Norway by soldiers who had been serving on the continent or the Eastern Front, and by some of the many compulsory workers from abroad.

One of the main reasons for the increase in infectious diseases was poor nutrition weakening the immune response. Dietary deficiencies developed in many sections of the population. There wasn't famine in Norway, but there was a shortage of food. Strøm thinks that the calorie content of the diet was 10–20 per cent lower than before the war. Most people grew thinner. On the other hand, he claims that the quality of the diet was good enough, as there were sufficient proteins, minerals, and vitamins. Therefore, there were hardly any deficiency diseases. Gogstad disagrees, maintaining that the food was worse both in quantity and in quality, and he points out that there were illnesses caused by vitamin deficiency.

Sexually transmitted diseases rose sharply, especially syphilis. The German soldiers who were spread throughout the country brought the infection with them everywhere. Whereas there were 335 reported cases of syphilis in 1940, the numbers rose to 2,056 in 1943 and 1,864 in 1944. The number of women reported as infected rose much more than the number of men, but this was because in most instances the man was a German soldier whose disease was not reported to the Norwegian authorities. The German doctors in Norway attended to that.

Since 1932, there had been more and more marriages. Then the number of marriages fell each year from 1940 until liberation. This was to be expected, given the uncertainties of life under occupation and the poorer living standards. Following liberation, the number of marriages rose in 1945, rose sharply in 1946, and stayed high thereafter. Reticence disappeared when peace came.

Figure 3 The Norwegian state in exile controlled a navy, an air force, and an army, but the leading section of the 'fighting forces' was the merchant fleet. This was the part that made the biggest contribution to the Allied war effort. This Norwegian ship is crossing the Atlantic in convoy in autumn 1941, its deck loaded with planes. © KRIGSARKIVET/NTB.

The trend in births was quite the opposite. The population increased by 125,000 during the occupation, and this was mainly because of the sharp increase in the number of births. This is the most striking feature of the demographic changes during the occupation. There was still some restraint, however, prior to the famous 'Baby boom' in 1946. In that year, a record was set that has never been broken: 70,727 live births. Many couples had obviously been waiting for peace to come.

There is something fascinating about the population curves that show the long, continuing trends of demographic change. Right throughout the war years, women gave birth as never before. This more than made up for the 10,000 war deaths. Military operations and occupation did not seriously disturb the continuation of family lineages in occupied Norway. To do that, the war would need to have hit a lot harder than it did, with widespread fighting, massacres, famine, or major epidemics. This was not the case.

PART III
WAR AND RESISTANCE

In a sense, Norway was divided into three parts. The first part was the Norwegian state in exile that was fighting the war in the wider world. The second was the non-Nazi public at home who resisted the occupation regime set up by the Germans and the Norwegian NS Party. The third was the illegitimate Norway – NS Norway and the NS state – that supported the German war effort and fought for a National Socialist Revolution. This tripartite division may be a small footnote in the annals of the world war, but The Resistance Movement at home and the Norwegians serving in the war abroad are towering landmarks in the history of Norway.

CHAPTER 10
NORWAY IN EXILE

When the British cruiser HMS *Devonshire* brought the Norwegian king and government and officers and officials to the port of Greenock in Scotland on 10 June 1940, something unique in Norwegian history occurred. There was no longer one Norway, but there were two: 'Norway at home' and 'Norway abroad'. It is, of course, nothing new in Norwegian history for Norwegians to be found beyond the bounds of Norway. The novelty was that one part of the state left its territory behind and established itself on another nation's territory. Two of Norway's most important institutions of state went into exile, where they would operate outside Norway for five years.

The great majority of Norwegians still lived in Norway at home, which was ruled by an occupying force. The Norwegian state abroad could not govern the land it had left. Nevertheless, Norway abroad would play an important role in Norwegian history. The history of these times can therefore not be written without including – to put it a little paradoxically – both a Norway outside Norway and a Norway inside Norway. The main difference was that Norway abroad was a nation at war on the Allied side. There is a direct connection between the resistance that the government declared in April 1940 plus the campaign that followed with the war that the government then fought for five years outside Norway. Occupied Norway was never at war in the traditional sense. Norway abroad was.

A major trend in the development of the two Norways is their gradual rapprochement. In 1940 they were far apart, but five years later they were almost united. The constitutional status of Norway abroad was clear from the beginning. It had its legal institutions, the king and the government, who claimed to represent Norway as a whole, even though they could exercise their authority only outside Norway at home. Norway at home, on the other hand, no longer had legitimate, representative bodies that could express the will of the nation. For the two Norways to come closer together, Norway at home would need organizations to take shape that had sufficient authority to be able to represent the population under occupation. In other words, it would need to grow a territorial resistance movement or 'Home Front'.

If Norway abroad's relationship to the population at home was crucial, the relationship to the host country, Great Britain, was at least as important. What's more, these two relationships were dependent on each other. Without a reasonably good relationship with Norway at home, the Norwegian authorities abroad would have difficulty relating to the British, who naturally wanted a Norwegian partner firmly connected to its homeland. And if the authorities in exile did not have the ear of the Allies, The Resistance Movement at home would have difficulty respecting them.

One of the necessary conditions for a good relationship with the British was that Norway abroad took part wholeheartedly in the Allied war effort. This required a change from Norway's pre-war policy of neutrality to an active war policy. There was agreement in principle on this, but it required a difficult change of mental attitude. Moreover, the change of policy required an expansion of the military organization that would lead and co-ordinate the military input. It would become apparent that two ministerial changes would need to be made for the change in policy to have the necessary weight and legitimacy.

King and government

In Great Britain, the Norwegian government in exile faced two big tasks. First, it should carry on 'the struggle to win back Norway's independence', as it had expressed itself in its proclamation when it left the homeland. The exact meaning of the word 'struggle' was not specified. It could mean a struggle to promote Norwegian interests around a negotiating table where the warring powers were haggling about a compromise peace. But 'struggle' also had a military implication from the start, and it soon came to mean mainly that – to continue the war from the campaign in Norway beyond the national boundaries.

Second, the government should take care of Norwegian interests beyond those directly related to the war. It must make links with the homeland. It needed to nurture the diplomatic relationships with other countries that were important to Norway. A growing number of refugees in Sweden needed help and support from Norwegian authorities. Welfare work was needed among the Norwegians who were gathering in Britain from many quarters.

The government did have control over some resources to enable it to carry out these tasks. Above all, it had at its disposal the Norwegian merchant fleet, the fourth biggest in the world. During the Norwegian Campaign, the government had already taken steps to put the fleet under state control. An important reason for the decision to leave Norway had been that this was the only way it could retain control of the fleet, which otherwise would probably have been requisitioned by the British. The building up of the new national shipping company had already begun. Income from shipping would make the authorities in exile independent and enable them to finance their war and other activities themselves. They had also succeeded in bringing Norges Bank's gold reserves out of the country, which further secured their economic position.

Constitutionally, the king and government were in a strong position. There was no doubt that they were Norway's legitimate authorities. King Haakon's position as Norway's monarch was rock solid. The government had been appointed from the Labour majority in parliament, in accordance with normal parliamentary procedure, and it had also, as most people saw it, been strengthened by the authorization given to it by parliament at Elverum on 9 April. To further strengthen its political position and to be seen as a fully representative national government, it had also asked the king to appoint four non-socialists as ministers without a portfolio. Its aim was to follow policies in the national interest, above party politics.

Johan Nygaardsvold remained Norway's prime minister until the end of the war, when he had been in the post for ten years. His long tenure of office was a decisive contribution to making the government a stable institution representing the continuity of the state. Nevertheless, this government had experienced a very unusual break in continuity. Until 9 April 1940, it had been a government of social reform, for which it has a secure place in Norwegian history. Then it became a wartime government, something for which it was neither appointed nor prepared, and it would wage war for as many years as it had promoted social reforms. There is no agreement about its performance as a wartime government, but it has certainly not had the same praise for its war as for its social reforms.

Not everybody in the government managed to cope with the harsh transition from peace to war equally well. Nygaardsvold coped indifferently. He was not a great war leader, and it worried him that the government must expect to meet harsh criticism when the war was over. Though weak himself in some ways, he had the good sense to put a strong man in each of the most important government positions, as foreign minister and defence minister. He also used his talents to handle the difficult relationship with The Home Front patiently and wisely.

From a military point of view, the government was underpowered. It had not brought many personnel, warships, or planes from Norway. It was also weak politically. The significance of the non-socialist ministers in the government was limited. They could not prevent the Labour majority from being criticized for its foreign and defence policies before the war, for its inept performance during the critical days in April 1940, for its military campaign or for having left its people in the lurch when they abandoned the country. The authorities in exile were further weakened by events at home in the summer 1940 when leading politicians, led by *Stortinget*'s presidency, advocated that the king and government should be dismissed, and that parliament should recognize a new government that would work with the Germans. The king and the government had no difficulty rejecting these demands from home. They had chosen their line, and they stuck to it. But they were weakened by the fact that leading circles at home demonstrated so clearly that they were willing to abandon them and let Norway at home take over the responsibility of government, based on collaboration with the Germans.

Under normal circumstances, the supreme governing authority is referred to as 'the king in council', which in practice means the government, and the authority ruling the country is simply referred to as 'the government'. Already during the military campaign, and even more evidently in exile, the expression 'the king and government' came to be used. After 9 April 1940, the king came to play a much more central role than was usual in normal times. This did not mean that he took over more governmental power than before. He did not try to push his will through the government but accepted what it decided. He rejected suggestions that he should pursue a more independent, regal policy.

The need for a unifying symbol at a time of national crisis was what made the king so prominent. King Haakon symbolized both Norway at home and Norway abroad. At home, pictures of him and of other members of the royal family were displayed in private premises in a country where the Germans forbade all propaganda for the royal family. He was photographed on his many visits to Norwegian ships and camps. The pictures were reproduced in publications for Norwegians in exile and in pamphlets that were smuggled home to occupied Norway.

Other members of the royal house were also significant. Crown Prince Olav often accompanied the king on numerous visits when they were photographed side by side. In the last year of the war, Crown Prince Olav was given the title of Supreme Commander of the Armed Forces. Crown Princess Märtha was brought into a political role in the summer of 1940 when she was living in Sweden. During the rest of the war when she was in the United States with the children, working for the Norwegian cause there, she was able to make use of her close relationship with the American president.

The government and The Home Front

The government worked to improve its relationship with the people whom it had left behind but still sought to represent. It was painfully aware of the danger of becoming even more isolated from the homeland than it was already, and it tried to reach out in various ways to the population in Norway at home. The most important channel of communication was the Norwegian transmission from the BBC, popularly known as 'London Radio', which maintained an important link between the people at home and the Allied world abroad. These broadcasts were significant both prior to August 1941, when listening to the radio was allowed, and thereafter when radio receivers were confiscated.

Two of the most important ingredients in the Norwegian broadcasts were news from Norway and messages home from Norwegians abroad. The news from Norway was obtained through the press office at the Legation in Stockholm, which had its own secret contacts across the border. In this way, people living under repression received news about themselves that was either not published in the newspapers at home or had been altered by the Norwegian broadcasting organization NRK under Nazi control. The broadcasters from London were careful to be factually accurate, but they were not balanced and neutral. London Radio was an institution for a country at war. Many people listened to the king's speeches and the government ministers also spoke, but it was mainly two of NRK's own presenters, Toralv Øksnevad 'The voice from London' and Arne Ording, who connected with people at home. London Radio became particularly important during the last year of the war when it broadcast the most important messages from the leadership of The Home Front.

It was already clear by autumn 1940 that there were activists at home who were willing to resist the occupying authority and the NS government in various ways. A 'Home Front' was coming into being, a counterpart to the government's 'Overseas Front'. The government naturally wanted to have links with The Home Front, but who were they and who could speak on their behalf? Individuals were regularly arriving from Norway, able to express what they thought were the prevalent trends in the occupied region. Via

Stockholm, the government received reports of an attempt in the winter of 1940–1 to create a united Home Front Leadership. However, no authoritative organization grew out of this that could speak to the government on The Home Front's behalf. Nor could the government do anything actively to assist the establishment of such organizations. It would have to wait until requests came from home that could be considered as more than just individual opinions.

Such a request came in summer 1941 from a group that has come to be known as *Kretsen* ('The Circle'). It originated from a patriotic milieu of high-status people from law, public administration, finance and the social-democratic labour movement. Paal Berg, chief justice of the Supreme Court, was a central figure. *Kretsen* was rather bourgeois, but it also included labour representatives, which guaranteed a political balance. Some of the people in what would become *Kretsen* had since autumn 1940 acted as recipients of money which via Sweden was smuggled from the government abroad to the incipient Resistance Movement at home.

When *Kretsen* approached the government, it was concerned about the government's poor standing in public opinion at home, which it wanted to strengthen by sending a representative from home. This was, as far as it went, an offer of help to the government, which the government accepted. The city treasurer of Oslo, Paul Hartmann, moved to London and joined the government, first as a minister without portfolio but soon after as finance minister. He regarded himself as a representative of The Home Front within the government, but he did not play the same role in connections with the homeland as Nygaardsvold, Lie and Torp.

Nygaardsvold was sceptical about the group behind the approach from home, with its bourgeois elite character. If it had not been that it also included representatives from the political and trade union arms of the labour movement, he might well have rejected it. The message that Hartmann brought from *Kretsen* also created ill-feeling. The first request was that the government must resign as soon as the war was over. That was not an invitation to work together. *Kretsen* accepted the government, but only because of necessity and only for the duration of the war.

The government recognized that it would have to resign after the war, and it knew that it would face criticism. But it had expected *Kretsen* to consider it of mutual benefit that it represented Free Norway and was taking part in the same fight against the same enemy as The Resistance Movement back home. From the government's point of view, it seemed a strange procedure for a self-appointed group at home to ask for one of their own people to be included in the government while at the same time emphasizing its mistrust.

Kretsen came into being through its approach to the government, but only from spring 1942 did a more regular correspondence develop between the parties and they were not fully bonded until the winter of 1942–3, when their relationship changed. By its big successes in the civil resistance campaign in 1942, The Home Front won a degree of prestige that carried weight with the government. On 8 February 1943, the government promised in a letter to *Kretsen* that it would resign as soon as the war was over. This removed a stumbling block that had lain between the government and *Kretsen*.

In February and again more clearly in early summer 1943 the government formally recognized *Kretsen* as its civilian counterpart and working partner.

During 1942 the government and *Kretsen* exchanged correspondence about various issues at home and abroad. Both parties considered the uneven and rather informal relationship between them at that time important but not particularly binding. Their most meaningful interaction was an exchange of letters in August–September 1942, when they found themselves in agreement in their criticism of the communists' violent approach in the resistance activity. Apart from that, the two parties each made their own decisions about how to direct the war that each was conducting in its own remit and with its own objectives. *Kretsen* expressed no opinion about how the merchant fleet should be used or how the defence forces should be deployed. They considered these to be the government's business. The government, for its part, did not involve itself in the civil resistance activity back home. It gave no directions for it, nor was it asked to do so. The government had to avoid interfering if it was to continue to be trusted by the civilian leaders at home.

From 1943 onwards the exchange of letters between the parties became more frequent and more committed, while they prepared for their most important shared operation, arrangements for the transition from war to peace. They planned what the role of parliament should be during the transition. They negotiated about who should lead the central administration after the occupier had left power but before the government could be in place in Oslo and before it had submitted its resignation. They also considered the arrangements for local government during the transition phase. There was almost a split in summer 1943 when *Kretsen* finally faced the government with an ultimatum that the government felt it had to accept.

It can seem strange that the problems of transition were so prominent and caused so much friction, whereas, in the event, the transition from war to peace occurred so painlessly in 1945. One reason is that it was far from certain that the change would be so peaceful. Other possibilities, including military actions, chaos, or German collapse, were very real and had to be considered thoroughly. Another reason is the method of communication between the parties. They corresponded without meeting face to face. The problems could undoubtedly have been resolved faster and more effectively through face-to-face negotiations. The differences between them on the structure of local government, for example, were quite small but nevertheless contributed towards pushing them apart.

The main explanation, however, is to be found in the very different ways the government and *Kretsen* saw themselves. The government was conscious of its position as the nation's legal ruler and considered it important that this status should not be weakened. It wanted to maintain the constitutional forms as much as possible. *Kretsen* felt that The Home Front through its resistance campaigns was the leading representative of the Norwegian people and must therefore take the lead in the transition period.

The relationship between the government and the civilian home front was largely a matter for the Norwegians. It was not something that the British felt they should become involved in. The relationship between Norwegian authorities abroad and the military resistance movement at home was, on the other hand, made more complicated, because the British followed their own policies in the first years of the war. British policy challenged the military resistance movement that was slowly and uncertainly growing in Norway and made its relationship with the Norwegian authorities abroad more difficult.

Alliance

From 9 April 1940, Norway at war could be considered as allied with Great Britain, even though they never entered a formal alliance treaty. Both parties were content to have a practical working alliance with specific agreements on particular issues. This informal alliance signified a sharp break with Norwegian foreign and defence policies before the war when Norway had stayed out of alliances and wanted to remain neutral in wartime. After 9 April the policy changed completely. Norway had suddenly become a combatant on the Allied side.

The switch from non-alliance and neutrality to a working alliance and warfare raised a heated debate in the government in autumn 1940. There was no disagreement about going to war, but how closely should Norway ally itself to Great Britain and how far should it enter the war? Some of the members of the government who clung most strongly to the old neutrality policy with its distrust of all great powers wanted to seek assurances from Britain in exchange for Norway's participation in the war. They wanted guarantees of Norway's position in the final peace negotiations. Foreign Minister Koht in particular did not want to commit himself too strongly to Great Britain. He supported an active war policy for as long as the war lasted, but he considered that the relationship with the Soviet Union required a delicate balance between West and East.

The majority in the government chose a different line. They would ensure Norwegian influence without making any initial demands to the British. On the contrary, they would meet with the British, concentrate on actions that would increase trust and wait to make requests and suggest changes until the British had firm confidence in their Norwegian counterparts and would be more favourably disposed to Norwegian demands and interests. Norway would gain negotiating power by becoming a good ally, hopefully, one of the best. The switch to this new policy of active alliance required a change of foreign minister. Koht resigned in November 1940 because he was associated with the neutrality policy and because he was a convenient scapegoat for all that the government had done wrong or was thought to have done wrong. The new foreign minister was Trygve Lie, who remained in office for the rest of the war and became one of the government's strongmen.

Lie had his own way of creating a good relationship between Norway and Great Britain. He not only cultivated close contact with his friend Anthony Eden, the British foreign minister. He also sketched out a policy for a post-war alliance. Norway would be an ally not only during the war but also afterwards. Lie acted boldly and went far. The government, in general, was reluctant to anticipate post-war policy, but Lie was less reticent. He proposed setting up a post-war defence alliance of the countries around the

North Atlantic. Lie wanted a wider alliance of which Norway would be a part, with Great Britain and the United States as leading members and smaller nations as partners. The alliance should build up a network of military bases, and in private conversations with the British, Lie indicated that such bases should also be set up in Norway.

In retrospect it is easy to see that this Atlantic policy anticipates the Atlantic Pact in 1949 and the formation of NATO. At the time, though, it was gradually put aside. It had, however, achieved its immediate objective, by creating in the British Foreign Office goodwill towards Norway as an active, positive, and creative partner. Norway could benefit from this goodwill when the two countries had to discuss difficult questions.

Foreign policy was one issue. The war policy to decide Norway's military contribution was another. This too required Norway to have a good relationship with its ally. From summer 1940 the Norwegian army, navy and air force were gradually built up. A military agreement between the British and the Norwegians on 28 May 1941 set out the principles for the organization and use of the Norwegian armed forces. They were to be deployed either to defend Britain or to recapture Norway. In practice, the parties went beyond the terms of the agreement and allowed the air force and the navy to take part in operations that were not directly related to the defence of Britain or the recapture of Norway. So far as possible, the forces should retain their Norwegian identity and character and be led by Norwegian officers, but they would be under British command when taking part in operations. Disciplinary regulations would be in accordance with Norwegian law. The Norwegian government would pay all costs, but the British promised to help with equipment and training.

One problem in the relationship with the British was that new questions which cropped up were difficult to resolve with the traditional division of the armed forces into separate branches under a single defence ministry. The first such issue was planning and preparation for the liberation of Norway. The British would have to provide most of the forces needed to achieve this, and British generals would need to have not only supreme military command but also civil authority within the war zone. This called for delicate and co-ordinated staff work from the Norwegian side to be able to influence the planning. The second question was about being able to influence the operations that the British were carrying out against Norwegian territory. Finally, a Norwegian resistance movement was developing, and the military authorities needed to assess how the military part of this movement should be incorporated into Norwegian and Allied war plans.

Defence Minister Birger Ljungberg had since his appointment in December 1939 been out of his depth in the Labour Party government. His weak performance in connection with the mobilization on 9 April and during the Norwegian Campaign was an easy ground for criticism. In October 1941 Oscar Torp took over as defence minister, becoming the second strong man in the government. As a political heavyweight, he provided the Defence Ministry with the authority it needed.

Torp realized that the Supreme Command needed to be reorganized to win the trust of the British and bring sufficient weight to bear in dealing with all the new issues that arose. The government, therefore, re-established the Supreme Command – *Forsvarets Overkommando (FO)* – in February 1942 under a new chief, Wilhelm Hansteen. The Supreme Command would have authority over all the branches of the defence forces and would also deal with the many new questions that had arisen. Torp put younger officers at the top levels of the Supreme Command, bypassing more senior officers with greater experience. He was convinced of the need for new brooms and fresh eyes.

It took some time for the command structure to take shape, but by the end of 1942, its two most important sections were FO 2 and FO 4, both with occupied Norway as their areas of responsibility. FO 2 saw to the intelligence service, which was growing fast. Extensive, detailed information about occupied Norway was needed to prepare for the liberation, plan operations in Norway, work with The Resistance Movement and gain the confidence of the British, who could expect to get better intelligence reports from the Norwegians than they could produce themselves. FO 4 was given responsibility for all operations involving Norway prior to the final liberation. These included both operations initiated from outside with little or no contact with people at home and operations that involved setting up or supporting resistance groups in occupied Norway. The operations required detailed collaboration with the British, who provided the necessary material resources and who had their own ideas about how the resistance activities should be carried out.

Participation in the wider war

When the Norwegian authorities arrived in Great Britain, they expected to continue the war by traditional means. The defence forces would carry on from where they had left off in the Norwegian Campaign. The navy was in operation less than three weeks after the capitulation. Personnel and equipment that had fought in the campaign were rapidly put into use. However, there were many limitations to what was available initially. The number of personnel and the quantities of equipment that came over from Norway were limited. Rearmament in exile had to start almost from scratch. Officials and staff in the Defence Ministry were few, and the officer corps was small. Much depended on the British, who controlled the supply of military materials, weapons and ammunition and decided how to utilize Norway's military contribution. The government was still a group of civilians who were unfamiliar with military conditions and unaccustomed to dealing with military problems.

The strategic situation and political circumstances were decisive factors. In the summer and autumn of 1940, it was uncertain how Great Britain would fare in the war. The damaging German air raids in the autumn suggested that a German invasion of the British Isles was imminent. The Norwegian government in exile had to make plans for a possible further journey to Canada. It would not have been easy to put full energy into building up a military force in these circumstances.

In the summer of 1940, the government's position in its homeland was at its weakest, and it only strengthened slowly thereafter. At that time, the government could not count on any great support from home for its war policy. None of that made it turn back. If it had been dismissed by the parliament at home, which was a real possibility that summer, it would undoubtedly have continued its work of raising a Norwegian fighting force abroad. But awareness of how weak it was back at home led the government to proceed slowly and cautiously. It did not impose conscription but relied on voluntary recruitment. After the campaign in eastern Norway, 5,000 men had been interned in Sweden. The government could have tried to have these brought over to Great Britain, but instead, they were encouraged to make their way back to Norway.

That same summer, the government turned down a quick opportunity to arm and train Norwegian troops. The British were keen to carry out raids on the Norwegian coast and they wanted Norwegian commando troops to take part, in exchange for the British providing weapons and the necessary training. This was the government's first encounter with British activism, and it declined the offer. They were afraid that people at home would not approve of the government agreeing to Norwegian soldiers taking part in attacks against Norwegian territory. Six months later the government became a little more proactive. On 13 December 1940, it instituted compulsory service for Norwegian men abroad but implemented this in practice only in Great Britain.

In assessing how they could contribute to the Allied war effort, the government could count on four branches of the defence forces – the three regular arms of navy, army, and air force plus a civilian 'defence arm', the merchant fleet. Of these four, the merchant fleet was the most important and was fully ready, while the other three had to start from scratch. There was an important difference between the navy and air force on the one hand and the army on the other. There were yet no land-based military operations that a Norwegian army could take part in. The army had to content itself with being held in readiness for the liberation of Norway and the defence of British territory. On the other hand, the war was expanding at sea and in the air, where there were roles for the navy and the air force right from the start. They couldn't just stand by in readiness; they had to take part as Britain fought to survive.

Recruitment was a limiting factor in building up the armed forces. Some Norwegians could be recruited because they were already abroad, but altogether not as many as could have been hoped for because it was possible to bring in only a few of the many Norwegian Americans. Further availability of recruits would depend on Norwegians leaving Norway, either by coming over the North Sea, escaping through Sweden or by returning with the British after a coastal raid or the evacuation of Svalbard. The government never actively encouraged Norwegians in occupied Norway to abandon the country to join the Norwegian forces in exile. Those who came did so of their own will because they wanted to play their part in the war abroad.

The shortage of available manpower raised the important question of how recruits should be allocated between the forces. The merchant fleet was prioritized, along with the navy and the air force who were actively engaged in the war. The army-in-readiness had to wait. By the end of the war, the Norwegian armed forces in Britain amounted to almost 15,000 men.

The merchant fleet

The investigating commission after the war gave the government a good report in respect of its management of the merchant fleet. It praised the government, the ship owners who had built up the fleet and made it available, and the sailors 'who had performed their arduous and dangerous duties with such great self-sacrifice'. It is the sailors who come first to mind when we think about the merchant fleet because it was they who felt the terrors of war and sailed with their lives at risk. However, the role of the government and the shipowners must also be recognized.

The Norwegian merchant fleet was the world's fourth biggest, and it included a large and modern fleet of tankers, the world's third biggest, which would prove to be especially significant. During the Norwegian Campaign, the government had already taken measures to gain control of the fleet. It was concerned lest the Germans get their hands on the ships through the many shipping companies situated within the part of the country that they occupied. They also feared that the British might requisition the fleet and sail it under the British flag, as they did with the Danish merchant fleet. At Stuguflåten in Romsdal on 22 April 1940, the government made a historic decision. The merchant fleet would be brought into what was a national shipping line, to be known as Nortraship. By this means, the government gained control of the fleet and was able to use it in the continuing struggle.

Nortraship became a big organization with about 1,000 ships and a corresponding number of employees, who worked in 50 local offices in the world's most important ports. The head offices were in London and New York. Though London was more important, the two were of equal status, which would cause difficulties later. There was a certain amount of tension between the government and the national shipping line. The government was mainly interested in the fleet as an instrument of war and put less emphasis on profit. The managers of Nortraship wanted to take profit more into consideration, and they also complained that the minister of shipping, Arne Sunde, involved himself too much in the management of the company.

The background to these disagreements was that it was shipowners who had been recruited to the management of the new, nationalized organization. They were the people with the necessary technical knowledge and commercial experience to manage a shipping fleet, and who therefore filled the top posts in Nortraship. They agreed that the fleet should serve in the war effort, but at the same time they were concerned about the economic aspects of the operation – that money had to be earned for building new ships both during and after the war. The ship owners were unaccustomed to the bureaucratic procedures of a nationalized industry. They didn't take orders readily from a ministry that had formal authority over them. In several instances, and particularly at first, leading ship owners within Nortraship had difficulties distinguishing between their own interests and those of Nortraship. It was, after all, their ships that Nortraship was deploying.

In autumn 1939, Norway had made a shipping agreement with Great Britain which meant that when Norway came into the war, 40 per cent of the Norwegian merchant tonnage was already sailing for the British. This agreement then gave a basis for new agreements with the British and later with the Americans. In the negotiations about such agreements, there was a noticeable difference between the British and the Americans, between London and New York. Nortraship in New York and Nortraship in London worked in very different circumstances, which partly explains the disagreements between the two offices.

The merchant fleet was most important in the first years of the war, and especially on the route over the Atlantic between Great Britain and the United States. This was the lifeline for Great Britain, which was dependent on getting supplies in from North America. In the early years of the war, one-third of Britain's oil and petrol was brought in by Norwegian ships. In publicity statements, the British claimed that the Norwegian contribution was of equivalent value to a million Allied soldiers. Lines of Norwegian ships travelled in convoy across the ocean, unloaded in British harbours and turned back to the United States for more.

The transatlantic route was the most important and was dangerous all throughout the war. The Mediterranean route was also important and just as dangerous. Norwegian ships sailed through the Mediterranean taking supplies and military equipment to Malta. The convoys were not only attacked by planes, submarines, and surface ships when they were at sea, but they were also continuously bombed while they were in harbour in Malta. Only a few Norwegian merchant ships took part in the convoys to Murmansk.

Norwegian ships also operated as support vessels for military operations. Nortraship's vessels took part in the evacuation from Dunkirk in May 1940. In the Mediterranean, they transported troops and equipment to war zones in North Africa, and they assisted the Allied landings in North Africa in November 1942. They were present at the landing in Sicily, the invasion of mainland Italy and the landing in Normandy in June 1944. Some ships were involved when the Allies landed in southern France. Several Norwegian ships formed part of the supply lines to the army and navy units that were fighting the Japanese. Two large liners were converted to troop transporters that carried tens of thousands of American soldiers from the West Coast of America to Australia and the Philippines, and Norwegian ships took part in the many invasions of Japanese-occupied Pacific islands.

After 9 April, there were 24,000 Norwegians working in the merchant fleet overseas. This number fell to 14,000 by the end of 1942 and remained at that level for the rest of the war. The number of foreigners employed rose, to comprise as much as a quarter of all the crews onboard Norwegian ships in 1943. Sailing for one side in the war was to expose oneself to the same dangers as soldiers in the field. Most of the ships did have some protection, though, sailing in Allied convoys escorted by warships and planes, and eventually, the merchant ships were also equipped with guns, anti-aircraft guns and trained gunners. This was not enough to protect them from German U-boats and planes, however. Many ships were sunk by gunfire, bombing or torpedoes, or, in some cases, blown up by mines. The losses were particularly bad in 1942 and in early 1943 until 'The Battle of the Atlantic' suddenly ended in May that year after a particularly critical month in March. From then on, it was the Allies who were on the offensive at sea.

The losses were great. As a result of shipwreck or other effects of the war between 9 April 1940 and 8 May 1945, 2,200 Norwegian merchant sailors died. That is over a fifth of all Norwegian war deaths in the same period and double the losses among Norwegian armed forces outside of Norway. In addition, 900 foreign sailors died. Four hundred and thirty-two of Nortraship's vessels were lost, with the result that by 1945 the fleet had declined to 565 ships. Nearly half of the tonnage had been lost.

Those who crewed Nortraship's boats were both 'wartime sailors' and 'seamen'. As seamen they carried out the regular work of life onboard, continuing to relate to each other as crew members did before, during and after the war. As wartime sailors, they were Norway's warriors standing face to face with death and experiencing the stresses and horror of war.

The navy

When the government moved to Great Britain, the naval officers and crews in northern Norway were ordered to follow with the warships that survived after the campaign. Norway would continue to fight the war at sea. The navy's starting point at that time was about 400 men and thirteen small naval vessels. By the end of the war, this had grown to 7,400 men, half of whom made up the seagoing part of the service, with 58 warships under Norwegian command.

Most of the navy operated from bases in Great Britain, but Norwegian warships were also stationed in Iceland, the Faeroe Isles, the East Coast of North America, and in the Mediterranean and the Persian Gulf. They escorted convoys back and forth across the Atlantic, when they could also protect Norwegian merchant ships, and they escorted convoys to northern Russia. It was while the destroyer *Stord* was escorting a convoy to Russia that she took part in the sinking of the German battleship *Scharnhorst* in the North Sea.

The navy participated in British raids on the Norwegian coast in 1941, and it also carried out one raid on its own. From then on, the Norwegian coast became a progressively more important area of operations. Alone or together with British vessels, submarines and motor torpedo boats attacked the German shipping that followed the shipping channels lying between the islands and the mainland coast. They also attacked German fortifications and signal stations on land and took part in setting agents ashore.

The navy's operations in Norway led to the loss of Norwegian lives over and above the navy's own losses. The demands of war were relentless in this respect. The Allies had no desire to destroy Norwegian ships with Norwegian crews that were sailing along the coast with goods intended for Norwegians, but it was difficult to distinguish these from German ships when both were sailing together in convoy. Many Norwegian ships with Norwegian crews were requisitioned by the Germans and carried German cargoes. Norwegian submarines sank two Norwegian ships with the loss of fifteen Norwegian lives, and the torpedo boats sank three ships with the loss of seventy-seven passengers and crew. That made up 10 per cent of all the Norwegians in the Norwegian home fleet who died because of Allied air or U-boat attacks or mines.

The navy lost 20 ships and 650 men, which gives a fatality rate of 17 per cent among those who were in active, seagoing service. Those who survived, like their fellow seafarers in the merchant fleet, had been exposed to huge hardships. Some had survived the sinking of their ships. Many had experienced exhausting and nerve-wracking turns on sea watches with the constant fear of enemy attack and with little sleep over long periods of time.

The air force

Like the navy, the air force was actively engaged in operations throughout the war, over a wide area and including actions on the Norwegian coast. It operated under British command when in action, as did the navy. And just as the British and Norwegian navies had a good relationship, so did the British and Norwegian air forces; they were brothers in arms.

The air force established a training school in Canada, with the nickname 'Little Norway', as early as autumn 1940, and during the war, the air force grew to comprise four squadrons. The first one that was established operated over the North Atlantic and the sea areas outside Norway, engaged in escorting convoys, hunting for U-boats and reconnaissance. A second squadron performed duties along the Norwegian coast, took agents to Norway and brought others back. In 1943 the squadron was provided with Mosquito fighter-bombers for their reconnaissance work along the coast. They fought German planes and attacked U-boats by opening fire with their cannons and machine guns and dropping depth charges. After the invasion of Europe, the Mosquitoes had a special role as pathfinders for British bombers. In these operations, the air force faced the same dilemma as the navy. Attacks on German shipping also destroyed or sank Norwegian boats and led to the loss of Norwegian lives. It is not known whether the Norwegian Mosquitoes caused such losses by direct attacks, but it is clear that they showed the way for Allied attacks that cost Norwegian lives.

Altogether, Norwegian ships and planes attacked or took part in attacks on German shipping along the Norwegian coast. A battle of life and death continued here in the air and on the sea for five years. It was mainly fought by the navies and air forces of the great powers, with the Germans on one side and the British on the other, plus the Russians in the North. However, units from the Norwegian navy and air force also took part, like a little brother alongside his elders.

Two squadrons took part in the defence of Great Britain and in the war in the air over Europe. The squadrons were recognized for their contribution to the Allies' large, but unsuccessful, commando raid on the French port of Dieppe in August 1942. The Norwegian squadrons provided cover for the ships and for the landing troops. They shot down at least fifteen German planes and were commended by the British. Before D-Day, 6 June 1944, these two squadrons were transferred to the Channel Coast and took part in the weakening of German positions prior to the Allied invasion. The lead-up to D-Day, the squadrons' contributions on D-Day itself and their active participation in the fighting on the continent in the months that followed became high points in the squadrons' histories.

Measured by the number of men, the air force was the smallest of the three armed services. It consisted of 2,600 men at the end of the war, but it had the biggest losses – 288 men who died out of 650 serving in the air, giving a fatality rate of 44 per cent.

The army

The army was the branch of the armed services that with a few exceptions was never in battle. It could take part in the defence of Great Britain, but apart from that, the government was not willing to use it for anything other than the liberation of Norway. It was a question of having a land-based military force ready to take part in the liberation. As the liberation was achieved peacefully, the army was not required to fight but was used for sentry duties in the same way as The Home Forces and police troops that were trained in Sweden.

At about the same time as the establishment of the navy and the air force was starting, the government set about raising what in March 1941 was called the Norwegian Brigade. There was not much left to build upon after the Norwegian Campaign, other than a few officers and some items of equipment that were brought over to Britain. On the other hand, there were several hundred whalers, seamen and various other Norwegians abroad who had volunteered for war service during the fighting in Norway and who could form the basis of the new army unit that was posted to Scotland, where it would be based for the rest of the war. As the army had the lowest priority among the forces it grew only slowly, from hardly more than 1,000 in summer 1940 to barely 4,000 men in 1945. Because members of the brigade only exceptionally took part in the fighting, the losses were not so great, around 100 men.

At first the plan was to create a combined unit that could act independently during the liberation, but this approach was changed after the Supreme Command was set up. If Norway was to be freed by military operations as part of an Allied invasion, this would have to be done mainly by Allied troops. The Norwegian army should act first and foremost in support of the Allies, by taking on operations for which the Norwegians were particularly well suited. So, in August 1942 the brigade was divided into independent companies that were slightly larger than a normal infantry company. These 'mountain companies' each consisted of 260 men. They would be associated with Allied units in different places. In this way, they would also be evidence of a Norwegian military presence over a wider area.

A parachute company was also set up within the brigade, as was a commando unit of a hundred men. These commandos took part in the motor torpedo boat operations on the Norwegian coast in 1942–4, and in autumn 1944 the unit participated in the fighting on the continent. The army also had smaller units deployed to several places. From May 1942, Norwegian troops occupied part of Svalbard. In September 1943 they suffered a raid by the Germans when fourteen Norwegians fell and thirty-three were taken prisoner, but the Germans withdrew, and the Norwegian garrison remained in place.

Operations in Norway

British operations in Norway presented the government and the military authorities with a problem at an early stage. German forces and installations in Norway were legitimate targets for attacks from Great Britain, but such attacks could also hit Norwegians and Norwegian interests. The British wanted to avoid that, but such collateral damage was a secondary consideration. When the British considered it appropriate to attack targets in occupied Norway, they would do so. As fellow combatants in the Allied camp the Norwegian authorities could not in principle take exception to such operations, but they could seek to have Norwegian interests considered.

As early as 1940, the British were beginning to plan and execute military operations in Norway. They carried out coastal raids. They organized resistance activity in occupied Norway. They bombed targets on Norwegian territory. The immediate intention was to damage the Germans, but there was also a wider purpose. In difficult times, it was a matter of carrying out offensive operations that could maintain morale and demonstrate a willingness to be proactive. Norway became a target area for such operations.

There was indecision about how extensive the operations should be. Churchill contemplated plans for a big landing in Norway and tried to get his generals and admirals to agree. They resisted but had to agree to do something on a smaller scale. British ships executed raids on the Norwegian coast and agents who were sent to Norway organized resistance groups, received weapons and carried out acts of sabotage, all in anticipation that this could be the preliminary to a bigger invasion that would soon follow. The British and the German sides both considered the possibility of an Allied landing in Norway in 1941–2. After that, the invasion plans were put aside by the British as the Allies landed in North Africa in autumn 1942.

The operations had consequences for Norwegians in the occupied zone. Raids could lead to destruction that was harmful to Norwegian interests and could entail German reprisals against the civilian population. Mass arrests and punishment invariably followed resistance actions. Bombing could lead to the loss of Norwegian lives and cause material damage. Norwegian authorities, therefore, had an obvious interest in being informed about the operations, influencing them and perhaps even taking part in them as part of their own military operations.

It was easier said than done at first. Norwegian representatives had no automatic place in the planning and execution of these activities. From a British point of view, the Norwegians could be considered a hindrance to this work. The British were disinclined to include them in their military secrets and had some mistrust of their ability to keep quiet. Thus, there was little or no communication between British and Norwegian authorities in connection with the operations. However, a collaboration did gradually develop and become closer, first in relation to the raids and later about the organization of resistance. On the other hand, there was never any close and confidential collaboration about the bombing, though the Norwegian authorities were able to exert some influence.

Coastal raids

At a time when Britain was mainly on the defensive, the British set up two new and innovative organizations that would initiate and co-ordinate offensive action. The Directorate of Combined Operations (DCO) organized raids on the coasts of occupied countries, carried out jointly by the navy and specially trained army personnel. DCO worked alongside the Special Operations Executive (SOE), which organized resistance in occupied zones. In 1941, SOE's main activity around Norway was to facilitate the raids.

The British undertook three big raids in 1941. The first, on 4 March, was directed against Svolvær and three other harbours on the Lofoten Islands. Five hundred British commandos and fifty of the Royal Engineers landed and overpowered the German garrison. They destroyed herring oil and cod liver oil processing factories and sank German ships. They also sank the Norwegian coastal steamer *Mira*, on which four Norwegian passengers were killed. The British took German soldiers as prisoners, along with 12 NS members, and they also brought a total of 314 volunteers to Britain.

In autumn 1941, after the Soviet Union had entered the war, Churchill was keen on further operations against the Norwegian coast, preferably in the North. In addition to showing a will to attack, he needed to demonstrate to the Russians that the British could lighten the pressure on them by attacking the Germans in the rear. The military was sceptical about Churchill's ideas, but two new raids were carried out around Christmas 1941. Almost 300 men landed at Reine in Lofoten without meeting any resistance, at the same time as a big diversionary operation with almost 600 men took place at Måløy on the island of Vågsøy in Sogn og Fjordane. This led to pitched battles with losses on both sides. German prisoners, NS members and Norwegian volunteers were again brought to Britain.

DCO needed Norwegians to take part in these raids as pilots, local guides, and regular soldiers. Norwegians, therefore, took part in all three of them. There were fifty-two Norwegian soldiers on the Svolvær raid, recruited from the army and led by Martin Linge. SOE gathered seventy-seven Norwegians for the raid on Reine. Thirty-three Norwegians took part in the attack on Måløy and were led by Linge, who died during the action.

The German reprisals after these raids caused concern within the Norwegian government, which had been poorly informed, and after the last two raids, they expressed their concern to the British. At the same time, some of SOE's men who had taken part felt qualms of conscience and rebelled. They were saddened and discouraged by Linge's death and found it difficult to take part in operations that affected the civilian population unless they were approved by some Norwegian authority.

To improve co-operation between British and Norwegian authorities working on Norway, the British proposed setting up a joint organization, the Anglo-Norwegian Collaboration Committee (ANCC). This held its first meeting on 16 February 1942 with representatives from SOE and FO. This new co-operative organization discussed the planning of raids, and there was no longer such sharp disagreement about DCO's operations. The raids still continued for about a year, but they were on a more modest scale and were more like sabotage actions. On 20 September 1942 ten British commandos and two of SOE's Norwegians carried out a sabotage attack against the power station in Glomfjord. One of the last operations was an attack on the Stordø pyrite mines at the end of January 1943 by British and Norwegian commandos.

Resistance behind enemy lines

The organization of resistance in occupied Norway had been part of SOE's remit right from the start, and after 1941 this became its main activity in Norway. With its headquarters in London and a significant presence in the British Legation in Stockholm, SOE followed a triple programme. First, it would build up resistance groups that could spring into action when the time came for Norway to be liberated. In 1941–2 people thought that this liberation could happen soon and would take the form of an Allied invasion, with Norwegian sovereignty regained by military action. Second, SOE wanted to establish resistance groups in the occupied territory that would organize a continuing programme of sabotage. Third, such sabotage could also be done by special groups who came in from outside to perform their mission and then escaped without taking part in other resistance activities.

SOE needed help from Norwegians for its activity on Norwegian territory, and it set about recruiting them. Until autumn and winter 1940–1 it had not attracted very many, but from April 1941 and for two years thereafter twenty to twenty-five men per month attended courses to acquire the necessary skills to take part in raids along the Norwegian coast or work as agents on Norwegian territory. They constituted a 'section' which had no official name meantime, but which for simplicity we shall here call *Kompani Linge*, which was the name the 'section' later received.

SOE needed help from Norwegians for this recruitment but was reluctant to enter into any institutional collaboration with Norwegian authorities. Instead, the British put their faith in contact with individuals within the Norwegian establishment whom they trusted. On the political level, they had some connections with Lie and a few with Ljungberg. In the military sphere, the head of the army's High Command, Major General Carl Gustav Fleischer, was sometimes involved. On lower military levels, SOE worked closely with Martin Linge, who became their man while also maintaining some connection with the Norwegian military administration. Linge saw to the recruitment of Norwegians who would be trained by the British and used in their operations.

SOE's relations with the Norwegians in 1940–1 took place on British terms. They did not invite Norwegian organizations to join in planning or implementing their projects in Norway or to take part in the training of Norwegian personnel. They remained very reticent about their activities. The Norwegians who met with the British were also very cautious in talking about what they knew. The result was that seen from the Norwegian side, the British activities in Norway in 1940–1 appeared unclear. The government knew little and the military authorities not much more.

To set up resistance groups and carry out sabotage, SOE sent in missions with soldiers from *Kompani Linge* – sometimes by plane, occasionally overland from Sweden, but most often by boat. In autumn 1940 SOE and the Secret Intelligence Service (SIS) jointly established a base on Shetland to facilitate sea transport. This was initially a purely British enterprise using fishing boats that came over from Norway. Later, faster and converted submarine chasers were used. The base hired Norwegian crews to operate what came to be known as 'The Shetland Bus'. British and Norwegian authorities gradually found themselves working together in connection with the base on Shetland. The 'Shetland Bus' made numerous journeys carrying agents and weapons to Norway and bringing returning agents and refugees back. For a couple of years, SIS also ran its own base at Peterhead in Scotland.

A mission sent to Norway to set up resistance groups generally consisted of two or three men who provided weapons training, established radio contact with London and received and stored weapons sent from abroad. In 1942 there was hectic activity in anticipation of the expected invasion. Up to and including August 1942, a total of fifteen expeditions set foot on Norwegian territory, and large quantities of weapons and ammunition had been taken to northern Norway. SOE's first sabotage action, in November 1940, was organized from Sweden and was directed against the Bergen railway line. The first sabotage group from Great Britain was sent to Norway in April 1941, and six more in the course of 1942.

SOE soon encountered the Norwegian military resistance groups that were forming and that came to be known as 'Milorg'. SOE had to relate to this organization, and the two parties came to play important roles in each other's development. The Norwegian government was also necessarily interested in a closer relationship with this part of The Resistance Movement. The same applied to the military Supreme Command, *Forsvarets Overkommando* (FO). This led to a complicated situation in the years 1941–2 and early 1943. All four agencies – SOE, Milorg, the government and the Supreme Command – had to clarify their relationships with each other. They finally completed this process in spring 1943, when all the disagreements and confusion between them were resolved.

SOE's activity in 1942 had drastic consequences. Their increased activity in the spring led to exposures of both SOE groups and Milorg networks, in addition to reprisals against the civilian population. The losses were great, with particularly harsh reprisals against Televåg as we have seen earlier. The setbacks led to SOE deciding in August/September 1942 to change its policy. From now on, the British would work together with Milorg. It had been shown to be too dangerous to have parallel organizations in occupied Norway. SOE would now base itself on Milorg and support Milorg's work of setting up resistance groups that would come into action at the liberation.

British actions in north Norway and Trøndelag in autumn 1942 led to further brutal reprisals. An exchange of fire with *Sipo* at Majavatn on the boundary between Nord-Trøndelag and Nordland and two sabotage actions prompted a state of emergency in Trøndelag in October. Thirty-four people were executed. SOE/FO was also unsuccessful with an expedition code-named 'Bittern', which roused criticism both at home and abroad. Some of the participants were careless, and one of them was a former criminal. Bittern's programme included the killing of informants and the expedition brought over a long list of people to be targeted. The planned killings and the behaviour of some of the expedition members caused dismay at home. Both *Kretsen* and the Milorg leadership reacted against Bittern with complaints to the government and FO, respectively.

The arrangement that evolved under all these difficulties and that the parties agreed from spring 1943 onwards was that SOE expeditions that were sent to Norway should be put at the disposal of the local Milorg leader, train his people and let Milorg have control of the weapons that were brought in. Action plans would be worked out by SOE and FO together. Where there was no Milorg unit, SOE and FO could set up resistance groups on their own initiative. SOE would still carry out acts of sabotage independently of Milorg by sending in their own sabotage parties.

Bombing

The Allies bombed military targets in Norway on land and sea. In the North, Soviet planes attacked German ships, harbours, and airfields. No Norwegian towns suffered as many air raids during the war as Kirkenes, Vardø and Vadsø. In the South, Sola, Kjeller and Værnes airfields, the U-boat harbours at Bergen and Trondheim, German warships in Norwegian harbours and German convoys in Norwegian shipping lanes were all bombed or otherwise attacked. Norwegian lives were also lost in these attacks – 750 between the end of the Norwegian Campaign and the end of the war.

The Allies held full command of their bombing activities. The Norwegian authorities had no influence on the bombing policy. They just had to accept that there were important military targets in Norway and that Norwegian lives could be lost when these were attacked. The only exception to this was towards the end of the war, in respect of Norwegian coastal shipping. The Allies wanted to obstruct the transfer of German troops from northern Norway back to continental Europe, and in autumn 1944 they stepped up their actions against shipping along the Norwegian coast. FO asked for fishing vessels, smaller boats, and the surviving coastal ferries to be spared, and in October the Allies recognized the Norwegian concerns by promising to restrict the actions against coastal traffic.

Other targets were in a different category, such as manufacturing industry that was important to the war but did not have the same immediate military significance as an airbase, a U-boat bunker or a ship carrying German troops. There were inevitable controversies between Norwegian and Allied authorities about the bombing of industrial targets. The Norwegians agreed in principle to Norwegian industry being bombed, even though that could lead to loss of human life and destruction of factories that would be important after the war. However, they wanted to have a part in the evaluations of what industry was important for the war, and how it could best be attacked with the least possible damage to Norwegian interests. As soon as FO was established, it took up the task of surveying the Norwegian industry and suggesting which industrial targets should have the highest priority and how best to attack them. Then they entered a discussion with the Allies to try to influence their choice of bombing targets.

Bombing, organized resistance and combined operations were assessed together. When something was chosen as a target for destruction, the question arose what would be most effective – sabotage, a combined operation or bombing. SOE and FO generally advocated sabotage, DCO favoured a combined operation and the Allied air forces preferred bombing. For the famous operations against the heavy water plant at Rjukan in Telemark, all three methods of attack were evaluated and used in turn, with the objective of stopping the production of the heavy water that could be used in the development of an atom bomb.

Norway in Sweden

Not only was there a 'Norway abroad' in Allied countries with its centre in London where the king, the government and a growing civil and military bureaucracy were located. There was also a 'Norway abroad' in neutral Sweden. This had its centre in Stockholm, where the Norwegian Legation and a steadily increasing number of associated agencies operated.

In occupied Norway, the German occupation set constraints on Norwegian resistance activity. In Great Britain, the constraints were set by the Allied war policy. For Norway in Sweden, the limiting factor was Sweden's neutrality policy. As a participant in the war, Norway abroad wanted to make use of Swedish territory in its war operations, as did the resistance organization in Norway at home. The question that they faced was how much they could do within the limitations set by Swedish neutrality. In the early years, they could not do very much, but their scope for action increased steadily in the second half of the war.

A prime objective of neutrality policy is to keep one's own country out of the war. In practice, this means aligning oneself with the strongest of the combatants without going so far as to become exposed to the other side's military actions. During the First World War that was what happened with Norwegian neutrality policy, which inclined steadily more in favour of the Allies. During the Second World War, Swedish neutrality followed a similar trend. It shifted from an obvious pro-German leaning in the first half of the war to an even stronger pro-Allied tendency in the second half. This move was a direct consequence of how the war developed, from German domination to Allied progress and final victory.

The relationship between Norway and Sweden was difficult in the first years of the war. Sweden granted Germany significant concessions. The Germans were able to use the Swedish railway network to transport hundreds of thousands of troops on leave to and from Germany. They could thus avoid sending them by the sea route, where ships could be attacked by the Allies. They moved tens of thousands of men between Trondheim and Narvik on Swedish railways, avoiding the dangerous sea passage. Not only civil goods were sent through Sweden, but also war materials. The pro-German policy had its counterpart in a reluctance to accede to Norwegian and Allied wishes.

Most of this can be explained by Sweden's exposed geographical position, surrounded as it was by German forces on all sides – in Norway to the West, in Germany to the South and on the German side of the Eastern Front against the Soviet Union. It can also be explained by a fear that Germany could invade and occupy Sweden without warning, as it had invaded Norway and Denmark. It was important not to provoke the unpredictable German dictator. With the benefit of hindsight, it seems unlikely that Germany would have squandered its energies on taking Sweden, but at the time the Swedish government was not so sure.

Not everything can be explained in this way, however. In the early years of the war, many leading Swedes anticipated a German victory. They wanted to align themselves accordingly and accommodate the future victor with a view to working together after the war. This attitude was not unknown in Norway either, especially among business people. There were strong pro-German voices in parts of the Swedish elite, not least among military officers and in the police. King Gustav V was friendly towards the Germans. Few people were national socialists, and the national socialist parties in Sweden were small and insignificant, but there was widespread admiration for Teutonic efficiency, strength, and culture.

Many middle-class Swedish citizens who didn't like dictatorship nevertheless preferred a German to a Soviet one. In these circles and more widely in the older generation there was still a residual grudge against Norway following the dissolution in 1905 of the union between Norway and Sweden. The great majority of the Swedish people supported the government's line on neutrality, though there was a small, but noticeable, opposition calling for a more pro-Norwegian policy. Scepticism towards Norway was strongest around Stockholm and in southern Sweden, whereas people along the west coast and around Gothenburg were more positively inclined.

During 1943 Swedish neutrality policy changed in line with the shift in the fortunes of war throughout the world. The many concessions granted to the Germans were gradually withdrawn. Now it was the turn of the Allies and the Norwegians to be granted favours. Among Norwegians, the critical, if not to say hateful, attitudes that many had developed towards Sweden were modified. People understood better how difficult Sweden's situation had been in the face of a dominant Germany and how Norway had benefitted from Swedish neutrality. By May 1945 the two nations could be united in their joy that the war was over, but on the Norwegian side, there remained a certain reserve in their view of the Swedes, reinforced by a traditional 'little brother' complex, until this ill-will eventually subsided.

Sweden was important for Norway in three ways during the war: the country received an increasing number of refugees from occupied Norway; important communication lines between Norway at home and Norway abroad ran via Sweden; and between 1943 and 1945 the Swedes allowed a Norwegian military force to be raised in Sweden.

Refugees

During the Norwegian Campaign in 1940, between 10,000 and 15,000 Norwegians crossed the border to escape from the battle zones. Most of them soon returned to

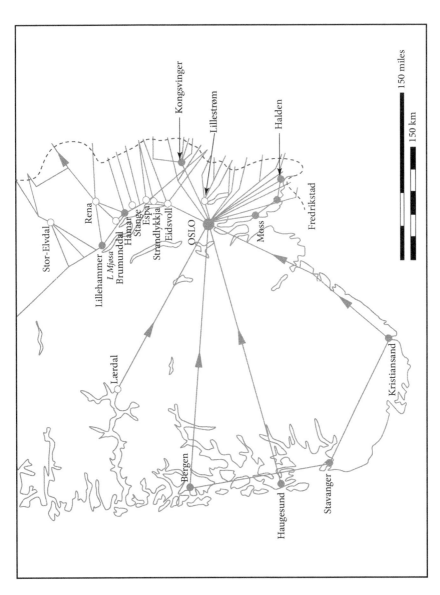

Map 4 Escape routes, south Norway. Escape to Sweden. The map shows the main escape routes in south Norway. The capital city of Oslo was the centre of the network.

Norway. In 1941–2 it was usually young men in the age group eligible for military service who wanted to go to Sweden. They left not to escape persecution at home, but because they saw Sweden as a staging post on the way to Britain. They wanted to travel on and to play their part in the wider war. Until Germany attacked the Soviet Union on 22 June 1941, it was possible to travel via the Soviet Union. In a few months, 500–600 men followed adventurous routes around the world to reach either Great Britain or 'Little Norway' in Canada. After the invasion of the Soviet Union this route was closed, and very few succeeded in leaving Sweden. However, it took time for the news to reach Norway that people were not able to transit through, and most of the refugees who crossed into Sweden in 1941 and well into 1942 did so in the hope of continuing their journey.

Right from the start, some people fled because the Germans were hunting for them, and the number of these gradually increased as The Resistance Movement grew. In the winter of 1942–3, 930 Jews escaped avoiding arrest and deportation. The following year, a thousand students fled when the Germans closed Oslo University in the autumn and arrested all the students they came across. Many young people fled to avoid the regime's compulsory labour service. During the forced evacuation of Finnmark and Nord-Troms in autumn 1944, some Norwegians crossed the border to escape. In time, an increasing number fled because they yearned for the meat casseroles and the brighter life in Sweden as living standards gradually fell and life in gloomy, occupied Norway became more burdensome.

The stream of refugees was limited in the early years, but then swelled and reached its height from August 1944 onwards until the end of the war, when there were never less than 2,000 arriving every month. Between August 1940 and the end of the war, 50,000 refugees were registered. Some left Sweden in various ways so that by the end of the war there were 43,000–44,000 Norwegian refugees living in their neighbouring country.

Not everybody who wanted to go to Sweden was able to cross the border. From 1 April to the beginning of December 1941, 797 people (27 per cent of applicants) were refused entry. The Norwegian Legation in Stockholm protested against this, claiming that all should be allowed in. This became accepted Swedish policy in the following years. Norwegians trying to go to Sweden were still turned back, but these were not refugees; they were young people who fancied a little trip over the border or local residents who wanted to visit relatives or go shopping in Sweden.

The border between Norway and Sweden is 1,600 kilometres long, and people fled over it throughout its length. At the Idde Fjord in the south, one could walk over the border on the ice in winter or be rowed across in summer. There was a sea route from Fredrikstad through the Hvaler archipelago to Sweden, and in the last year of the war, several thousand refugees journeyed by boat over the Oslo Fjord from harbours in Vestfold. But the great majority crossed the border on foot. A minority crossed at the long section between Røros and Kautokeino. Here, travellers had to make their way over bare mountains. The further north, the more demanding were the escape routes. In north Norway, refugees could walk for several days from their start in Norway before they reached any human habitation at the Swedish end. That was not the norm, however. The great majority travelled through the forest regions of eastern Norway along the many escape routes in Østfold, Akershus and Hedmark. Most of the refugees crossed the border without the backing of any organization. They set out on their own initiative or received more or less coincidental help on the way. The resistance organizations, however, gradually developed their own sections whose main role was to assist the flight of refugees.

It was difficult for the Germans and NS to control the long and largely uninhabited border zone, and the Germans did not put much effort into stopping the flow of refugees. The border patrols were too small to cover the sections for which they were responsible. Relative to the large number of refugees, the losses were therefore small. Ninety-six refugees died or were executed as prisoners or perished by being shot or as a result of other hazards on their journey to Sweden. Twenty-nine people who acted as guides to refugees died while providing assistance, or were executed or died in captivity, and fifty-five helpers were executed, died in captivity or were killed as they were being arrested. The combined total of deaths was 180, but many hundred refugees and several hundred helpers were arrested and imprisoned.

From spring 1941 onwards, the refugees were sent to the Norwegian reception centre which was first located at Öreryd in Småland but was later moved to Kjesäter. There they were registered, given a Norwegian passport, and questioned. Through these numerous interviews, the Norwegian authorities were able to gather information about conditions in Norway. If there had been mass arrests, the interviewers could uncover the reasons for them, and warnings could be sent home about who was in the danger zone. NS members or other unpatriotic individuals were turned down by the Norwegian authorities, were not given a refugee number and were turned over to the Swedes.

From the reception centre, most of the refugees were sent out to work in the woods. The Swedish authorities set up special camps with an instructor and a cook, where the refugees lived, ate, and were taught the skills of forestry. The work was unaccustomed and hard for most of them, but it seemed even harder because the young men were not able to travel on to take part in the war. From 1943, most of them worked in industry or at a trade or joined the police troops.

Sweden and Norwegian resistance

Support could be provided from Swedish territory for the Norwegian resistance, but the Swedish policy of neutrality set limits to this, tight in the early years of the war though steadily loosened thereafter. At first, Norwegians who supported resistance activity from Sweden risked being arrested by Swedish police and perhaps being brought to court. Between 1940 and 1944, 395 Norwegians were arrested for pro-Allied activity that was contrary to Swedish law, and 89 were sentenced to several months in prison. Most of these arrests took place in 1940–2. Several of Norway's resistance heroes served time in Swedish prisons early in their careers.

Nevertheless, there were connections right from the start between Norwegians in occupied Norway and in neutral Sweden. During the war, the border was more closely controlled on the Swedish side than on the Norwegian. However, it did not present insurmountable obstacles, and there were many possible routes to go across. Norwegians travelling legitimately between Sweden and Norway could also play their part in maintaining connections between home and abroad.

Because it was possible for people to cross the border, the Norwegian Legation in Sweden was able to act as an important link between The Resistance Movement and the Norwegian authorities abroad. Until spring 1942 there were two Norwegian government ministers resident in Stockholm and one of them, Anders Frihagen, began as early as autumn 1940 to transfer money secretly to Norway. These payments would continue until the end of the war and comprise most of the forty-five million kroner that the government sent home during the war. Frihagen also sent his own couriers to Norway to investigate how the resistance was developing at home. The correspondence between *Kretsen* and the government always went via Stockholm. On the military side, reports and information coming from Norway were sent on from Stockholm to authorities in London, who responded with answers, questions, or orders. Much of the communication, however, went just between Norway and Sweden. Not everything had to be sent on to London.

This all had to be done with great secrecy, discretion, and conspiratorial technique. Reports had to be coded and often microfilmed. Hiding places had to be chosen carefully. Caution was required in recruiting Swedish assistants, border officials, police officers, railway personnel, customs officers, drivers, and others. Somebody had to check that couriers did not give themselves away by wearing a wedding ring on the wrong hand or smoking British military tobacco, which smelled quite different from the Swedish utility tobacco. The normal postal service had to be avoided because the Security Police were intercepting letters. Loud-mouthed people and overenthusiastic patriots were not suitable for such work.

In summer 1941 the Legation set up a small military office that handled communications with Milorg and the military intelligence agency XU. From 1943 this activity increased significantly, and the military office was split into sections that matched the divisions within FO. MI 4 would link with Milorg and MI 2 with XU. At an early stage, in 1941, the military office established connections with a clandestine part of the Swedish intelligence service, the 'C-bureau'. The Swedes had just as much interest as the Norwegians and the Allies in acquiring information about the *Wehrmacht* in Norway, and the C-bureau, therefore, initiated a cautious collaboration with the military office. The bureau was willing to allow Norwegian couriers to cross the frontier independently of the border guards, in exchange for receiving copies of their reports on German military matters. Similarly, the Swedes would get copies of reports from interviews at the reception centre, if these contained useful military information. The modest co-operation in 1941 was gradually extended, becoming very comprehensive by the end of the war.

Alongside MI 2 and MI 4, the press office ran a very extensive communication service with Norway. The press office was interested in all sorts of news from occupied Norway, except for what was of direct military interest. The office had its own Swedish helpers at the border, managed its own routes and gathered material from a network of informants in Norway. In winter 1941–2 it set up special postal routes between Stockholm and

Oslo that ran at least once a week. Couriers travelled about once a month to Norway – preferably to Oslo but sometimes further north. To support the news work at home, the press office arranged for cameras, film, photographic paper, and duplicating equipment to be taken over to Norway. News bulletins and magazines were also taken across. At the reception centre, the press office interviewed newly arrived refugees to get the latest news from home.

The material that the press office gathered was distributed to Swedish newspapers to keep them informed on the situation in Norway. It was also forwarded to the Norwegian government's information office in London, was included in the press office's publication for the refugees, *Norges Nytt*, and was in various ways returned in adapted form to a news-hungry Norway. The editing had to be carefully balanced with respect to the Swedes, who referred to protests from the German Legation and urged the Norwegians to be more careful. The judgements to be made with respect to Norwegians in the occupied zone were just as difficult. Material from home had to be published in a way that did not put lives at risk.

Working closely with the military office and the press office was the legal office, which had a supervisory function. It ran a security service to ensure that the routes over the borders were safe, but first and foremost it had the task of identifying NS members and other suspects who came over the border. This could be a delicate matter, and the office was naturally controversial. It used military channels for its correspondence with illegal groups in the police at home. Other offices within the Legation also needed to gather information from home or send reports homeward, generally through the Communications Office (*Sambandskontoret*), which also saw to money transfers home. The Confederation of Trade Unions had its own courier lines across the border to the illegal trade union movement at home, as did the communists. Particularly towards the end of the war, it became an increasing problem to organize the many routes so that they did not coincide and hinder each other.

As the communication services became better and more systematically organized, several main channels developed. 'Full-route' couriers travelled the whole way from Stockholm to selected locations in Norway. They were usually bringing particularly important information or special equipment. A lot of material was sent by so-called 'relay routes', when messages and materials were sent in several stages until the consignment reached its destination. At the border, items were hidden at an agreed place and fetched from the other side. Post routes were direct, usually by train. The despatcher hid the post in an agreed place on the train between Stockholm and Oslo, and the recipient retrieved it when the train arrived. At the end of the war, there were sea routes from the West Coast of Sweden to landing places in Østfold, Vestfold and Telemark. These carried goods one way and usually brought refugees back.

The police troops

For Norway at war, it was important to mobilize all the Norwegians of eligible age who were in Sweden, but this was impossible, so long as Swedish neutrality was inclined in favour of the Germans. When the policy began to swing in the opposite direction in 1943, moves were made to establish Norwegian military training in Sweden. At the start, these were disguised by making the programme as civilian as possible. In summer 1943 the refugees were summoned to what was described as a health check but was, in reality, a military recruitment programme. During sixteen days they underwent medical checks that basically were a military medical assessment with a view to calling them up for military service later. Simultaneously, they were given a sort of elementary military training over several days. The 'health camps' continued through the autumn and became the starting point for the first military camps and regular enlistment early in 1944.

Another way to disguise military instruction was to call it police training. Police are civilians, but they receive weapons training. This training could be extended within the ambit of civilian policing. In summer 1943, fifty-five men attended a order police course with distinctly military features, located at remote Johannesberg manor house near Gottröra, north of Stockholm. This was the start of building up a bigger military force in Sweden. The Swedish police commissioner Harry Söderman, an unconventional and energetic man who supported the Norwegian cause, now became the driving force in this work. He wanted to extend the police training and militarize some of it further under the description of 'reserve police'. Building works were started at Gottröra, and a new police course with 250 men plus an officer training course for 40–50 men could begin there in the first half of October.

When Justice Minister Terje Wold arrived from London that same month, the plans grew and crystallized. One thousand and five hundred men would be summoned to Gottröra for combined police and military training. They became known as the *Rikspoliti* ('National Police') and would come under the National Police Chief and the Justice Department in London. A further 8,000 men would be called up to purely military service, disguised under the description of the Reserve Police. They would come under the Military Inspector, later the Military Attaché, in Stockholm, and the Military Supreme Command and Defence Ministry in London.

Swedish authorities had agreed to the plans for the health camps, and initially, the combined police and military training was given the necessary camouflage through Police Commissioner Söderman's efforts. But when the plans expanded in the autumn with little reference to the Swedish military authorities, a disagreement arose and at that point, the Swedish government stepped in to take control. Many members of the government did not want to give a warring nation such as Norway the opportunity to carry out military training in neutral Sweden. On the other hand, it could become difficult to keep the Norwegian youths under control if the occupation's end phase in Norway became violent. In that case, it was better to keep them in camps under military discipline and give them a minimum of military training.

The government considered it best to approve the Norwegian plans, but to restrict them so strongly that the purely military aspect of the project was limited. When the government gave its official approval on 3 December 1943, it emphasized that what was intended was a police force that would have guard duties and was not to be thought of as fighting units. It made it clear that the troops could not leave the country without Swedish approval. Weapons should be made available only for training and would be kept under Swedish control until they were to be used in Norway. The weapons training should only include light arms such as pistols, sub-machine guns and hand grenades, including a light mortar.

Personnel were called up for 5 January 1944, and training of the Reserve Police was considered to have begun from 15 January. Refugees who were already in Sweden were gradually called into service. Newcomers were sent directly from the reception centre at Kjesäter to one of the fifteen military camps that were gradually being set up throughout Sweden.

The various restrictions that were set on the police troops were slowly lifted. The Norwegians pressed to have them removed, while the Swedes held their ground but gradually gave way. Until summer 1944 the Reserve Police units were loosely constituted and of a mainly civilian nature. From the autumn they began to assume a tighter and more overtly military form. On 9 August the Swedes gave permission for marches and larger exercises. They were no longer so concerned that the training would attract attention and provoke German protests. The following month, the police troops were given permission to use heavier weapons such as automatic rifles, machine guns, heavy mortars, and automatic and anti-tank guns. In the end, nearly all the camps got weapons, and the earlier distinction between armed and unarmed units disappeared. The Swedish military was now taking an active part in the training. A number of Swedish instructors were assigned to the Reserve Police battalions. The Swedish defence staff held two large field exercises for the troops: one with 4,800 men in Dalarna at the beginning of December 1944 and another with 6,000 men in Hälsingland in April 1945.

The police troops comprising the National Police and the Reserve Police finally amounted to some 14,000 men, almost as many as the Norwegian armed forces in Britain. They were mainly intended for guard duties but could also carry out military operations. From a starting point of nearly zero in summer 1940, by the time of liberation the Norwegian government had at its disposal almost 30,000 men, shared between the 'Norway in Britain' and the 'Norway in Sweden'.

CHAPTER 11
NATIONAL SOCIALISM – AN ATTEMPTED REVOLUTION 1940–2

After 25 September 1940, Quisling's NS Party faced the formidable task of carrying out a National Socialist Revolution in Norway. Compared with other occupied countries, the way of going about this was unique. Norway was the only German-occupied country where an indigenous national socialist party got hold of state power and used it to try to promote a revolution. The Nazi movements in other occupied countries never assumed office and never acquired the same grip on power as NS did.

NS itself usually called this revolution 'the new order', but the word 'revolution' was also used, a 'national revolution', since the NS people saw themselves as revolutionaries. They would change a divided and declining nation into a new, united, and harmonious fellowship on a national socialist foundation. 'Revolution' is, therefore, a better and more meaningful word than the more opaque 'new order' to express what the NS Party was setting afoot.

In retrospect, it is easy to see that NS had no chance of success. Their attempt at a National Socialist Revolution was bound to fail. That was not how it appeared at the time, however. The NS Party had the backing of all-conquering Germany and was confident of success. In less than six months, it had gone from being an insignificant political sect to becoming the party of government. 'History' had placed it in the middle of one of its great tides of development, which would generate a national socialist Europe. The NS Party embarked on its historic mission with shining optimism and bright confidence in future progress. They were on course towards their place in a Europe fashioned by the fascists' political and ideological entrepreneurial talents.

Nor was there any feeling within the general population that the revolution had no chance of success and that they could just wait passively for its inevitable collapse. On the contrary, the advances towards The National Socialist Revolution were seen as so threatening and the possibilities that they might succeed were taken so seriously that a storm blew up against them. It could not be taken for granted that the attempt at a National Socialist Revolution in Norway would fail. It would need to be resisted and rejected. People felt that the underlying values and basic ideology that bound Norwegian society together were under threat. This feeling unleashed powerful forces.

This situation sets one of the main themes of Norwegian history in the years 1940–2: an NS state in conflict with its own population; a state without a people against a people without a state. The state had at its disposal all the means of power and all the levers of control that are available to a totalitarian government. It was opposed by a population that could mobilize nothing more than their own strengths and talents. The state was secure on its perch as long as it was steadied by an occupying power. The population had no possibility of recapturing their state. They would need to pursue a different approach – to demonstrate how little progress the new state was making in connecting with its people. The strength within their powerlessness would thus become apparent.

The *Nasjonal Samling* (NS) government

The new NS Party government that was to implement The National Socialist Revolution was organized as Terboven had decreed on 25 September 1940. NS had been given all the ministerial appointments apart from the three economic departments. The ministers answered individually to the *Reichskommissar*, from whom they derived their authority. They could be appointed or dismissed only by him, and he directed and co-ordinated their activity with the help of his staff in the *Reichskommissariat*. That was the external and official aspect of the new order. Internally, however, Quisling also had a hand. He didn't have any formal position in relation to the ministers appointed by Terboven, but the NS ministers were members of a *Fører*-led party and Quisling was their *Fører* to whom they had sworn allegiance. Quisling met once a week with the NS ministers so that he could lead and co-ordinate their activity.

This arrangement was obviously considered as a prelude to the anticipated transfer of power to a government headed by Quisling. One day, the party *Fører* would step forward from his informal position as the ministers' Norwegian chairman and become the nation's official leader. It is not known to what extent Quisling managed to act as an informal head of government, how much initiative he took or to what extent he operated as a co-ordinating agent. He was now participating in the arena of practical politics, which was not his strong point. Some of the government ministers, possibly influenced by the commissariat's advisers, were probably at least as important in the attempt to carry out a National Socialist Revolution in Norway as Quisling himself.

The occupation regime that was introduced on 25 September 1940 was changed only once. That happened on 1 February 1942 in a state ceremony at Akershus Castle, when Quisling became prime minister of a government that consisted of only NS members as ministers. Sources of information about what led up to this ceremony are obscure. It has therefore been difficult for historians to follow the developments towards this new arrangement, to point out which people were decisive or to assess the influence of external circumstances on the result.

Some general underlying factors can be sketched out, however. Terboven probably wanted to get away from Norway and was interested in preparing for that. In his own interest, he opted for an arrangement that would make it possible for him to withdraw. As usual, Quisling persisted with his requests: the setting up of a formally sovereign NS government with himself as the leader; the end of the state of war; the establishment of diplomatic relations and a Norwegian army. The membership of NS had continued to increase, although more slowly than before. The time was therefore ripe for NS to be given more power. Paul Wegener, head of the *Einsatzstab*, had already declared in May 1941 that NS was now strong enough to form a government.

There were signs in autumn 1941 that something was afoot, but the changes did not get moving until January 1942. Terboven was undoubtedly behind them. He came back from a visit to Hitler with authority to report that the *Führer* had approved a change of regime. He then used Wegener as his envoy to Hitler. Terboven, Wegener and Quisling at this time had several meetings about the proposed new arrangements, while at the same time Quisling and Hagelin kept their supporters in the navy informed. During these meetings, and especially after Wegener's meetings with Hitler, it became clear that the change of regime would be rather less than what Quisling was asking for and could have had grounds to hope for. The obstacle was Hitler's fear of an Allied invasion. The Allied raids on the Norwegian coast around Christmas 1941 had scared him, and in January 1942 he gave orders to move large parts of the navy to Norway and accelerate the building up of *Festung Norwegen*. So, it was not opportune to give a Norwegian government too much independence. What was chosen instead was a compromise that gave Quisling and NS something, but not as much as they had hoped for or reckoned on.

Blended into the compromise solution there was an expectation that further developments could follow that would satisfy Quisling's demands. Quisling may have been given assurances of such developments, or he may have understood vague statements or imprecise formulations from the Germans too literally. At any rate, he presented his demands to Hitler several times in the following months. For a while, Terboven also considered how the compromise arrangement could develop into something more. He appears to have thought that some of Quisling's demands could eventually be accepted. If Terboven wanted to resign from his position in Norway, he too cannot have been satisfied with the compromise.

It all seems typical of Hitler's regime. The *Führer* was overloaded with important matters. His approval had to be obtained when an occupation regime was to be changed, but he gave his directives in several instalments that could be contradictory. Decisions were temporary and vague instead of permanent and well-defined. Final decisions were deferred, and those around the *Führer* strove to make sense of the confusion he had created.

The procedure for Quisling's assumption of power in February 1942 was chosen with care. It was important that the new government's legitimacy did not come from the occupying power. The government must appear not to have been installed by the Germans but to have been appointed on a legitimate Norwegian basis. The solution to this was that all the ministers resigned their appointments and the NS ministers then asked Quisling to form a government. The Nazified Supreme Court approved this procedure and pronounced that it was constitutionally in order. For his part, Terboven declared that he had accepted the ministers' resignations.

The ceremony at Akershus was performed with pomp and splendour, expressed in rituals framing it in historic Norwegian and Norwegian-German traditions. Norwegian and German symbols vied for attention. Norwegian flags hung from Romeriks Tower alongside the German flag. The wall of the great hall glistened with the NS symbol, the sun cross in gold and red, alongside the German national symbol, the swastika and eagle in gold. The rostrum was flanked by two arrays of flags where the Norwegian and German colours merged: the Norwegian national flag; the German swastika flag; the Norwegian sun cross; the German war flag and the banner of the Norwegian *Hird*. When everyone was in place the door opened and the assembly rose to their feet and raised their right arms in salute. Terboven and Quisling, who was in *Hird* uniform, came into view and strode across the room through a forest of upstretched hands, to the sound of Grieg's *Homage March*.

In his speech at Akershus, Quisling proclaimed that Norway again had a national government. He further asserted that there only remained one final stage before the country regained its full national liberty and independence. The present ceremony symbolized a temporary position on the road towards the definitive form of government. At the same time, he was quick to emphasize the extent of his power. The national government, he said, united the power of the king, government and parliament. From now on, the government would issue 'laws', not just 'decrees' as the ministers had done under Terboven. This relationship of NS to the state was soon formalized. A law on party and state dated 12 March 1942 confirmed NS as the official party of government, closely linked with the state. This signified clearly that the party stood above the instruments of state and could use them for its own purposes.

As both *Fører* and prime minister, the head of both party and state, Quisling could now live up to his position. He and his staff established themselves in the Royal Palace. Terboven and the *Reichskommissariat* had their offices in the Storting building a few hundred metres away. Quisling had his official residence outside the city centre at Gimle, 'the home of the gods', in an impressive building that now accommodates the Holocaust Centre. There, he and his wife Maria could welcome their Norwegian and German guests in tasteful surroundings. In addition, an 'Eagle's nest' was built for Quisling in the form of a country house in Asker district called Leangkollen, furnished with a banqueting hall in Viking style. Just as the king had his royal guard to protect him, so did Quisling have an armed guard on sentry duty at the Royal Palace and at Gimle.

Quisling went on a state visit to Hitler. He and Terboven travelled together to Berlin, each at the head of his large delegation. At the railway station in the German capital, they were welcomed by Hans Heinrich Lammers, head of the Reich Chancellery, with his entourage. The meeting with Hitler took place on 13 February. The following day, Quisling held a press conference and was guest of honour at an afternoon reception hosted by Göring. The news of the change in the form of government in Norway and Quisling's new role as prime minister was well written up in the press.

Quisling's new official image as a statesman and the publicity given to him in NS-dominated Norway and in German-dominated regions abroad bore little correspondence to the reality. The position he had attained and the power he had been given was strictly limited. Not much had really changed. Terboven continued as *Reichskommissar*, with the same powers as before. The German *Führer*'s decree of 24 April 1940, the formal basis of the *Reichskommissar*'s power, was not withdrawn. The SS and the police remained as strong as before. Norway's sovereignty was not restored, there was no peace agreement, and the dream of an independent Norwegian army was as remote as ever, no matter what great expectations Quisling and NS may have had that this was all just a temporary solution to be followed by something more.

Historians have pointed out how little the ceremony at Akershus really meant. However, Quisling's 'assumption of power' was not without significance. The appointment and dismissal of government ministers were now in the hands of Quisling as prime minister. Up to now, the *Reichskommissar* alone had appointed the ministers representing the commissariat. Now, the Germans could no longer appoint or dismiss ministers on their own initiative; they had to go through Quisling. They could enforce their will, but it could take time, require extra effort, and embitter their relationship with NS. The ceremony at Akershus did strengthen the power of the government ministers and the central administration. The Germans still had to govern through a Norwegian administration, and that administration was now under the control of a Norwegian prime minister and his government.

The ministers did enjoy more freedom of action for a while. Terboven told his heads of department that the aim was 'an independent Norwegian regime' and that they should patiently bide their time. After the ceremony, the ministers no longer had to submit their proposals to the *Reichskommissariat* beforehand. Several of the ministers did act so independently as to rouse concern among the Germans. But most important of all: the state ceremony on 1 February 1942 opened the way to a new strength and scope in the NS Party's efforts to bring about The National Socialist Revolution.

The Nazification campaign

The National Socialist Revolution was promoted on two fronts. One of these was an ideological movement, to convert Norwegians to national socialism. The other was to create a new political order. Both objectives were pursued through a campaign of Nazification that started immediately after 25 September 1940, was conducted with considerable energy in 1940–1 and reached a climax in 1942. The opposition that the campaign generated followed the same course, following it like a shadow.

The Nazification campaign was promoted in several ways. Norwegians were to be persuaded. With the help of propaganda, several different means of influence and the suppression of opposing viewpoints by censorship, NS would convince the population that national socialism was the right course. The party sent out speakers; held well-advertised meetings; made national socialism visible through public marches; posted pictures of Quisling on walls and lampposts; and launched big recruitment drives. For a while in autumn and winter 1940–1 the *Hird* was especially aggressive, with the aim of winning the campaign in the streets as the German *Sturmabteilungen* (*SA*) had done in the years before Hitler's coming to power.

A second line of approach was infiltration. NS would insinuate itself into society by filling existing positions with its own people and setting up new institutions that would be staffed by NS members from the start. From these bridgeheads, the tenets of national socialism would be spread downwards and outwards throughout society. A third line used physical force to crush the opponents of Nazification.

Most of this could be carried out only using governmental power, which was now in the hands of NS. The ministries led by NS were the most important tools available to the party in its work to transform society, which would be changed by the laws and regulations they issued. Among the total of thirteen ministries, there were only three that had not been led by NS ministers prior to 1 February 1942 and that did not take part in the Nazification campaign up to that time. These were the three economic Ministries of Finance, Trade and Supplies that Terboven wanted to keep out of the hands of the national socialist revolutionary movement. The other ministries all took part, though they were not all equally important. The four new ministries that were established specifically to promote the new order played especially important roles. These were: the Ministry of the Interior; the Ministry of Culture and Popular Enlightenment; the Ministry for Labour Service and Sport; and the Police Ministry. A fifth, pre-existing section of government, the Ministry of Justice, also played an important role in Nazification. The Church and Education Ministry was involved in 1940–1 but became a key agency only the following year.

Terboven supported the campaign in principle, though he felt obliged to intervene when the revolutionary movement threatened German interests such as peace and good order in workplaces and industry. The numerous German advisers also influenced the campaign. The whole of the large *Einsatzstab* under Paul Wegener in the *Reichskommissariat* sought to advise NS centrally, as did the German advisers spread throughout the ministries and local organizations.

The ministries were not the only agencies driving the revolution forward. The process of Nazification also applied to central and local government administration. As early as 4 October 1940, Terboven had issued a decree that public servants could be moved or dismissed if they did not support the new order. The Ministry of the Interior followed this up by instructing all public servants in both central and local governments to support NS and its subsidiary organizations. Recruitment to official positions came under political control. A special office, the *Nasjonal Samling*'s Personnel Office for Public Servants (known for short as NSPOT), had to approve all appointments and promotions within the administration, to keep opponents of NS out and help supporters of the new regime to advance. Within central government administration, the process of Nazification continued throughout the occupation, with the result that by 1945, 40 per cent of the civil servants in the ministries were adherents of the party.

The Ministry of the Interior

In the early years, Viljam Hagelin was the most influential man in NS after Quisling. He was the *Fører*'s deputy and as head of the Ministry of the Interior he had an obvious impact on the implementation of The National Socialist Revolution in central and local governments. He admittedly left much of the work to his officials in the ministry, but it was Hagelin who impatiently pushed the initiatives forward and carried the ultimate responsibility.

The Ministry of the Interior set about Nazifying local government. The communal self-government that had played so big a role in the development of Norwegian democracy was abolished in record time in the winter of 1941. From now on, the local communities would be governed by a mayor who was a member of NS, provided such a person could be found. The new mayor would follow the *führer* principle in carrying out his duties. He alone would make all decisions. Hagelin made use of both state and party to bring about the new order. The state civil servant for the districts, that is the county governor, and the NS county *Fører* would together nominate who should be the mayor. The ministry then took the final decision. The county governor would also select the members of the new local council.

The county governors were not members of NS, but their traditional loyalty to the state, even now that it had become an NS state, made them effective instruments for bringing about the new order. After the county governors had assisted at the birth of the new arrangements, they themselves were removed over a year and replaced by NS members. The new appointees would also govern on the *führer* principle. Dissent was pointless.

The Nazification of the local councils continued throughout the whole of the occupation. Seventy per cent of the mayors were NS members in summer 1942, 82 per cent in April 1944 and nearly 100 per cent by the time of liberation. This was perhaps The National Socialist Revolution's biggest triumph, based on quantitative measures such as the number of NS members in mayoral positions. A qualitative assessment is more difficult and requires more thorough investigating. The question then becomes to what extent the Nazified local government managed to carry The National Socialist Revolution further forward, set its mark on the districts and reshape them towards a national socialist pattern. The new government hardly reached that far.

An important way to reach out to the public was through existing organizations: large and heavyweight organizations such as the trade unions and chambers of commerce; medium-sized and less influential trade organizations; and all the small associations of nearly every kind. NS went along this route to win influence, to gather mass support and to give the party a more solid basis. The party's interest lay not only in getting a grip on individual organizations but also in taking a corporate view of the whole gamut of organizations. The labour, business and cultural organizations would form the basis for the new national assembly that NS wanted to set up, *Rikstinget*.

The NS state with its ministries played an important role in the Nazification of the organizations. The Ministry of the Interior was the most important, but several other ministries were also engaged in the process. At the same time, the party set up its own trade unions, and representatives from the party made direct approaches to organizations that were to be won over to NS. But above all, as we shall see, the Nazification was advanced through two drastic interventions by Terboven.

The Ministry of Culture and Popular Enlightenment

After Quisling as premier and Hagelin in the Ministry of the Interior, Gulbrand Lunde was the most prominent person in the first two years of the NS government. His department became the Ministry of Culture and Popular Enlightenment, with overall responsibility for reforming cultural life and the media in the spirit of the new regime. Lunde had developed a strong NS presence and a platform of local support in the Stavanger area. He had a notable talent as an orator and writer. Within NS, he was the leading representative of the party's nationalist wing.

Lunde was enthusiastic about all aspects of the national culture – Norwegian history, Norwegian nature, Norwegian language. He thought that Norwegians had abandoned their distinctive culture. Marxism and psychoanalysis had taken over the theatres, and cinema had become a tool in the hands of Jewish speculators. The country was flooded with Hollywood films, full of gaudiness and glitter. Now all alien 'culture' was to be cast aside. People must appreciate the worth of their national culture and advance the national ideals through film, theatre, art, literature, the press, and broadcasting.

The ministry established the National Film Directorate, which gradually acquired control of all aspects of the cinema industry. The theatres were brought under the control of the ministry. Theatrical performances, revues, songs, public readings, and other forms of public presentation of text were all censored beforehand. In spring 1941 a National Theatre Directorate was established to supervise this. The theatre directors had to be approved by the ministry and were held responsible for the content of performances.

The NS leadership in the National Gallery thought that what the party regarded as the time of national decline had been expressed in visual art. They would clear the gallery of degenerate art to protect the nation's cultural heritage. The exhibition of 'Art and Degenerate Art' opened in the National Gallery in spring 1942. All the 'degenerate art' was displayed in one of the rooms, and the good and ideal art in the others. Henceforth, it was the latter that the National Gallery would promote and display. Pictures by artists such as Reidar Aulie, Arne Ekeland and Per Krohg were branded as degenerate.

The Publishers' Association was Nazified in autumn 1941 and given greater authority over the publishing houses. In March 1942, Knut Hamsun's son Tore Hamsun, who was a member of NS, was commissioned as a director in the Gyldendal publishing company, assisted by an active senior consultant from NS. In summer 1943, Aschehoug also had a director similarly appointed, though he was less active and influential. The two biggest publishing houses thereby came under control by NS. The ministry also supported three NS publishing firms that grew rapidly and published NS literature, children's books, and fiction.

The Germans and NS both wanted to ban books. The Germans were first to act against publishers, booksellers, libraries and newspaper kiosks. Books by numerous anti-German authors were proscribed, mostly well-known writers, Marxists, Jews and anti-Nazis. NS took part in this purge and then started a campaign of its own. On 17 February 1941, the ministry issued a regulation about the protection of Norwegian literature, to the effect that books that were damaging to the national and social advancement of the Norwegian people could be confiscated. The ministry set up a list of such books and followed it with supplementary lists in the following years.

Lunde's ministry got an early grip on the main news media organizations. It took over NRK, the Norwegian Broadcasting Corporation, only three days after the regime change of 25 September 1940, dismissing the management and replacing it with a head appointed by the ministry and several members from NS. The Norwegian News Agency had already been Nazified the day before by order of the ministry. The news on NRK was given a pro-German and pro-NS slant and the men promoting the new regime were given broadcast time. The competition from London Radio was strong, however, and after radios were confiscated in autumn 1941 the NRK broadcasts no longer reached out to Norwegians in general but only to NS members, who were allowed to keep their radios. German programmes gradually took over more of the broadcast time, until they filled about half in 1941. NRK largely became a forces radio for the German troops in Norway. As a component of The National Socialist Revolution it lost its significance early on.

The press was censored. Journalists were instructed what they should write, how they should write it and what to leave out. The press department in Lunde's ministry attended to censorship from the Norwegian side, sending out daily directives to the papers. The department also appointed managers in the districts, who supervised the local papers and could intervene if necessary. However, it was primarily the Germans who exercised censorship. The press was subject to both the *Wehrmacht*'s military censorship and the press department in the *Reichskommissariat*. All information considered important for the conduct of the war was blacklisted, and there was much of this: weather forecasts, mention of the many German building projects and news about the tens of thousands of soldiers who could be seen throughout the country. The press department required the press to write in a way that served German interests and told the journalists in detail how they must do so.

The Ministry for Labour Service and Sport

The Ministry for Labour Service and Sport was led by Axel Stang. The ministry's two areas of responsibility were very different, but what they had in common was that they were both concerned with young people. Through compulsory labour service and organized sport, the youth of the nation would be brought up in the spirit of national socialism.

In autumn 1940 the ministry was busy developing plans for a new, compulsory labour service, modelled on the German *Reichsarbeitsdienst*. This soon came into being, with the short and appropriate name *Arbeidstjenesten* (*AT*). Regulations about compulsory registration and service obligations followed in March and April 1941. The necessary apparatus for call-up was established, work camps were set up and the first recruits assembled in May. Compulsory service in AT was for three months, later extended to six. With some exceptions, the work consisted of building and maintaining roads, draining marshes, helping farmers in spring and autumn and similar work. About 40,000 young people did compulsory labour service between 1941 and 1943. *AT* was largely run by officers, and it had a clear military flavour. The workers wore uniforms. They were not armed, but they paraded and marched with shouldered spades.

AT did have a potential and a real role in The National Socialist Revolution. It created a ready-made process that could be used for enlistment and included an officer corps that could transfer over into the future army. Nothing ever became of this, but *AT* continued as a civil institution and a channel for Nazification. Most of the officers who served in *AT* joined the NS Party. The Nazi salute was instituted, the *AT* songbook included NS songs and there was NS propaganda in a handbook that was issued to every recruit. To assist the cultural nurturing, a 'Word for the Day' was published, with contributions from Hitler and Quisling. Sections from *AT* were included in big NS events. On the anniversary of the Akershus ceremony in February 1943, there was a big contingent from *Arbeidstjenesten* in the parade in Quisling's honour at the Palace.

There were, however, limits to the NS propaganda and the national socialist rituals. The Nazi salute was introduced for the officers, but not for the rank and file. The teaching that took place in the work camps was not particularly coloured by propaganda. The songbook also included neutral songs, and 'Word for the Day' included excerpts from Bjørnson and Ibsen. The officers, whether NS members or not, were trained that politics should be kept out of the military service and now the labour service. They were concerned that ideological lectures and active political recruitment would create unrest and harm the work.

Stang was interested in the labour service but had little commitment to the development of Norwegian sport. So, other people led the attempt to Nazify sport, particularly the German adviser Willy Wagner, who was responsible for sports matters in the *Reichskommissariat*'s propaganda department and worked alongside the head of the sports section in the Ministry for Labour Service and Sport. The ministry put its full weight into an initiative when it called the chairmen of the various sports associations to a meeting in the ministry on 22 November 1940. It announced that it would set up a new Norwegian Sports Association as an organization for all sports. The ministry would set the rules for the new association, and all types of sports organizations must belong to it. They should continue their activities as before and could not be dissolved without approval from the ministry. The association was constituted on the *führer* principle. The ministry would appoint a supremo and leaders under him for the various branches of sport. Election and self-regulation on Norwegian sport's traditional principles were set aside. The ministry would put sport under state control.

The Ministry of Justice

The Ministry of Justice under Sverre Riisnæs was responsible for implementing The National Socialist Revolution within the legal system. A decree from the *Reichskommissar* on 25 October 1940 established a new Norwegian court, *Folkedomstolen*, which became active a few months later. This was to be a political court, 'the national socialist state's special protection against forces hostile to the state and the people'. Within the court structure, it was parallel to the new State Police (Stapo) in the police system. The idea was that in cases of civil resistance, Stapo would make arrests and carry out investigations. A new public prosecutor who was a member of NS would bring charges and *Folkedomstolen* would judge the case and pass sentence.

However, the new court and public prosecutor gradually became irrelevant. Instead of making use of *Folkedomstolen*, Stapo placed political opponents in prison or in camps as 'security prisoners' for variable lengths of time. From August 1943, more serious cases could be heard by specialized courts. People who fled to Sweden also ran the risk of the police taking their close relatives as hostages and imprisoning them with the intention of deterring others from leaving.

In autumn 1940 the regime made a three-pronged attack on the independence of the courts, with two initiatives from the Ministry of Justice and one from the *Reichskommissar*. On 14 November Riisnæs issued a decree that gave him authority to appoint lay justices, and on 5 December the Ministry of Social Affairs reduced the upper age limit for public officials to sixty-five years. Eight of the Supreme Court's eighteen judges were over this age. Riisnæs now wanted to clear them out and replace them with judges who were pro-NS. A letter from Terboven on 3 December delivered the most decisive blow to the independence of the Supreme Court when he stated firmly that the Supreme Court could not take a position on any of the decrees issued by himself or his appointed ministers. The court could not re-examine them either under Norwegian law or under international law. By this move, Terboven greatly reduced the authority of the court and removed a legal barrier to Nazification campaign.

The Police Ministry

The Police Ministry had a narrower remit than the other ministries, as it was responsible for only one public institution. The SS had brought this about and placed their man, Jonas Lie, at the head of the ministry. In this way, the police became subject to SS influence. It was reorganized on a German model and became subordinate to the German *Sipo*. The Norwegian police became the most strongly Nazified of all the agencies of the state, and a new NS branch of the police, the State Police (Stapo), became the NS state's most important police resource for persecuting political enemies.

By autumn 1940 many in the police were joining NS. Jonas Lie and other leading police officers were at the head of this trend, putting strong pressure on their subordinates to become NS members. Terboven's statement that the road to Norwegian independence lay through NS made an impression. After a while, some of those who had joined in 1940 regretted having done so and withdrew, but Nazification continued. In round figures, about 40 per cent of the employees in the police and the sheriffs' offices joined NS during the war. There was a parallel movement among the military officers, who were serving in the army, the other public authority that could legally exercise coercive power. The percentage who became Nazified was high, though considerably lower than among the police. Among both the officers and the police, there were those who admired their German counterparts on professional grounds.

The ministry oversaw the new political police force, Stapo, that had been under development from autumn 1940 but was formally established on 1 July 1941. Membership of NS soon became obligatory for Stapo personnel, and many of them were convinced national socialists. Stapo's role was to suppress resistance to NS. This could involve dealing with simple cases, such as arresting people who demonstrated by wearing red knitted hats or sporting a paperclip in their buttonhole or tearing down pictures of Quisling, but it could also involve more serious and complicated matters such as preventing flight to Sweden or hunting down illegal organizations. It would not be long, however, before the *Gestapo* intervened and took over. Military resistance quickly became a matter for the *Gestapo* or *Abwehr*, but the *Gestapo* also worked to combat civil resistance. There was close co-operation between the *Gestapo* and Stapo, and the *Gestapo*'s use of brutality and torture gradually came to be copied by many Stapo men.

Altogether, the use of political police and police persecution of political opponents were the aspects of The National Socialist Revolution over which the Germans had the strongest control. NS had wider freedom of action in other fields, even though the Germans always set the boundaries and could always intervene when they saw their primary interests threatened. In the matter of policing, the day-to-day control, and the close, subordinate relationship of the NS-Norwegian police forces to their German counterparts gave little scope for NS to take an independent line.

Resistance

Terboven's political revolution on 25 September 1940 did not invoke any immediate opposition. The sudden eradication of Norwegian democracy was not met with a wave of protest. What the new order was met with was paralysis. Throughout the autumn and winter of 1940–1 this paralysis began to lift and there were signs of a shift of public opinion. The sense of defeat, the feeling of helplessness, the confusion throughout spring and summer and the shock after 25 September began to recede. More people wanted to express their opposition to the new regime.

In an open society, a change of mood such as this would probably have been expressed in the organization of a popular movement with a defined leadership and registered members. In the winter six months of 1940–1 there were signs of such a development. Activists tried to bring scattered initiatives and different ventures together into a united organization. It was all rather loose, and the circumstances prevented activists from operating as a protest movement can do in peacetime. 'Politics' was forbidden outside NS and was clamped down upon by the police. Halfway through 1941 the organization was already breaking apart. Arrests and escapes into exile finished it off.

It is obvious that an opposition front was developing, but it is equally clear that it was fumbling, scattered and going in different directions. Some initiatives were civil, others of a military nature, some were about purely symbolic resistance, others about organized services. Only gradually would the many initiatives be brought together and gathered within the frame of a comprehensive resistance movement.

In the years 1940–2, however, there was one central line of development that can be seen from an overall point of view, namely the struggle against Nazification. In this struggle, the resistance did not move first and foremost against the new order of 25 September as such. There was no frontal attack directed against Terboven's obvious breach of international law, with his total rebuilding of Norwegian society's national constitution and internal politics. The protests were more limited, and the most important opposition came from a few sectors that had certain connections between themselves but at the same time had an opinion-forming influence that extended over society as a whole. This pattern of sectoral resistance influencing wider opinion continued throughout the whole duration of the civil resistance to Nazification.

The conflict over The National Socialist Revolution was primarily between the NS state and the public. This could be seen as a Norwegian internal political struggle, but with the occupying power in the background providing a political and physical guarantee for the Nazification campaign. The Germans wanted to let it remain like that. NS should so far as possible be given the opportunity to show that the party was able on its own to reform and Nazify Norwegian society. On the other hand, the Germans could also take part or intervene in the conflict. How, when and on what level they chose to join in were not specified beforehand, not for NS and certainly not for the activists in the resistance campaign. This made the conflict unpredictable, with unexpected interventions and surprising turns.

The four most important parts of the resistance in 1940–1 were: a mass protest from the sports sector; a protest from a central public institution, the Supreme Court; a protest from another central public institution, the church; and fourth, a joint protest from a number of organizations.

Sport

In the interwar years, the sports movement had been divided between the working class and middle class. Each organized its own association. On 13 September 1940, an interim management committee was set up to prepare for and implement the establishment of a new, united sports association. The chair of the interim committee was army officer Olaf Helset, and the vice-chair was the labour leader Rolf Hofmo. Both fully supported the union. They feared that developments in Norway would go the same way as in Germany, where the working-class sport was banned and the leaders imprisoned, while the middle-class sport was gradually Nazified. Activism among the Germans and NS on one side and the strong will to resist among the sports officials on the other were the most important reasons why the process of Nazifying the sports movement was started so early and the opposition was so strong.

The interim committee refused to recognize the new, NS association that the ministry had proclaimed, and they organized a public boycott of it. This led to a 'sports strike' over the next six months. Nobody would allow themselves to be nominated to any position in the new association. All sports events promoted by the association would be nullified. Nobody would arrange or take part in official competitions. The interim leaders continued their activity in the form of an illegal committee that continued to function until the end of the war. As NS gradually tried to force its way into the local sports clubs, they either had an NS leader imposed, or they were dissolved. In spring 1942, 324 clubs were NS-led and 250 were dissolved. Membership was minimal. In autumn 1944 the membership in the Sports Association was not more than 1.3 per cent of what the membership had been in the old National Sports Association.

The top-heavy sports association with all the subordinate Nazified associations and the poorly supported NS sports clubs at ground level tried to promote Nazified sport with competitions, sports meetings and combined Norwegian-German events. These were all boycotted by the great majority of participants and the public. On the other side, there was quite a lot of 'patriot-sport' with competitions held in secret. However, it was not the illegal sports activities that made the sports resistance into a mass movement, but the almost total boycott of all NS-organized sport. The sports strike was the first big, collective protest in the civil resistance, and it was unique in Europe, without parallel in any other country's sports movement.

The Supreme Court

The Supreme Court, with Chief Justice Paal Berg as its central figure, protested against all three of the regime's initiatives that threatened the independence of the courts. It opposed the decree about the lay justices and appealed to the Ministry of Justice to have the decree about the age limit changed. Above all, the Supreme Court directly challenged what Terboven had decided. The court must be able to test the validity of the occupying power's decrees under international law. This was a provocative point of view. The courts in the Netherlands, Belgium and Denmark made no claim to have any right to test the occupier's decrees.

What the Supreme Court primarily wanted to do was to make it clear that the new regime had no legitimate foundation. On the other hand, the judges did not really think that their protests would have any effect on the new holders of power. On 12 December 1940, they declared that they could not continue in their positions in these new circumstances, and they resigned from public office. In a few months, the court had demonstrated emphatically that after political democracy had been abolished the state was no longer a legal state, a state of legitimate law (*Rechtsstaat*). Terboven allowed the Ministry of Justice to follow up on the resignations by appointing new, pro-NS Supreme Court judges. The Supreme Court was thereby able to continue its activity but as a Nazified agency. The lower courts were not subjected to any significant attempts at Nazification, and they continued to function as before.

The church

NS's Nazification campaign did not include the church. The church and education minister, Ragnar Skancke, said early on that the party had no plans for the church beyond what was printed in the NS manifesto, which stated that basic Christian values would be protected. This was, however, conditional on the church not attacking or being hostile towards the new NS state. The priests were warned that they must stick to the edifying and the 'eternal' in their preaching, and not be 'political'. The church continued its activities as before. The government ministry made no attempt to reorganize it, and no bishops or priests were dismissed. In the German Lutheran Church, forces that wanted to unite Christianity and national socialism gained the upper hand. There were few such tendencies in NS.

When the Lutheran established church launched its first resistance action in the new year of 1941, its criticism was therefore mainly not about matters concerning itself but about issues in society. By then a meeting of bishops and mission society leaders had founded the Christian Consultative Council (*Kristent Samråd*). This was a combined church council for the established Lutheran Church and the non-established Christian organizations, and it would come to play a big part in determining the church's line of resistance. It was led by the bishop of Oslo, Eivind Berggrav.

On 15 January 1941 the bishops wrote an important letter to the government minister. By then it was clear that the state had violated both international and Norwegian law, and this was the starting point for the bishops' protest. Was the state a state of legitimate law in which the exercise of power was constrained by the law? If it was, the church had an obligation to obey it, as the bishops equated a state of legitimate law with Christian norms. If it was not, the church had an obligation to be disobedient. The population had now been put in doubt, the bishops said, about whether the state would uphold law and justice as the church's confession of faith required. The church, therefore, needed clarity about whether the state accepted and felt bound by the legal and moral obligations that were grounded in the foundations of the church's faith, the Bible, and the Confession.

The bishops' views were expressed in a 'Pastoral letter to Our Congregations from the Bishops of the Church of Norway', dated January/February 1941. In the letter, the bishops were able to refer to numerous declarations of support from non-established Christian organizations and faith communities. Fifty thousand copies of the letter were printed, and their distribution to priests and congregations throughout the land started at the beginning of February. Then the police and *Gestapo* in Oslo and Aker took a hand and confiscated the letters. Thirty-six thousand copies had already been sent out, but police throughout the country also tried to confiscate them or prevent them from being discussed. Nevertheless, many priests did receive the letter and read it out during or after the church service on Sunday, 9 February. The bishops protested against the confiscation in a letter to Skancke several days later and at the same time sent a letter to the deans in each diocese, advising them about the confiscation.

The Supreme Court and the church were both important public institutions with great symbolic authority and the capacity to influence public opinion. The Supreme Court's action was just about the court and the court system, but it had a wider influence because the legal system has an essential place in a democratic society. The church's protest was chiefly about what it considered were unsupportable conditions in society but also about violations of its own position. The Supreme Court did not do anything to publicize its action, but the church did. Through priests and congregations, it addressed all Christian

Norway, at a time when religion still had a strong position in the community. By its action, it branded The National Socialist Revolution as ungodly and the NS state as non-Christian, even though it didn't use such strong words.

Sport, the Supreme Court, and the church were pioneers in the civil resistance, largely because they had persistent and committed leaders. One of them, Rolf Hofmo, was removed from the field early and remained out of action throughout the later resistance campaign. He was arrested in February 1941 and later sent to Germany, where he remained in prison until the war was over. The three others continued as prominent resistance leaders; Paal Berg right up to the liberation and Berggrav until he was interned in spring 1942. Helset continued, including a year in prison, until in May 1943 he had to flee to Sweden, where he became second in command of the Norwegian police troops.

Helset had been involved in the military resistance right from the start, first in the Norwegian Campaign in 1940 and then as a key person in the development that led to Milorg. In autumn 1940 he combined this activity with his leadership position in the sports movement's resistance. In summer 1940 Berg and Berggrav had supported a policy of co-operation, up until Terboven's political revolution. Thereafter, they followed the mainstream in the internal political development from collaboration to resistance.

The organizations

The number of social organizations had grown in the interwar years. Numerous large and small organizations had acquired greater power and more influence. In spring and summer 1941, many of them took part in a protest that would have dramatic consequences for themselves, for the Nazification campaign and for the development of an organized resistance movement. The protest took the form of three petitions, which this time were not addressed to any government ministry, but to the *Reichskommissar* himself. The purpose, at any rate of the first two petitions, was not to get Terboven to change his policy. The signatories reckoned that was impossible. The purpose was to influence opinion and strengthen the developing resistance front. Altogether the three protests, the Germans' reaction to them and the later fate of the protesting organizations were decisive in the development of a civil resistance movement.

The first letter of protest from the organizations to Terboven was dated 3 April 1941 and signed by leading representatives of twenty-two organizations, protesting about political appointments to public office. The next letter to Terboven was dated 15 May and signed by representatives of forty-three organizations. It started with a general criticism of how NS had acted since coming into power. The ministers had in several instances made decisions that were in obvious conflict with international law, Norwegian law, and Norwegian public understanding of the rule of law. The letter specially mentioned regulations issued by the Ministry of Justice and by the Police Ministry that were not consistent with the purpose of the legislation to protect personal security. It gave examples of how NS had advanced its cause, referring to the behaviour of the *Hird* and the pressure on public officials to join NS. The letter then concluded that all this had led to increasing unrest in all sections of society.

Nearly all the organizations behind the first letter of protest were also signatories to the second, plus a further twenty-three that came in the second round, corresponding with the broader content of the second letter. The most important addition was that the Federation of Norwegian Commercial organizations and the Association of Norwegian Insurance Companies were now among the signatories. On the other hand, the big three business organizations were conspicuous by their absence – the Employers' Federation, the Federation of Norwegian Industries, and the Association of Trade Guilds. They didn't want any confrontation with Terboven. The 43 signatory organizations represented about 700,000 members. The most powerful of the organizations, the Confederation of Trade Unions, was a signatory to both letters.

Terboven responded to the protests not with any counterargument but with a blatant display of power. The forty-three signatories were summoned to a meeting on 18 June in the parliament building, where Terboven started by giving a thundering speech. Then six of the organization leaders were arrested and taken away by German police. Hagelin then stepped forward and referred to a decree that had been issued the day before. This gave the Ministry of the Interior the right to reorganize or dissolve associations and to dismiss and replace leaders. Using the authority given by the decree, the ministry had decided that eleven of the protesting organizations were to be dissolved and twenty-six others would have a leader appointed by the ministry. The appointed commissars were present at the meeting, and each left the meeting together with the leader who was being replaced, to complete the formal takeover in the organization's offices.

The third letter of protest came from the Confederation of Trade Unions alone. Developments in the trade union movement since 28 September 1940 had been complicated. At the head of the legally constituted confederation, there were three new leaders who had been appointed by the Germans. These were not members of NS, but they were regarded by the Germans as co-operative. Under them, the members of the old secretariat continued in office, willing to make considerable concessions to keep the organization functioning and accepting the leaders appointed by the Germans without protest.

Three different groups each tried to pull the union movement in their own direction. One group was NS, which had some members in the movement. The second was the communists, who had considerable influence. They wanted to keep NS out but were otherwise willing to co-operate with the Germans. The third group was the Labour leaders who had followed the government north during the military campaign in 1940 and then turned back to Oslo. Back in Oslo, the Germans had forbidden them to resume their work. The most important of these were the legitimate chairman of the confederation, Konrad Nordahl, the vice-chairman Lars Evensen and Einar Gerhardsen who was vice-chairman of the Labour Party. They were part of a milieu that was outside the confederation's secretariat but tried to influence the leadership from outside and win them over to a less compliant policy towards the Germans. In January 1941 this faction was behind the founding of the illegal newspaper *Free Labour Movement* which continued until the end of the war, with great sacrifices, as the illegal organ of the labour movement.

One man who gradually came to play a key role was the confederation's lawyer, Viggo Hansteen, a former communist. His policy was a mixture of collaboration and cautious resistance, and he won influence by cultivating links with all relevant sectors: the leaders appointed by the Germans, the members of the secretariat, the communists, the circle around the 'Free Labour Movement' and resistance groups outside the labour movement.

Inside the confederation, the will to resist grew throughout the spring of 1941. Nevertheless, the Germans allowed the confederation to continue as before and did not intervene. On 30 June the confederation sent a protest letter of its own, signed by the whole secretariat. The labour leaders complained that the organization now had so little influence on pay rates and was so subject to detailed control that it could hardly function as its members' representative organization any longer. If the authorities did not allow the labour movement 'satisfactory opportunities to do its work', the members of the secretariat could no longer continue in post. The confederation had now expressed an indication of protest three times.

The time for writing protest letters was now over. The first and the last protests had expressed professional interests but the middle one, 'the protest of the 43', included a broader complaint about the behaviour of NS. Taken together, the letters of protest were a comprehensive demonstration of the organizations' collective opposition to the NS state and the institutions of the German occupation that were behind it. The organizations' leaders backed the protests with their signatures.

Even though the resistance to the regime's Nazification campaign came from sectors and did not indicate any generally formulated platform or manifesto, the resistance from these groups was nevertheless an obvious defence of important aspects of the nature of Norwegian society and the culture of Norwegian democracy. The Supreme Court and the church had shone a light on the need for legitimate government in a liberal democracy. The democratic principle that the administration should be politically neutral had been pointed out. The organizations had demonstrated how democracy is anchored in a civil society alongside and independent of the state. So long as the organizations were intact, their democratic, electoral principles were a challenge to The National Socialist Revolution's *führer* principle. All the four sectors had demonstrated how democracy had a broader basis that quickly became evident when the uppermost political institutions disappeared. The sectors expressed oppositional views that in a free society would soon have been passed on into the political system but that had been blocked when the political level was occupied by NS and Germans.

Terboven's show of power in the parliament building on 18 June was nothing compared with the violence he now directed against the labour movement. He declared a state of emergency. From the early morning of 10 September 1941, armed police units patrolled the streets of the capital. Posters announcing the state of emergency were evident on house walls, and the newspapers gave it prominent coverage. Any disturbance of industrial calm was strictly forbidden, anybody who opposed the emergency regulations would be court-martialled and resistance would be crushed by armed force. At the same time, the *Gestapo* moved against the labour movement. By the evening of 10 September news came that Viggo Hansteen and senior shop steward Rolf Wickstrøm had been tried by court martial, condemned to death and executed. More sentences followed the next day. A further three people were condemned to death but reprieved, with the sentences reduced to life imprisonment. The *Gestapo* rounded up all the members of the confederation's secretariat that they could get hold of. 250 were brought in for questioning and at least 120 arrested, including several leading shop stewards. In all, twenty-two were given long sentences in *Zuchthaus* and sent to Germany. The state of emergency was lifted after six days.

The state of emergency was directed particularly against the trade union movement but was obviously also intended to have a deterrent effect on the whole Norwegian public. As he had done with the meeting in the parliament building on 18 June, Terboven used the opportunity to take Nazification a step further. The trade union organization was now put in the hands of NS. The head of the NS union organization was appointed as leader of the Confederation of Trade Unions, and numerous individual trade unions got new NS or pro-NS leaders. In the two big business organizations, the Employers' Federation and the Association of Trade Guilds, the chairmen were replaced by new leaders from NS. The Germans instituted a ban on resigning from these organizations or from the Confederation of Trade Unions, and subscriptions still had to be paid. *Nordmannsforbundet* ('The Norse Federation') had a new leader appointed by NS. *Norsk Folkehjelp* ('Norwegian People's Aid') and the Scout organizations were dissolved.

At the University in Oslo, the Germans dismissed the elected rector, Didrik Arup Seip, and replaced him with an NS man, Adolf Hoel. The education minister, Ragnar Skancke, summoned the teachers and students to a compulsory meeting in the main assembly hall, amid an ominous display of the authority supporting the state of emergency. Heavily armed German policemen were posted along the walls of the room, and machine guns mounted in the galleries pointed down towards the assembled crowd. The head of the *Gestapo* spoke first and ended by declaring that the rector had been dismissed. Then he handed over the leadership of the university to Skancke, who now became rector and in turn appointed Hoel as his deputy rector; he later became rector. The university was now to be run on the *führer* principle. Seip was arrested and later sent to Germany, and three other anti-NS professors were also arrested.

Terboven's support of the Nazification campaign was a two-edged sword. It gave NS new positions in organizations and institutions, but the way this happened, with compulsory appointments, was not designed to increase support for NS and give The National Socialist Revolution a broader basis. Terboven's primary motive for forced Nazification can hardly have been to support NS. Rather, by installing NS leaders into organizations he wanted to ensure that the organizations and institutions did not develop further into centres of unrest.

What Terboven probably had not reckoned on was the reaction that Nazification at the top of the institutions evoked among the rank and file. Most of the members resigned from or left their Nazified organizations and no longer took part in their activities. Among the sports organizations, the demise of the new, Nazified association was already well underway. Over the whole range of organizations, most of those led by NS seemed to be empty vessels. Parallel to the resignations from and inactivation of the organizations, another and even more important development was taking place. In autumn 1941 new, illegal organizations or networks sprang from the old organizations, with similar vocational bases but often with new leaders and new connections. At the same time, some of the leaders in these illegal organizations sought to find ways of working together. An organizational basis for a civil resistance movement was laid down that autumn.

Victory in the civil resistance campaign

In the time after the ceremony at Akershus in February 1942, The National Socialist Revolution was approaching its climax. The new NS government was full of enterprise and initiative and seething with proposals and actions. Its hour had come. Lawyers would be obliged to be members of The Norwegian Bar Association. The law on Norwegian press associations and the law on the work of advertising imposed obligatory membership on two new groups of workers. *Noregs Ungdomslag* (a cultural youth organization) was reorganized. *Noregs Mållag* (an organization promoting the *Nynorsk* language) was later incorporated into the *Ungdomslag*. Anyone who wanted to publish had to be a member of the Norwegian Publishers' Association, which was under NS leadership. Several associations got new chairmen or new management. The list of planned, half-implemented or fully realized initiatives was long. There were plans to gather all the business organizations into ten 'national commerce and industry groups'.

Only five days after the inauguration ceremony at Akershus, the new government passed two important laws. The first said that all young people in the age group ten to eighteen must serve in *Nasjonal Samlings Ungdomsfylking* (*NSUF*), the NS youth organization modelled on Hitler Youth. NS wanted to have a hand in the upbringing of young people. The second law was about setting up a new professional organization for teachers, *Norges Lærersamband*. This was to be headed by a national leader nominated by the prime minister. The man selected for this post was Orvar Sæther, a teacher from Lakkegata School in Oslo and a former chief of staff in the *Hird*. Membership of the new teachers' organization was compulsory.

These were two separate laws, but they were linked together in the way they were presented to the public and in the directives that The Resistance Movement issued opposing them. The crux of the matter was the nurture and education of young people. NS wanted to get a hold of the new generation and reform them in the spirit of national socialism. This would be brought about through National Samling's youth organization and via the NS-led teachers' organization through which the party would be able to influence young people in school. The youngsters were to be faced with national socialism in an organized form, both in their free time and in school.

For Quisling, the corporate aspect of *Norges Lærersamband* was important. His projected national assembly, *Rikstinget*, would consist of representatives of organizations from the various sections of society and working life. The teachers' organization fitted well into this mould. It would be one of the many mandatory organizations that would form the basis of the assembly.

In the week after the announcement of the new laws, people in resistance circles discussed how they should respond. The outcome was a carefully worded resistance directive for use by the teachers, in two parts. In the first part they refused to co-operate in bringing up young people along the lines that were specified for the NS youth organization. In the second part, they refused to become members of *Norges Lærersamband*. The directive was delivered through various channels to teachers throughout the country. They were encouraged to send a signed copy to *Norges Lærersamband* on 20 February. Now it was no longer the organizations as such that were protesting via their leaders. The rank and file of the membership were being mobilized. This initiated the most important counterattack on NS's Nazification campaign and triggered off a set of dramatic events in spring 1942. The directive succeeded in mobilizing most of the teachers to take part in a large demonstration of disobedience against the government's Nazification campaign.

Quisling and the Church and Education Ministry could have chosen to ignore the protests and not make them into a big issue, or they could have negotiated, coaxed, and compromised. Instead, they did the opposite. They acted quickly, indeed rashly, obviously without having thought carefully through the consequences. Quisling wanted to force the teachers to their knees. On 23 February they were informed that withdrawal from *Norges Lærersamband* would be interpreted as resignation from their posts. Teachers who had not cancelled their protest by 1 March were dismissed. On 25 February it was announced that all teachers who still protested against membership would have their February salary cut off. This did happen in Oslo and a couple of other places.

Quisling and his colleagues obviously reckoned that under such pressure, the teachers would surrender and withdraw their resignations. When they didn't do that, the ministry found itself in a difficult situation. To save face and gain some breathing space the ministry pointed out the need to restrict the use of fuel and declared a month's 'fuel holiday' from school, starting on 27 February. During the 'holiday', the authorities turned up the economic pressure. Ten thousand teachers were unpaid in the months of March and April, while most schools remained closed. The police took action. Teachers were arrested, questioned, and possibly imprisoned for a while, to find the ringleaders of the protest and deactivate them.

On 14 February, the bishops protested about the obligation on young people to serve in the NS youth organization. The mass protest about this, however, came from the parents. At the beginning of March, a group of women initiated an act of protest by parents, encouraging them to send a message to the ministry: 'I do not wish my child to take part in NSUF's Youth Service, because the guidelines drawn up for this work conflict with my conscience.' The parental action was widespread, was probably the biggest of all the mass actions in 1942 – and was a formidable success. The numbers are uncertain, but there is no doubt that tens of thousands sent in their protests. This was a specific action, directed solely against the compulsory youth service and carried out by a specific social group, parents. But the parents, the teachers and the clergy had one common purpose – to protect the upbringing of children from the NS government and national socialist influence.

Throughout the first weeks of March the political situation within the country was extremely tense. The teachers stuck to their opposition to membership of *Lærersambandet*, most schools were closed, and the teachers didn't get any pay. Tens of thousands of parents protested that their children would not serve in NSUF, and the church was about to break loose from the NS state. Then Terboven intervened, as he had done the previous year. He met with Quisling, and they both agreed that they must hit back hard. A thousand male teachers throughout the country were arrested on 20 March in a joint action by Norwegian and German police. Stapo, the normal police forces and sheriffs in rural communities all took part in the arrests. Then the *Gestapo* took over and placed the teachers in internment camps.

In the camps, the *Gestapo* put hard pressure on the arrested teachers. Living circumstances were wretched, and the food was poor. The teachers were interrogated and threatened, and in the camp at Jørstadmoen the teachers were kicked and beaten and subjected to punishment exercises of crawling face-down through the snow.

> A very frequent punishment exercise was to make the whole group lie face-down and then – with their hands behind their backs – crawl forward through the snow. This is very difficult even under normal circumstances. What it was like for the teachers in normal civilian clothing and in 30-40 cm. of wet snow, is easier to imagine than to describe.

The Germans' demand remained unchanged. The teachers must state that they agreed to join *Lærersambandet*. Then they would be set free.

As the arrested teachers were scattered in different camps, it was difficult to unite them in a shared response. At Falstad and at Sydspissen, the teachers submitted to the pressure, joined *Lærersambandet* and were allowed to leave the internment camp. When those at Jørstadmoen continued to refuse, the Germans tightened the thumbscrew. Five hundred teachers were sent north to Trondheim, where the *Reichskommissariat* had requisitioned the boat *Skjerstad*. The teachers were now to be sent to Kirkenes to do forced labour. In Trondheim, some of them were prepared to give up, but Terboven turned a deaf ear. On 15th April, *Skjerstad* left Trondheim on a seventeen-day voyage north. Around 490 teachers were crammed together on a vessel that was authorized for 250 people and that could be considered at risk of Allied attack along the coast. In Kirkenes, the teachers were handed over to the *Wehrmacht*, who set them to work. Most of the government ministers protested in the cabinet meeting about the maltreatment of the teachers but without effect. They didn't have Quisling on their side, and anyway, the matter was now in the hands of the Germans.

The school situation remained deadlocked until the end of April. The teachers refused to teach, and most of the schools were closed. Two factors led to the teachers surrendering and the schools being able to reopen. On 21 April Terboven gave a speech in which he interpreted the resistance by the teachers as an attempted strike that disrupted public peace and order. This could be understood as a signal of more drastic measures, with the possible use of death sentences. The second factor was that the Church and Education Ministry retreated. In a circular on 25 April, they declared that the teachers were automatically enrolled in *Lærersambandet*. It was no longer necessary to submit any individual declaration of membership. The teachers should return to their teaching posts and would be paid from 1 May.

The teachers maintained their protest against *Lærersambandet* and refused to acknowledge that they automatically were members, but in practice, they accepted the compromise and the schools gradually opened again. The teachers who had been taken to Kirkenes, however, had to continue their forced labour in the north. The Germans would not abandon the requirement that they must join *Lærersambandet*. After internal discussions, the teachers decided to sign a statement that they were becoming members. After that, they were sent south in three groups throughout the autumn and were able at last to resume their work as teachers.

The teachers' protest was the collective act of resistance that aroused the greatest attention and had the strongest influence on public opinion in spring 1942. There were teachers throughout the country, and in many rural districts especially they were key people in the local community. Whether they had children in school or not, most people were concerned about what was happening with the teachers. Moreover, the teachers' plight called for aid that involved the wider community. The teachers were unpaid for two months, and collections and other assistance were started to help them and their families. What made the teachers' action particularly important was the feeling that those who helped the teachers not only supported them and took part in defending how young people were to be brought up but were also working together in the whole of society's resistance against the NS state.

The stubborn church

The conflict between the NS state and the church ran parallel to the conflict over education and was almost equally dramatic. The church wanted to break away from the state because it was no longer a state of legitimate law. On 24 February the bishops resigned from their appointments as state employees. Most of the priests and many parish councils sent statements to the Church and Education Ministry to say that they still considered their bishop as legitimate. The question now arose of whether the priests should also resign, and it was agreed that they should. The underlying reasons for this action would be set out in a comprehensive statement of faith, 'The Foundation of the Church', explaining the theological reasons for resigning.

At Easter, the priests read out the statement to their congregations. They then declared that they were resigning from their appointments but would continue to carry out all the work in the parish that could be done by a priest without an official state appointment. The statement was widely supported by parish councils and by non-established Christian organizations. In the history of the Lutheran Church, this mass resignation was a unique event. No established Lutheran Church has detached itself from the state in this way before or since.

The previous year, the church had protested against a state that infringed the law. Now, the church bore the full consequences of its protest. From now on, bishops and priests would have to get by without their state salary but continue to hold services, give spiritual guidance, and take part in the work of the parish. They continued to live in their vicarages. However, they could no longer perform legal weddings. Couples wanting to be married had to do so in a civil ceremony for the marriage to be legal. They could then follow this with a blessing in church.

Quisling again wanted to react harshly. He responded to the resignations with an urgent telegram to every priest, in which he described the resignation as an act of rebellion that would incur the law's strongest punishment. The leader of the church, Eivind Berggrav, was arrested and later interned, and all the bishops in turn were dismissed and banished from their dioceses. But the Church and Education Ministry did not remove the great majority of the priests who had resigned their official appointments – and that was nearly all of them. By 1 March 1943, 645 priests out of 699 (92 per cent) had resigned. During the war, eighty-seven of these (12 per cent of those who were in service prior to the ceremony at Akershus) were dismissed and in most cases also banished from their parishes.

The State Church, which was now an NS church, continued to function as best it could. The ministry appointed new bishops and priests to replace those who had been dismissed or had reached retiring age. There were not many to choose from, and the ministry had to reduce the required theological qualifications to fill the vacancies. In place of the traditional Council of Bishops, Quisling set up a new institution, the Church Advisory Council, which included not only the NS-appointed bishops but also Quisling and Skancke. Support for the NS State Church was minimal. The result here was the same as in other areas. NS could demonstrate a foundation in formal institutions, but it was a weak foundation.

There were now two Lutheran Churches in Norway: an NS State Church with a sparse following, and an autonomous church with its own leadership serving the great majority. On 20 June 1942, the bishops decided to set up the Provisional Church Leadership and sent out a notice about this. A month later, the new leadership introduced itself by publishing an explanation of the church situation. As members of the leadership group were imprisoned, new members stepped forward. From May 1943 this group became fully illegal. Prior to that, it had on several occasions acted openly with names mentioned. Thereafter, it operated 'underground' like other illegal resistance leadership groups.

The churchmen were treated less harshly than the teachers. The work of the autonomous church was obstructed or disturbed in various ways, but not to the extent of preventing it from functioning as a church for the great majority of the population. The reason for this difference in response lay in Germany, where there had been a conflict between church and state throughout the 1930s. When war broke out, this conflict was abandoned. Hitler wanted to postpone the big confrontation with the church until the war was over. This policy spilt over into Norway, where Terboven had

NS under his thumb and did not want to act so harshly against the clergy as against the teachers.

The church's act of resistance had the same effect on public opinion as the actions by the teachers and the parents. The church had its own channel of public communication, the pulpit, which was unique in the one-party state. The resistance by the church added a wider dimension to the protests by the teachers and the parents. The church's principled rejection of the NS state became united with the teachers' and the parents' more specific protests.

The effectiveness of the civil resistance in spring 1942 lay in the interaction between the teachers', the parents' and the clergy's actions and their influence individually and collectively on the public in general. The issue at stake was the future of The National Socialist Revolution. The German security service wrote in its situation report on 26 April that both in Quisling's government and in leading resistance circles the conflicts in the current situation were 'considered to be the decisive confrontation over the new ideological and political order in Norway'.

In spring 1942, the fight about The National Socialist Revolution in Norway attracted attention beyond the borders of the country. Somebody succeeded in sending out reports of *Skjerstad*'s voyage, which became front-page news in the Allied press. This publicity called up images of the little, defeated, unarmed nation that was turning against the dominant occupying force. The events in Norway reminded people that the war was not only military but also ideological, a campaign for the democratic and constitutional values that the Allies saw themselves as fighting for. This came at a time when the Allies were still on the defensive and Germany was at the height of its power. Usually, The Resistance Movements throughout Europe developed in line with the fortunes of the war. They strengthened as the Allies strengthened. The Norwegian civil resistance in 1940–2 broke this mould. It reached a climax and won on The Home Front while the Germans were still winning on the external fronts.

NS's national assembly is buried

In early summer 1942, the situation calmed down. The teachers' mass protest had run its course, and none of the parties in the church dispute provoked the others with new initiatives. Quisling then started a new offensive on two fronts, which was carried out in summer and autumn 1942. First, in a memorandum on 9 June to the German *Führer*, Quisling pointed out that the strife with the teachers and the church was over and suggested that the time might be ripe for peace negotiations. Hitler's reply in a letter of 29 June was negative. The war situation was such that a peace agreement would not be appropriate.

Another cold shower from the *Führer* followed soon after. In a meeting in his headquarters on 11 August, Hitler again asserted that there would be no peace negotiations during the war. The relationship between Germany and Norway should not be discussed at all. Germany would decide about that unilaterally when the war was over. Terboven was given the task of sharing this information with Quisling clearly and sharply. In a letter of 17 September, Quisling was explicitly requested to put a stop to all discussion in NS about changing Norway's political position and status according to constitutional and international law.

The second front that Quisling opened was to try to set up the combined parliament consisting of a cultural assembly and a business assembly, known as *Rikstinget*. This had remained on his agenda since the ceremony at Akershus and had provided the overall perspective behind the many moves in spring 1942 to take control of the organizations. What he needed to do was to establish a set of loyal organizations that could serve as a foundation for *Rikstinget*, and to select representatives from them.

When the resistance leaders got to hear of this plan at the end of August, it provoked a massive wave of protest, reminiscent of events in the spring. Tens of thousands of workers and business people gave notice individually that they would not be members of any organization that was represented in *Rikstinget*. This time, Terboven intervened almost immediately. Mass resignations could lead to industrial unrest that would hurt production, the Germans' vulnerable area. *Gestapo* and Stapo rounded up a number of business leaders and trade union officials for interviews, and some of them were detained. The police demanded that the resignations be withdrawn and threatened drastic reprisals. The public still had ghastly memories of the terror during the state of emergency the year before. The resignations were withdrawn, and people continued formally as members of their NS-led organizations. However, NS also had to make concessions. It gave up attempts to establish *Rikstinget*, which received its death blow on 25 September 1942.

The mass resignations by workers and business people were more widespread than the protest actions by the teachers and the priests. Hundreds of priests, thousands of teachers but tens of thousands of workers protested. Only the action by the parents of school children could muster as many people. However, the action in the autumn did not have as strong an impact as the dramatic events of the spring. One reason for this was that the workers' action was incomplete and was weakened by the division between the social democrats and the communists. Another, more important, reason was that the mass resignation action was quelled so quickly that it never fully developed. It did have a role, however. It was seen as an addition to the acts of protest in the spring and like those, it demonstrated the strength of the resistance to the NS state and The National Socialist Revolution.

The return home from Kirkenes in November 1942 of the last of the teachers can be seen as the end of two years of increasingly intense confrontation between the NS state and the Norwegian public over the future of The National Socialist Revolution. The public emerged as winners and NS as losers. The public had not allowed itself to be converted to the national socialist ideology, and NS had not managed to consolidate any public basis of political support. The division between the 'Nazis' on one side and the 'Patriots' or 'Good Norwegians' on the other became more acute because of the confrontation. NS did admittedly continue promoting its Nazification campaign almost until the end of the war and membership increased slowly right up until autumn 1943, but after 1942 public awareness of the need to resist the progress of Nazification was so widespread that NS made little headway.

The triumph of the civil resistance movement stands in sharp contrast to two other events at the end of 1942. The same month as the last of the teachers came home from Kirkenes, the Germans carried out their action against the Jews, which took the lives of a third of the Norwegian Jews. For the military resistance movement, 1942 was far from a triumph. It went from one catastrophe to another. The last chapter in this tragedy was the bloody defeat of Milorg in Sørlandet.

After their defeats in the conflicts about school and church in the spring and about *Rikstinget* in September, NS had every reason to put all their strength into making a success of the party's national conference on 26–27 September. The thousands who flocked to the capital at the end of September 1942 must have felt a growing sense of isolation. The successful resistance campaign had shown that most of the population was steadily turning against them. At the national conference, the delegates were able to emerge briefly out of isolation and feel strengthened by the elaborate arrangements. The party could still reap the benefits of being connected with an occupying power at the height of its strength. The Germans had been advancing in the East since summer. Pan-Germanism reached its high point in the party just at the time of the conference. One leader after another referred in his speech to the Germanic fellowship that bound Norwegians and Germans together.

However, the party was at a watershed. From late autumn the fortunes of war elsewhere in the world changed and NS was now being backed by a losing, rather than a winning, Germany. The party conference at the end of September was the only one held during the war. Thereafter, the external opposition became too strong and the internal capacity too weak for the party to attempt such a show of strength again. There had been high emotions and enthusiastic responses to the pan-German speeches during the heady days of the conference but after the party was over, the German security service reported that doubt was beginning to grow. Within NS, Norwegian nationalism and doubts about the Germans grew stronger. The summary executions during the state of emergency in Trøndelag a fortnight later reinforced this trend. These shocked all Norwegians, both NS supporters and their opponents.

Resistance leadership

During 1942 a civil resistance leadership developed that would take its final shape the following year. It consisted of two groups that were held together by a few key people, but the leadership as such was never formalized. The two groups were *Koordinasjonskomiteen* ('The Co-ordination Committee', known as *KK*) and *Kretsen* ('The Circle').

There were five social groups who mobilized in 1942 – the teachers, the parents and the priests in the spring and the workers and business people in September. There was no overall leadership behind the actions. Each had its own leadership. Considered together, they formed a rather diverse picture. Nevertheless, there were links between them. In the school and church protests, events in one sector affected developments in the other. The pioneer status of the teachers and the priests in the resistance was held up as an example to the workers and the business people when they were preparing themselves for their protest. There were channels of communication between the various leaderships. Important leaders knew each other and conferred. The core groups behind the teachers' and the parents' actions were quite close, even though it was a question of two separate actions and there was some disagreement initially about the parents' actions. There was communication between these groups and the churchmen about the Youth Service, which everybody objected to.

At the same time, the Co-ordination Committee (*KK*) was functioning as a cross-sector organization. This had its roots in the protest by the organizations the year before and in the underground leadership groups that were set up in autumn 1941. The *KK* system was established by New Year 1941–2, when six different professions were represented on the committee. The committee included trusted men throughout most of the country, mostly people from the same professions that were represented on the committee and especially teachers. In summer 1942 the workers and the business people each got a representative on *KK*, in preparation for the protest about *Rikstinget*. The workers' representative's constituency was the illegal trade union movement, and the business representative was supported by an illegal committee of business people. Later, agriculture and public administration were also represented. For security reasons, the committee didn't grow any bigger than that. *KK* was sufficiently representative to give the civil resistance legitimate breadth.

KK also had links with illegal leaderships that were not directly represented in the committee: from 1941 with the illegal student leadership and the teaching staff leadership at the university; from 1942 with an illegal group for civil servants and public officials; and from 1943 with the 'Culture Group' that aspired to lead the resistance in the field of art and culture. Finally, there were variable, but eventually good, relationships with the illegal press.

KK had a secretariat who attended to connections with the committee's local representatives through a dedicated communication service. It was not safe to use the telephone, telegraph, or ordinary post, which could alert police attention. *KK* was also cautious about using couriers. It mainly made use of postal and railway workers who alongside their ordinary work passed messages on between *KK* centrally and the representatives in the districts. The man behind the initial set up of this intentionally conspiratorial communication network was the first general secretary, Ole Jacob Malm.

This illegal technique was later developed further, enabling the secretariat to become more professional. The first three general secretaries also represented their professions in *KK*, but this ended in summer 1943 when Tore Gjelsvik took over the position. The previous general secretaries had been known by name within the *KK* organization, but Gjelsvik saw to it that the members of *KK* and the local representatives knew only his codename. Through *KK*'s secretariat, the civil resistance leadership gradually acquired access to important resources such as the illegal press and transport of refugees. Over time, the secretariat came to operate with a significant role of its own in relation to the larger committee.

The representatives in *KK* exchanged reports from the various branches of civil resistance and monitored the situation. Basically, *KK* was still no more than what the name indicated – a co-ordinating group but not a higher-level organization. Nor was it only *KK*'s network that was used to spread directives and information during the big actions. The church and the illegal trade union movement each had their own lines of communication. The parents' action was started and partly carried forward by women who conveyed the directives from one to another on their own initiative.

The other leadership group, *Kretsen*, with Paal Berg as its central figure, came into being because of its connection with the government in exile. However, the men who comprised it were also active in The Home Front and exerted an influence on various sectors of the resistance and in relation to *KK*. So, from the beginning of 1943 at the latest, the civil resistance leadership consisted of two defined groups: *KK*, which had been in existence for a year; and *Kretsen*, which first became an established organization in the winter of 1942–3, because of its connection with the government in exile. Through *Kretsen*, the leadership encompassed a political balance between non-socialists and social democrats, an access to social prestige and constitutional legitimacy and an authorized connection with the government in London. Through *KK*, the leadership had its roots in the organized civil resistance.

CHAPTER 12
THE HOLOCAUST IN NORWAY

The German programme to eradicate the Jews was in a way part of the Norwegian National Socialist Revolution. Quisling and NS admittedly did not intend to eliminate the Jews as the Germans did, but they assisted the German action against them, and they instigated a policy that envisaged Norway without any Jews. The antisemitic vision of a future national socialist society without Jews in Norway was realized in autumn 1942. Like the policy to attempt forced Nazification of society, the anti-Jewish policy aroused resistance. However, this resistance took a different form. It consisted of helping the Jews to flee.

The Hitler regime's antisemitic policy evolved in stages. The final step in this development was the decision that all European Jews should be eliminated. By spring and early summer 1942 the way this was to be done had finally been decided: gassing in special camps in Poland. The Germans would eradicate all the Jews they could get their hands on, including Western European Jews in occupied countries. In June and July 1942, they began transporting Jews from France, the Netherlands and Belgium to extermination camps in the East.

Although the German eradication programme applied to the whole of Europe, it could not be carried out in the same way everywhere. It had to be adapted to local circumstances and different occupation regimes. In France, the Netherlands and Belgium the Jews were separated out from the rest of society over a period and deprived of their assets, their livelihoods and their freedom of movement. Only after that did they st' being removed in batches, with transport after transport to the extermination cam' the East. In Norway, the occupation regime did not try to isolate the Jews in the years of the war and discrimination was limited, except in Trøndelag. On the oth' the mass arrests and deportations struck suddenly and forcibly, concentrated few months.

The number of Jews in Norway was relatively small; well over 2,000 at th' occupation. Most of them lived in and around Oslo, plus a fair number i' but there were a few spread throughout the country. The great majorit' lower middle class, and few or none of them could be counted among N economic, or cultural elite. From a German point of view, it could th' be said that there was no 'Jewish problem' in Norway.

Nearly all the source material that could throw light on h' level decision about the arrest of the Jews in Norway was mad' sources available are about its implementation. However, the occupation regime was such that the decisions must have

Rediess and Fehlis, or must at least have been approved by these three, who controlled the regime's security apparatus. It is doubtful whether they received any direct orders from Himmler or *Reichssicherheitshauptamt* (*RSHA*) about the time and place for arrests and deportations. The German *Führer* state didn't work like that. It is more likely that Terboven and the others knew that the Third Reich had now started a European mass extermination campaign and that Norway was expected to take its place in this action against the Jews. The Holocaust in Norway was set in motion in a way characteristic of national socialism: a mixture of planning, improvisation, and dependence on the circumstance.

The action against the Jews in 1942–3 took place in four stages. The first stage was the state of emergency in Trøndelag in October, where Terboven, Rediess and Fehlis were all present. The state of emergency was not primarily directed against the Jews, but these three made use of the opportunity to hit them also. One Jew was among those executed, but apart from that the Jewish men were arrested and sent to the German internment camp at Falstad, while the women and children were gathered in three flats in the town and kept under police observation. Although this was a local action, it showed some features that would be repeated later. Only the men were arrested in the first instance, but the women were kept under observation. The Norwegian police followed German orders in carrying out the arrests. This too became a pattern.

The next stage was the big action against the Jews. This was triggered by an incident on the train to the border town of Halden on 22 October, when a guide who was travelling with a group of escaping Jews shot and killed a border policeman. On the evening of the following day, preparations were started for bigger action, and in the morning two days later an urgent telegram was sent from the head of Stapo to the police offices. All adult male Jews were to be arrested early the next day, 26 October and gathered in Oslo. In the capital city itself, Stapo saw to the arrests but had to call on help from the Criminal Police, the Germanic SS Norway and others. Elsewhere, responsibility for the arrests was given to the police office or the local sheriff's officer. From Oslo, the arrested Jews were taken to Berg camp near Tønsberg, a new and as yet incomplete establishment that was under the control of the Police Ministry. The women were not arrested but were required to report to the police.

Obtaining sea transport between Norway and Germany was always a bottleneck, and the *Gestapo* did not have any ships available when the men were arrested. The third stage started when the German Navy made a ship, *Donau*, available at short notice. Stapo was now ordered to deliver all the Jewish men on 26 November to Oslo Harbour, where the *Stapo* took over. All the women and children were to be arrested the same day and then to the harbour, where they were herded aboard *Donau* along with the men and to Poland. There, most of them were immediately exterminated in the gas chambers Auschwitz while the rest were set to work where most of them sooner or later met their ends. This time too, Stapo needed help and was assisted by other branches of the police, and the Germanic SS Norway.

The deadline for embarkation was so short that the Jews from outside Oslo did arrive in time. So there had to be a fourth stage. The remaining Jews were held in detention until they could be sent with a new transport on 24 February 1943. With that, the Holocaust in Norway was largely completed.

The Germans arrested the men and the women in two stages, the men first and then the women. There is nothing in the sources to say why they divided the operation in this way, but it may have been to carry out the action against the Jews with the least possible disruption to general public order. If everybody in the family was arrested at once, this could more easily be seen as the prelude to deportation with all that implied and could give rise to protests. So long as only the men were arrested, it could seem as if the Germans would be content just to put them to forced labour in Norway.

The NS state and the police

The Germans initiated the arrests of the Jews, but the NS state implemented them. As with the arrests of the teachers six months earlier, the Germans found it convenient to let the Norwegians themselves do the rounding up. The NS state's police carried out all the arrests and except in Trondheim, they saw to the internments. They also arranged the transport of the Jews to the quay at Oslo Harbour, where the *Gestapo* took over. The *Gestapo* controlled the action but otherwise stayed in the background. In Stapo, they had an obedient and national socialist-oriented tool that could draw in other branches of the police as required.

The police forces were the main agencies implementing the Holocaust in Norway, but in the process, they made use of public transport services. Norwegian Railways took the arrested Jews to internment camps. The railway carried them from Trondheim and from Bergen to Oslo. A hundred taxis booked by Stapo took women and children from their homes to Oslo Harbour.

The Quisling government provided a formal basis for the arrest of the Jews, in a new law dated 24 October which referred to suspicion of activity inimical to the people or the state, without naming the Jews specifically. The NS government also issued a law on 26 October that all Jewish assets should be confiscated, for the benefit of the Norwegian treasury. The names of the Jews who had their assets confiscated were published as this proceeded, in order that potential creditors could lodge their claims. This law was probably directed not only against the Jews but also against the Germans. The NS government wanted to ensure that the Jews' assets did not fall into the hands of the Germans but were applied to the benefit of the NS state. Nevertheless, there was a tug of war between the parties, as it was soon decided that the Germans would get the Jews' gold, silver and wristwatches while the NS authorities got their hands on the rest of the booty.

There is nothing to suggest that Quisling resisted the German demands for all Jews to be arrested and then deported. On the contrary, the Germans probably found in him a willing partner who had no qualms about collaboration. It was natural for Quisling to make the resources of the NS state available for the arrests of the Jews. NS had been an antisemitic party since 1935, and antisemitism was a central part of its ideology. In March

1942 the NS state revived the clause in the constitution that had been abolished in 1851 excluding Jews from the country. In a speech on 6 December 1942, Quisling said that 'the only possible solution is for the Jews to leave Europe and go elsewhere – preferably to an island'. Quisling had no wish to protect Norwegian Jews from deportation. It may also have been important for him to show a willingness to co-operate with the Germans in a matter that was important to them.

It is a debatable question who knew what about the eradication of the Jews. The Germans wanted to keep it secret and never said anything about the real purpose behind the arrests and deportations. We don't know how much the top echelons in NS got to know, but it seems unlikely that none of them knew or guessed the Germans' intentions. The most important point, however, is not what Quisling and his henchmen knew about the final fate of the Jews, but that they too wanted the Jews out of Norway and therefore collaborated in their deportation. Then, as soon as the Jews were out of the country, it became a purely German matter in which Quisling no longer needed to take an interest or become involved.

Jewish escape

Many Jews, probably most of them, were secretly warned beforehand of the arrests both on 26 October and a month later. These prior warnings came in the first instance from police personnel and in the second instance from taxi drivers who knew what was likely to happen. These were not co-ordinated reactions but responses by individual police officers and taxi drivers who gave quiet warnings that spread further through various social networks.

The warnings put the Jews in a desperate situation. Trying to escape was at any time a dangerous and uncertain undertaking that families with children and elderly members readily rejected. The women did not want to flee, for fear of putting their arrested menfolk in danger. However, the number of Jewish refugees arriving in Sweden did start rising before the first arrests, and between the first two actions about 230 managed to escape. Then came the big stream of escapees at the end of November and into December, coming to a halt in January. Altogether, 930 Jews escaped between October 1942 and January 1943.

Nearly all the refugees got help to escape. In the beginning, most assistance came spontaneously from friends, neighbours, or relatives, but sooner or later most of them received organized help. The Resistance Movement took part in providing this help and in doing so it extended its scope. It already had a system for transporting refugees from the Oslo district, shared between Milorg, Sivorg (the civil resistance organization), Komorg (the communist organization) and XU (the intelligence organization). It had been necessary to build up such escape groups to take the resistance organizations' own members to safety when the authorities were after them. Altogether, these escape channels had a capacity of fifty to sixty refugees per week.

In autumn 1942 this capacity was too small. Towards the end of the year, the system was under heavy pressure from two-quarters – not only from the Jews but also from

The Resistance Movement itself, which was being extensively dismembered in Sørlandet. Individuals and small groups started helping. A new escape group known as 'Carl Fredriksen's Transport' took 350 Jews plus several hundred other refugees to the border during one and a half months, until the group was exposed and the members themselves had to flee.

Organizing mass exodus was no easy matter. Safe hiding places had to be found at short notice for Jews awaiting transport. Travel out of the capital had to be arranged, with all that entailed, including vehicles, driving permits, fuel, choice of an escape route, messages to people along the way and messages to guides who would escort the refugees across the last stretch towards the border. The remarkable thing is that hardly anybody was caught. It is amazing how ineffective *Gestapo* and Stapo were in their hunt for escapees.

The work was not without problems and friction. People fleeing from the rounding up of resistance groups were given priority, while anxious and terrified Jews had to wait in overcrowded apartments. The escape groups were mostly accustomed to helping young, fit men with experience in resistance groups. With the Jews, they also had to deal with children and old people not suited to the long, arduous routes that had been in use until then.

The Holocaust in perspective

The Holocaust in Norway struck hard – harder than in France and Belgium but not so hard as in the Netherlands. A total of 776 Jews were deported, of whom only 38 came back. The Jews made up as much as half of the approximately 1,450 Norwegian prisoners who were sent to Germany and who either perished or were killed there. On the other hand, the majority got away. Of the 2,000 or more Jews who were in Norway at the start of the occupation, a good 1,200 managed to escape to Sweden during the 5 years of the war; 124 avoided deportations because they were married to non-Jews.

A historian balances between seeing the past as it would have been seen at the time and viewing it in the light of our knowledge of what has happened since. Good historical understanding is built up in the tension and interchange between these two points of view. In the case of the wartime history of the Jews, the tension is particularly strong and the historian faces special challenges. We now know that the Germans' project was mass extermination and that the action against the Jews in Norway must be understood accordingly. But it must also be understood from the perspective at the time when most people knew nothing about the extermination plans. For them, the action against the Jews was just one of a long series of actions against the population in the occupied zone.

The action against the Jews came at the end of a year that had been full of dramatic events and harsh reprisals. The teachers' revolt, the mass arrests and the church resistance had dominated public life in spring and summer, along with the violent reprisals over events at Telavåg and the death sentences of eighteen people who had tried to escape to Britain. Then in autumn, these horrific events were followed by the bloody state of emergency in Trøndelag with thirty-four executions. People were able to learn about these events through reports in the papers but not so with the arrest of the Jews. The only authorized information regarding the treatment of the Jews was about the confiscation of their assets.

However, the illegal press and London Radio carried news both of the arrests and of the deportation. The arrest of the men also featured in the protest dated 10 November that the Provisional Church Leadership sent to Quisling and that was read out in many churches and prayer houses in November and December. Many people must have known at least about the arrests of the Jews, even though the Germans and the NS state kept quiet about them. However, some of the illegal newspapers did state that the Jews would be exterminated.

There has been a long and intense discussion about the Holocaust. A basic question has been why so many Jews were captured and whether more could have been saved. In retrospect, the civil resistance leadership has been criticized for doing so little to save them. One response to this criticism has been to point out that the leadership had come into being as part of the struggle against Nazification, and that its activity had been limited to that. It was not yet ready to take on other, wider tasks. It had only scant resources to assist escaping refugees. Another question has been the reliability of the information they received about the impending action against the Jews. Was it accurate enough to initiate a rescue operation, or was it too vague and uncertain? A third issue is what role antisemitism played. If there was antipathy, to what extent was this antisemitism and to what extent was it just a dislike of everything that was foreign to homogeneous Norwegian society?

In this debate, much has been made of the fact that it was not German, but Norwegian, police who made the arrests. That is true, but it is only one side of the case. The other is that the branch of the police that took the lead in the action was Stapo, a newly created, Nazified branch that operated as an underling of the *Gestapo*. Stapo led the action and made the arrests under German control, and when their own resources were insufficient, they brought in other branches of the half-Nazified police, the *Hird* or the Germanic *SS* Norway. It was a Norwegian police force that made the arrests, but a force that had been extended with a political arm, Stapo. That was not what one usually understands by 'Norwegian police'.

If we compare the Holocaust in Norway with the way things developed in Denmark, it becomes clear how much events were influenced by the type of occupation regime. Until the end of August 1943, the Danes still had their own democratic government that protected the Jews. Then when the government resigned and no new one was appointed the German security police went into action, though with little effect. The German civil and military authorities in Denmark were not interested in persecuting the Jews, so long as they disappeared from the country. So nearly all the Danish Jews fled over the sea to Sweden.

The Danish Jews had a longer history in Denmark than the Norwegian Jews in Norway, had higher social status and were better integrated. The Danish population and

The Resistance Movement mobilized in support of the Jews in a way reminiscent of the school and church protests in Norway. The Danish population identified with its Jewish members and saw the attack on the Jews as an attack on themselves. This was not the case in Norway, where the action against the Jews was perceived not as an attack on Norwegian society in general but as an attack on a particular group within that society.

CHAPTER 13
COMPULSORY LABOUR AND MASS ARRESTS IN 1943

Towards the end of 1942 Germany and Italy were forced onto the defensive. They failed to halt the Allied landing and advance in North Africa, and on the Eastern Front, the German advance was brought to a halt. The definitive turning point in the Second World War came on 2 February 1943 when Field Marshal Paulus and the German 6th Army surrendered at Stalingrad. Germany had clearly suffered a serious setback. For the first time, the German leadership had to admit to its public that it had a problem.

The regime's response was to demand more. Every effort and all resources had to be applied even more intensely in the fight against the Bolshevik mortal enemy who was now on the offensive. Goebbels expanded on this theme in hypnotic turns of phrase in a famous speech in the *Sportpalast* in Berlin on 18 February. It was here that he launched the catchphrase about 'total war'. 'Do you want total war?' he appealed to his packed audience. 'Yes', came the resounding, almost hysterical reply. The meeting was a great success in influencing public opinion. Goebbels succeeded in bringing the Germans together to reinforce their input to the war effort.

Goebbels's call for an even greater effort was also followed up in the occupied zones. On 19 February Terboven laid out his plans in a meeting with Quisling, and on 22 February they shared the platform at a large German–Norwegian gathering in Klingenberg Cinema in Oslo. Quisling spoke first, rising to a conclusion with his support for the great project that was now being launched. Terboven supported the scheme with all his German weight and authority. Both presented the fight against Bolshevism as the main motive. In Terboven's speech and in the joint telegram that they sent to Hitler and published, they declared that the call to total war had been heard and understood in Norway. Amid storming applause, the prime minister had announced a basic law on the concentration and total commitment of all the country's labour force.

The law about the national labour service was launched at the meeting in Klingenberg Cinema on 22 February 1943. In addition, three supplementary laws were issued specifying how labour service was to be implemented. The law declared that the aim was to deploy parts of the workforce that were not being fully utilized or were being applied to non-essential tasks. The workforce thus made available would ensure the availability of necessary supplies, which would be to the benefit of both Norwegians and Germans. In practice, this meant employment in agriculture and forestry. Workers would also be diverted to the defence of the country, in the form of work on German military building and construction sites.

Quisling can hardly have had strong objections to Norwegians responding to the German demand for a greater mobilization of resources. He was probably also attracted by being given the same status as Terboven in announcing the new law. It was not often that the Norwegian *Fører* and the German *Reichskommissar* appeared on an equal footing in public. Anyway, it was Quisling's and NS's policy that Norway should stand together with Germany in the world war and that the NS state must contribute to the German war effort.

The law about the national labour service was not the first law affecting the labour market. The difference was that this law had a new political and ideological basis and presentation. The earlier regulations had not been presented as matters of a major political nature and grafted into a speech about a major European war. The new law presented the NS authorities with a formidable task, as the labour market was already tightly regulated, and unemployment had long since disappeared. The task now was to seek out workers who were already employed but could be spared, and to transfer them to workplaces with higher priority.

The law was implemented in two stages. All men and women were required to register during the month of March. The newspapers carried instructions about how and where in each community those to whom the law applied should report. By 31 March, 320,000 men and women were on the register, but this number was incomplete because the Labour Directorate still lacked returns from Oslo Commune. In April, the employment offices started allocating people to jobs. Workers were instructed to report at a specified location, from which they were sent to their places of work. These could be far away, often in north Norway.

The authorities used two methods to get hold of workers who could be released from their current employment. Under the new laws, the ministry had been given full powers to close, scale down or merge companies and businesses to release workers. Already on 27 February the Ministry of Commerce had announced that all bars, nightclubs, and luxury restaurants should be closed. Then they started the process of finding businesses that could be closed, scaled down or merged. The ministry's other method was to initiate a 'combing out' campaign. Employees whom firms could dismiss without too much harm to the activity of the business would be 'combed out' and enlisted. Both methods were complex to put into effect. Deciding how a particular business could release some of its workers required detailed business knowledge and good judgement.

The enlistment faced opposition and progressed slowly. Nevertheless, 56,000 people were compulsorily transferred to other work in 1942 in accordance with earlier regulations, and 85,000 in 1943 after the law on the national labour service came into force. According to one source, approximately 11,000 employees from different businesses had been transferred to important wartime production by summer 1944. Trading and banking sectors had yielded most, amounting to 8,500 personnel. Two thousand seven hundred businesses had been wholly or partly closed or had been merged.

The law about the national labour service was the Quisling government's most important initiative in 1943. It was a step forward on the radical course that the government had set with the laws and regulations issued between 1940 and 1942. But this legislation was in a different category. It was not about measures to spread a new ideology and create a new political order. This time, it was about the economy and the maximum possible mobilization of a vital economic resource, labour. The immediate demands of the war were making themselves felt. The moves towards Nazification and a permanent new order were not abandoned, but they were given lower priority and they became progressively less effective.

The campaign against the labour service

The civil resistance leadership was very unsure how to react to the law about the national labour service. Their problem was that the real aim of the law was so unclear, which made it difficult to know how to oppose it. The civil leadership therefore hesitated and debated back and forth, while the illegal newspapers each reacted in their own way.

At the time, many people were frightened that the workers who had been called up would be sent to Germany. We now know that this was unlikely because the Germans needed all the workforce they could get in Norway. However, there were persistent rumours that the labour conscripts would be sent to Germany, and at one time people in the resistance leadership regarded as genuine, reports that this had happened in some cases.

Another concern was that when the Germans or NS first took control of the workers, they would be organized into fixed units, given military training and transformed into military detachments that could be sent to the front. From today's perspective, it is easy to see that this too was unlikely. It was also conceivable that the workers would be sent to German construction sites in Norway, and when the resistance leadership got their hands on a couple of circulars from the Labour Directorate in late March, they had evidence that this would indeed happen. It appeared from the circulars that 10,000 men would be allocated to German military construction sites and that the directorate should concentrate exclusively on this process until 15 April. However, conscripted workers were also being allocated to agriculture and forestry, and it was not so easy to protest about these two fields of business activity.

After much fumbling and extended discussions, the civil leadership decided first to encourage a boycott on registration. Then they agreed on their final and definitive directive on 13 April: Nobody should report for any type of registration. Nobody must turn up if called to a labour office, a departure point or a workplace. The farmers were instructed not to accept conscripted labour. Women were warned against taking up posts left vacant when men were conscripted. Judges and police officers got specific orders, as did parents. Not least, the directives to the business community were emphasized. The campaign against the national labour service that this started would last through the end of that year and into the next.

The German security service's report from July 1943 shows that the campaign against the national labour service must have had an effect. Many of the difficulties that the NS authorities faced and which are evidenced in the report can probably be traced back to

The Resistance Movement's orders and the encouragement by the illegal press. On the other hand, there has always been some uncertainty about what the campaign against the national labour service achieved in 1943 and the beginning of 1944. How many people evaded labour conscription because of the resistance campaign, and how many for other reasons? It certainly didn't lead to the same widespread mobilization of resistance as in 1942, and it did not have the same wide reach as the corresponding wave of resistance that arose in spring and summer 1944.

In its action against the national labour service, the civil resistance campaign retained some important characteristics from the previous years. The resistance arose as a reaction against a specific move by the NS state, not as a campaign against NS as a whole. With the campaign against the national labour service, the leadership had moved the civil resistance into an economic and potentially military field. As before, the focus was on NS, not the Germans, and the resistance was aimed most directly against what the NS state was doing, not against the *Reichskommissariat* or the *Wehrmacht* that stood behind NS.

Home Front Leadership

The civil resistance leadership's launch of the campaign against the national labour service changed its position and status. Prior to 1943, the leadership had not on its own initiative issued directives that it urged the civil resistance organizations and the public to follow. The directives now came from a central leadership that addressed itself to the whole population, both the people who had been called up and the many others who were asked to help. The leadership did try to get the public to follow the directives, but it would achieve full coverage only the following year. It had, however, taken a big stride when on its own initiative it launched a resistance campaign that rose above the sectoral pattern that had typified the civil resistance until now.

Having achieved this overall position in the civil resistance movement, the civil leadership combined with the military leadership in 1943 to create 'The Home Front Leadership'. The two groups had each been growing independently during 1941 and 1942, and there had been little contact between them. During 1943 they came together, started co-operating and agreed on the basic direction of The Resistance Movement. In doing so, they created a political focal point for the movement which it is convenient to call 'The Home Front Leadership', even though it had not yet been given that title by either of its two sections and neither leadership group was known to the public in general. They all operated under cover of the inclusive description 'The Home Front'. The clarification of the relationship between the two groups proceeded simultaneously with and depended on them sorting out their relationships with the authorities in exile.

This process was started by a crisis in the relationship between the two groups. At the beginning of 1943, the civil leadership could look back on a series of triumphs in the civil resistance campaign that was in stark contrast to the bloody defeats that the military resistance had suffered. The civilian leaders knew little about the military leadership and therefore regarded them with some distrust. At the start of February 1943, *Kretsen* sent its 'partisan letter' to the government in exile. In the letter, it not only expressed doubt about the military resistance work. It explicitly opposed any resistance work aimed at raising guerrilla or sabotage groups behind the German lines in the event of an Allied invasion. *Kretsen* thought that it would not be possible to give underground troops the necessary military training under the circumstances prevailing in occupied Norway. A 'rising' would therefore become 'a sheer children's crusade' for the participants and immediately provoke violent reprisals with mass shootings of the civilian population.

After this outburst, *Kretsen* held fast for a while to the view expressed in its 'partisan letter', though without extending its criticism further. Following several rounds of clarification, the parties agreed to work together. Two representatives from *Kretsen* would meet with the military leadership when matters of common interest were being discussed. The process was finally completed when the civil leaders committed themselves to the strategy for the military resistance work in a letter of 15 November 1943 which the civil leadership, the military leadership and the illegal police leadership jointly sent to the prime minister in London.

This letter finally established which platform of resistance politics the 'Home Front Leadership' stood on. There had not been any conflict about the civil resistance campaign. The conflict had been about the military resistance, and it was the policy about this that was finally resolved in the letter. This was the strategy that the military authorities abroad and the military resistance leadership at home had already been working towards, but now it was also accepted by the civil resistance leadership. What was established was that the resistance campaign needed to have both a civil and a military side. As military resistance led so readily to roundups and bloody reprisals, it would need to be restricted to preparations for the eventual liberation. Acts of resistance that aroused attention and influenced opinion would continue to be initiated by the non-violent arm of The Resistance Movement.

The setting up of The Home Front Leadership was a big step on the way towards integration of the civil and military resistance. There was, however, a limit to how far this integration could go. The civil resistance campaign was in essence a domestic matter that the authorities in exile supported but otherwise did not become involved in. The military branch answered to a Norwegian and behind that an Allied command abroad. The Home Front Leadership could therefore never function as an overall leadership for the military resistance but had to be content with expressing its points of view and helping to co-ordinate the civil and military resistance work.

For security reasons, The Home Front Leadership that had now been created did not publicly acknowledge its existence. The extent to which people, in general, reckoned that there was such a body must have varied greatly. What is certain is that the leadership worked under a handicap while it had not openly proclaimed its existence. Many people assumed that the directives came from 'London', because they were quoted in 'London Radio' without being attributed to any authoritative leadership at home.

It was also difficult for The Home Front Leadership to combat opposing groups so long as it 'didn't exist'. It faced opposition from the start. Part of the opposition took its starting point from what it knew of *Kretsen*'s opinions about the problems of switching from war to peace. There were thought to be undemocratic and dictatorial tendencies in the way *Kretsen* wanted to organize the transitional government. Much more important was the communist opposition that The Home Front Leadership faced right to the end of the war.

The development of The Home Front Leadership was a process that extended throughout the whole occupation. Some of its origins date back to 1940. Important parts of its foundation were the civil and military resistance leaderships that were established in 1941–2 and that both acquired their final form in 1943. The combined leadership's big breakthrough came in spring 1944 when it finally revealed itself to the public as The Home Front Leadership (HL), became associated with important resistance events and received widespread public support. Finally, it underwent an internal reorganization and formalization of its structure over New Year 1944–5. Altogether, it is remarkable how gradual the development was, how harmonious it appears retrospectively despite a series of setbacks and hard-won experiences, and how clear the pattern finally became: a well-founded Home Front Leadership with all-round public support and an equally well-established and permanent opposition, the communists.

In Denmark, developments were quite different. Most of the Danes supported the country's democratic government which distanced itself from any resistance against the Germans. However, in the course of 1943 popular resistance became a major factor based on sabotage and strikes. The Germans demanded that the government clamp down on this, which it refused to do. They then forced it to resign and for the remainder of the war, the country was ruled by civil servants. The resistance continued to grow, however, and so did the reprisals against it. During the breakthrough in 1943, a resistance leadership was set up rapidly and in September announced publicly in the form of Denmark's Freedom Council, six months before the Norwegian Home Front Leadership became public knowledge. In comparison with the Danish Resistance Movement, the Norwegian started earlier but developed more cautiously, with less use of strikes, sabotage and assassinations and a later announcement of the resistance leadership to the public.

Three mass arrests

In August 1943 the Germans arrested police personnel and military officers, followed by an arrest of students in November. These actions appear to have been initiated by German authorities inside Norway without influence from abroad, and one of them led to strong criticism of Terboven, who fell out of favour with Hitler for a time. German police carried out the arrests without making use of their Norwegian colleagues. Many of the people arrested were deported to prison camps in Germany.

The arrests were directed against groups where the Germans thought they had detected resistance activity. The arrests of police and students were triggered by particular acts of resistance. They could be considered as a collective punishment for continuing resistance activity, but they were primarily a preventive manoeuvre against a possible Allied invasion. By sending many or most of these groups out of the country, the Germans wanted to secure themselves against being attacked in the rear in the event of an Allied landing. The three groups were not considered to be political prisoners, and in Germany they were better treated than political prisoners.

On 16 August 1943 and the following days, about 500 policemen were arrested. The same day that this campaign began, the whole Oslo police force of 600–700 men were called together at the Guards' barracks near Majorstua in Oslo. Jonas Lie gave a speech in which he told them that a policeman had been shot that morning for refusing to obey orders and he demanded a declaration of loyalty from all present. Under pressure and threats, with suggestions that more could be executed, they all signed a declaration of loyalty apart from sixteen men who refused and were imprisoned.

Of those arrested, 271 men were sent to Stutthof Concentration Camp near Danzig, where they were relatively well treated. The SS arranged a re-schooling course intended to convert them to committed national socialists and get them to report for service with the Nazis. None of this succeeded.

At that time the police had long been a strongly Nazified institution. A new political police force, Stapo, had been founded, many policemen had joined NS and a good number of NS members from outside had been recruited into the police. But there was also another side to the police during the occupation. Nazification was extensive but varied. There was a wide range of NS members within the police, from convinced national socialists to pure opportunists who joined to advance their career, to lukewarm and passive adherents. Despite everything, a good half of the police were not in the NS. Some members of the police were clearly in favour of resistance, and there were connections between them and the growing resistance movement.

Terboven had noted the growing tendency to resistance, and he wanted to suppress it. He would do this both by arrests and by executions. The Germans carried out the arrest of the police officers, but Terboven preferred to leave the business of execution to the Norwegians. Police Officer Gunnar Eilifsen had refused to follow an order to bring in some girls who had been called for compulsory labour. Terboven wanted to use this to create an example. Eilifsen was to be shot, and Terboven insisted that the Norwegians must do this themselves. This was an absolute order. If the Norwegians wouldn't do it, the Germans stood ready.

Under strong pressure and short deadlines, the Norwegians accepted that they would have to carry out the execution. Under trial in 1945, Quisling said that if he had handed Eilifsen over to the Germans something much worse might have happened. The result would have been a German military dictatorship with bloodshed, arrests and so on. He may have thought like that, but it is more likely that he had other motivations in August 1943. Quisling wanted to advance and strengthen the NS state that he headed. It needed to show itself so far as possible as a sovereign state with the functions and agencies that pertain to such a state, including the power to condemn and execute in serious situations such as those that can arise during a war. Always leaving it to the Germans to punish and execute people merely showed the powerlessness of the NS state.

A new law and a new court were hastily created to have Eilifsen condemned and executed. This law, which could be applied retrospectively, came to be known as *Lex Eilifsen*. It established that offenders against the military criminal law would be dealt with by provisional special courts and Lie now arranged for such a court to be set up, 'the Police Special Court'. Lie and Riisnæs put such intense pressure on the three judges that two of them finally voted for the death penalty. Eilifsen was condemned on 15 August, Stapo executed him the following morning and on the same day, Lie used the execution as a means of putting pressure on the policemen who were assembled in the barracks at Majorstua.

The action against the police was not intended as part of the advancement of national socialism, but *Lex Eilifsen* had that effect. The NS state's judiciary apparatus was extended. *Folkedomstolen* had already been established. Now came special courts, first the Police Court and later others. They pronounced death sentences and other sentences in both political and criminal cases. Eighteen death sentences were pronounced and executed in cases against members of the resistance, and four in criminal cases. The new law was intended to demonstrate to the Germans that the NS state could maintain discipline among its own citizens, and to the citizens that the power of the NS state was on a par with all other states. The NS state could pass sentences and punish physically, even to the ultimate punishment.

Many military officers were arrested the same day as the police. The Germans combined the actions under the codename *Aktion Polarkreis*. On 16 August 1,500 officers were arrested. Five hundred of them were later released, but the remainder were sent to Schildberg in Poland. It was fortunate for the officers that it was the *Wehrmacht* that arrested and dealt with them. Terboven regarded them as civilians and would have handed them over to the *Gestapo*'s rough treatment, but the *Wehrmacht* regarded them as officers and treated them in accordance with international law.

The arrest of the students followed a crisis at the university. There had been conflicts about student admissions the year before. The Church and Education Ministry wanted to give NS students priority for courses with restricted numbers. The disagreement blew up again in autumn 1943. In August the university received from the ministry a new regulation about admissions, to the effect that the ministry and the rector would decide how many applicants and which ones were to be admitted to courses in the various faculties. The deans and the teachers' illegal leadership group both feared the political motivation behind this move, and they opposed the regulation. As before, the deans wanted to negotiate and seek compromises. The teachers' leaders were set on a decisive struggle.

The will to resist was rising that autumn, and all the faculties agreed on a sharp protest. In the middle of October, Terboven and Quisling agreed that action must be taken. If the NS state did not intervene, the Germans would. Stapo went into action and arrested about seventy male and female students and eleven university teachers. On 10 November the faculties agreed to protest against the arrests, and the students followed with their own protest five days later. Two thousand students signed a declaration in which they opposed the imprisonment of the students and asked for them to be set free.

It is difficult to say what the outcome of the dispute at the university would have been if developments had not suddenly taken a harsh turn. Terboven intervened after a sabotage incident. On the night of 27/28 November, four men broke into the university's assembly hall through a back door. They poured petrol and paraffin over the aisles leading to the podium and set it alight. Many people thought at the time that this was an act of provocation: it must have been done by the Germans to give them an excuse to make arrests. Only after the war did it become clear that the perpetrators were resistance members, connected with the illegal newspaper *London News*. What has never become clear is their motive, and if or how the fire-raising was intended to contribute to the resistance struggle at the university. Two days later, on 30 November, the *Gestapo* went into action, assisted by soldiers from the *Wehrmacht*. The university was surrounded, and all the students found on the premises were arrested. The *Gestapo* got hold of 1,100–1,200 students in all, about a quarter of the total student numbers. Most of the male students were then sent to a camp at Stavern.

The arrests of the students attracted international attention and showed the Germans in a bad light. The reaction in Sweden was particularly important. Swedish newspapers gave the arrests prominence, which aroused anger and led to many protests. The gradual readjustment of the Swedish neutrality policy now made it easier to express anti-German opinions. On 1 December the Swedish foreign minister communicated with the German minister in Stockholm, urgently requesting that the Germans suspend their action against the students. For Hitler, the relationship with Sweden was a delicate matter. In August the Swedes had withdrawn the permission for German troops to travel through Swedish territory, and it was conceivable that they might also reduce the vital export of iron ore and ball bearings to Germany. There was a risk that anger over German behaviour in Norway could push the Swedes in that direction. Hitler was therefore greatly displeased about Terboven's action, and Terboven fell into disfavour for a while.

Hitler's displeasure affected the way the students were dealt with after the arrests. At first, instructions came from Berlin that they should all be released. Then came counter-orders because Hitler had been exasperated by the sharp reaction from Sweden. The students should still be sent to Germany, though in smaller numbers. The NS leaders, NS students and Rector Hoel and the deans all tried to influence the Germans to free as many as possible. The outcome was that something under half of the students were set free, while the rest were sent to Germany in two batches. Like the officers and the police, the students received better treatment in Germany than the political prisoners. Like the police, they were also subjected to an unsuccessful course of indoctrination that was supposed to convert them into national socialists.

The mass arrests in 1943 did not lead to any protests of the broad, collective sort that was typical of the civil resistance. However, one of the mass arrests created a need for help to flee. The Jews had been helped to get across the border the previous year. Now it was the students' turn. The escape organizations helped as many as they could and about a thousand students crossed into Sweden, where most of them joined the police troops.

By closing the university as a teaching institution, Terboven created a barrier to any further development of national socialism through it. There was no longer anybody there to Nazify. There was little purpose in directing new actions against unwilling professors, and experience showed that newly appointed, incompetent NS followers had little chance of success.

CHAPTER 14
THE HOME FRONT AND THE RESISTANCE MOVEMENT

'The Home Front' is an expression characteristic of the time of the occupation. It is a broad concept, embracing two main ideas. In one sense, 'The Home Front' includes all the non-Nazi members of the population. Everybody who does not support or identify with the German occupier and NS is part of 'The Home Front'. In this broad sense, 'The Home Front' is equivalent to 'the nation minus the Nazis'. In the other sense, 'The Home Front' is something narrower, more like 'The Resistance Movement' with all that implies of organization, acts of opposition and open conflict. The term itself – The Home *Front* – leads one's perception in that direction. 'Front' suggests action.

The expression became popular precisely because it was so comprehensive and flexible. At one moment 'The Home Front' could be associated with the majority of the Norwegian population, and in the next with a 'movement' among the people. At one moment it was like 'The Resistance Movement' and in the next, it also included the supportive society around the movement. 'The Home Front' meant both the great majority of the population and an active minority within it. The constantly resonating level of contact between the anti-Nazi public in general and an actively resisting minority within it gave the expression 'The Home Front' a particular intensity.

Nowadays the term 'The Resistance Movement' is used more than 'The Home Front' in talking about the time of the occupation. For post-war generations who have not experienced wartime, 'The Resistance Movement' seems more concrete and understandable than the diffuse and elusive 'Home Front'. During the war, it was the other way round. 'The Resistance Movement' was used, but 'The Home Front' was the more common expression.

The first element of 'The *Home* Front' implies an opposite concept, 'The *Overseas* Front' ('Utefronten'). This refers to constitutional Norway in exile with its merchant fleet, the armed forces and the backing of the Allies. Some fought 'abroad', others 'at home', but they were all engaged in the same struggle. Despite the initially large gap between The Home Front and The Overseas Front, the shared element of these terms expressed the idea of unity in the struggle at home and abroad, a common front against the same enemy, whether in the form of an occupying power at home or a military force overseas.

A country such as Denmark had a resistance movement but not a home front, as there was no Danish front outside the country to contrast it with. There was no constitutional Denmark in exile. We could also speak of a home front in other countries that were engaged in the war, but then it refers to the 'front' that the women created by looking after households in hard times, holding the family together and filling the workplaces made vacant by men going away to war. When *Norges Hjemmefrontmuseum* is translated into English, it cannot be called 'Norway's Home Front Museum'. That would give a visitor a false impression. It should be 'Norway's Resistance Museum'.

The Home Front built up the sense of national identity from something more than the cultural and political identity of the pre-war years. This sense of identity was actively cultivated. In the privacy of their homes, people sang patriotic songs more than ever, decorated their Christmas trees with Norwegian flags and celebrated most of what the earlier nation-builders had created. The ultimate political goal was the re-establishment of a democratic society. But the most immediate and most dynamic factor was the campaign of resistance against the regime. This was what now mainly gave the nation a shared sense of purpose.

On The Home Front, there were three types of resistance activity, defined by general form rather than by specific types of action. First, people could express their opposition to the regime individually and spontaneously. The best-known form of this was what is called 'symbolic resistance'. Norwegians wore badges, flowers, paperclips or other accessories to show their national solidarity and their distance from the regime. These actions exposed the protesters to some risk of arrest and imprisonment. Quite a few were arrested for wearing flowers in their buttonholes on the king's birthday. Those who were arrested were usually released after quite a short time.

The second type was collective resistance when a socially defined group took action in protest against an initiative by the regime. This was the form of action most characteristic of the civil resistance. Central organizers and illegal networks contributed to the collective civil resistance, but the main actor was the protesting group itself.

Organizational resistance was the third type, in which the main resistance action was carried out by an organization or by an organized network set up specifically for this type of protest. These were active more or less continuously. The most important expressions of organizational resistance were the Co-ordinating Committee (KK) with its secretariat and network of local representatives; Milorg; the illegal press; the intelligence service; refugee transport and, in a category of its own, the communist resistance. 'The Resistance Movement' in its narrowest sense was like the organizational resistance. The full-time illegal workers, the committed core who dedicated their whole existence to the resistance campaign, were generally to be found within this type of resistance. These were also the people exposed to the greatest risks and to suffering the greatest losses.

The civil resistance

The Home Front started from absolutely nothing. Nobody had the experience of how to act in relation to an occupier. One had to go back to 1814 to find the most recent instance of foreign occupation, which was only on a small part of Norwegian territory. The time horizon was short. People continued to think that the war would soon be over. The Home Front in the sense of 'The Resistance Movement' started small and lacked clear divisions between different types of resistance. What would later become separate fields of activity were at first mixed together. One and the same person often participated in several areas at the same time.

In retrospect, however, we can see how the pattern was set at an early stage for a basic division of The Home Front into two parts, a civil and a military resistance movement. The most typical expressions of civil resistance were the big collective actions. They were reactive. An initiative from the NS state – either implemented or planned – provoked and aroused the resistance which came in two waves. The first wave arose during the struggle against NS's Nazification offensive in 1940–2. The second followed in 1943–4 and was directed against the regime's compulsory labour conscription.

Protest often took the form of refusal to follow an NS state regulation or law. The collective resistance largely consisted of civil disobedience actions against a state that was not acknowledged as legitimate. Different groups were mobilized in each of the waves of protest. Larger or smaller sections of society were engaged in support around each group, and this influenced the non-Nazi population in general.

The protest by the legally constituted organizations in spring 1941 was an important trigger for the civil resistance movement, even though it was only the leaders of the organizations who had signed the letters of protest. A new and decisive phase in the development of the civil resistance followed when Terboven sidelined these organizations, which had the effect of creating new, illegal leadership groups. The protests purely by organizations were now replaced by collective protest actions, which no publicly recognized organization and no specific personal leadership claimed to have initiated.

The church differed from this model because it functioned as an institution and not as an occupational group. As an institution, the church operated openly when it protested. Bishops and priests declared publicly that they were resigning from their appointments. But the church too had its anonymous leadership in the form of the Christian Consultative Council. This decided on a strategy and discussed drafts of letters and statements, though the council itself was not known to the public. When the autonomous church set up its own governing body, the Provisional Church Leadership, this functioned initially with a named membership, until it too was finally forced to go underground.

The call to take part in protest action was set out in *paroler* ('directives'). This term was a typical feature of The Resistance Movement. A directive specified what one should do in response to an initiative by NS, and this became the characteristic link between a group who aspired to leadership and the people for whom the directive was intended. A directive was usually anonymous and was not personally signed. Recipients followed it when they agreed with the content, and it was communicated through channels that confirmed that it came from an authoritative leadership.

The big challenge in developing the civil resistance was to create respect for the legitimacy of groups issuing directives, despite their anonymity. This challenge embodied the democratic element in the system. The civil leadership groups and the combined civil resistance leadership were undemocratic in the sense that they were secret and not elected. The democratic feature was that they left it to the recipients of a directive to decide whether or not to follow it. Directives had to land on fertile ground. They had to correspond with a readiness to protest on the part of the recipients. They could be reinforced only by moral force, not physical force.

There could also be counter-directives or conflicts about the directives. Just as the school's dispute was coming to a climax, a headteacher sent a telegram on 5 March 1942 that was published in the press, advising the teachers to withdraw their protest about membership of *Lærersambandet*. In musical circles, there was heated discussion in autumn 1943 about a directive that KK had approved. This came from the cultural group and urged musicians and the public to boycott all public concerts. The counter-directive opposed the boycott. There could also be doubt about the extent of the resistance directives. Sports competitions arranged within the national labour service were not boycotted in accordance with the sports strike in other fields.

In the university, two conflicting lines of policy developed. One was the collaboration line, sometimes called 'the deans' line', which advocated asserting the university's interests by co-operating with the institution's NS rector. The other was the resistance line, which held that the university should take a leading role in the civil resistance campaign similar to the Supreme Court, the church and the schools. The university must not hold back from a break with the NS state if necessary, in order to put strength behind its demands.

The civil resistance evolved on three different levels, which interacted with each other and made it a wide-ranging societal phenomenon. The big collective actions operated on the most spectacular and influential level. The next level consisted of the directive-led resistance stemming from illegal sector leaders. This continued even after the big collective actions had waned. Many smaller initiatives by NS gave rise to specific resistance directives.

On the third, grassroots level, a day-to-day resistance sprouted unorganized, spontaneously and individually. Some wrote 'Long live the King!' on house walls; others secretly read illegal newspapers. The most widespread and typical resistance on this level, however, was the social boycott of NS members and Germans, often called 'the ice-front'. On this level, the boundary of what can be defined as 'resistance' was fluid. The distinction between resistance and other expressions of national solidarity is not easy to trace. The new type of social togetherness with indoor gatherings on national festival days, community singing and reading of patriotic poems within the home was an expression of national awakening during the years of occupation. It was not necessarily the same as 'resistance'.

At the time, the expressions 'Civil Resistance' and 'The Civil Organisation' (shortened to 'Sivorg') were not in common use until the final year of the war, when they came to be used to distinguish the civil resistance from the steadily more dominant military resistance. The most usual description of the civil resistance at the time was *holdningskamp* ('attitude battle'). In retrospect, this can seem a rather vague expression. It says nothing about what attitude it refers to, about the relationship between attitude and action, or about what sorts of actions the right attitude should lead to. At the time, *holdningskamp* did not seem so imprecise. In changing situations, each individual had to find his or her own way of expressing resistance against the Nazification measures of the new regime. The 'attitude battle' was also a call to individual engagement.

This battle was directed not exclusively against NS but also against the Germans. There were social norms for how one should behave in relation to them. One should not fraternize with German soldiers or welcome them into their home and should keep their distance from them as from NS members. The Home Front's humour was directed just as much against the Germans as against NS. Some people needed in the course of their work to have relationships with Germans and maintain a necessary administrative or economic co-operation. In this situation, the *holdningskamp* norm was that one should not have private interactions with them. Irrespective of whether they were NS members or not, women who associated with Germans or had intimate relationships with them were deviating from this norm and experienced a correspondingly severe social boycott.

The civil resistance was unarmed and non-violent. Although it was supported by sabotage actions after 1942, the core of the civil resistance remained non-violent. This was not on grounds of principle. People supported The Overseas Front's military action, and after some hesitation, the civil resistance leaders also supported Milorg's policies. The policy of non-violence was partially based on tactics. Acts of violence readily provoked German reprisals. For the same reasons, the civil resistance movement did not encourage strikes.

The civil resistance embraced the great majority of citizens in a way that the military resistance did not and could not. It penetrated society as it evolved on three levels. It was primarily the civil resistance that made 'The Home Front' such a widespread, but fluid, phenomenon; sometimes heroic as 'the fighting nation', sometimes less dramatic as just 'the non-Nazi public'.

The civil resistance was overshadowed by the military resistance in the last year of the war and has continued thus in the post-war years. The best-known resistance heroes are from the military arm of The Resistance Movement. Shooting and explosions have seemed more exciting and have attracted more interest than unarmed mass actions of an ideological and political nature. This is a pity because for a long time it was the civil resistance that was the stronger of the two and had a wider reach. It is also the element of the Norwegian resistance that most specifically distinguishes it from other countries' resistance movements.

The difficult military resistance

The military resistance movement differed from its civil counterpart in important ways. The military resistance looked to the use of weapons and acts of violence, which required military knowledge and weapons training. It was directed against the physical power of the Germans, whereas the civil movement was aimed against NS as its most immediate target. The civil movement did not have great material needs, whereas the military needed weapons, ammunition, explosives and communications equipment.

The reprisals against the military resistance operations – and particularly against those connected with Britain – were drastic. The razing of Telavåg, the deportation of the inhabitants there and the executions of the eighteen who had tried to escape to

Britain demonstrated that, as did the thirty-four executions in Trondheim during the state of emergency. The civil resistance was usually not confronted with death sentences, physical damage or states of emergency, nor to a great extent with deportation to prison camps in Germany. The Germans usually satisfied themselves with arrests, periods of imprisonment, internment and deportation within Norway, though the resistance in the trade union movement was met with drastic reprisals during the state of emergency in September 1941.

In the civil campaign, organization-building consisted of setting up a nationwide network to disseminate directives encouraging resistance. The organization was just a means of reaching out to the public. In the military arm, it was the core underground organization itself that would go into action. Most of the military resistance work was secret organizational activity, whereas the civil resistance activities manifested themselves openly.

The two resistance movements comprising The Home Front' also had very different relationships with The Overseas Front. The civil resistance campaign stayed decidedly home-based throughout the whole war. The aims or the directives for this part of The Home Front were never discussed with the government in exile. The aims of the military campaign, on the contrary, were formulated in an interaction between home and abroad. Milorg had no ambitions to operate independently of the authorities in exile. It needed The Overseas Front's constitutional legitimacy and Allied backing, and it needed direction, military training, and military equipment from The Overseas Front. The civil movement had its first big triumph in 1942 and its second in 1944. The military struggled with great difficulties for several years; its time did not come until the last year of the war.

The military resistance operated on three levels from the start. Small and active local groups were formed into squads. They often started by hiding weapons from the 1940 campaign and trying to keep themselves fit for action until the time was ripe. On the regional level, officers and others tried to organize on a bigger scale. Much of their work consisted of setting up contacts roundabout in the districts. At the highest level, several officers felt the need to create a leadership structure that could bring together and direct an organization that covered the whole of southern Norway. This led to the formation of the first Milorg leadership group in spring 1941.

The purely military aspect of this diffuse and tentative activity was limited. The work of establishing contacts was in many ways the most important, though some small-scale training activities were organized. Field exercises and orienteering races were arranged cautiously in woodlands and remote countryside. Something like manuals or instruction leaflets started circulating in autumn 1941, but the first real directives for a united military organization came in 1942.

Those who had aspirations to function as a central leadership strove to create a policy-making body. They worked to shape the future military organization and develop some sort of pattern for its activity. They tried to acquire an overview of what was happening out in the districts and to define more closely what the relationship should be between Milorg at home and the authorities in exile.

The first Milorg leadership felt a strong need to be relieved of the ultimate responsibility for military resistance work. It did not have ambitions to stand at the head of an independent resistance movement. A report dated 10 June 1941 that landed on the desk of the Special Operations Executive (SOE) stated that their intention was to put a physical force at the disposal of a government at home that would be recognized by the king. The government in exile was not mentioned, and there is little doubt that the Milorg pioneers regarded it sceptically. The government at home would decide if and when the force would start to function. The Milorg leaders thought that a clandestine government at home led by Paal Berg already existed, and they wished to place their organization under this.

When they realized that no such government at home existed, they concluded that their organization would have to take orders from London via the Army High Command. Milorg leaders who had to flee from Norway and arrived in London in October 1941 expressed this point of view. The government acceded to their wish rather reluctantly and recognized Milorg on 20 November 1941. In principle, this implied that all resistance activity that could be defined as military should thereafter be under the aegis of Milorg. Military resistance would need to follow the guidelines that Milorg set down.

In 1942, Milorg was confronted with almost insurmountable problems as a result of the operations in Norway organized by SOE and the Norwegian Supreme Command (FO). In spring there were violent reprisals following the skirmish at Telavåg, and in autumn these were followed by other drastic punitive measures during the state of emergency in Trøndelag. The reprisals after the Telavåg affair and the thirty-four executions in Trøndelag cast dark shadows over all military resistance work. Then came the problems with the Bittern expedition that SOE and FO mounted in autumn 1942, which created difficulties for the Milorg leadership. It was not made any easier by the communists following their own programme of sabotage. To top it all, there were widespread exposures of Milorg in Sørlandet, leading to six people being executed and seventy-six dying in prisons or prison camps. The organization there had become overexposed because of expectations of an imminent invasion.

So, at the start of 1943 the situation was that while the Defence Ministry, the Supreme Command and Special Operations Executive worked well together on operations in Norway, the government and the civil resistance leadership were sceptical. They were doubtful about the operations, and also about the value of military resistance work in general. Nor did SOE/FO and the Milorg leadership have a close relationship.

However, they would come together in spring 1943. A meeting held in Sweden in May that year was particularly important in establishing trust between the military leadership at home and abroad and for the final formulation of the guidelines for Milorg and for SOE/FO's work on Norway. The meeting confirmed what had in practice been the case for some time; that Milorg was a preparatory organization that would come into action only at the final liberation and would not carry out acts of sabotage before then. Sabotage was the job of SOE/FO and would as before be carried out by groups that were sent in from outside and had to leave the country after completing their mission. In the event of invasion, only the authorities in exile would have command authority over Milorg. SOE/ FO could organize military resistance groups on their own initiative in regions where there was no Milorg presence. The authorities in exile would work towards every Milorg district having radio communication links with London and being able to make direct agreements about the supply of weapons, equipment, instructors, and radio operators.

The young lawyer Jens Christian Hauge played a key role in the rapprochement between the Milorg leadership at home and the Supreme Command abroad. In the course of 1942–3 he became Milorg's undisputed leader and worked deliberately to create a good relationship with the authorities in exile. He also sought co-operation with the civil resistance leadership, and towards the end of the war, he would become a key person in the combined Home Front Leadership (HL).

The illegal press

The illegal press can be considered as part of the civil resistance, but can also be dealt with as a branch of its own within organizational resistance. It arose from the need for a news service that told what the censored press did not tell. The censored press and broadcasting provided only such news and opinions as the Germans and NS wanted to transmit. The public reacted by boycotting broadcasts from NRK in Oslo. People no longer listened to them.

One might have expected that they would also have boycotted the pro-German and pro-NS newspapers, but many people continued to subscribe to or buy them. They contained interesting local news and published regulations and ordinances that affected daily life and that people needed to know about. The papers also printed adverts for the exchanges that were so important in a society where most things were in short supply. But the official press was biased and needed a counterweight.

The Germans and the NS state persecuted the illegal press, which was regularly broken up by Stapo, but especially by the *Gestapo*. The most drastic regulation regarding the illegal press was issued on 12 October 1942 and stated that anybody who published, distributed or received an illegal newspaper was liable to punishment by death or in lesser cases by imprisonment. The regulation was not in fact enforced fully. The number of death sentences was relatively small in relation to the threats in the regulation, though 3,000–4,000 people were arrested for having published or received an illegal paper, and many of them were sent to Germany.

There was a change in the development of the illegal press when all radio owners apart from NS members had to hand in their radio sets in autumn 1941. The regime wanted to stop the groundswell of pro-British sentiment that the broadcasts from London were promoting. However, quite a few people hid their radio sets away, some people who had two surrendered only one, and some looked out their old crystal sets from the early days of radio. People listened secretly to the broadcasts from London, wrote them down and spread the word. Numerous radio newspapers sprung up between August and October 1941. The one that was probably biggest, *London News*, was established on

15 September 1941 and was published intermittently either every day or two to three times a week in a print run that varied from 1,000 to 4,000 copies. It collapsed when it was brutally broken up in February 1944.

The radio newspapers passed on the news that had been broadcast in Norwegian from the BBC. The progress of the war interested people intensely, because that would decide what the future would be like. Although the radio newspapers mainly included material from London Radio, they also commented on current events and published The Home Front's directives. In this, they were more like the newspapers that most reported and commented on the local news.

Nowadays, newspaper publishers would prefer to have a subscription for every single copy, but with the illegal press, it was the other way round. The illegal papers were like a sort of chain letter. They should be read by as many people as possible and passed from hand to hand. The papers themselves constantly reminded people of the duty to pass them on to others: 'The paper is not a museum display. Let it circulate.'

The civil resistance leadership understood the importance of the illegal press as a means of communication and wanted to make use of it. As early as autumn 1940 an unnamed paper was published that later came to be known as *The Bulletin*. It originated from central resistance circles in the capital, for whom it was a sort of communication outlet. It was not intended to be distributed widely, but to give signals and directions to key people. It developed to become a sort of authoritative mouthpiece for the civil resistance leadership.

From 1942, the civil resistance leadership tried to maintain regular contact with the illegal press. This took a more permanent form the following year, though it was set back several times by arrests. In spring 1944 a system was established that was secure enough for The Home Front Leadership and the illegal press to have regular contact without the risk of arrests affecting one group spilling over onto the other. By the summer the leadership had secure connections with eighteen to twenty newspapers in and around Oslo. The papers published the leadership's directives and became an important communication channel to the population, as most of the papers were produced in Oslo and were distributed across the country from there. In return, they received material help in the form of radios, paper, copying machines and money. The relationship between the leadership and the press did not change the basic character of the press. On the one hand, it was not subordinate to the leadership and it continued extensive, decentralized and varied activity on its own. On the other hand, it became progressively better integrated with the civil resistance movement through its links with the leadership.

The intelligence service

The military intelligence service supplied the Allies with information of military value from the occupied territories. This was a combination of civil and military activity. It was unarmed, like the civil resistance movement, and its core activity of gathering information seems more like a civil than a military function. However, its ultimate purpose was military and the recipients of the information were military authorities. The intelligence service was the part of The Resistance Movement that made the most important contribution to the Allied war effort.

The intelligence service had two branches, each working for a particular authority abroad. One was the operational intelligence service. This dealt with information necessary for ongoing Allied operations, particularly against German shipping. News of the location of German ships, how many there were, their intended route along the Norwegian coast and the state of the weather was important for planes and ships attacking the German convoys. Information of this type had to be sent quickly to be of any use. This was achieved by sending in agents from abroad with radio equipment to transmit up-to-date information over the airwaves. The British Secret Intelligence Service (SIS) was responsible for the shipping information, working alongside the Norwegian Defence Ministry's E-Section. This service was set up early, with four radio stations linked to Great Britain in existence by 1940. In 1941 there were six and by 1945 there were forty-six. Few of the stations operated for more than a year.

The SIS agents, who were all Norwegians, were mostly brought to Norway by plane or by boat, but many were also sent in from Sweden. They were usually located along the coast, where they generally lived in simple cabins, tents or caves. They used binoculars to observe and report directly on the movement of ships. Sometimes they were able to watch the ships being attacked soon afterwards, as a direct consequence of their transmission of information. In principle, the agents were supposed to be self-sufficient with the equipment and the provisions they brought in from outside, and they were to have as little contact with the local people as possible. In practice, they did meet people and the presence of radio stations in or near towns usually led to the growth of a supportive local network. This enabled the agents to get lodgings, extra supplies and information that could not be gathered by observation alone, as, for example, when harbour employees were able to report on German ships in port or the departure times of German convoys.

There were radio agents along the coast up as far as Finnmark. After the big German battleships and cruisers were sent north in 1942, SIS prioritized the operational intelligence about these ships. Several SIS agents from as far north as Alta followed the movements of the ships. The radio reports from the agents were important components of the picture that the British were building up of the movements of the big ships, which led to the battleships *Scharnhorst* and *Tirpitz* being sunk.

The Soviet Union was also interested in acquiring information about shipping along the coast of Finnmark. This was the easiest place for Russian planes and submarines to attack the German convoys to Kirkenes and Petsamo. The Soviet North Fleet and the Soviet Security Service (NKVD) recruited Norwegians to its intelligence service, gave them the necessary training and landed them by boat or parachuted them into position. These men are generally referred to as 'partisans', but they were in reality intelligence agents. They radioed information about shipping and other matters to Murmansk.

Norway in the Second World War

In autumn 1941 there was one radio station operating in North Norway, in 1942 there were seven and until summer 1943 there were still seven. Then they were almost totally eliminated, and thereafter there were probably only two stations. About a hundred people worked for or were associated with the Soviet intelligence service in Finnmark and Troms. They suffered great losses. Of the hundred, twenty-three were executed, ten fell in attacks, two perished and eleven fled.

The Norwegians whom the British or the Soviet intelligence services sent into Norway must be considered as part of The Resistance Movement, but they were on its fringe. They were few compared with The Resistance Movement as a whole, and in principle, they were expected to keep their distance from the rest of the movement. On the other hand, the agents were fighting the same enemy as other members of the resistance and they shared the same motivation. The aim of their service united them with others who chose resistance rather than passivity. When we see the intelligence agents in the context of their contact networks, they are clearly part of The Resistance Movement.

The other type of intelligence service was static. This was not intended to support ongoing operations but to gather information about all important aspects of the *Wehrmacht* in Norway. The main purpose was to give the Allies as much as possible of the information they needed to build up a picture of the German forces and incorporate this into the overall picture of the German forces in Europe. The secondary intention was to provide intelligence that could be needed for future operations.

Various specialized groups gradually evolved within the intelligence service. The biggest and most important intelligence organization was XU, which had its origins in two groups. One consisted of officers who had taken part in the Norwegian Campaign in 1940 and who initially worked with both the intelligence service and Milorg. The other was made up of academics and students who gradually came to form the backbone of XU as the officers disappeared because they either had to flee or were taken prisoner. During 1941 the XU central core in Oslo acquired a network of individuals or groups in all districts of southern Norway, though the coverage was uneven. The build-up continued in the following years and was steadily extended, despite exposures and losses. Eventually, XU covered both southern and northern Norway.

XU had access to a few radio stations, but most of the information it sent out went overland to Sweden and was then sent on by plane to London. This was partly because of necessity, because much of the static intelligence information was extensive and was unsuitable to be sent by radio stations that could not transmit too much content or for too long at a time. Also, there was less urgency with static information. It could be carried by couriers, but the safest way was to use the train. Microphotographed information was put in specific hiding places in trains crossing the border, to be retrieved by the recipients in Stockholm.

About 5,500 people took part in the intelligence service, for shorter or longer periods of time. Of these, about 1,800 were involved with the radio stations and 2,400 with XU throughout the country. The combined losses in the intelligence groups amounted to 267. Of these, 102 were executed, 94 died in prisons or prison camps, 67 died in action or while under arrest, and 4 when trying to flee.

Escape

War, flight and refugees go together. In Norway, people fled from the towns in the first days after the German invasion. In Oslo and other places, the 'Panic Day' was 10 April. Most of them soon came back, but some continued living out in the country throughout the summer. During the military campaign in 1940, 10,000–15,000 Norwegians fled over the border to Sweden, but most of them also came back the same summer. Later, towards the end of the war, 25,000 Norwegians fled from the Germans' forced evacuation of Finnmark and Nord-Troms in the winter of 1944–5. Some of them made their way over the border to Sweden, but most of them stayed on in caves and turf huts in regions the Germans had abandoned. These were 'internally displaced persons', to use a modern expression. The biggest flow of refugees, however, was out of the country in either of two directions: an early and smaller flow westward over the sea to Great Britain; and a large and prolonged exodus eastward to Sweden.

Organizations or networks that made arrangements for flight and helped people to escape must be considered part of organizational resistance. Whether to West or East, most of the refugees made their own way without such help. They acted spontaneously and individually. But organizations, groups or networks soon developed who saw it as their duty to organize other people's escape. In the terminology of The Resistance Movement, they operated in the field of 'export' as 'export organizations'.

The North Sea route

Between spring 1940 and early 1942, about 3,300 Norwegians in almost 320 vessels escaped across the North Sea to Britain. This traffic reached its high point in autumn 1941 before coming to a halt the following year because of the high losses it entailed. Most of the refugees landed on Shetland or on mainland Scotland. As the term 'England' was widely used at that time to signify 'Great Britain', these sea journeys were generally referred to as *Englandsfarten* ('the English Route'). Most of the voyagers were young men who wanted to take part in The Overseas Front. As time went on, others took this route because they were in danger of arrest and needed to get out. The voyages usually set off from the west coast. There were several starting points, but the activity was to a large extent centred around Ålesund.

People embarking on the journey faced great challenges. First, they had to acquire a boat. One could buy a boat, friends or relatives could make a boat available, and sometimes young people stole a boat. The vessel was usually small, carrying ten to fifteen refugees. It had to be acquired secretly so that people didn't get wind of the plan. The next secret move was to have the boat at the right place at the right time and gather the group of escapees. The third challenge was the voyage itself. German reconnaissance planes, German ships and German mines were a constant danger, but the weather was often even more dangerous. Some people had a quick and easy voyage without great problems. Others ran into rough weather and had to wage a fierce struggle against the forces of nature. Around 16 boats with a total of 137 people were lost, most of them because of bad weather.

The *Gestapo* and *Abwehr* put a lot of effort into stopping escape to Britain, including the use of Norwegian agents who joined their service and infiltrated groups involved in the traffic. These agents tried first to win the confidence of their countrymen before betraying them to the *Gestapo*. The Rinnan Gang stretched its tentacles along the west coast and was the source of several betrayals. Those voyages to Britain, sometimes involving other illegal activities, led to the loss of 160 lives in this way. The victims were executed, died in captivity or were shot as they tried to flee.

Escape groups gradually developed who focussed on the organization of the voyage to Britain. They organized escape for people in the neighbourhood but also for people who came from further away. In Ålesund, connections were set up between such escape groups and resistance circles in Oslo who sent their people there to have them taken over to England. People also came to Ålesund from Bergen and from Trondheim. It was typical of the escape groups that they were not only engaged in the journey to Britain but also involved in other resistance work. Such overlapping of activity was usual everywhere in the pioneering days, but it was especially prevalent on the west coast and it gave the resistance there a characteristic regional flavour: seaborne escape, intelligence gathering and military activity combined.

The North Sea route was interwoven with the activities of the British in Norway. SIS and SOE organized 'The Shetland Bus' that carried agents and weapons over the North Sea. On the journey back, they brought returning agents and refugees. The British used refugee Norwegians for this, and in the early years, they also used the fishing boats in which they had come over. This interweaving of civil and military traffic was the reason why the Germans put so much effort into stopping the voyages to Britain.

Escape to Sweden

The biggest flow of escapees was eastwards to Sweden. The route to the West lasted only for a couple of years, but the flow to the East never stopped, and for the most part, just increased. It was easier to get to Sweden than to Britain. On the westward journey, storms could be fatal. Travelling east, the weather could be a threat on the barren mountain routes but not in the forests through which most people travelled, and not over short sea crossings. The Germans concentrated on stopping travel to the enemy in the West but put less effort into blocking the flow of refugees to neutral Sweden in the East.

Most of the refugees managed to cross the border without the backing of any organization, but specialized escape organizations gradually developed. Here as along the west coast, escape, intelligence, military resistance work and the illegal press all merged in the early days. Several groups sprung up that were active in all or most of those fields. These later either disappeared or became the starting points for bigger and more stable escape organizations. Between 1941 and 1943 a specialized escape network was created, linked to the bigger resistance organizations. In this way, the civil resistance movement,

Milorg, XU and the communists' resistance group came to include their own escape organizations. These were initially intended to help their own people who had come into danger, but the civil escape apparatus and the communists' network in particular also started taking other categories of refugees. The central organizations were all in Oslo, where they received refugees from most of southern Norway and sent them on their way. The various groups worked together, and escape as a whole was a particular, specialized field of resistance activity.

A fully developed escape organization had several parts. The setting up and maintenance of escape routes was, of course, central. These varied according to what sort of refugees would be following them. The forests in Østlandet contained many different routes. Of sixty routes altogether, a few were in use throughout the occupation and the rest for shorter or longer periods. Some were very long, included substantial days' marches and were generally safest. These were appropriate for important people, who had to be in good shape. Others were short and required less physical exertion. Some routes required walking from the start right to the frontier, but most of the refugees travelled by train, car or bus for part of the way. There were nearly always guides associated with the routes.

In Oslo, the refugees were distributed in concealment flats where they had to stay until the route was clear. They had to be provided with food and sometimes also clothes or shoes, which was dependent on the organization having the necessary ration cards or being able to acquire food, clothing or shoes in other ways. The refugees also had to be given the necessary papers, which required the escape organizations to have good relationships with the police who issued these.

The escape organizations were not initially designed to cope with a mass exodus. In autumn 1942 the escape groups in southern Norway had a normal capacity of fifty to sixty refugees per week. Two years later they had grown to 22–25 routes with a combined capacity of 1,000–1,200 people per month. That was about half of the total number of refugees who crossed the border every month. Most of the routes were not fully used for more than short periods. Sometimes the organizations had to assist larger groups at short notice. The first instance of this was when hundreds of Jews had to flee in autumn 1942. The second time was when about a thousand students had to do the same the following year. The escape organizations also had to respond during the dispute over the national labour service in 1944. On such occasions when they were dangerously overloaded, they had to utilize their capacity to the full while at the same time reaching out to expand it.

CHAPTER 15
THE NORWEGIAN COMMUNIST PARTY

The status of the communists during the occupation was unique. In contrast with the other political parties, which suspended their activities, the Norwegian Communist Party (NKP) continued in existence throughout the war. NKP developed a radical resistance policy that differed from the mainstream policy of The Home Front and its leadership. This led to a permanent division between two camps in The Resistance Movement.

In the early post-war years, the writing of history about the communists suffered from the effects of the Cold War and the lack of sources. Cold War politics determined the attitude towards the Communist Party. The communists' role in the war was overshadowed, toned down and criticized. This has changed in more recent years, and the communists' resistance is now receiving its deserved place in the historiography.

The enthusiasm for revision should not, however, cause us to lose sight of the communists' particular starting point. From the start, the Norwegian Communist Party was subordinate to a communist world movement. The line that the Party followed was therefore determined not by circumstances in Norway but by what Comintern thought was right at the time. The distant aim was the world communist revolution. But as the revolution had to wait, Comintern's policy in the meantime concentrated on defending the Soviet Union. In other words, Comintern was primarily a tool of Soviet foreign policy.

Comintern's control over the Norwegian Party increased steadily throughout the 1930s. Several of the party faithful were sent to Moscow to attend Comintern's political schools and came back imbued with Communist Party discipline and culture. The composition of the Party's leadership had to be approved by Comintern, which could intervene directly in the appointments of leaders. At the same time, NKP had to follow the vagaries of Comintern policy, which usually corresponded poorly with political reality in Norway. The result was that the Party declined significantly. Like NS, it was reduced to a mere sect.

A new turn in Soviet and therefore Comintern policy was brought about by the non-aggression pact that Germany and the Soviet Union signed on 23 August 1939. Germany and Russia had been irreconcilable enemies throughout the 1930s, and the defeat of fascism had been one of Comintern's major tasks. The communists now had to do a U-turn overnight. Germany and the fascists were no longer the great enemies. Great Britain, France and Germany had suddenly become tarred with the same brush, three imperialist great powers who were fighting for supremacy in a war that had nothing to do with the communists. When the Soviets attacked Finland and the Winter War broke out on 30 November 1939, NKP supported the Soviets. This further reduced its popularity. Nor did Germany's invasion of Norway change the situation from a communist point of view. The invasion was just a part of the war between the great powers which was not Norway's concern. NKP dissociated itself from the Norwegian government's resistance policy and wanted an end to the military campaign as soon as possible.

The non-aggression treaty did not protect Communist Parties in the occupied countries. NKP was banned on 16 August 1940, over a month before the other parties. The question then was whether it should go underground. Doing this was by no means new among Communist Parties; clandestine operation had been an everyday activity for many of them. It was therefore quite natural for NKP to continue as an underground party.

Even though recruitment of members to the Party had declined steadily, it had kept a foothold in the trade union movement, where the communists had played a role in the trade union opposition of 1940 and continued to exert influence on the new trade union leadership that Terboven set up. The aim was to preserve the trade union movement as a means of protecting the workers' interests. This required some collaboration with the Germans, who must not be offered any excuse for stepping in to ban the movement. At the same time, NS had to be kept out. This policy was supported by Comintern in the two directives that NKP received from Moscow at that time, calling for more effort in the struggle against NS and Nazi ideology.

The banned NKP was thus both collaborating and resisting. The resistance consisted of the Party defying the Germans' prohibition and pursuing an anti-NS policy. As the non-aggression treaty underlay this policy, there were tight limitations to what resistance could be undertaken and NKP became sidelined from the general development of The Home Front. The communists could not align themselves like most Norwegians with the war the British were fighting or honour the king as a symbol of unity. They could not take part in military resistance or support preparations for renewed participation in the war in the event of the British trying to recapture the country. Nevertheless, the communists did have a connection with the rest of The Home Front through their opposition to NS and their ideological anti-Nazism.

The Radical Resistance Party

The German attack on the Soviet Union on 22 June 1941 changed the communists' position completely. The Soviet Union and Great Britain immediately became Allies against Hitler's Germany. The war was no longer an imperialist conflict between bourgeois great powers, but a war between the Soviets and Great Britain on one side and Germany on the other. The war waged by the British and by the Norwegian king and government had suddenly become the communists' war too. This would require a change of NKP's policy. Two delegates from Comintern came to Oslo in July. NKP now received orders to work for a national unity front and collaborate with all forces that opposed fascist Germany. The political mass struggle must be combined with direct action that would create chaos behind the German lines and obstruct the Germans' supply lines and troop transports.

It took six months for the Party to agree to the new policy. The person who carried it through was Peder Furubotn, a man with long experience both in the Party and in the communist world movement in Moscow. Since coming home from Russia in 1938, Furubotn had been stationed in Bergen as the Party's secretary in Vestlandet (Western Norway). He had always been critical of the Party's leadership in Oslo, and after 22 June he pressed hard to get the Party to take up the new resistance policy. The Soviet Union was now fighting a battle of life and death, and it was the Party's duty to attack the enemy on Norwegian soil.

On 31 December 1941, thirty to forty people gathered for an extended central committee meeting that was held in Oslo, disguised as a new year party. The meeting approved Furubotn's 'war policy' and elected him as the Party's leader to put it into action. It was not enough just to oppose NS's Nazification programme. NKP supported the civil resistance but considered that civil acts were not sufficient. The resistance must be directed primarily against the Germans' military and economic interests.

'We face the reality in Norway today that all manufacturing is devoted to production for Hitler-Germany's war and war objectives and that its relatively few occupation troops remain unchallenged,' Furubotn wrote. Therefore, a military resistance movement should be established that could carry out sabotage and engage in partisan warfare. The communists were not against raising military units that would prepare themselves for an Allied invasion, but they also wanted to attack the occupying army in the meantime; a policy like that of SOE at the time. In industry, silent sabotage should be practised and the allocation of Norwegian labour forces to German workplaces boycotted.

This was an extremely radical policy that NKP was now proposing for the direction of the resistance. It was adopted at a time when people still had fresh memories of the state of emergency in September and had over several months been able to read regularly about further executions. Nobody who took part in the meeting could have been in doubt that this policy would lead to more reprisals. Nor could anybody have doubted that it corresponded poorly with opinion among the public, who had little inclination for armed conflict and its bloody consequences.

NKP had been politically weak for more than a decade and had not yet strengthened its position during the occupation. There is only one explanation why the Party nevertheless committed itself to its dangerous new policy: its commitment since its birth in 1923 to serve the communist world movement and Soviet state. The central core of communism was in mortal danger, and the Party's contribution to its defence must be correspondingly fearless.

The Party took on an overwhelming task with its new policy, but there was one point of view that could be used to appeal to the Party members. It had always been easy for the Party's opponents to criticize it for being unpatriotic because it acted as a tool for Soviet interests. The struggle for international communism and support for the Soviet Union could now for the first time be combined with a struggle for national liberation.

The fight for the communist fatherland became the fight for the national fatherland also. For the first time, NKP could now hope to attract patriotic support.

Right to the end of the war, NKP followed the Comintern directive and the programme that it had adopted on New Year's Eve 1941. There was no question of changing it, just of making the necessary tactical decisions. These would necessarily be hard decisions, because of the big gap between NKP's guiding policy and what most people could be willing to sacrifice on the altar of the resistance. NKP, therefore, advanced slowly, to begin with, both because it took time to expand the Party's organization and because public opinion was little prepared for the radical elements in the policy.

NKP maintained its Party organization during the war. Under the Party leadership there was a Party apparatus with district leaderships and local branches, organized according to residential district or workplace. Under these, illegal working groups or 'cells' operated. The work of the Party included traditional political and ideological indoctrination with studies of Marxism–Leninism, the history of the labour movement and Russian party history. The real leadership lay with Furubotn and a circle around him. This consisted at first of pre-war communists, but as many of them were arrested and possibly executed they were replaced by young people turning to NKP. In spring 1942 Furubotn set up his headquarters at Krosstølen in Hemsedal. The HQ later moved camp several times, always in mountainous areas for reasons of safety. It was attacked several times by the *Gestapo*, but Furubotn and several of his colleagues always managed to get away.

NKP was both a Party organization and a resistance organization, two sides of the same coin. Several important parts of the resistance became linked with the Party organization. In industry, the Party promoted the establishment of 'national committees' that would take part in the resistance and organize silent sabotage clandestinely, creating delays in production. A bigger and more important field was the illegal press. In autumn 1941 some Party veterans started two newspapers that would become among the largest of the illegal press. One was *Radio-nytt* ('Radio News') which produced almost 300 issues from when it started right until the end of the war. It was printed using a stencil on a duplicating machine. The other was *Friheten* ('Freedom'), which was printed from spring 1942 onwards. *Friheten* served in effect as the Party's organ till February 1944 when *Alt for Norge* ('All for Norway') took over as the Party's main mouthpiece. The editing took place at Furubotn's headquarters.

To play its part in the militarization of the resistance, NKP started organizing military groups that were known as 'The National Guard'. The Party worked in the same way as the pioneers in Milorg: setting up units, recruiting volunteers and arranging for some military instruction. The communists did not insist on keeping their units separate from Milorg but tried to work together, and in the course of 1942–3 the communist military groups were either integrated into the Milorg structure or broken up by the *Gestapo*. The communists eventually gave up promoting this form of military organization. Their work with military groups was never a great success. NKP never came near to creating a guerrilla movement of its own.

One part of the reason for this was the regular breaking up of units by the Germans. Another and just as important explanation was that the communists had difficulty competing with a military organization that was legitimized by the authorities abroad, had direct connections with them and received instructors, radio operators, technical equipment, weapons, and ammunition from outside. From the Soviet side, the communists received nothing.

Therefore, it was not military groups or partisan operations that were the most prominent feature of the communists' resistance activity, but sabotage. One man, Asbjørn Sunde ('Osvald'), played a key role in this. He had experience from the Spanish Civil War and from the end of the 1930s, he belonged to a secret sabotage organization that the Russians set up in Western Europe, the 'Wollweber Organisation', which had a branch in Norway. Then in July 1941 he too was visited by the delegates from Stockholm and given orders that the organization in Norway must be activated. Explosions started that same month, and Sunde continued working on sabotage from then on. The organization that he established with local branches undertook well over a hundred operations during almost three years, mostly sabotage but also several assassinations plus thefts to acquire money, ration cards or explosives. That was many times more acts of sabotage than SOE/ FO's sabotage parties carried out in the same period.

Sunde's final loyalty was always to those in the Soviet Security Service (NKVD) from whom he received his orders. He led the sabotage campaign rather independently of the Party, and he was not even formally a member of it. For a time, he took on assignments for Milorg and the illegal police group that worked with Milorg. In March 1944 his relationship with the Party leadership broke down, and in June he received orders from his Soviet masters to dissolve the sabotage organization. He obeyed this order, and thirty-five of his men travelled over to Sweden, where they joined the police troops. Others continued the campaign of sabotage but under different circumstances.

NKP continued working on sabotage and succeeded during autumn 1944 in setting up four regional sabotage organizations that carried out fifty to sixty operations. The biggest and most dynamic of these groups was the organization in Oslo, known as the Pelle Group and led by Ragnar Sollie. The organization in Bergen District was unique in that it worked with both SOE agents and Milorg and functioned as their sabotage group.

The communists set up their own escape organization. In some places the local Party branches also organized transport for escapees. The escape organization existed to serve the communists, but in practice it received more of its clients from Sivorg, who paid for them. Just as in Milorg and Sivorg, the organization had to acquire concealment flats, messengers, lorries, supplies, guides, and couriers.

The communists and The Home Front Leadership

The communists worked on two fronts simultaneously. They took an active part in the resistance movement at the same time as looking for arenas where they could make their influence felt and have a say in the direction of the movement. They sought constantly to be represented in the illegal leadership of the trade union movement, *Faglig Utvalg* ('Trades Committee'), which was dominated by social democrats. They were represented there from October 1942 to February 1944 but were excluded before and after that time. The Party worked mainly towards achieving membership of a combined leadership for The Home Front.

The two groups were far apart, however. The Home Front Leadership (HL) came into being on a policy platform that emphasized civil resistance against Nazification, alongside military preparations for the final liberation. This was very different from NKP's policy of partisan action and sabotage. In autumn 1943 NKP became more insistent in its agitation for this policy. Communist newspapers turned to open polemic against The Home Front's 'passive' line, while Sunde's organization carried out a series of sabotage actions. The blowing up of the railway line at Mjøndalen on 7 October attracted the greatest attention because it led to the execution of five hostages from Drammen.

There were signs that the communists' radical resistance policy was now beginning to have a wider appeal. The Home Front came to a bit of a standstill in autumn 1943 and the first months of 1944. The communists' agitation for a more military resistance and their acts of sabotage to some extent filled the gap this created. The Home Front Leadership might therefore be interested in coming to an agreement with the communists to tame them if possible, and the communists were still interested in being represented in the leadership. Discussions between them were, however, unproductive. The communists did not gain a place in the civil or military leadership.

They then switched over to calling for a new leadership to be created, a Freedom Council on the Danish model. The Home Front Leadership that had been formed the year before had not yet let its existence be publicly known, and the communists could imply as part of their agitation that no such leadership existed. Then when The Home Front Leadership publicly acknowledged its existence during spring 1944, the communists gradually abandoned their agitation for the Freedom Council and demanded instead to be represented in HL. Their demand was not accepted. In contrast with other occupied countries in Western Europe, NKP remained isolated within The Resistance Movement right to the end of the war. The social democrats had opposed the communists during many difficult pre-war years, and they now continued the fight by denying them a place in the leading organizations of The Resistance Movement.

NKP underwent great changes during the occupation. It grew to a membership that it had not had before the war and would not have again later. The increased support was due primarily to the Party's radical resistance policy and practical activity, rather than communist ideology. The many resistance activities started by the Party created numerous opportunities for people who wanted to play a practical part in the resistance. The Germans created impressive communist martyrs when SS and Police Court death sentences specifically identified those among the condemned who were communists.

Another factor, just as important, was that the Party abandoned the world revolution. Comintern was dissolved in 1943. NKP turned to supporting the king and the government and hoped for a restoration of democracy after the war. Many who had initially been sceptical about the Communist Party were now less fearful of it. Its association in the public mind with the Soviet Union became an asset rather than a liability as public admiration for the Soviet war effort increased. Thoughts of the Soviet state's many totalitarian features and memories of the Moscow Trials, purges and red terror faded and were replaced by a tendency to regard Soviet Russia as a social experiment that could have its good sides.

During this process, the origin of the communist resistance policy was either forgotten or seen in a new light. When it was adopted on New Year's Eve 1941, it was based primarily on the defence of the Soviet Union, irrespective of national needs, Norwegian public opinion or The Resistance Movement that was taking shape. The many new people who flocked round to support the Party's resistance activities had little or none of this background. Some of them did not even know that the activity in which they

Figure 4 People leave the mine tunnels at Bjørnevatn outside Kirkenes, where they have been sheltering for several weeks. The battle for Kirkenes is over, Soviet soldiers have taken the town and most of Øst-Finnmark has been liberated – six months before the rest of the country. A Soviet film team recorded the occasion. © NORGES HJEMMEFRONTMUSEUM.

were taking part had been initiated by the communists. Others knew without thinking it important, and yet others were sympathetic towards the socialism that they felt the communists somehow stood for. The idea that the communists' resistance struggle arose first and foremost from a duty to protect the Soviet fatherland was remote from the great majority who gradually found themselves within the communist orbit.

The increased support for the communists was expressed in measurable form after liberation when they won slightly under 12 per cent of the votes in the parliamentary election in 1945 and had 34,000 members in 1946. Then came the Cold War, and things didn't go so well. One might have thought that NKP would then have honoured the communists who had been in the front line of the resistance campaign and given them leading positions in the Party, but things did not work out like that. During an unusually bitter disagreement at the end of the 1940s, reminiscent of the bloody purges in Eastern European Communist Parties at the same time, the 'War-time Communists' with Furubotn at their head were forced out of the Party while a group of pre-war communists took over power. NKP then continued its slow downward march towards ruin, obedient to the Soviet state as always.

PART IV
TOWARDS THE END

The closing stages of the war in Norway began in the North, and they began violently. Soviet troops drove the enemy out of Øst-Finnmark, while the Germans devastated Finnmark and Nord-Troms, and the members of the local population were evacuated by force or fled. Abroad, Norway's soldiers and seamen continued serving as before, and at home, The Resistance Movement reached its high point in the last year of the war. Meanwhile, people struggled in the grimness of everyday life. Living conditions grew steadily worse, and goods became more and more scarce. When would the liberation come, and what form would it take? Among the Germans and within NS, competing factions clashed ahead of a defeat that was difficult to confront.

CHAPTER 16
THE OVERSEAS AND HOME FRONTS IN THE LAST YEAR OF THE WAR

In 1944–5, the Germans were fighting against superior Allied forces in the East, South and West. The Allies would sooner or later reach Germany's borders and start occupying the German homeland. The Germans only managed to strike back briefly, in the Ardennes Counteroffensive between December 1944 and January 1945. Then their fate pursued its course as before. The Germans retreated on all fronts. The alliance between the Soviet Union, the United States and Great Britain would inevitably win. The only question was how the endgame would work out. Would the Germans surrender before they were finally defeated, would the German *Reich* collapse or would the Germans defend themselves until there was nothing left to defend? These were the questions that dominated everybody's thoughts.

The Allies put nearly all their military resources into continental Europe. Other regions were of secondary importance. This determined Norway's situation in the last year of the war. Neither the Western powers nor the Russians were prepared to put anything into a denouement in Norway while the battles were raging on the continent. Only when Germany was broken there would they turn to considering what had to be done in Norway. Perhaps the situation would resolve itself by Germany surrendering Norway without a fight. But one could not be sure. There were 300,000–400,000 German soldiers stationed in Norway, available to fight back.

There could be no doubt about the outcome of such a scenario, but it would convert Norway into a battlefield and cause great suffering for the Norwegian population. Right to the last days of the war it was an open question whether the end would be peaceful or violent. The Norwegian authorities in exile also experienced this uncertainty and felt frustrated by their difficulty in getting the Allies to take an interest in Norwegian affairs.

Participation in D-Day

Early on the morning of 6 June 1944, Operation Overlord started. This was a massive landing of British, American, and Canadian invasion troops on the Channel Coast of northern France, between Caen and Cherbourg. D-Day had come; the liberation of Western Europe had started. Three of the four Norwegian defence forces, if the merchant fleet is included, took part in this enormous mobilization. The Norwegian participation was microscopic in relation to the total muster of Allied strength, and only part of each of the Norwegian armed forces was involved. However, the modest Norwegian contribution to D-Day was significant. For once, the Norwegian forces were operating as part of a combined operation. On 6 June the air force, the navy and the merchant fleet were taking part in a massive enterprise. They were enhanced by being part of a bigger whole. The enormous scale of the landings gave even the modest Norwegian participation greater status.

The air force was the branch of the services that made the biggest contribution to the D-Day landings and the subsequent fighting on the continent. Half of the squadrons – the two fighter squadrons – served in the war over Europe continuously from the landings until liberation. From November 1943 they had been organized in a Norwegian wing that in reality consisted of two Norwegian and eventually two British squadrons, plus a fifth, Dutch squadron from January 1945. The Allies had mastery in the air, and the squadrons did not face any German planes in their overland sorties, just anti-aircraft fire from the ground. After the first days of the invasion, the squadrons continued regular raids across the continent from bases in England, attacking German troops, vehicles, trains, and tanks.

On 20 August the wing was transferred to France. The Norwegian units, 331 and 332 squadrons, took part in the battles against the retreating Germans for eight months. This hectic and eventful time until April 1945 became a high point in the squadrons' history. The planes operated in turn from seven different temporary airbases on the continent. The crews had to cope with living in tents, barracks, and self-built huts. Four hundred lorries carried equipment and personnel from place to place, and the men faced an enormous task in all types of weather to prepare each new base and maintain the aircraft. The wing carried out its first bombing raid over Germany on 17 October. During the campaign, twenty-six Norwegian airmen in the Norwegian wing lost their lives and eleven were taken prisoner.

In spring 1944 the navy had at its disposal about fifty warships. Ten of them were present at the landing operations – three destroyers, three corvettes, three motor launches and a patrol boat. Two ships were lost. One was the newly built destroyer *Svenner*, which was lying off the coast early on the morning of 6 June, waiting for the passage towards the land to be cleared of mines, when it was torpedoed amidships, broke in two and sank. From a crew of well over 200 men, 34 lost their lives. *Svenner* was the first casualty among the Allied landing fleet. The other ship that was lost was the destroyer *Glaisdale*, which survived D-Day but struck a mine off the French coast on 23 June, was damaged without any loss of life and was taken out of service.

From the merchant fleet, Nortraship provided forty-three coastal ships for the Normandy invasion. The crews joined voluntarily, and six of the boats took part in the action on the first day. They anchored as near the beach as possible to unload troops, ammunition, petrol and provisions. Soon, the ships were able to sail in at high tide and remain on the beach until low tide, so that the transport vehicles could drive right up to the ship and transship directly. Nortraship also provided some older ships to be used as breakwaters. These were sunk to provide shelter for ships unloading. After D-Day, Norwegian boats took part in shuttle traffic convoys between England and France to carry supplies to the troops at the front. Of the forty-three vessels provided by Nortraship, two were sunk with the loss of three lives, and twenty-six were slightly damaged.

The army was the branch of the defence services that did not as a whole get an opportunity to serve in Normandy. After D-Day, both officers and men in the Norwegian Brigade wanted to take part in the fighting on the continent. In August 1944 the mountain companies asked to be allowed to take part in the campaign in France. Their request was considered by the Supreme Command, the Ministry of Defence and the government, but the conclusion was 'No'. It was not advisable to send the small Norwegian forces onto the continent. They could suffer severe losses, leaving few troops left for operations in Norway. As before, they had to be held back in readiness for the liberation of the homeland. A mountain company that was sent to Finnmark in November 1944 was the first to take part in this liberation.

The Norwegian participation in the Normandy invasion did not signify any fundamental change of policy. It was just one of many outcomes of the war policy that the government had adopted on 9–10 April 1940 and had developed further when it came to Britain. The practical application of this policy lay in the air force's and the navy's continuing operations, the army's preparations, and the merchant fleet's voyages in Allied service. The war policy was now going further along the course that had been set previously. The many questions of a military nature were mainly decided by the military authorities in consultation with the Allies. The government's primary concerns now were how they could come to the aid of northern Norway, prepare for the end of the war and be ready for the final homecoming.

The royal family was a big asset to the government in holding The Overseas and Home Fronts together. King Haakon was just as popular abroad as he was at home, and he strengthened the government in its relationships with The Home Front. In the last year of the war, the government also wanted to expand the role of Crown Prince Olav, by appointing him as head of the Allied army of liberation that would sooner or later recapture Norway. In this, however, they were aiming their sights too high. The Western powers were not interested in having a Norwegian crown prince as commander-in-chief of a combined liberation force.

However, the crown prince did get a new appointment that gave him a more significant role. On 30 June 1944, he was appointed as Supreme Commander of the Norwegian Defence Forces. This made him overall leader of all Norwegian armed forces, both the traditional forces abroad and Milorg at home – The Home Forces, as they were now called. He functioned as a unifying chief of defence for both The Overseas and The Home Fronts. His position was not merely symbolic. Olav had military training, was interested in military matters and was a real military leader.

The government and the military authorities continued to work with The Resistance Movement on how best they could prepare themselves for the conclusion of the war, depending on what form that would take. Through personal meetings between representatives of The Home and Overseas Fronts and lengthy correspondence, the parties came to an agreement about a machinery of government to be prepared in readiness to manage the country after liberation. This would consist of a triumvirate in each district: a county governor selected beforehand by *Kretsen* in consultation with the government; a head of The Home Forces and a chief of police selected beforehand. In the government ministries, advisers were selected who would govern alongside The Home Front Leadership (HL) until the government could be in place, ready to take over.

The civil resistance movement's second victory

In the last year of the war, The Home Front and The Resistance Movement achieved unprecedented breadth, depth, and strength. Spring and summer 1944 were a turning point when the civil resistance culminated in a widespread and successful offensive whose effects were apparent right to the end of the war. The military resistance movement was also much more prominent in the final year. From spring 1944 it grew continuously in strength and scope while increasingly influencing the broader Home Front.

The offensive against the national labour service law had started the year before. It continued into 1944 and intensified with a simultaneous boycott of labour conscription in *Arbeidstjenesten (AT)*, which had been introduced in 1941 as described in Chapter 11. The leaders of the resistance feared that the NS state would use *AT* as a back-door method of military conscription and mobilization.

The leadership launched a comprehensive campaign against *AT*. Nobody should attend for assessment or work. The directive was disseminated via *KK*'s network of contacts, published by the illegal press and broadcast by London Radio. The directives against *AT* then ran in parallel with the directives against the national labour service, which still applied. The new campaign was not an immediate success. Only about 30 per cent refused to attend. On the other hand, it was an important forerunner to the third and most important phase in the fight against compulsory labour.

The third phase began in May 1944, when the NS state launched a big new offensive. Under the provisions of the law about the national labour service, all men aged twenty-one to twenty-three were summoned to report to employment offices on 19 May. When they attended, they would be registered and possibly sent to work for six months in agriculture, forestry, building and construction work or important industries, in other words, a large-scale mobilization of labour. The summons to attend was issued at short notice, obviously in an attempt to forestall possible opposition. The resistance leaders were again concerned that labour conscription would be converted into military conscription with organization of military units.

KK had got to know about the coming call-up on 12 May. They asked London Radio to 'send the strongest possible propaganda against any form of attendance'. Within Norway, KK itself started working tirelessly to have the directive against labour mobilization distributed. Young people were urged to scatter and so far as possible to go into hiding individually. Special directives were issued to different groups of the population, advising how they could help the young men to boycott the call-up. Parents, priests, teachers, lawyers, doctors, employers, farmers, and others all received their own directives. This was followed later in the summer by instructions that the boys could go to Sweden, where they could join the police troops. In spring 1944, Milorg began setting up permanent resistance cells in the forests, where the members would live like soldiers in the field. Some of the young men who avoided the labour mobilization joined these cells.

In spring 1943, sabotage had been used on one occasion as part of the fight against the national labour service. In May and June the following year, sabotage became more widespread when employment offices and other parts of the registration system were blown up. The sabotage also had a psychological effect, creating an impression that there was physical power behind the civil directives.

The opposition provoked by the mobilization of labour became the second high point of the civil resistance campaign during the war. Young people and society in general came together in their opposition to the mobilization initiative. As in 1942, this became a struggle which both parties, the NS state as much as The Resistance Movement, regarded as a decisive trial of strength. As in 1942, the NS state lost. The police were not able to stop the flood of young people evading the labour mobilization.

One result of the long-running campaign against the national labour service and *Arbeidstjenesten* was that the Germans got fewer workers for their military construction sites. Another was that the successful action against labour mobilization strengthened morale among the population during the last year of the war. There were no new major offensives. The civil resistance levelled off, but it continued. The civil leadership regularly sent out directives about how people should behave in relation to NS and the Germans. Constant, encouraging messages were needed along the many 'fronts' in domestic and business life. The strength that The Resistance Movement had shown in the opposition to labour mobilization gave these messages increased acceptance and effect.

The Resistance Movement is militarized

In spring 1944, while the campaign against the national labour service and labour conscription was fully underway, the policy for the military resistance was revised and the movement started a period of growth that would continue until the end of the war. In March 1944, a fourteen-day meeting was held in Stockholm between representatives of the Supreme Command (FO) and the national police leadership in London, and the Milorg leadership in Oslo. The meeting confirmed the core of Milorg's present and future policy. As before, the organization should prepare for action during the liberation. The new element was that it should also to some extent carry out operations meantime. This addition to the policy was the result mainly of demands from within Norway. There were obvious tendencies towards a radicalization of the resistance in 1943–4. Many people were calling for more than just civil acts of resistance. Impatience was growing within Milorg's ranks and many people wanted action, not just training and readiness. There was growing support for the communists' policy of sabotage.

One form of action that resulted because of the Stockholm meeting was assassinations, and the other was sabotage. The number of assassinations now grew sharply. There were sixty-five in 1944–5, compared with a previous total of only seventeen. Members of Company Linge, Milorg fighters and sometimes the communists carried out the assassinations. These were directed against informants and policemen who were a threat to the resistance organizations. The German police and German soldiers were not targets.

The first sabotage actions following the new policy came about at the beginning of May as part of the campaign against the national labour service and mobilization of labour. The actions were mainly carried out by members of Company Linge, sometimes with help from local Milorg fighters. It was through these actions that the scattered Company Linge personnel in the Oslo area who worked on different missions came together under Gunnar Sønsteby's leadership to form a unit that came to be known as the Oslo Group.

The other type of sabotage was purely military, directed against targets important for the war. The meeting in Stockholm did not come to final decisions about this type of sabotage, which needed Allied approval first. The Western powers' highest military command, SHAEF, now kept tight control of The Resistance Movements in the various countries, and neither FO nor SOE could give permission for military sabotage without approval from SHAEF. The order from FO to set Milorg's military sabotage in motion in the last year of the war first came out on 26 July. Milorg should attack petrol and oil installations at every opportunity. Throughout the autumn several other types of targets were added, such as vehicle workshops, while permission had to be obtained in individual cases in respect of industrial enterprises. The first sabotage actions followed soon after the order.

After that, sabotage in Norway was performed by three different groups – Linge personnel, Milorg fighters and the communists. SOE/FO continued sending in expeditions of Company Linge people who carried out sabotage independently of the military resistance movement. Milorg did extensive sabotage either alone or in collaboration with Company Linge. As before, the communists followed their own programme and ran their own sabotage groups. Bergen was an exception, where the communists, Milorg and Linge personnel worked together on sabotage.

Railway sabotage was in a category of its own. The Allied Supreme Command had asked on 18 October 1943 for preparations to be made for such sabotage in Norway. So, in winter 1943–4 several groups from Company Linge were sent into Norway with all the necessary equipment, to lie in wait near the most important railway lines. In autumn 1944 these groups had orders to continue to lie low. The Allied generals preferred to bring German troops from Norway onto the continent to defeat them there. From Norwegian quarters, however, there was now pressure to get permission for railway sabotage. On 26 October SHAEF gave way a little and ordered a limited campaign of railway sabotage, mainly to maintain morale among the men from Company Linge who had been waiting so long.

On 5 December, SHAEF did a U-turn. Railway sabotage should now go full steam ahead to delay the transport of German troops from the North. New sabotage parties were brought in to supplement the existing ones. The last reinforcements came in March 1945, when three groups of about fifteen men each were brought in to attack the Northern Railway. One was an American-led unit consisting of Norwegian-Americans and Norwegian seamen, the second was made up of members of the parachute company and the third was from Company Linge.

During the last five months of the war, a series of sabotage attacks were carried out against the railways. One of them was the blowing up of Jørstad Bridge by the Woodlark Group. On the evening of 12 January, they were able to place their explosive charges under the bridge. At 2.30 am the charges went off and the bridge was destroyed. Several hours later a locomotive and the first seventeen wagons plunged into the river. A Norwegian engine driver and fireman and over seventy German soldiers were killed.

Local Milorg groups carried out two sabotage attacks on the Dovre Railway in January. On the night of 14 March Milorg carried out its big, co-ordinated *Operasjon Betongblanding* ('Operation Cement Mixing') against the railways when the Southern, Western and Eastern Lines from Oslo were damaged in numerous places and NSB's headquarters in Oslo was reduced to rubble. This large-scale action was valuable both for the damage that it caused and as a demonstration of Milorg's strength shortly before the final stages of the war.

Many of the young men who evaded the labour mobilization initially hid in the forests. The question arose as to whether The Resistance Movement should organize them militarily. The communists worked towards this for a while and considered their escape as part of an incipient partisan movement. The Milorg leadership thought that it was not realistic to take them all in hand but decided that Milorg should allow selected groups to remain in permanent hiding in the forests. They slept in small self-built huts, trained for military action, received airdrops, and tried to acquire necessary supplies for themselves.

For its part, FO worked on a bigger plan that originated from the campaign against *Arbeidstjenesten* and the national labour service. The Supreme Command wanted to set up its own bases in isolated regions and recruit young men to them. The bases would operate as centres for the training of guerrilla units. They would be FO's extended arm in occupied Norway and would at the same time be part of The Home Forces. Five bases were planned, of which two were fully built by the time of liberation. One was 'Elk' Base, which was divided into four parts in the forest and mountain areas around Hallingdal and Valdres, with headquarters in Vassfaret. The other was 'Bear West' in the Matrefjell mountains north of Bergen.

The bases were organized from London and were directly under FO's administration. The staff who were sent in from abroad consisted of members of Linge Company and army officers. The bases received their supplies of weapons and ammunition from Great Britain. Bear West was supplied both by the Shetland Bus's converted submarine chasers and by airdrops, whereas Elk was supplied only by air. The personnel lived spread around in huts and mountain farms, and most of the provisions had to be secured from neighbouring districts.

Bear West recruited people from Milorg and elsewhere, building up to an establishment of 250 men by the time of liberation. Elk did not build up such a force. Milorg fighters were sent to attend courses there and some of them became permanent members of the base, but most returned to their own districts to put their new skills into practice locally.

The courses lasted for up to four or five weeks. The first one was in January 1945 for sixty men, who were trained as platoon leaders and communications personnel. The courses took place in areas so remote that both shooting and explosives exercises could be mounted. The head of Elk Base was also the operational leader of the surrounding Milorg districts.

The bases followed the same aim as Milorg, to prepare a force ready to act when the occupation was coming to an end. They should not go into action before then but should work as quietly as possible and attack only in self-defence. Thus, the military authorities in London managed to run a couple of guerrilla bases in occupied Norway quite unchallenged for several months. Only a short time before liberation did the Germans start trying to eliminate them. Both bases then came under attack. The assault on Elk lasted only a short time but Bear West had to defend itself for almost a week.

The strong growth of the military resistance movement in the last year of the war occurred partly because of an increasing will to resist among the general population. After four years of occupation, there were more and more who supported the idea of resistance, including military resistance, and were willing to risk taking part in or assisting The Resistance Movement. People had become more accustomed to resistance activity being followed by reprisals and harsh punishments and were more willing to accept the consequences. They were also motivated by news of resistance in other countries. Reports of all the sabotage in Denmark fanned the flames.

However, the growth was also due to the abundant help that was flowing in from abroad. There was an essential difference in this respect between the first four years and the final year of the war. In the course of the war, 717 successful supply operations were carried out by air. Of these, 682 were in the final year. The Shetland Bus brought in 137 tonnes of cargo by sea in 1944–5, compared with 83 tonnes throughout the 4 earlier years. At the time of liberation, The Home Forces had 40,000 men, three quarters of whom were armed. The availability of weapons was mainly the result of the big import of arms in the last year of the war.

In addition, 132 men were parachuted during 1944–5, compared with a total of 76 in the previous years. The Shetland Bus brought in about as many agents in the final year as in all the previous years. The Home Forces received a supplement of instructors and material supplies that converted them into a much more battle-ready entity than before. The big sabotage campaign in March and the successful defence of the Elk and Bear West bases at the end of the war are evidence of that.

In the last year of the war, some of the aid to The Home Forces and to various intelligence and sabotage operations came from Sweden. One of the police troop camps, Älgberget at the south end of Siljansjøen (Lake Siljan), was converted into a training camp for Milorg people. At Ählby outside Stockholm and at Skeberg in Leksand, special training was provided for people who then went on operations in Norway. Food and clothing were transported over the border to the Milorg districts in Østlandet. In New Year 1945, the Swedes gave permission for weapons to be taken over the border, too. Large quantities of arms and ammunition were transported, mostly from Gothenburg and Bohus Counties: 1,240 crates of explosives; 48 crates of weapons and ammunition; and 151 tonnes of food.

Along the Swedish border, bases were set up as starting points for operations in Norway. In the regions bordering Nord-Trøndelag, five such bases were established on either the Swedish or the Norwegian side of the border. Their role was to carry out sabotage against the Northern Railway, and in the last nine months of the war, they performed nine explosions on the line between Steinkjer and Mo i Rana, one of which was the sabotage of Jørstad Bridge. Further north, on the Swedish side in the areas facing Nordland and Troms, four 'Sepal' bases were established in tourist huts and mountain lodges. These came about through a close collaboration between the Norwegian intelligence section MI 2 and the Swedish intelligence service. The bases would provide help from Sweden for the organization of military resistance in Nordland and Troms. Especially in Troms, Milorg activity was largely organized and equipped from the bases. The Milorg fighters sabotaged railway junctions and German stores depots. They also had to help escapees to cross the border. All the bases had direct radio connections with London, from where their activity was controlled.

SOE and FO's sections in the Swedish capital were not the only agencies involved in organizing this activity. In the last year of the war, the Americans came in with their full weight. The American Office of Strategic Services (OSS), which was the equivalent of Britain's SOE and SIS, established a department of its own in Stockholm, the Westfield Mission, which had Norway as part of its remit. SOE, OSS, and FO worked together in London, and their regional offices in Stockholm did the same. Westfield Mission would concentrate on northern Norway. It was responsible for the Norwegian-American base that sabotaged the Northern Railway, and it financed and supplied the Sepal bases. From New Year 1944–5, American planes brought weapons and ammunition into Stockholm camouflaged as diplomatic mail. The equipment was gathered in a villa at Lidingö which served as a weapons depot, before being transported out to the bases and to The Home Forces in southern Norway. The Americans made a massive contribution to air transport in the last year of the war, with the transport of personnel from Sweden to Great Britain and to Finnmark, plus airdrops over Norway.

None of this would have been possible without Swedish aid. Help came from the Swedish intelligence service, the military, the police, and many civilians. It was provided in a country that officially maintained its neutrality policy right to the end of the war, though tending steadily more in favour of the Allies. Help from the authorities was mainly mediated by individuals rather than coming from the authorities as such, but it could not have been given without the authorities either approving or turning a blind eye.

In this respect, the circumstances in Sweden during the last year of the war were rather strange. At the government and senior administrative level, the Swedes tried to hold their ground against persistent and demanding Norwegians, Americans and British who tended to go their own way. At lower levels in the system, the increasing sympathy for Norway and the knowledge that despite everything senior authorities were well inclined led to an urge to respond to the Norwegians and bend the rules. It was a hectic, nervous time when many activists – Norwegian, British, American, and Swedish – ran ahead of the government while the senior bureaucrats tried half-heartedly to work through the regular channels.

Milorg's system of central resources was greatly expanded during the last year of the war. The central leadership had at its disposal numerous concealment flats that were used by the leaders themselves and by the associated escape group that helped Milorg people to escape if they had come into danger. The organization could acquire false passports, identity cards and ration cards. It handled the correspondence with Stockholm and London, and it had its own encryption office that ciphered and deciphered the messages. It had access to a special listening service that tapped Stapo's telephones, and through the postal system, it was able to exercise some surveillance over the mail and pick up letters that could represent a threat to The Resistance Movement. It also set up secret supply stores in the capital to meet its own needs and help the neighbouring districts.

The growth and expansion of The Home Forces changed the pattern of the resistance and the perception of The Home Front in the last year of the war. Previously, the civil resistance campaign had dominated. It was visible and it engaged many people, both those who were directly involved and those who supported the civil actions in various ways or were affected by them. The military resistance work had been going on underground and had not mobilized so many people. From summer 1944, it was the military actions and the build-up of military strength that made the biggest impression and surpassed the civil mass actions as the strongest influence on public opinion. The building up of forces prior to the liberation phase did not leave such visible traces as the assassinations and sabotage, but it still made an impression. There were rumours about men who disappeared into the woods and about the increasingly frequent nocturnal airdrops.

The Home Front Leadership steps forward

In the last year of the war The Home Front Leadership let its existence be known to the public. This first happened in connection with the campaign against *Arbeidstjenesten* in March 1944, when the directives were reported to be coming from 'The Home Front Leadership', usually shortened to 'HL'. From then on, this title was promoted in the three media to which the leadership had access – London Radio, the illegal press and the civil leadership's network of contacts. Nothing was said about who was behind HL. It was mainly the civil leadership, who needed to put some authority behind their directives against *Arbeidstjenesten*. Neither the military resistance movement nor the Milorg leadership was mentioned, though they were presumably associated with HL in the minds of the public.

From the time its existence became publicly known, HL was in a strong position. Its authority stemmed from the successes in the civil resistance campaign and was further strengthened by the growth and expansion of the military resistance movement. It was recognized as having not only civil and moral authority but also military and physical power. It benefitted from the growing prestige of the Allied camp and by the fact that its directives were broadcast from London.

The last phase in the development of The Home Front Leadership came at New Year 1944–5, when it became centralized and formalized. 'The Home Front Leadership' now incorporated *Kretsen*, while KK and the Milorg leadership each appointed their representatives. It embraced a political balance between non-socialists and the labour movement and also included a representative of the farmers to add further social breadth. It was chaired by Paal Berg, who stepped forward at the time of liberation as 'The Leader of The Home Front'. Jens Christian Hauge became a key person in the reorganized leadership while continuing to lead Milorg, and both the civil and the military organization served as the leadership's secretariat.

It proved to be possible to create a leadership that spoke to and on behalf of both The Resistance Movement and The Home Front, even though it was not elected. It was not only self-appointed but also anonymous. None of the public and only very few people in The Resistance Movement knew who was in the leadership. For obvious reasons, HL had to withhold any identification of the leaders, which is usually such an important aspect of most types of leadership. Nevertheless, it managed to achieve widespread support for its faceless leadership team. The need to have somebody who could be seen as the leader in the resistance against the NS regime and the occupying power was big enough to trump the inevitable scepticism about a secret leadership.

German counter-sabotage

The increasing incidence of sabotage and the growing number of assassinations worried the German authorities. The Norwegian communists organized an extensive sabotage attack against the two biggest shipyards in Oslo – Aker and Nyland – on the night of 23–24 November 1944. According to German reports, 23,500 tonnes of shipping was sunk and 25,800 tonnes damaged. This hit the Germans at a critical moment, when the divisions from Finland and the Murmansk Front were due to be transferred by sea from Norway to the battlefields on the continent.

The Germans discussed how they should respond to the increasing sabotage. As the most important sources about this topic are preserved, we can follow the discussion. It shows how several organizations within the Third Reich were involved, and how the debate evolved against the broader background of Germany's situation.

The discussion had started because of increasing sabotage in Denmark, but it took a new impetus from the sabotage at the Aker and Nyland shipyards. The day after these attacks the head of the German Navy, Grand Admiral Karl Dönitz recommended to the head of the *Wehrmacht* High Command, Wilhelm Keitel, that the shipyard workers should be held responsible for any acts of sabotage at their workplaces, and that the responsibility should extend to their families and relatives. They should be liable to punishment even if they had had nothing to do with the sabotage. The High Command accepted Dönitz's recommendation. Keitel wrote immediately to the supreme commanders in Norway and Denmark respectively, instructing them to work with their civilian counterparts: Terboven in Norway and Reich Plenipotentiary Werner Best in Denmark. Terboven and Best were asked to issue regulations in accordance with the military's wishes. Every worker should understand that sabotage at his workplace could have very serious consequences for himself and, if he fled, for his loved ones.

The question involved the Security Police, who also expressed their opinion. On 7 December the head of *Reichssicherheitshauptamt (RSHA)* Ernst Kaltenbrunner wrote to Keitel, saying that *Sipo* had a bad experience with reprisals in the occupied territories. *Sipo* considered that the solution was to keep a better watch, but that this would require the military to make the necessary personnel available. Kaltenbrunner enclosed an instruction he had sent to the heads of *Sipo* in Denmark and Norway. This disagreed with taking punitive measures against shipyard workers when it could not be shown that they had taken part in sabotage. The businesses risked losing valuable workers, whose arrest and possible imprisonment in concentration camps would harm wartime production.

Alongside sabotage of shipping, the increasing sabotage of railways in both countries was giving grounds for concern, because the transport of troops from the North was just as dependent on railways as on ships. On 25 January 1945, Fehlis sent a long list of Norwegian sabotage attacks to *RSHA*. The sabotage of Jørstad Bridge on 13 January, where so many German soldiers lost their lives, made a particular impression.

Terboven did not let himself be put off by statements and directives from the heads of the High Command and the Security Police. He went directly to the *Führer*. Hitler received a report from him at the start of December. Terboven began by outlining briefly concerning the sabotage attacks against the Aker and Nyland shipyards. Then he started evaluating countermeasures. He had no confidence in counter-sabotage as practised by the Germans in Denmark, where the Germans' response to The Resistance Movement's acts of sabotage was to blow up objects selected at random. Nor did he support counter-terror, another method used by the Germans in Denmark, where they reacted to the Danish Resistance Movement's assassinations by killing Danes at random.

Terboven's rejection of counter-terror may seem strange, as the *Gestapo* in Norway had followed such a policy for some time. As part of a special programme called *Blumenpflücken* (picking flowers), a total of eleven Norwegians were assassinated in the course of six months. Terboven may have thought that the experiences with *Blumenpflücken* had not matched the expectations, which tallies with the fact that the *Blumenpflücken* programme was abandoned at that time. Anyway, he claimed in his report to Hitler that counter-terror would not achieve the objective and pointed out that Himmler and Kaltenbrunner thought that it would have harmful consequences.

On the other hand, Terboven believed that there was something to be said in favour of the High Command's suggestion about shared responsibility. People in the workplace must be liable to punishment even if they had not taken part directly in an act of sabotage, the condition being that Terboven got permission to follow up with executions. By this Terboven obviously meant the killing of hostages and making it public in order to create an impression. This was his 'old method', as he wrote, probably thinking of the executions in Trøndelag in autumn 1942. The *Führer* had banned such executions.

Terboven wrote that a new regulation would only have the necessary weight and be a success if he could again use his 'old method'. This was the heart of his report. He wanted the ban on the execution of hostages and publication of death sentences to be lifted. The High Command agreed with Terboven's assessment. Reprisals would be effective only if they were carried out ruthlessly, and Terboven was given full authority to start executing hostages.

In the second half of January 1945, Terboven and Quisling met with Hitler in Berlin, where they discussed the counteroffensive against sabotage and assassinations in a wider context. At a meeting with Hitler on 21 January, Terboven proposed what should be done to bring an end to the acts of violence. He distinguished between two types. Sabotage and assassinations carried out by parties coming in from Britain or from Sweden should be dealt with by the military and the *Gestapo*. The fight against acts of violence performed by home-based groups, on the other hand, should be dealt with politically.

Terboven wanted to make use of the differences between the non-socialists and the communists in The Resistance Movement. He pointed out that behind the sabotage and assassinations there were a non-socialist national majority and a communist minority. There had been disagreements between them, but in the last year, the non-socialist opposition to the communists' sabotage campaign had weakened. He maintained that this was mostly because of the lack of effective response from the German side. Now he wanted to deepen the gulf between the two groups. He would frighten the influential leaders in the non-socialist camp to get them to turn against sabotage again. Terboven recommended shooting particularly influential anti-Nazi industrial leaders without trial and sentence. They should be blamed for supporting the sabotage. In particularly suitable cases, trials by the SS and Police Court would be arranged, with the implementation of the sentences and appropriate publicity.

In Berlin, Quisling was faced with Terboven's request for drastic measures in the fight against sabotage. There are post-war sources from *Nasjonal Samling* about these requests and Quisling's reaction to them. The sources are dramatic, but they are not easy to interpret. It seems clear at least that Terboven wanted to push Quisling to support his proposal in some form or other, and that Quisling resisted this. His resistance cannot have been absolute, however, because the NS state would soon co-operate in executions.

According to a report from the High Command to Böhme on 2 February, Hitler only partly accepted Terboven's recommendations. Hitler did not want hostages to be taken as a means of avoiding sabotage attacks. He also rejected shooting influential citizens without a legal trial. Such shootings could create martyrs. Nor did Terboven get permission to use SS and police courts. However, Hitler did approve the use of courts-martial, which obviously implied that the sentences could be announced publicly.

After The Resistance Movement had assassinated the Stapo and *Hird* leader Karl Marthinsen on 8 February 1945, the papers reported that a German court martial had pronounced twenty-one death sentences – of which sixteen were carried out – and NS's Norwegian special court had brought about twelve death sentences with subsequent executions. It was obvious that four of those who were executed belonged to the non-socialist national elite whom Terboven wanted to scare. In the announcement of the sentences, they were named individually, and their high status was mentioned. They were executed the same day as they were arrested.

The executions apparently reflected a compromise between Hitler and Terboven. The victims had not been treated as hostages but had been tried by a court and officially executed for specified resistance activities they had perpetrated. Some had done things that were so serious that they could probably have been executed anyway, but that did not apply to all of them, and certainly not the four high-status non-socialists. Nobody was officially executed for Marthinsen's assassination. None of them had been involved in that. They were sacrificed as part of a collective retaliation that was intended to have an extra effect. Hitler's requirement that influential citizens should not be shot without trial had been met. They all had their cases tried in court, though the court was a court-martial that was appointed by Terboven, delivered summary judgements, and was expected to pronounce harsh sentences.

New death sentences were announced the day after the big railway sabotage that Milorg carried out on 14 March. The SS and Police Court sat as a court martial and condemned fourteen men to death. They were all presented as saboteurs, but they were not expressly linked to the railway sabotage or condemned for taking part in it. As with the death sentences following Marthinsen's assassination, the purpose was deterrence. Those who were responsible for assassinations or sabotage should know that others could lose their lives as scapegoats for their misdeeds.

With this, an important line of development came to an end. It had begun with the ship sabotage in Denmark and at the Aker and Nyland shipyards on the night of 23–24 November. It had continued with a couple of months of top-level discussion among the Germans about what should be done to stop the sabotage. This had swung between a soft line that emphasized maintaining a better guard and police investigation, and a hard-line that involved reprisals and the execution of people who were not guilty of the relevant sabotage actions. In Norway, the hard-line was expressed in two declared mass executions in February and March, respectively. But that was an end to it. There were no further deterrent mass executions, indeed no more executions at all. The deadly days of the reprisals policy were past.

CHAPTER 17
THE NORTH NORWAY NARRATIVE

North Norway has distinctive characteristics that set it apart from the rest of the country, and there is a special north Norwegian thread woven into the narrative of the war years. Narvik was the site of the longest and hardest battles of the Norwegian Campaign in 1940. Then in 1942, north Norway was a priority zone as the British planned an invasion and precipitated the growth of a resistance movement that became exposed to bloody dismemberment. It was in north Norway that the Germans worked on their insane Polar Railway project that brought so many prisoners of war into the country and so many to their deaths. The proximity to Russia, always an important factor in north Norwegian history, was especially apparent during the Second World War. The region was adjacent to an active battlefront, a situation unparalleled in the rest of the country. There were more German soldiers in proportion to the local population than elsewhere in Norway.

During the last, long six months of the war, events in the most northerly counties took a new course. Northern Norway was the only place where Norwegian territory was liberated by military action and the Germans withdrew their troops before the war was over. The Germans submitted the local population to treatment that was unlike anything experienced further south. Not only did they withdraw back from the Murmansk and Finland Front across north Norwegian territory; they also razed to the ground the settlements in their wake. The inhabitants were forced to evacuate, and the Germans hunted down those who tried to escape the compulsory relocation.

The *Wehrmacht* and the liberation of Finnmark

Along the coast, the Germans still needed their planes and warships to attack the Allied convoys and protect their own shipping. In summer 1944 the U-boat bases in Norway became even more important when the Allies captured the German-occupied ports in France and the U-boats were moved to Norway. Above all, however, the *Wehrmacht*'s role was to be prepared for an anticipated invasion. Right to the end of the war, Hitler believed that the Allies would try to invade Norway. He would therefore not allow any reduction of the *Wehrmacht* on Norwegian territory. At the time of liberation, the German troops in Norway numbered about 350,000 men.

Norway was now not only a base for an army of occupation but also a transit zone for German troops being pulled back from the Northern Cape of Scandinavia. Three days after the D-Day landings in Normandy, the Russians went on to attack the Finnish positions along the Karelian Isthmus, north of Leningrad. The Finns were driven back.

About the middle of July, the Russians ceased their offensive. Stalin did not want to divert forces to occupy all of Finland. The Finns then abandoned their alliance with Germany. On 2 September Finland broke off diplomatic relations with the Germans and asked them to withdraw their troops. Two days later, the Finns agreed on the terms of a truce with the Russians, according to which the Finns would disarm the German troops and hand them over to the Russians as prisoners of war.

The Germans now began pulling their troops back to the northernmost regions of Finland. As the Germans withdrew, they carried out a scorched earth policy, destroying bridges and laying mines under roads behind them. Finnish soldiers followed their progress, at first allowing the Germans to retreat at their own pace. The Finns also agreed with the Germans that the population in the retreat zone would be evacuated. Finnish authorities arranged for over 100,000 of their people to be evacuated to Sweden and southern Finland.

The Russians did not approve of the Finns' leniency towards the Germans and urged the Finns to drive the Germans back with force. So, from 1 October there was a full-scale war between the former brothers in arms, in what was known as 'The Lapland War'. The Germans extended their scorched earth policy. All buildings in the retreat zone were to be destroyed.

So far, these developments had only applied to the situation in Finland, but now Norway was dragged in. On 4 October, Hitler gave orders for the whole of the 20th Mountain Army – the 'Lapland Army' – to be withdrawn to a new defence line in the Lyngen area in Norway. All German troops in the Northern Cap should leave Soviet, Finnish and parts of the north Norwegian regions.

The Russians went onto the offensive at the Murmansk Front on 7 October and quickly forced the Germans back. Soviet troops crossed the border into Norway on 18 October, and on 25 October they captured Kirkenes. Then they halted at the Tana River, 150 kilometres inside Norwegian territory. Soviet and German troops were in battle in Tanadalen for the last time on 6 November. As in Finland, the Russians did not want to have large armies tied down in Norway. They did want to have control of the Kirkenes region, which along with Petsamo had been central to the German campaigns in the North. But once that need was met, most of the forces should be sent south to take part in the fighting there. The Russians did not trouble to pursue the Germans further west through Finnmark.

The German retreat approached Lyngen along three lines. The first led north-westward directly from Finland across the Norwegian border into the Lyngen area. The second route took them northward through Finland to cross the border near Karasjok on the Finnmark Plateau and down to Lakselv at the head of the Porsanger Fjord. There they joined with the forces who had made their way along the third line of retreat, westward from Kirkenes. Around 200,000 German soldiers and several thousand Russian prisoners of war marched along these three routes, together with 60,000 horses who were also part of the retreat. During the withdrawal the *Wehrmacht* did as they had done in Finland, destroying almost everything in their wake.

Behind the protection of the Lyngen Line, many of the troops from the Finland and Murmansk Front were sent south. They would not form part of the defence of *Festung*

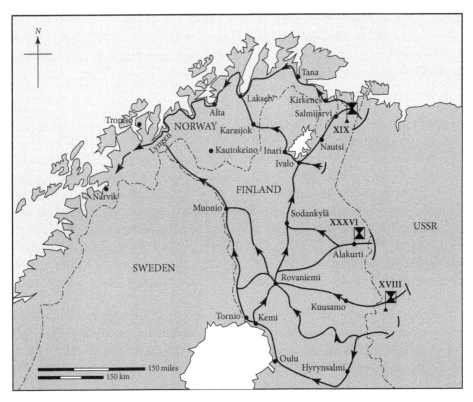

Map 5 German withdrawal through north Norway 1944–5. The German withdrawal from Soviet and Finnish territory was a complicated and logistically very demanding operation. Militarily, it was successful, but it severely affected the Norwegian population in Finnmark and northern Troms.

Norwegen but would be taken over to the continent to fight there. They marched along endless rough roads to Lyngen and continued southward on foot to Mo. There they boarded Norwegian Railways' troop trains to be transported to southern Norway and then carried by ship to Denmark. Finally, they were despatched to the battlefields on the continent. One division took part in the Ardennes Offensive, and three divisions took part in the final battle for Germany. As part of these redeployments, the German army in Norway was integrated into the 20th Mountain Army, led by Lothar Rendulic. He replaced Falkenhorst on 18 December and was himself replaced in January by Franz Böhme, who set up his headquarters in Lillehammer and remained there until the end of the war.

For a good six months, until the country was liberated, the *Wehrmacht* in Norway was, therefore, a mixture of a retreating force in transit from the Northern Cape to the continent, and a stationary army. Nobody could know what this combined stationary and retreating army would do if the Germans surrendered on the continent or the Third Reich fell apart in chaos, but this was the question that concerned most people. In the meantime, the *Wehrmacht* army of occupation continued to perform its military duties as before. The clear order from Böhme was that any attack would be resisted, whether it came from outside or from The Resistance Movement. The Germans also prepared plans for how they would destroy harbours, power stations, telecommunications, and railway networks if they were driven back in battle.

Forced evacuation and cave-dwellers

The *Wehrmacht* continued its scorched earth policy during the retreat through Norway from the northern Finland and Murmansk Front. As in Finland, the question arose of evacuating the civilian population from the ravaged areas. In Norway, the *Reichskommissariat* and the NS state saw this as their responsibility. After Hitler had ordered the withdrawal to the Lyngen position in Norway, Terboven took the initiative for a voluntary evacuation. As usual, the *Reichskommissariat* needed to use the NS state's administrative apparatus to implement its policy. On Terboven's recommendation, Quisling appointed the police minister and the minister for social affairs as superintendents to oversee the evacuation.

It immediately proved difficult to get the process started. The populace did not want to move, and the *Wehrmacht*, the *Reichskommissariat* and the NS representatives did not co-operate well. When Terboven visited north Norway at the end of the month, he became convinced that more effort was required. The people must be forcibly evacuated, and all the houses burnt. On 26 October he sent a telegram about this to Hitler's powerful secretary, Martin Bormann. Hitler heeded Terboven's request. On 28 October the military received orders that the whole population east of the Lyngen Fjord was to be forcibly evacuated and all dwellings burnt down. The *Wehrmacht* would be responsible for ensuring that the order was carried out ruthlessly. 'There is no place for leniency towards the population.' Terboven had gone directly to Hitler, over the heads of the military authorities.

At the same time as the *Wehrmacht* was bringing its marching columns of soldiers and Soviet prisoners of war southwards along National Highway 50, the military set about destroying and burning everything behind them: roads, bridges, telegraph poles, quays, boats, business premises, schools, churches, houses, and outhouses. Alongside the ravaging of the infrastructure, 40,000–50,000 people were forcibly evacuated from Finnmark and Nord-Troms. At every place, people were given a short deadline and further instructions on where to report. When the deadline expired, they had to leave the site. German demolition squads then blew up or set fire to everything they found and slaughtered or appropriated all the livestock. People were transported to special evacuation centres, from which they were sent onwards by boat. About half of them were dispersed throughout Sør-Troms and Nordland, while the rest were mainly allocated to Trøndelag and Østlandet.

German soldiers often came back to search for and remove people who had hidden away in the first instance. Total devastation usually accompanied total forced evacuation, but not always. In the eastern parts of Finnmark, the Germans were driven back so rapidly that they didn't manage to carry out the scorched earth policy. Here, however, the Soviet bombing had destroyed much of Kirkenes, Vadsø and Vardø. As the Germans had little time to evacuate the population, a majority remained in Sør-Varanger and nearly all on the Varanger Peninsula. The buildings in Tana were burnt down, but two-thirds of the population managed to escape into the hills. On the Finnmark Plateau, Kautokeino and Karasjok were almost totally razed, but the great majority of the people avoided evacuation and remained in the area.

There were four parties responsible for carrying out the evacuation and providing the administrative resources. The *Wehrmacht*'s main interest was in clearing Finnmark and Nord-Troms of all inhabitants and getting the whole population away. The *Reichskommissariat* representatives tried to influence the *Wehrmacht* and the NS state and to mediate but had no means of their own to implement an evacuation. The third party was the two NS superintendents and the NS state's local officials, whether they were members of NS or not. From the start, they faced major difficulties with a population that did not want to be evacuated.

The fourth party was an efficient civilian evacuation bureau that came into being in Tromsø. It met the need for sea transport by acquiring a fleet of cutters, provided accommodation and food, and did its utmost to solve all sorts of practical problems. The leader of the bureau faced the classic problem of administrative collaboration. Helping with the evacuation meant co-operating in a process that had been started by the Germans. On the other hand, the evacuees badly needed help. This was the crucial consideration for the leader of the evacuation bureau. He tried to distance himself from NS, but he took part in meetings with the NS county governor where the NS overseers might also be present. Outside the meetings with the county governor, he had daily discussions with a representative of the *Reichskommissariat* about transport problems.

The Home Front Leadership was poorly informed about the situation in the North and thought it was wrong to assist the forced evacuation in this way. In mid-November, they issued a directive that people must not help Nazi authorities and organizations with the evacuation, but the directive did not match the public mood and had to be retracted after less than two weeks. The evacuation bureau never complied with the directive. The bureau's policy was that the forced evacuees must be helped, even if that involved contact or co-operation with German military and civil authorities and the NS administration.

Twenty-three thousand Norwegians refused to be forcibly evacuated and hid away. Some slept under upturned boats, others slept in tents, some managed to build a simple hut, but most sought shelter in *gamme* – simple earth huts built up around a framework of posts, covered with earth or turf and with a smoke-hole in the roof. People in Finnmark and Troms combined working in fishing and agriculture. They had hayfields in the remote countryside where they might already have a *gamme*, or they could build a new one now when they needed to hide there. They had to be careful, though, not to light a fire in case the smoke was visible from the sea.

Why did people flee from the forced evacuation? Why did they expose themselves to such hardships that they could more easily have avoided? One answer is that many people reckoned that Soviet and Norwegian forces would soon arrive to drive the Germans out, or that the war would soon be over. To submit to evacuation did not necessarily appear a better alternative. They could face the danger of being torpedoed or bombed during a sea voyage. It was uncertain what sort of accommodation awaited them when they left home.

Another answer can be found in the lifestyle. Those who escaped evacuation had lived from a combination of fishing and crofting, largely independent of supplies from outside. They were accustomed to a hard life at sea and in the remote countryside. So, it was not so frightening for them to turn to outdoor living as it would be for town dwellers and others who lived fully in a cash economy. Basically, this can be seen as a homeland protest. The people of Finnmark were bound to their special lifestyle and emotionally connected to their scattered dwelling-places. They would rather defy an alien physical power than allow themselves to be plucked out of a countryside and a fishing and farming economy that had so fundamentally shaped them and their existence.

The sweetness of the first meeting: The Overseas Front returns home

The government in London was deeply concerned about developments in north Norway. In the first years of the war, it had assumed that the liberation of Norway would take the form of an Allied invasion and military action. The British would land and throw the Germans out. From winter 1943 it was no longer so certain that the Western powers would be the first to liberate Norway. There was an increasing likelihood that it might be the Russians. If the Russians attacked the Germans on the Murmansk Front and drove them back, they might follow the German troops into Norwegian territory.

These prospects alarmed the government. It had throughout the war been closely connected with Britain and had gradually developed a good working relationship with the British. It was content that it would be British and possibly American soldiers who liberated Norway. The government had had little to do with the Soviets, and the Russians had not been part of the government's plans for the liberation. It was unsure of the Russians' intentions. The government thought it best to approach them to form better relationships and learn something of their intentions. Foreign Minister Trygve Lie proposed that Norwegian forces should fight alongside the Soviets. The answer he received from the Soviet ambassador in London was effusively positive. The Russians were eager to accept this. The Norwegian force should be the biggest possible, several battalions or a whole division who would be supplied with the most modern equipment from the Red Army. The Russians were exaggerating; the Norwegian government did not have a division available.

Lie's other proposal was that Norway and the Soviet Union should come to an agreement about what the relationship should be between Soviet troops, who might be operating on Norwegian soil, and Norwegian authorities. The government had no hesitations about making a similar agreement with the British and the Americans, but it was unsure how wise it would be to enter an agreement with the Russians. The British were not enthusiastic about the Norwegian proposal, as Norway would thereby be distancing itself somewhat from Great Britain. On the other hand, the proposal for an agreement could generate goodwill among the Russians, which the Norwegians might now need. The Russians responded quickly and positively to the Norwegian approach, and the Soviet–Norwegian agreement was soon signed. On the same day, 16 May 1944, similar agreements were made with Great Britain and the United States. The Russians were obviously pleased to be treated on a level with the Western powers in this way, at the same time as Norway was slightly loosening its ties with them.

But then the difficulties began, and a picture of a powerless government began to emerge. The government was faced by the obvious unwillingness of the Western powers to become engaged in Norway. It was not clear whether north Norway or Finnmark were to be seen as the Western powers' or the Russians' area of operations. After the signing of the agreements on 16 May, the government was paralysed by the Russians' icy silence. The Russians had eagerly accepted the Norwegian offer to send troops to fight alongside them, but the Soviet ambassador told Trygve Lie that the details of this could be negotiated only with the military authorities in Moscow and that was the end of the matter. No negotiations took place. It was impossible to find out anything about the Russian plans in the North.

The Russians broke their silence only when Russian troops crossed the border into Norway on 18 October. Foreign Minister Molotov had a discussion that evening with the Norwegian ambassador in Moscow, telling him that Soviet troops would very soon be driving the Germans into Norway. It would then be important both for the world and for the Norwegian people that the Norwegians took part and could raise the Norwegian flag on Norwegian soil. Only when people in Moscow publicly celebrated the capture of Kirkenes on 25 October did Norwegian authorities learn that there were Soviet troops on Norwegian territory. The most important thing from the Norwegian point of view, however, was that the Russians had now at last broken their silence to bid Norwegian authorities and Norwegian troops welcome to a region of Norway. This resolved the difficulty. The government could send Norwegian forces to the Soviet-occupied areas in the Kirkenes region, where the Russians would welcome and assist them.

The problem was how to assemble the necessary troops and how to get them to Finnmark. The Norwegian fighting forces in Great Britain amounted to some 12,000 men. Of these, the British would not release the Norwegian air force and the Norwegian navy, who were both actively engaged in the Allied advance in Europe. The Allied Supreme Command only allowed the navy to send a small fleet to the North – two corvettes and three minesweepers. The Norwegian Brigade in Scotland consisted of 3,500 men, a standby force ready to be sent into Norway at the time of liberation. The biggest obstacle to sending such a force to Finnmark was the lack of transport. The Western powers could not immediately release Norwegian merchant ships that were sorely needed in other places, and they were reluctant to deprive themselves of naval forces. Only a military mission and a single mountain company of 233 men were able to travel with a fast convoy headed for Murmansk. They arrived in Kirkenes in November.

In autumn 1944 the Norwegian police troops in Sweden numbered 11,000–12,000 men and the government wanted to transfer some of them to Finnmark. The Swedes agreed with this and were willing to supply them with weapons and necessary equipment. American planes started flights from Luleå in northern Sweden to Kirkenes in January. Several hundred men were also brought from northern Sweden across Finnish territory and onto the Finnmark Plateau. A total of 1,300 men from the police troops were transported to Finnmark by the end of the war.

The arrival of the military mission, the mountain company, the naval detachment, and the police troops signified the return of part of Norway abroad back to Norway at home and established a legal Norwegian authority in areas that had been liberated. Volunteers joined on the spot and men eligible for conscription were called up, to create the Varanger Battalion, which in May 1945 amounted to 800 men. Eventually, there were 2,700 soldiers under Norwegian command. The military mission appointed a new county governor, and the military and civil administrations worked together to establish a local leadership in areas the Germans had abandoned. Local mayors and district sheriffs were appointed. Military and civil administration went hand in hand. The first traitors were arrested.

The military mission and the mountain company ran into big problems initially. The relationship with the Russians was fine, but the Norwegians did not have vehicles or horses of their own and had little equipment. They were totally dependent on material support from the Russians. The Russians were amazed that they were so few, as were the local population who were hoping for supplies from outside to relieve distress in the bomb-ravaged and devastated areas. The Norwegian soldiers who came from Britain had spent the past few years training themselves for warfare. They did not understand a population who did not want to fight and who they thought had shown a feeble attitude towards the occupying forces. Despite these big initial differences between the people of Finnmark and the soldiers from Britain, the situation became easier as people received supplies from abroad. The Norwegian troops gradually became visible over larger areas and demonstrated that they were able to provide help to the population.

The mountain company was under Soviet command initially and was sent out on reconnaissance patrols to gather information about the Germans' forces and intentions. On 6 February, District Command Finnmark took over command and set about establishing a base in Skoganvarre and assembling troops in the Porsanger area. There were clashes between German and Norwegian patrols, but the losses were small. The region between Lyngen in the West and Tana in the East is often spoken of as a 'no man's land'. There were, however, thousands of refugees in this 'no man's land'. German patrol boats and landing parties operated along the coast from a few bases that the Germans held onto almost to the end of the war, while Norwegian soldiers slowly made their way into the 'no man's land' from the East.

Finnmark and Troms are part of a multi-ethnic region that includes a majority of ethnic Norwegians; Sami; and Kvens (who are of Finnish origin). In NS there was a tendency to look at the Sami as an inferior race. The Germans regarded the Sami more as an exotic people, with whom officers and men were happy to be photographed. Mixing German and Sami blood was something else, however. The *Lebensborn* programme would not help Sami women who had had children by German soldiers. Some of the

Sami and the Kvens who were forcibly evacuated and sent south experienced language difficulties because their Norwegian was poor. Apart from that, the reindeer-herding Sami on the Finnmark Plateau have their own history of forced evacuation. The Germans were interested in acquiring reindeer meat and German and NS authorities wanted to evacuate the Sami and their reindeer to Helligskogen in Troms. Instead, they disappeared eastward to another place also called Helligskogen, near the Finnish border, without the NS authorities or the Germans being able to stop them. Almost 1,500 Sami escaped in this way with their reindeer.

With their boycott of the forced evacuation in turf huts, caves, upturned boats and tents, the people of Finnmark created an epic north Norwegian narrative. Their act of disobedience has not usually been seen as part of The Norwegian Resistance Movement but must be considered as such. The boycott was a form of collective resistance, without any leadership or any connection with the organized Home Front. The fugitives neither followed directives from the civil resistance leadership nor followed instructions from any military leadership. They mounted a spontaneous resistance front in the wilderness, directed against both the *Wehrmacht* and the NS state, but without any pretensions other than to defy the order to move away from their homelands. In the history of resistance, they have a place alongside the 'partisans', the north Norwegian intelligence agents who worked for the Russians.

CHAPTER 18
THE GERMANS AND NS FACE DEFEAT

Terboven's situation did not basically change during the last year of the war. He still held the same full authority from Hitler to govern the civilian population of Norway autocratically. His crucial relationship with the *Wehrmacht* was still difficult and demanding. As before, he faced a military colossus over which he had no authority.

Terboven remained dependent on the SS police system with his continuing close connection to it through Rediess and Fehlis. Combatting The Resistance Movement was a continuing preoccupation as always, but it was now more pressing than ever, for two reasons. One was that the resistance grew strongly in extent and power during the last year of the war, with increasing use of military means. The other was the thought of the impending endgame. Terboven and the police would need so far as possible to ensure that The Resistance Movement did not fall on the retreating Germans from behind.

Böhme as head of the *Wehrmacht* preferred to wait and see how the denouement would work out and did not recommend any aggressive policy in the meantime, but Terboven was belligerent. He made no secret of the fact that he wanted to fight. The Germans in Norway should put up a fight and continue the struggle. His view was shared by some of the officers: You don't give up until you are defeated. Nazi ideology and military honor both required that they should not abandon Norwegian territory without a battle.

Terboven's problem was that he controlled so little of what was needed for the battle. He could reckon on 2,000–3,000 men at most in the German Security Police and Order Police, a couple of thousand Norwegians returned from the Eastern Front, and another couple of thousand from the armed units in the *Hird*, making up 6,000–7,000 men altogether. He was dependent on the *Wehrmacht* and would need to exert influence on the colossus to stimulate it into action at the end.

Terboven had previously tried without success to secure his own area of authority behind the front in the event of an invasion. In March 1945 he tried again. If the end of the war in Norway took the form of active hostilities and Norway became a battle zone, Terboven and his civil administration would become subordinate to the military authorities in the area of operations. So, Terboven suggested that he should become Böhme's deputy. The appointment would not involve tactical and operational leadership. Terboven would not get involved in military matters but would take his place as a sort of political commissar alongside the head of the military. This would enable him to take part in the discussion among the officers about what the *Wehrmacht* should be doing in Norway and encourage them to continue the war on Norwegian soil. Again, he got nowhere. The military was having none of it, and Hitler finally refused his request.

In the last six months of the war, Terboven would be aware of Fehlis distancing himself from him. As head of the Security Police and the Security Service, Fehlis tried to restrain Terboven on two occasions when he wanted to be more aggressive. When Terboven recommended forced evacuation of the population from north Norway, Fehlis and the head of the *Einsatzstab* sent a joint telegram to Hitler's headquarters, advising against Terboven's proposal. The second occasion was at Easter 1945 when Terboven wanted to start large-scale raids in the forests north of Oslo, where Milorg was at its most active during the last months of the war. Suspicious characters would be arrested and some of them shot. With support from both his own and the central branches of the Security Service, Fehlis managed to foil Terboven's plan. The Head Office of German Security (RSHA) ordered the action to be canceled, and Terboven had to give in.

Quisling and NS

Quisling still clung to the hope that there was something to be gained from the Germans. In autumn 1944 he worked on plans for a new meeting with Hitler. He and Terboven were finally able to appear before Hitler at the end of January. Quisling put forward the same requests as before: for a peace agreement, full sovereignty, withdrawal of the *Reichskommissariat,* and the establishment of normal diplomatic channels between Germany and Norway.

The new element was the emphasis he placed on plans for a European treaty and a Germanic agreement that would lay the foundations for a nucleus of Germanic states in a European federation. Both these ideas implied that Germany would be less dominant than before. Hitler had less interest than ever in such proposals. The Germans were suspicious about an initiative that could be understood as an incipient detachment from Germany. Quisling achieved nothing. He and leading circles in the party had rather naively had great expectations of the meeting with Hitler, and they were very disappointed when these were not fulfilled.

The *Hird* continued as a section of the party, with Quisling as overall leader. Since 1943 it had been defined as a part of 'the state's armed forces'. It still provided a starting point from which to work towards creating the army of the future. In February 1945 the *Hird* consisted of 8,500 men. Of these, 3,700 were not available for *Hird* duties because of service in the police, Eastern Front units, *Arbeidstjenesten* or elsewhere, and 4,800 were considered as active members. The active membership was now more strongly militarized. Two new sections were created in 1944: *Hirdens Bedriftsvern* and *Hirdens Alarmenheter*. There was some overlap between the duties of these sections, but *Bedriftsvernet* was intended mainly to protect important industrial enterprises from sabotage and *Alarmenhetene* was more like emergency response units that could be called out at short notice. Members of the *Hird* were required to serve in these, receiving military training and bearing arms like regular soldiers.

During spring 1945 an elaborate plan was developed to mobilize NS by expanding the *Hird*. As many as 21 battalions would be set up, amounting to 12,000 men in total. The

Germans approved the plan, on the condition that the troops would be under German command when they were in operation. NS members between the ages of 18 and 25, who were eligible for service in the *Hird* were registered by the NS county *Fører*, and about 2,000 men were called up. The plans met strong opposition from the party members. A significant proportion of those who were called up went into hiding to avoid military service.

The NS state took part in the reprisals after Marthinsen's assassination. Its special court pronounced the death sentences. Terboven took the initiative, but it appears not to have been too difficult to engage Quisling in the actions. According to what Quisling said at his own trial after the war, it can appear that he reasoned approximately the same way as he probably did after the death sentence against Police Officer Eilifsen. To allow only the Germans to punish and execute would have exposed the powerlessness of the NS state. The matter could not possibly have been left entirely to the Germans. 'That would have been giving up.' The NS state too needed to be able to condemn and execute harshly and mercilessly.

Many NS people felt insecure in the last year of the war when the internal political conflicts became progressively more acute and The Resistance Movement and the NS state confronted each other more bitterly than ever before. State and party leaders demanded extra security measures. Quisling's bodyguard was enhanced with a third company of police in spring 1944 and a fourth made up of former front-fighters in the autumn. Several NS Party officials asked to be provided with weapons. Their request led only to long debate as the *Wehrmacht* and *Sipo* were opposed to arming the Party, though when Quisling visited Berlin in January 1945 he gained approval from Hitler, who promised to send 10,000 pistols.

The Resistance Movement's assassinations caused particular alarm. They were not directed against NS members as such but against informers and the NS state's police. Ten police officers and district sheriffs were assassinated in autumn 1944 and five in spring 1945, with Marthinsen's assassination as a high point. As the Stapo men were always members of NS, the assassinations could be seen as an attack on the Party and committed Party members were disturbed. Some of those who had been assassinated were officially honored, were given state funerals, and were promoted as martyrs in the fight against the internal enemy.

The ideological system that Quisling had built up and that depended so heavily on the concept of fascism's inevitable triumph and NS's mission as a handmaiden of history was shattered. Quisling had no alternative ideological structure to offer. Instead, he extracted the strong anti-communist element in national socialism and emphasized it even more. In the last year of the war, Quisling spoke powerfully about how the war that Germany and NS Norway were fighting together had now become a war of defense against Soviet communism that threatened to overwhelm Europe and European culture. It was a notion that when carried to its extreme concluded in the idea that the endgame should take the form of an alliance between Germany and the Western powers against the Soviets. At the end of the war, there were not a few in NS who thought that after Germany's collapse the Western powers and the Norwegian government in London would be dependent on support from the NS members to protect themselves against the Bolshevik advance.

The final months of the war were a time of confusion in NS, with conflicting trends, lack of realism, and flight into alternative worlds. The thought that Hitler would give the Party what he had always refused before was naïve. The idea of the party as a member of an anti-communist alliance with the Western powers and the Norwegian government in exile was sheer utopia. Quisling's dream in quiet moments that he could retire as a priest in Fyresdal was far from reality. His unofficial 'foreign minister' toyed with lofty plans for Norway to declare neutrality and join with Sweden, Denmark, and Finland in creating a Nordic bloc. Quisling's proposal in May 1945 that as the leader of an 'outgoing' government he should hand over power in an almost regular manner to an 'incoming' government was totally unrealistic.

There was, however, some basis underlying the imagination and fiction. Neither the ordinary Party membership nor the leadership in NS was prepared for any ultimate fight for survival. Only the small group inclined towards the SS had thoughts of fighting to the last man. The others feared and wanted to avoid a civil war. The militarized sections of the *Hird* were not intended to enter the field against invasion forces and The Resistance Movement. Quisling saw them rather as a bargaining chip. They gave the government a semblance of power. The *Hird* could be envisaged to function as a guard in a time of difficult transition. NS wanted to finish its work without bloodshed. That became the party's contribution to the peaceful conclusion in Norway.

The last days

It would not be long before the Third Reich collapsed. Germany was being pressed from all sides. On 16 April Soviet troops mounted a fresh attack with the aim of surrounding Berlin. On 24 April they reached their goal. Then they fought their way through the streets into the city itself.

The Western powers could no longer avoid the question of what would happen to Norway if the Germans put up a fight there. At the beginning of April General Eisenhower, supreme commander of the Western Forces finally received orders to develop a plan for the liberation of Norway in the event of German resistance. Previously, an Allied landing by sea or air would have been the basis of such a plan, but another possibility was now open: Norway could be liberated from Swedish territory. The Allied plan that was presented at the end of the month presupposed that Sweden not only agreed to but also took part in such an operation with its own troops. On 30 April the Allies requested negotiations with Sweden about possible operations against the Germans in Norway, and the Swedes answered 'Yes' the same day. An Allied military mission should come to start the discussions.

On the afternoon of 30 April, Hitler committed suicide. Previously, he had unexpectedly selected the head of the navy, Grand Admiral Karl Dönitz, as his successor. Dönitz now became both head of state and supreme military commander of what was left of the Third Reich. He set up his headquarters in the town of Flensburg, just south of the Danish border, where German forces were still in control.

Dönitz held meetings in Flensburg on 3 May with representatives whom he had summoned from the occupying authorities in several countries. He wanted to inform them about the current situation, to assure himself of their loyalty, and to be informed about local circumstances. Terboven and Böhme came from Norway. Dönitz did not wish to carry on some desperate final battle, but he did want to win time so that the stream of German refugees from the East could reach West Germany and the German armies on the Eastern Front would be able to withdraw and avoid becoming prisoners of the Soviets. To achieve this, he needed the armies in Norway and Denmark as bargaining counters. The military chiefs must therefore retain full control of their forces and hold them in readiness. Böhme's order of the day to the troops in Norway on 5 May reflected this, stating that Dönitz wanted to save as many Germans as possible from Bolshevik chaos and that the soldiers in Norway must therefore be ready to fight. In the hands of the head of state, they were an important instrument that must not lose a fraction of its weight and worth.

To strengthen Böhme's position and to restrict any tendency for the different services to go their own way, Dönitz ordered that the navy and the air force should be directly under Böhme's authority. By this move, Falkenhorst's old dream was fulfilled. *Wehrmachtbefehlshaber Norwegen* had finally become a real supreme commander. To prevent Terboven from interfering, Dönitz dismissed him on 7 May and transferred his duties to the Supreme Command at Lillehammer; another fulfillment of Falkenhorst's dreams.

Dönitz made no headway with his policy and soon abandoned it. The Allies refused to negotiate and would accept only an unconditional German surrender. On the night of 6 May, Germany capitulated under Dönitz's leadership. During 7 May the news spread and people in Norway started celebrating the victory. Only late that evening did Böhme receive orders from the German High Command to lay down arms. The capitulation began formally on the night of 8 May.

One important reason why the liberation of Norway – apart from in the North – happened peacefully was that there was a legitimate state authority in Germany the whole time, even after Hitler's death, able to take the necessary decisions and have them implemented. Another was that discipline held in the *Wehrmacht* right to the end. Also, the government in exile in London and The Home Front Leadership in Oslo had prepared very thoroughly for the transition from war to peace and had taken a lot of care in the last weeks to avoid actions that could provoke the Germans.

Terboven gave up his plans to continue the struggle. His loyalty had always been to the *Führer*. So long as Hitler urged continuing war, so did Terboven. When Hitler gave up the struggle and committed suicide, so did Terboven soon afterward. On 8 May he took his own life at Skaugum. Rediess did the same, and Fehlis followed suit several days later when he was found among *Wehrmacht* soldiers in Porsgrunn, where he had hidden away.

Of the NS leaders, Lie and Riisnæs barricaded themselves in Skallum Farm in Bærum, outside Oslo, together with Henrik Rogstad, the County *Fører* for Sør-Trøndelag, who had recently been a rising star in the Party and was now head of both Stapo and the *Hird*. The three were committed to dying together. It ended with Lie dying of fever, stress, lack of sleep, and a poison pill, while Rogstad shot himself. Riisnæs surrendered without resistance. Quisling put suicidal thoughts aside. He wanted to be judged, not so much by a judicial court as by the Verdict of History. Together with most of his ministers, he left Gimle early on the morning of 9 May and reported to the police station in 19 Møllergata, where they were imprisoned.

Others soon took over the government. Until 7 June, Norway was formally an Allied operations zone subject to Allied rule. From the Norwegian side, The Home Front Leadership now stepped forward, presenting its members to govern for a few days alongside the previously appointed advisers in the various ministries. On 13 May, Crown Prince Olav arrived at the head of a government delegation and took over, while HL withdrew permanently. The rest of the government arrived later, and on 7 June the Allies ceded power the same day as the king came back. Then when *Stortinget* was assembled again for a short sitting, all of the country's constitutional authorities were back in place. Full normality was only restored, however, after the elections in the autumn.

Norway had become a participant in the Second World War on 9 April 1940, and it emerged from the war in Europe five years and one month later. Hostilities continued in Asia for a while, and Norwegian ships continued to serve in the war against Japan. Several hundred Norwegians were in Japanese prisons. To be better equipped to seek war indemnity, Norway declared war on Japan on 6 July. The government affirmed that there had been a state of war between Norway and Japan since the Japanese attack on Pearl Harbor in December 1941. On 15 August 1945, Japan capitulated. Norway's participation in the Second World War was over.

SELECT BIBLIOGRAPHY

Dahl, Hans Fredrik. *Quisling: A Study in Treachery*. Cambridge: Cambridge University Press, 1999.

Derry, T. K. *The Campaign in Norway*. London: H.M.S.O, 1952.

Frøland, Hans Otto, Mats Ingulstad, and Jonas Scherner (eds). *Industrial Collaboration in Nazi-Occupied Europe: Norway in Context*. London: Palgrave Macmillan, 2016.

Gjelsvik, Tore. *Norwegian Resistance, 1940–1945*. London: C. Hurst, 1979.

Hassing, Arne. *Church Resistance to Nazism in Norway, 1940–1945*. Seattle: University of Washington Press, 2014.

Hoidal, Oddvar K. *Quisling: A Study in Treason*. Oslo: Norwegian University Press, 1989.

Insall, Tony. *Secret Alliances: Special Operations and Intelligence in Norway 1940–1945 – The British Perspective*. London: Biteback Publishing, 2019.

Kersaudy, François. *Norway 1940*. London: Arrow, 1991.

Kiszely, John. *Anatomy of a Campaign: The British Fiasco in Norway, 1940*. Cambridge: Cambridge University Press, 2017.

Mann, Christopher. *British Policy and Strategy Towards Norway, 1941–1945*. Basingstoke: Palgrave Macmillan, 2012.

Milward, Alan S. *The Fascist Economy in Norway*. Oxford: At the Clarendon Press, 1972.

Rhys-Jones, Graham. *Churchill and the Norway Campaign, 1940*. Barnsley: Pen & Sword Book Limited, 2008.

Riste, Olav. *The Norwegian Intelligence Service, 1945–1970*. London: Frank Cass, 1999.

Salmon, Patrick (ed.). *Britain and Norway in the Second World War*. London: HMSO, 1995.

Stokker, Kathleen. *Folklore Fights the Nazis: Humour in Occupied Norway, 1940–1945*. Madison: University of Wisconsin Press, 1997.

INDEX

Index

Index